Early Anthropology in the

Sixteenth and Seventeenth Centuries

Early Anthropology in the Sixteenth and Seventeenth Centuries

by

Margaret T. Hodgen

Philadelphia
University of Pennsylvania Press

To
M. A.

Foreword

IT HAS BECOME a convention in dealing with the historical careers of the social studies to fix their birth dates somewhere in the nineteenth century, when the academic departmentaliz-ation of the study of man had its inception; and then, when unfavorable comment is heard, to defend them singly or jointly on the score of their youth and immaturity.

This is unfortunate. The study of man in the Western world is not young. It is one of the oldest subjects of serious thought. Neither sociology nor anthropology sprang *de novo* and fully formed from the reflections of their presumptive "fathers," Auguste Comte and Sir Edward Burnett Tylor; and even those bold spirits who have recently traced the antecedents of the two disciplines as far back as the eighteenth century — to the Encyclopedists and the Scottish moral philosophers — have reached back only part of the way. To fix casually upon any handful of recent scholars as "founders" or "originators" is always a disservice to intellectual history. Only Professor A. Irving Hallowell, in his new and searching study, *The begin-nings of anthropology in America* (1960), seems happily to have avoided these pitfalls.

Though the present essay attempts to meet the situation in some degree by relating the study of human cultures to other man-centered themes, as well as to expose some of the evidence of reliance upon an extremely ancient humanistic inheritance, it should be clearly understood for what it is, namely, an exploration and nothing more. All that the reader may expect to find are a few broad strokes indicating the method or body of organizing ideas by which problems and solutions of a broadly anthropological nature have been set forth during one small segment of the past, together with some of the reasoning which supported them. Should any of these earlier ideas bear

7

a family resemblance to procedures lately in use, it will not be a mistake to regard them also as very old and very persistent.

Apart from a few introductory remarks upon Herodotus, Pliny, Solinus, and the medieval encyclopedists, in what has been called a medieval prologue — apart from discussions of Platonism and other earlier systems of thought — this essay deals with the organizing ideas employed by students of man and culture in the sixteenth and seventeenth centuries. During these critical years curiosity concerning the strange customs of mankind in faraway lands and times was immeasurably sharpened. For one thing, the hobby of collecting curios was extended to human manners. These were gathered not only from among newly discovered tribes but also from the literatures referring to antiquity. A massive volume of materials was soon made available. This was given a more or less orderly presentation in the "treasuries," "mirrors," and "fardels," which paralleled in the humanities the better-known collections of flora and fauna. A little later, the same type of material found its way into popular geographies and cosmographies, the attention of some scholars being focused upon certain larger constellations of ethnological traits, which may now be called social institutions, such as religion, marriage, the family, and government or the state.

This sixteenth- and seventeenth-century literature, which laid the foundation of modern anthropology, comparative religions, anthropogeography, and many other related studies, exhibits the emergence of what must now be regarded as scientific method in the study of culture and society: first, in a definite transition from the motive of entertainment to that of organized inquiry; second, in the more or less clear statement of questions or problems of importance; and third, in the choice of organizing ideas to be employed in dealing with the problem of the origin of man, the diversity of cultures, the significance of similarities, the sequence of high civilizations, and the course of the process of cultural change.

But while scientific inquiry aims at the presentation of things as they are, things are not always seen as they are, even by scientists. The mind of the inquirer is never a *tabula rasa*. Only too often phenomena come to be viewed through the media of old and congenial ideas : among early anthropologists, through *ideas* of manners and customs, or by virtue of problems and solutions already in being. Moreover, it is worth remembering that the intellectual reservoir from which organizing principles have usually been drawn has always been Europocentric. They have been derived, almost without exception, from Western philosophy or the Judeo-Christian Scriptures, never from Asiatic, African, or native American sources. One example is the theory of diffusion, so much in evidence during the Renaissance and subsequent periods. Another is the principle of order so often imposed on cultural materials — or that serial, genealogical, hierarchical scheme for the spatial and temporal arrangement of things which has entered so smoothly into current theories of conjectural history or theories of social evolution. The latter doctrine, to press it back no further, is derived from scholasticism and neo-Platonism.

Any book is the fruit of many decisions, small and large. Obviously this one might have been written by half a dozen other authors, in half a dozen other ways, and for as many purposes. For this reason several features require comment. In discussions of the literature bearing on the cultures of diverse peoples, many of whom may be unknown to the lay reader, it has seemed necessary to preserve a few familiar land-marks, even though for the professional reader they have already assumed the complexion of historical clichés. The periodization of the book is a case in point. Granted that "truer" or more representative divisions of intellectual history are desirable to replace the hackneyed intervals marked by the terminal dates of the conventionally numbered centuries, it will be acknowledged that these are not discoverable all at once.

A new scheme would require much study. It will be noted also that for the sake of convenience in communication the sixteenth and seventeenth centuries are sometimes included under the rubric of the Renaissance, while the term "Middle Ages" is more or less loosely used. Both usages need defense, but the battle will not be fought out in these pages.

Since the history of anthropological thought is so intimately allied with many other fields in the humanities, such as theology, philosophy, geography, history, and even poetry and the drama, there has been no attempt to compile a complete bibliography apart from those titles which appear at the ends of chapters. Other titles might have been added, but the words of men tend to be repetitious. For the same reason, there has been no effort to come at the first title on any subject, or the first statement of any idea. The book at its best is an outline of possibilities for future studies in the history of ideas, not the final study.

A glance at the footnotes will show how much the following pages are indebted to the work of others. I have been assisted by two fellowships: one from the Henry E. Huntington Library and one from the John Simon Guggenheim Memorial Foundation. To the late Godfrey Davies of the Huntington Library and to many members of its staff I owe a great personal debt. Friends in other fields have also been very helpful. I doubt whether Dr. Sherna Vinograd and Dr. Ellen Douglass Leyburn, so generous in sharing their gifts of mind and spirit, have any idea of how much they have contributed to these pages. Ruth Tormey Pchelkin and Dr. Kenneth E. Bock were good enough to read the manuscript in one of its more inchoate forms and to give me the benefit of their advice. Lastly, to Dr. A. Irving Hallowell and to Dr. Loren Eiseley must go my deep appreciation for their unfailing kindness.

M. T. H.

Contents

Illustrations

14

The Medieval Prologue

CHAPTER I

The Classical Heritage

"What is new usually wins its way by disguising itself as old."
—C. S. Lewis

When "a certayne Caravelle sayling the West Ocean . . . was driven to a land unknowne, and not described by any Map or Carde of the Sea," medieval conceptions of savagery began slowly to lose their hold on the European mentality. For it was not so much that a Genoese sailor became the discoverer of new lands across the Ocean Sea, or that a little band of European seamen looked for the first time on the Red Men of America. It was rather that for once savagery was seen, at least in a measure, through eyes unblurred by medieval fantasy, and that it was described with calm, expressive realism. One of the most arresting features of the Columbian account of the indigenous peoples of the New World is its friendliness, freshness, and modernity.

Writing in the *Journal* of his first day ashore on a Caribbean isle, the Admiral noted with composure and photographic detachment that the people who came swimming to his ships had very handsome bodies and good faces; that they wore their hair down over their eyebrows; that some were painted black, some white and red; that some bore spears tipped with fishes' teeth. Though he found them deficient in everything that made life worth while for Europeans, he was delighted with their generosity and ingenuity. They brought presents of

17

parrots and balls of cotton thread to his shipmates; when they came again, it was in boats made out of hollowed tree trunks, richly carved, and propelled with paddles not unlike a baker's shovel. Later on, the sailors came upon "a man alone in a boat," carrying a piece of the Indians' bread, "about as large as a fist," and a basket of their own make. Judging from homely details such as these, it seemed to Columbus that all the inhabitants of the several islands possessed the same language and the same manners, except that some were better bargainers. When his sailors ventured into their houses, they found them thoroughly swept and clean, with beds and coverings like nets of cotton. Nets of palm fiber, horn fishhooks, and bone harpoons were in use. Though it was impossible to determine whether or not land was held privately or in common, all Carib men seemed to be content with one wife, and, having no "creed," they seemed promising subjects for conversion to Christianity. A man by no means well informed or given to original ideas, the Admiral was none the less profoundly impressed with the moral and intellectual qualities of these good-natured savages. He noted their ignorance of the use of iron and of many other European customs, but he also remarked "the kindness with which they were ready to give away their whole property and their childish pleasure in receiving the trash distributed among them," the hawks' bells and colored beads given by their visitors.[1]

Despite the researches of scholars who have read and analyzed the Admiral's marginal annotations in the *Ymago mundi* of Pierre d'Ailly, in the *Cosmographia* of Enea Silvio Piccolomini, in Marco Polo and Pliny, there is little to suggest that he was greatly influenced in his description of the islanders by any of these popular sources of medieval ethnology. Here and there, to be sure, are a few descriptive phrases or epithets reminiscent of an older body of ideas. The unvisited island of "Quaris," for example, was said to be the habitat of a people

Hairy Amazons, from the Borgia Map drawn in the fifteenth century, before the great discoveries.

who had a taste for human flesh.[2] There were hesitant references to Amazons and to a tribe devoid of hair. In a remote part of western Cuba, tailed men were said to live.[3] It seems also to be true that after the later voyages, when the Admiral's position at home had become less secure, he retreated to an easily recognizable medieval mysticism. Though he himself was never wholly convinced, he referred then to the string of Caribbean Islands, thought falsely to be off the coast of China, as the site of that Paradise which was preached with resonant and apocalyptic overtones by all fifteenth-century theologians.[4] Whether his remarks on the presence of Amazons, tailed men, or this earthly Paradise were concessions to what he regarded as timely and necessary propaganda, or were parts of the considered views of an experienced voyager, is very difficult to say. Nor does it make much difference. His initial response to the peoples of the New World was different from that of

André Thevet, one of the earliest French explorers of South America, who saw marvels and monsters everywhere. It was less medieval than that of Sir Walter Ralegh, who reported on the people of Guiana a century later. Though the mind of Christopher Columbus may have been, as many now think, an inextricable mixture of ambition, cold scientific curiosity, and medieval credulity, the matter is not here of first importance. The more significant of his contributions to the history of ethnological ideas were his realistic, down-to-earth judgments of the Caribs and their culture. These, if the anthropology of Herodotus be excepted, were almost unique departures in ethnological attitude and method of inquiry. More important yet, were his simple descriptions of the customs and the appearance of the island peoples, to which were added the unequivocal statement that, so far as he knew, there were "no human monstrosities" such as thronged the pages of medieval cosmographies and travel tales. The whole population was said to be very well formed. Even those called cannibals were physically normal men, except that they wore their hair long like women.[5] Living at a time when most men's minds were swamped by religious and superstitious extravagances, and deprived of a good education, this sailor approached ethnological phenomena with an amount of tolerance and critical detachment unusual in his day — and possibly also in ours.

Apart from the Biblical account of the origin and "primitive" condition of mankind, the chief source of the medieval anthropological tradition, as it came to be transmitted under the names of Pliny, Pomponius Mela, Solinus, Isidore, Vincent, Bartholomew, Sir John Mandeville, and a host of lesser borrowers, was Herodotus of Halicarnassus. It was his hand, in the fifth century B.C., which first set down in an organized and vivid form a description of a series of human cultures, later to be deformed and disfigured to suit the twisted imaginations of his successors. It was his mind, brooding restlessly over strange cultural contrasts in Mediterranean lands, which first formulated some of the persisting problems of anthropological inquiry. Even though there were no medieval translators to make the details of Herodotus accessible to an age which knew little Greek, the pith and substance of his work, the names of the nations he visited, his institutional conception of the organization of these cultures, his choice of traits to be described, mysteriously survived in books of knowledge, and in the encyclopedias of the first and twelfth centuries.

Like so many who were to come after him, the author of the *Histories* was a great traveler. He is said to have covered 1700 miles east and west and 1600 north and south, no mean feat for his day and generation. His journeys, perhaps in the company of traders, took him as far east as Persia, and as far west as Italy. He knew the coast of the Black Sea. In Egypt he ascended the Nile as far as Assuan, and, though his voyages never took him where he could see them, he was the first of a long line of men to write of the Indian ascetics. He made the acquaintance of the inhabitants of more than forty Greek cities from Cyprus to Syracuse, and with those of more than thirty countries. True, the *Histories* had their focus in an account of a war, the struggle of the Greeks to throw off the Persian yoke; but the author also had something to say about over half a hundred tribes or "nations," among whom were the Scythians north of the Black Sea and the African tribes of Libya.

Though the air of the ancient world at the time he wrote was full of speculation concerning the origin of man, Herodotus was not one to spin theories about the Golden Age or the genesis of society. He was concerned primarily with human groups as going concerns; and he assembled his facts either as an "eyewitness" or on "hearsay," each procedure being checked by what he called "inquiry" or *historiê,* a word meaning literally "to track down."[6] Nor was his attention confined solely to nonliterate or savage man, though he shows clearly his power to discriminate culturally between the Ethiopian cave dweller, the Scythian nomad, the hunter, and the cannibal. He was interested in the culture of every kind of people, civil or uncivil. To him, the barbarian was not a curiosity, an exception, a thing apart. To all Greeks, their country was an island of civility in a sea of incivility. The barbarian or the savage was at the door; he was a member of the human family; and life was unthinkable without day-to-day intercourse with him.[7] It was a delight to Herodotus to study the minds of all kinds of men, to jot down their social usages, "their superficial tastes and decencies of life . . . as well as the greater things, marriage customs, diet, climate."

The length of the descriptions allotted to the two or three score cultures which made up his ethnological collection varies, depending upon their relative importance in the contemporary Mediterranean world, and on their roles in the struggle between Greece and Persia. Long word portraits of the Athenians, the Spartans, the Persians, the Egyptians, and the Scythians are occasionally made longer by the artful insertion of a tale intended to divert the reader, or a dramatic episode to make the historical narrative move. The descriptions of other peoples are often pithy and short, especially those of the lesser Scythian and African tribes. Of the Indian Callatiae, Herodotus says merely, though it suffices, that they were men who ate their fathers.[8]

It also seems clear that Herodotus approached the task of describing manners and customs with a fairly definite idea of what constituted a culture, and a fairly specific set of questions for evoking details from informants. The criteria which separated one group from another and gave individuality to his descriptive portraits were common descent, common language, common religion, and the observance of like manners in the smaller details of living, such as dress, diet, and dwellings. The Argippeans, who lived at the foot of the Ural Mountains, were presented vividly as being bald from birth, speaking a language of their own, using no weapons, dispensing justice in the quarrels of their neighbors, and dressing after the manner of the Scythians. They lived on the juice of a species of cherry, making the lees into a solid cake which they ate instead of meat. "They dwell each man," he said, "under a tree, covering it in winter with a white felt cloth, but using no felt in summer."[9] For each group, in other words, seven categories of cultural fact are given. We are told their geographical location and something of their environment. We are told of their language, their dress, their food, their dwellings, their form of self-defense, or their lack of it, their prestige as judges among other peoples. On the other hand, concerning Egypt, one of the more important culture areas, Herodotus says at the outset that he will have to extend his remarks to some length. This country — its climate, its people and animals — was a constant surprise and challenge to the observer, "very much as Japan with its customs and Australia with its fauna have challenged the modern traveller."[10] For the Egyptians the number of cultural categories evoked far exceeds the seven used in describing the Argippeans.

Among the various classes of information which Herodotus seems to have emphasized, thus suggesting a pattern for later descriptions, were marriage customs, religious rites, burial practices, and food habits. The description of these four categories of traits, or "social institutions," were not necessarily executed in the round for every tribe that happened to stroll across the pages of the *Histories*; but they were mentioned often enough to indicate the direction taken by his curiosity, and the content of the questions he probably put to informants.

It is obvious that the institution of marriage and the patriarchate were of profound interest. This was due, at least in part, to the proximity of fifth-century Greeks to other forms of social organization and the need for comparison and evaluation. A Greek had only to travel down the coast as far as Lycia to find a people among whom descent was reckoned through the mother.[11] Athenian poets wrote tragedies on the problem of whether a man was nearer kin to one parent than another. In Assyria and Thrace, bride-purchase was known.[12] The Libyan Adyrmachidae practiced the *droit de seigneur;* the Agathyrsi, the Nassamonians, and Massagetae were thought to be promiscuous; there was widow-burning among the Thracians, and plurality of wives among other peoples.[13] Herodotus also seems to suggest that marriage by capture was an element in the culture of the Pelasgians; while the Issedonians, who ate their dead parents, were otherwise civilized enough to grant a measure of equality to their women.[14] So complete is Herodotus' survey of the different forms of the existing marriage institutions in his world, says Sir John Linton Myres, that each one even now is typical of a widespread type, and all taken together form a series from promiscuity to patriarchal monogamy.[15]

On questions of religion Herodotus was curious but also somewhat hesitant, restricting himself to collecting as much as he could of the experiences and beliefs of others without betraying his own. His plan for dealing with informants, showing dimly through a multiplicity of details, seems uniformly to have included at least three questions : first, what gods were worshiped? second, what were their names? and third, what rites of sacrifice were practiced? In the longer descriptions, such as that given of the religion of Egypt, the dress and dietary laws of the priests were reported, together with the choice of sacrificial animals, their preparation and manner of sacrifice. But for many other peoples, it seemed to be enough merely to note the presence or absence of a temple, altars, or images.

Divine nomenclature, the giving of names to the deities of other peoples, or the problem of distinguishing between the gods of an investigator's own pantheon and those of others, has always been a delicate and difficult matter. Difficult for the investigator as a believer, because for him there can logically be but one pantheon of deities; delicate, because to acknowledge the presence of other divinities by other names, among first one people and then another and another, is to rock the very foundations of religion itself. Before this impasse, Herodotus established the canon of the equivalence of the gods, or what, under similar circumstances in Rome, came to be called the *interpretatio Romana*. That is to say, in naming and describing alien deities he did exactly what nearly all subsequent students of religion were also to do : he assumed that though names might differ, the gods of one race could be equated with those of another. Zeus was Zeus the world over; if not in name, then certainly in function.

But apart from all this, the most significant bequest made by Herodotus to subsequent thought was his use of comparison, and his recognition, even in the fifth century B.C., of some of the problems which have emerged whenever the comparison of cultures has revealed either similarities or differences. Occasionally in the *Histories* comparison was employed primarily as an aid to description, or was implicit in the describer's mind. Thus the historian could say with reference to Persian religious ceremonial : "It is not their custom to make and set up statues and temples and altars [as do other peoples]," or with reference to the Indians : they kill "no living creature, nor sow, nor are wont to have houses" [as we do]. Though not stated in so many words, comparison actually took place, apparently with a conceptual model of some other culture in mind, to which others were referred and found wanting. This negative type of description, implying comparison and the recognition of antithesis, will be met with again and again in the history of ethnological thought, not only among the Greeks but throughout the Middle Ages and the Renaissance. Then again the mental act of comparison was indicated by the affirmation of simple likeness. The Babylonians, observed Herodotus, buried their dead in honey, and had funeral lamentations like the Egyptians; the Abystae aped the manners of the Cyrenians; the Massagetae resembled the Scythians in their dress and mode of living; while each man among the Nassamonians had several wives, and in this resembled the Massagetae.

However, to note and enumerate similarities and differences in manners and customs is one thing; to grasp their historical or scientific meaning is another. This, many successors of the old Greek historian were to find out to their confusion, notably Churchmen in the Middle Ages, who felt obliged to reconcile cultural diversities with the assumed homogeneity and historical priority of the Judeo-Christian tradition, and those eighteenth- and nineteenth-century social scientists who attempted to make the discovery of similarities a confirmatory adjunct of some theory of historical or evolutionary succession. Fortunately, Herodotus was free of such an ambition. He expressed no desire to confer upon his own culture the honor of being the source or the pinnacle of cultural achievement. Indeed, similarities were usually cited with the more modest and mature intention of proving prior historical contact, the prior transmission of culture from group to group, the prior operation of a process of diffusion; or to interpret Greek culture itself as an amalgam of gifts from many donors. Apparently in fifth-century Greece, there was neither honor nor dishonor attached to worshiping borrowed gods, or in practicing borrowed customs. Likeness as the result of borrowing was recognised as the inevitable and common outcome of the migration and mingling of peoples.[16]

The pages of Herodotus thus abound with attitudes and descriptive details which illuminate by inference the life and mind of the Greeks themselves. When the author speaks of the manners of the Persians, or the ways of the Egyptians, or the customs of the Agathrysi, the Budini, the Garamantes, or the Scythians, the contrasts elicited convey much to posterity concerning the domestic habits and controlling ideas of his own people. With it all, he was cautious and frank. Over and over again he stated that he was merely trying to relate what he himself had seen or heard, without prejudice and with a mind free of preconceptions. When differing accounts of an event or a custom were given to him, he hastened to assure his readers, "I cannot positively state whether this was done or that"; or "for myself, my duty is to report all that is said, but I am not obliged to believe it all." This innate caution contrasts sharply with the attitude of the men of the Middle Ages, who were only too eager to swallow whole both fact and legend. Since nothing had been said of an hypothetical Hyperborean folk by presumably neighboring Scythians, nor by any other dwellers in near-by regions, Herodotus expresses doubt of their existence.[17] So too he is unable to persuade himself that there existed a race of men born with one eye, who in all else resembled the common run of mankind; though, in another connection, he seems to accept the presence of the one-eyed Arimaspi on the borders of China.[18] Apparently, remoteness lent a kind of plausibility. Such marvels might be possible in appropriately distant localities. For it seems to be true, he said, "that the most distant parts of the world, as they enclose and wholly surround all other lands, should have those things which we deem best and rarest."[19] The nearer he drew in his reporting to the fringes of the known world, the more his natural scepticism began to break down. Human phenomena took on stranger and more bewildering manifestations; until finally he allowed himself to tell of one people beyond the eastern steppes, in a region of which no one could give a coherent account, who had feet like goats, and of another who slept away half the year.[20]

Herodotus, the ancient Greek, was a cheerful, inquisitive, rationalistic extrovert who traveled over his world to discover the facts, who took delight in telling a good story but usually avoided the temptation to wander very far from sober common sense. Unfortunately, these qualities were not destined to persist in Western ethnological thought. In the confusion attending the transition to the patristic culture of the Middle Ages, they were lost. They were lost together with the *Histories* as a book and the *Histories* as the bearer of a conscientiously conceived and realistically executed descriptive procedure. According to the record of such matters, manuscripts of Herodotus may have been available in Byzantium in the twelfth century. During the thirteenth century they are known to have made an occasional appearance in the libraries of Italian collectors. But it was not until 1474, or after scholasticism had left its mark, that a first Latin translation was made in Venice by Lorenzo Valla, and the printing presses began gradually to make the whole text of Herodotus available to the learned.[21] By that time medieval distortions of his ethnological legacy, along with similar notions, had become entrenched in the European mind.

Thus, though some of the content of the *Histories* formed a part of the medieval heritage, it bore little resemblance to the spirit of the original. The scholastically minded men by whom the transmission was conducted were neither cheerful, inquisitive, nor cautious. Quite the contrary. The great corpus of Greek learning embodied in Herodotus and the ethnological observations of other historians fell into the hands of note-takers and epitomizers who, for reasons best known to themselves, preserved only certain parts of the originals, omitting others. Though some of the transmitters give the impression of having

Fellow, call'd Hear-say; his Mouth was slit up to his Ears, and in it were seven Tongues, each of 'em cleft into seven parts," with which he chattered and prattled with all seven at once and in diverse languages. A crowd of men and women stood about him, gaping and listening. Here, said Pantagruel, repeating the beadroll of Rabelais' medieval anthropogeographical sources, "I am much mistaken if I did not see among them Herodotus, Pliny, Solinus, Berosus, Philostratus, Pomponius Mela, Strabo, and God knows how many other Antiquaries" — including Albertus Magnus, Pope Pius the Second, Volaterranus, Paulus Jovius, Chaton the Armenian, and Marco Polo, all lurking behind a piece of tapestry, "privately scribling the Lord knows what, and making rare work on't and all by Hear-say."[26]

In sharp contrast to Martyr and Rabelais, Columbus was a modern, willing on occasion to make concessions to the legendary, but only under the pressure of circumstances, not because of ignorance or credulity. But old ideas die hard. It is not their nature, nor the nature of men, their carriers, easily to yield sovereignty. Whether medieval ethnology, or indeed the entire state of mind described as "medieval," was due to the erosion of time or to mental apathy; whether this in turn was due to the isolation of scholars, or whether, in the prolonged struggle with the barbarians, the Muslims, and the Tartars, all curiosity had to be subordinated to the needs of survival — one fact remains clear : until the sixteenth century little effort was ever made by anybody to take a long, fresh look at the way of life of any people, or to report results free of the misapprehensions attending an unswerving fidelity to tradition. Despite easy access to missionaries, pilgrims, and traders who traveled continuously on the continents of Europe, Asia, and Africa, who had many prolonged contacts with non-Europeans, and who must have known better, the legendary was preferred to the factual. Learned and unlearned alike chose to steep their minds in a stale decoction of cultural observations made long before by the ancients, which, sound perhaps in the first instance, had been transmitted in attenuated or distorted form by a succession of irresponsible imitators. Better sources were shunned in favor of compilations and epitomes which contained a diverting mixture of the marvelous and the monstrous. Having lost touch with the classics, medieval scholarship purveyed a preposterous and fabulous sediment of what had once been a comparatively realistic antique ethnography.

The pre-Columbian system of ethnological thought, if system it may be called, was composed of fragments of ancient learning and superstition, disfigured by careless repetition and invention. Not only were the ancient names of ancient peoples confused but so also were their cultures. Several distinct groups were often lumped together as one. A description of a tribe in Asia was often applied, without explanation or apology, to one in Africa. Further, in the take-over of anthropological tradition from antiquity, the feeling for elapsed time was lost. Medieval scholarship seemed to have no realization that a people described by the ancients one thousand years before might no longer exist; that it might have moved out of its earlier homeland, or have been swamped by an invading culture, or, as the result of a cloud of circumstances lost its old name and altered its old way of life. Though their interest for anthropologists, if any, should have been antiquarian and little more, these peoples of antiquity were still referred to as possessing living, functioning cultures, their habits unchanged, their habitats unmodified.

Nor was this all. Medieval copyists and epitomizers were anachronistic in another sense. They were incurious concerning the manners and customs of near-by European barbarians or savages. They preferred to deal with the cultures of the classical peoples, or to follow classical models of cultural description, restricting ethnological comment to the former inhabitants of the Mediterranean littoral, or adding to these the ancient empires of the Medes and Persians, the Babylonians, Assyrians, and Egyptians, with occasional references to obsolete customs of India and China. Even as late as the thirteenth century, Bartholomew of England, whose ambitious encyclopedia became widely known, found little he wanted to say about the cultures of the contemporary peoples of Europe. There was scant interest in the manners of the barbarians of northern and western Europe as reported so graphically by Caesar and Tacitus. Medieval man was indifferent to the ideas and behavior of the near-by European barbarian or savage — probably because medieval man was so often the very savage the ancients had seen fit either to eulogize or belittle.[27] The commentator preferred to dwell upon the savagery of antiquity. He was carried away by reports, gleaned from the classics, of the existence of human monsters. These creatures haunted the minds of Europeans. They could not be exorcised, but appeared and reappeared for centuries, in the work of would-be scientists, in the sermons of the clergy, and in poetry and the drama.

The first and possibly the most influential of the epitomizers of the manners and customs of mankind was a man of great and lasting reputation, Pliny the Elder (A.D. 23–79), who lived at the very beginning of the Christian era. These were stirring times. During the fifty-six short years of his lifetime, Jerusalem was taken and destroyed by Vespasian; London came into being as a Roman settlement on the Thames; an ocean route to India was opened by way of the Red Sea; St. Peter and St. Paul were martyred in Rome. As a soldier and a colonial official, Pliny enjoyed an advantageous position for collecting cultural information in a far-flung empire. He was also a great student. By his own reckoning, his encyclopedia was assembled from over two thousand works and by a hundred authors. But his talents were never those of an observer or investigator. Written in the first century, almose five hundred years after Herodotus, the *Historia naturalis* was sundered from the *Histories* not only in time but in temperament. Herodotus was an inquirer; Pliny was a collector.

This *Historia naturalis,* which appeared about A.D. 77, was not devoted to man and man's habitat, to anthropology or anthropogeography, alone. These subjects are considered in only four of the thirty-seven books. The remaining thirty-three constitute a vast collection of miscellaneous information on sculpture and the fine arts, the industrial processes of antiquity, Mediterranean trade, Italian agriculture and mining, the religious usages of the ancient Romans, invention, zoology, gems, and so on. When rarely a piece of ethnological description was undertaken, details were meager and subordinate to geographical interests. Except, indeed, as he transmitted to the Middle Ages certain of the more fabulous elements of Herodotus and others, Pliny expended little thought on the manners and customs of mankind.[28]

At the outset, the numerical dimensions of the task of describing the varieties of human activity were startling and discouraging. Human cultures, he remarked, were beyond counting and almost as numerous as the groups of mankind. As a result, there were hundreds of groups, tribes, and peoples, whose names are mentioned and who are located geographically with some care, but nothing more. Even in Hispania Terraconensis, where Pliny resided for some years as a Roman official, not one Spanish tribe is distinguished culturally from another. Having traversed Germany as far as the source of the Danube, all he cared to say of the inhabitants from his own observation was that there were five German races. Toward the peoples of the Crimea, his attitude was the same : its population, he said, "includes 30 tribes; of these 23 live in the interior, 6 towns are occupied by the Orgocyni, Characeni, Assyrani, Stactari, Ascisalitae, and Caliordi. . . ." When his own land of Italy was under examination, Pliny again acknowledged the same basic difficulty. "I may with justice be considered ungrateful or lazy if I describe in this casual and cursory manner a land which is at once the nursling and the mother of all other lands. . . . But what am I to do? . . . I must do what I did when I spoke about the heavens," with its myriads of celestial bodies, touch only "upon particular points and only a few of the stars." [29]

Having made this decision, descriptions of the geographical world external to man are substantial as compared to his treatment of cultural phenomena. Apart from occasional allusions to occupation, diet, types of dwellings, and general appearance, he neither sought nor employed consistent criteria for the separation of one culture from another. Cultural characteristics, when mentioned at all, were couched in epithets: the "cannibal" Scythians were descended from slaves; all human beings in Gaul were included under the term "long-haired"; in Cappadocia the Massyni were tattooed. Thirty other peoples were either plowmen, nomads, charioteers, foresters, or asphalt-makers; wagon- or cave-dwellers; fish-, lotus-, pineseed-, turtle-, or bird-eaters; dog-milkers; dark-haired, long-headed, or tattooed — and nothing more. The only human groups upon whom he bestowed anything other than such forms of verbal compression were certain Eastern folk — the Chinese, Arabians, Indians — and a few monstrous races.

After leaving the Caspian Sea, "the first human occupants [to the northeast]," said Pliny, were the people called the Chinese, who were famous for a woolen substance obtained from their forests. After soaking it in water, they combed off the white down of the leaves, and so supplied Roman matrons with transparent raiment to flaunt in public. [30] Though mild in disposition, they resembled wild beasts in that they shunned the company of the remainder of mankind, and practiced the silent trade. Concerning the peoples of that other Asian land, India, Pliny followed in the footsteps of Alexander, stating that the more civilized of its races were divided into many castes. There were those who cultivated the land; those who were engaged in military service; exporters and importers of merchandise; administrators of the government; devotees of wisdom who voluntarily ended their lives on burning pyres; and still another half-wild folk who hunted and trained elephants.

Apart from such snippets of ethnological information, and notwithstanding the title of his *Natural history,* Pliny, like many who were to follow and make use of him, was far more interested in the unnatural characteristics of beast and man than in the common and the usual. Just as his volumes on zoology dwelt with relish on fabulous animals, so in those pages devoted to mankind, no tale dredged up from mythical antiquity was too threadbare, too extravagant, or too fantastic, to receive a rehearsal. Some were recounted at considerable length and with far more literary embellishment than the author chose to allot to the day-to-day lives of normal human beings. In Africa, for example, there were the cave dwellers, who lived on the flesh of snakes, and being voiceless made only squeaking noises. There were the Garamantes, who, devoid of marriage rites, lived with their women promiscuously. There were also the Augiles, who worshiped the powers of the underworld; the Gamphastes, who went naked, refrained from battle, and avoided foreigners; the headless Blemmyae, with their eyes and mouths in their chests; the Satyrs, who, except for their shape, had nothing of ordinary humanity about them; the Strap-foots, with feet like leather thongs, whose nature it was to crawl rather than walk.[31] Placing all responsibility upon the Greeks, "because of their far greater industry or older devotion to the study," and with tongue in cheek, Pliny ex-

panded his museum of *mirabilia* with tribes already supposedly
made known by Herodotus. These included the cannibal
Scythians; the one-eyed Arimaspi; the men who used skulls
for drinking cups; the Thibii, who had a double pupil in one
eye with an image of a horse in the other; the Hirpi, who
walked on hot coals without discomfort; and so on and on.
India and part of Ethiopia were said to swarm with human
marvels, including men who were exceptionally tall or exceptionally dwarfed; the Monoculi and the Umbrella-footed. Not
without reason, the solitary Essenes were presented as "remarkable beyond all other tribes in the whole world," because they
had no women, no money, and "only palm trees for company."
So also certain of the African peoples received mention because one or another characteristic, considered common among
other human beings, was absent.[32] Megasthenes is made
responsible for first giving currency to the tale of the Indian
nomads who, like snakes, had only small holes for nostrils;
Isagones, for telling of a human race whose life span reached
140 years; and Onesicritus, for spreading the story of men
eight feet tall who lived to the age of 130 without ever growing old.

But Pliny's zeal for collecting instances of the abnormal in
man was devoid of curiosity. Not once did he ask himself how
the abnormal became abnormal. A credulous man, living at
the onset of a credulous age in European thought, he "harvested the tares of legend and magic along with the wheat of
historical fact and ancient science." Apparently believing
everything he had ever heard or read, his critical powers were
unaroused. Nor was he intellectually moved by the manifold
relationships which the Roman state was compelled to maintain with barbarian nations, and which led Roman jurists to
devise laws to fit the needs of strangers as well as citizens.
Unlike Herodotus, he found no reason to reflect upon the
differences among peoples, or to compare them. All in all the

ethnological section of Pliny's *Historia naturalis* is a bursting
storehouse of information and misinformation thrown together
hastily and indiscriminately.

With Pomponius Mela in the first century A.D. and Solinus
in the third, the impairment of ethnological competence in
Western thought, which had begun with the Roman encyclopedist, became even more pronounced. Both of these men, like
their master Pliny, were epitomizers of manners and customs;
both were more absorbed in the abnormally human than in
the normal; and both were popular literary channels along
which flowed the hypnotic tide of ethnological fantasy, myth,
and legend that was later to overwhelm the better judgment
of medieval Europeans.

According to Mela in his *De situ orbis,* a little book translated into English in the sixteenth century,[33] "to treate" with
"the situation of the worlde" was "a combersome worke." So
he made up his mind "to meddle" only with "the noblest
thinges, and that breeflie." Moved by this modest purpose, he
became primarily a geographer, whose descriptive excursions
into the domain of human behavior were few, unoriginal, and
preposterous, but unquestionably accepted as authoritative.

Beginning "where our Sea [the Mediterranean] entreth
first into the maine Landes, and especially [with] those
Countries that lye on the right hand as it cometh in," he dealt
first with the manners, apparel, and diet of the inhabitants of
"Affricke." On the coast of Cyrenica, the people were said to
be civil after the manner of Europe, saving that some of them
differed in language and in the serving of their gods. "The
Noble men and Gentle men," he said, "goe in Cassockes, and
the common people are cladde in skinnes of Cattell and wilde
Beastes : on the grounde is there bedde to reste on, and there
Table to feede on. Their vesselles are made, eyther of woode or
of barke : their drinke is milke, and the juice of berries. . . ."
The uplandish or inland folk, on the other hand, "doe yet after

a more rude fashion wander abroade following their Cattell : and according as pasturage leadeth them, so remoove they themselves and their sheddes from place to place. . . . And albeit that being thus everywhere scattered by householdes, and without any lawe, they consult not in common upon any thing : . . . for as much as everie of them hath manie Wives at once, and by reason thereof manie Children and kinsfolke, there never lieth any small Companie of them together in one place."[34]

Then pursuing a rather erratic course across northern Africa, Mela paused in Egypt to describe burial customs and religion; after which came Asia Minor, the Caspian region, southern Europe, England, and finally India and Arabia. Meanwhile, many of the same old tribes, nations, and peoples, who had made their entrances into ethnological *mirabilia* in the pages of Pliny and Herodotus, reappeared in *De situ orbis*; and much that had once been said fabulously was said again, heedlessly and without discrimination.

Mela's better-known successor, Caius Julius Solinus Polyhistor, lived well over a hundred years later and was the author of a similar volume, entitled *De mirabilibus mundi*. Intended to amuse as well as inform, it contained (as Arthur Golden, its translator, said in 1587) not only "the noble actions of humaine creatures," but "the description of Countries, the maners of the people : with many mervailous things and strange antiquities, serving for the benefitt and recreation of all sorts of persons."[35] Golden overestimated the proportion of the noble to the fantastic. For Solinus asserted, not without pride, that he had studied "certaine choyse Bookes, to the intent to digresse further from thinges knowne [than others], and to make longer tariance in things more strange." It was to be a geography, yes, but a geography filled to the brim with the entertaining but nonsensical extravagance of the antique mind.

Starting "at the head of the world the Cittie of Rome," Solinus first conducted his readers to various points of interest in the metropolis. But before very long he allowed himself a digression on the monstrous fruitfulness of some women, along with a general survey of obstetrical problems and superstitions. Resuming his role as geographer, he moved on to a description of the Italian peninsula and a narration of the history of its people. But again the thread of the argument, if any, was broken. This time the subject was the many peculiar things to be found in Italy, including a viper whose sting was incurable; a species of wolf which "if they see a Manne before a Man see them, he becometh dumbe"; and certain luck-bearing precious stones and minerals. Leaving Italy, he carried his readers to southern Europe : to the islands of Sardinia, Corsica, and Sicily, where without difficulty, he found magnetic stones, poisonous worms, plants possessing the power to afflict men fatally with lock-jaw; and valuable springs whose waters mended broken bones.

It was not until Solinus reached Thrace that he gave direct attention to the strange customs of mankind. But here, what he recorded, strongly reminiscent of Herodotus in his more credulous or anecdotal moments, was strange indeed.[36] The people of this nation were contemptuous of life.

They agree all to die willingly : some of them beleeving that the soules of them that decease returne againe, and othersome thinking that they die not, but are in a more happie and blisful state. Among most of them, the birth daies are sorrowfull, and contrariwise the burialls are joyfull. . . . When Women come to the time of marriage they take not Husbands at the appointment of their Parents : but such of them as excel others in beautie . . . [choose] him that is best Chapman.

In the country of the Neuers (said by the sixteenth-century translator to be part of Muscovy) men were transformed in the summertime into wolves. "The God of this people is *Mars,* in

stedde of Images they worshippe Swordes : they offer menne
in Sacrifice : and wyth theyr boanes make fire to burne the
Sacrifices wythall. Next Neyghbours to these are the Gelones,
afterwards called the Getes, and then Tartarians. They make
bothe rayment for themselves and furniture for theyr horses
of theyr enemyes skinnes."

When Solinus reached Africa, wonders, both human and
subhuman, increased. In these "waylesse wildernesses," the
Athlantians were described as altogether void of manners fit
for men.

None hath anie proper calling, none [a reminiscent touch] hath
any speciall name. They curse the Sun at his rising, and curse
him likwise at his going downe. . . . It is affirmed that they
dreame not." Here also the Troglodites dug themselves caves
under the ground. Among them, "there was no covetousnesse of
getting, for they have bound themselves from riches, by wilful
poverties. . . . All these live by the flesh of Serpents, and beeing
ignoraunt of speech, doo rather jabber and gnarre then speake.

Both Mela and Solinus, like Pliny before them, regarded
the normal as prosaic and humdrum. They dwelt by preference
upon the rare, unique, and eccentric, rather than the common,
habitual, and human. According to Solinus, even the cattle of
the Garamantes were deformed. They grazed "sideling" with
their necks awry, for their horns growing down to the ground
would not suffer them to face forward. The Essedones made
drinking cups of the skulls of their parents; and the daintiest
dishes of the Anthropophages were made of human flesh. It
was their custom "to follow the corses of their Parents singing :
and calling together a knot of their next Neighbours, to teare
the carkasses a sunder with their teeth, and dressing them with
the other flesh of beastes, to make a feast with them. . . . The
Arimaspes again were a people with only one eye. The ears of
the Phanesians were of such length that they could cover the

rest of their bodies with them, and needed "none other apparell to clothe theyr limbes with, then theyre owne flappes." [37]

Solinus, it has often been said, was Pliny's ape, using the *Historia naturalis* as a quarry for marvels of all kinds. It would probably be more correct to say, especially with respect to ethnological data, that Pliny, Mela, and Solinus, and all their kind, were borrowers from Herodotus, but only of those elements upon which the old historian put the least emphasis. [38] Perhaps the most important exceptions to this rule were Mela's descriptions of the peoples of Gaul, and Solinus' "other Worlde" of Ireland and England with their uncivil and barbarous inhabitants. Writing in the fifth century B.C. Herodotus had described, briefly or at length, some fifty or more peoples. Five to eight hundred years later, Pliny, Solinus, and Mela referred to thirty-four of the same peoples, and in terms that are either identical with or very similar to those used by the Greek hostorian. Though forgotten in name, the author of the *Histories* was honored in imitation. [39]

BIBLIOGRAPHY AND NOTES

1. Lionel Cecil Jane, *The voyages of Christopher Columbus, being the journals of his first and third, and the letters concerning his first and last voyages, to which is added the account of his second voyage written by Andres Bernaldez; now newly translated and edited with an introduction and notes by Cecil Jane* (London: Argonaut Press, 1930), 148–56, 165, 263; *Select documents illustrating the four voyages of Columbus, including those contained in R. H. Major's Select letters of Christopher Columbus; translated and edited with additional material, an introduction and notes by Cecil Jane* (London: Hakluyt Society, 1930–33), *passim*. For a somewhat different point of view concerning the ethnological observations of Columbus, see Samuel Eliot Morison, *Admiral of the Ocean Sea* (Boston: Little, Brown, 1942), I–II, *passim*; Salvador de Madariaga, *Christopher Columbus; being the life of the very magnificent lord Don Cristobal Colón* (London: Hodder and Stoughton, 1939), *passim*; Leonardo Olschki, "What Columbus saw on landing in the West Indies," *Proceedings of the American Philosophical Society,* 94 (1941), 633–59.

2. Jane, *Voyages of Christopher Columbus,* 263–64.

3. Jane, *Select documents,* I, cviii.

4. Leonardo Olschki, *Storia letteria delle scoperte geografiche; studie ricerche* (Firenze: L. S. Olschki, 1937), *passim*.

5. Jane, *Select documents,* I, 16.

6. Sir John Linton Myres, *Herodotus, father of history* (Oxford: Clarendon Press, 1953), 5, 9; see also Edward Ernest Sikes, *The Anthropology of the Greeks* (London: D. Nutt, 1914), *passim*.

7. Terrot Reaveley Glover, *Herodotus* (Berkeley: University of California, 1924), 115.

8. Herodotus, *Herodotus, with an English translation by A. D. Godley.* The Loeb Classical Library (London: William Heineman, 1921–24), iii, 38.

9. *Ibid.,* iv, 23–25.

10. Glover, *op. cit.,* 135.

11. Sir John Linton Myres, "Herodotus and anthropology," in *Anthropology and the classics,* edited by R. R. Marett (Oxford: Clarendon Press, 1908), 152–68; "They take their names not from their fathers but from their mothers; and when one is asked by his neighbor who he is, he will say that he is the son of such and such mother, and recount the mothers of his mother." (Herodotus, i, 173.)

12. Herodotus, i, 196; v, 6.

13. *Ibid.,* iv, 168; iv, 104; iv, 172.

14. *Ibid.,* vi, 138; iv, 26.

45

46 Early Anthropology in the 16th and 17th Centuries

15. Myres, *"Herodotus and anthropology,"* 155.

16. Lionel Pearson, "Thukydides and the geographical tradition," *Classical Quarterly* (London), 33 (1934), 49–55; Mikhail Rostovtsev, *The social and economic history of the Hellenistic world* (Oxford: Clarendon Press, 1941), 31.

17. Herodotus, *op. cit.*, iv, 32–36.

18. *Ibid.*, iii, 116; iv, 13–27.

19. *Ibid.*, iii, 116.

20. *Ibid.*, iv, 25.

21. A vogue for the classics in Byzantium stimulated a vigorous book trade and the production of new manuscripts. Herodotus, among others, was quoted by the poet Tzetzes in 1100 (S. K. Padover, "Byzantine libraries," in James Westfall Thompson, *The medieval library* [Chicago: University of Chicago Press, 1939], 321–22). Ciriaco of Ancona (c. 1391– c. 1450) collected Greek manuscripts, including Herodotus. (George Sarton, *Introduction to the history of science* [Baltimore: Williams and Williams, 1927–48], III, pt. II, 1321). Pope Nicholas (1447–55) sent Enoch of Ascoli to the Orient to seek manuscripts, and stimulated the translation of Greek authors into Latin, including Herodotus (Dorothy M. Robathan, "Libraries of the Italian renaissance," in Thompson, 518). See also Pearl Kibre, *The library of Pico della Mirandola* (New York: Columbia University Press, 1936), *passim*; "The intellectual interests reflected in libraries of the fourteenth and fifteenth centuries," *Journal of the History of Ideas* VII (1946), 257–97; Eva M. Sanford, "The study of ancient history in the middle ages," *ibid.*, V (1944), 21–43.

22. Henry Raupe Wagner, *Peter Martyr and his works* (Worcester: American Antiquarian Society, 1947), 15–16. The *First Decade*, finished about 1500 or 1501, related to Colón and Pinzon. A paraphrase in Italian was published in 1504, reprinted in 1507, and reprinted again in Seville by Martyr himself.

23. Pietro Martire d'Anghiera, *De novo orbe, or The historie of the West Indies, contayning the actes and adventures of the Spanyardes, which have conquered and peopled those countries, inriched with varietie of pleasant relation of the manners, ceremonies, lawes, governments, and warres of the Indians. Comprised in eight decades. Written by Peter Martyr a Millanoise of Angleria . . . Whereof three have beene formerly translated into English, by R. Eden, where-unto the other five, are newly added* (London: Printed for Thomas Adams, 1612), sig. C 4 r, C 6 v.

24. François Rabelais, *Gargantua and Pantagruel,* translated into English by Sir Thomas Urquart and Peter le Motteaux, annis 1653–1694 with an introduction by Charles Whibley (London: David Nutt, 1900), III, 77–78.

25. Abel Jules Maurice Lefranc, *Les navigations de Pantagruel: étude sur la géographie Rabelaisienne* (Paris: Henri Leclere, 1905), 109.

26. Rabelais, *op. cit.*, III, 341–48.

27. George Boas, *Essays on primitivism and related ideas in the middle ages* (Baltimore: Johns Hopkins University Press, 1948), 153.

28. In the Middle Ages Pliny's work had a direct influence upon thought. This is proved by the number of times the title of his *Historia*

naturalis appeared in literary catalogues. Manuscripts are numerous, as are also printed editions, which began to appear immediately after the invention of the printing press. (Herbert Newton Wethered: *The mind of the ancient world: a consideration of Pliny's Natural History* [London: Longmans, 1937] 2–6; Lynn Thorndike, *A history of magic and experimental science* [New York: Macmillan, 1923–1941], I, 46, 51–53; Eugene Willis Gudger, "Pliny's *Historia naturalis.* The most popular natural history ever published," *Isis,* 6 [1924], 269–81.)

29. Caius Plinius Secundus, *Natural History,* with an English translation in ten volumes, by H. Rackham. The Loeb Classical Library (London: Heineman, 1938–1956), IV. xii, 84–85; III. v. 36–45.

30. *Ibid.,* VII. xx, 53–54; IV. xvii, 106.

31. *Ibid..* V. viii, 43–46. Much of what appears in this section resembles Herodotus, with some displacements or misquotations. Similar instances are to be found in *De situ orbis* by Pomponius Mela, another first-century geographer.

32. *Ibid.,* V. xv, 73–74.

33. Pomponius Mela, *The rare and singular worke of Pomponius Mela, that excellent and worthy cosmographer, of the situation of the world, most orderly prepared, and devided every parte by it selfe: with the longitude and latitude of everie kingdome, regent, province, rivers, mountaines, cities and countries. Whereunto is added, that learned worke of Julius Solinus Polyhistor, with a necessarie table for thys booke: right pleasant and profitable for gentlemen, marchaunts, mariners, and travellers. Translated into Englishe by Arthur Golding Gentleman* (London: Printed for Thomas Hacket, 1590).
Little is known of Mela beyond the fact that he was born in Spain, not far from Gibraltar, and that he wrote his geographical treatise in A.D. 43. The *editio princeps* of this popular work was printed in 1471, supposedly by Antonius Zarotus under the title *Cosmographia.* Later editions appeared under the title *De situ orbis.* (Justin Winsor, *Narrative and critical history of America* [New York: Houghton Mifflin, 1884–89], II, 180–82.)

34. *Ibid.,* sig. C i r; D iii v.

35. Caius Julius Solinus, *The excellent and pleasant worke of Julius Solinus Polyhistor. Contayning the noble actions of humaine creatures, the secrets & providence of nature, the description of Countries, the maners of the people: with many mervailous things and strange antiquities. Serving for the benefitt and recreation of all sorts of persons. Translated out of Latin into English by Arthur Golding, Gent.* (London: I. Charlewoode for Thomas Hacket, 1587), sig. A i r.

36. In England in the sixteenth century, as often elsewhere during the same period, an historico-ethnological sense was lacking. Cultural descriptions made of the ancients in antiquity were implicitly accepted as currently true for contemporary residents of the once classical regions. So also was a description of the English during the Roman occupation, at least when included in the translations of such books as Mela and Solinus. Apparently readers were not troubled by the fact that Elizabethan England differed radically from Roman England. The translator

of Solinus tried to make an identification between the Muscovites of the sixteenth century and the Neuers of Solinus and Herodotus, but the description offered is still that by Herodotus, and referred to a people who lived over two thousand years before.

37. *Ibid.,* sig K ii v – K iii r; M iii r; W i v; T ii r; N i v; O ii v.

38. "Solinus hath drawn almost all his matter out of Plinies fountaines . . ." (*ibid.,* sig. A ii r). But he did not use the *Natural history* "without discrimination . . . he only laid under contribution those portions which contained a good store of marvels. Thus he turned especially to the geographical books (iii–vi), and to passages 'Concerning Man' (bk. vii), 'Concerning Animals' (bks. viii–xi), 'Concerning Trees' (bk. xii), and 'Concerning Gems' (bk. xxxvii). . . . In the same way, most of the thirty-nine chapters of Pomponius Mela which reappear in Solinus are from the second book of that compendium, where the manners and monsters of outlying countries are particularly dwelt upon." (Sir Charles Raymond Beazley, *The dawn of modern geography* [London: J. Murray, 1897–1906], I, 250–51). It was probably from lost classical works that he drew most of his additional facts or fancies, unknown to Pliny or Mela (*ibid.,* I. 251, note 1). For possible common sources of Pliny and Pomponius Mela, see John Kirkland Wright, *The Geographical lore of the time of the Crusades* (New York: American Geographical Society, 1925), 366, note 6.

39. Judging by agreement in the names of tribes, Mela or Solinus, or both, seven times mention and describe a people previously mentioned or described by Pliny, but not by Herodotus. In six cases Mela seems to be the source of the cultural description found in Solinus. This helps to indicate their ultimate indebtedness to Herodotus, though his work may have been transmitted to them indirctly through many hands.

CHAPTER II

The Ethnology of the Medieval Encyclopedists Pilgrims, Merchants, and Missionaries

"Doctors are dispersed everywhere in every castle, every burgh, and especially by the students of the Two Orders. . . . And yet there was never so much ignorance, so much error."

—ROGER BACON

ONE DIFFICULTY that besets the student of the history of ethnological ideas, especially during the pre-Columbian period, is that of placing himself in sympathetic rapport with the man of the Middle Ages, the credulous reader of Mela and Solinus; of coming to an understanding of why medieval thought, though grounded in the Hebrew Scriptures, contained so large an ingredient of the pagan, the fantastic, the monstrous, and the fabulous. It is possible, of course, that real sympathy with minds so far in the past is unachievable. Or perhaps we tend to make another error. Perhaps no such creature as medieval man, monolithic in thought and undifferentiated in opinion, ever existed except in the convenient typology of the historian or medievalist.

Be that as it may, historians and medievalists, most of whom are somewhat less concerned with the history of ethnological thought than with other early features of European culture, have not yet solved the problem. Furthermore, the difficulty has been compounded by the obvious presence in the literature of at least two distinct views of the medieval mentality, both supported with voluminous documentation and both, to all intents and purposes, equally sound.

According to some authorities, the medieval mind moved along channels far removed from independent inquiry or the detached scrutiny of nature and man. By those who have adopted this position, we are told that European life was stationary or retrograde; that the spirit of the age had turned the most talented minds to theological rather than secular problems; that among theologians the despotic operation of the processes of tradition embodied in religious dogma, had already snuffed out the least flash of curiosity. Though many a capital and boss in church or chapel, many a bench-end or roof beam, now testifies to the delight of the medieval crafts-man in foliage and in flowers, the culture of the Church Fathers was indifferent to natural beauty. Nature presented to the eye of faith a panorama of objects insignificant in them-selves unless interpreted with reference to the categories of salvation. If theologians ever doubted the tales of fabulous peoples transmitted from the ancients, they were restrained by a traditional classicism and scholastic logic from refuting their existence. As for man as a whole, the Fathers desired less to know him than to save him. And this point of view, narrow as it was, communicated itself to the masses of simple folk who knelt at many altars.

On the other hand, for other historians the dimness of the Dark or Middle Ages, especially as its shadow fell across the desire to accumulate fresh ethnological information, was never so unrelieved as some of their colleagues would have it. Given another collection of materials just as relevant and just as representative, indifference to new knowledge concerning the peoples of Asia or Africa was far from universal. Nor was new knowledge inaccessible. In the work of such men as Vincent of Beauvais, Bartholomew of England, Mandeville, and many of the later encyclopedists, who seemed to harp upon the culturally fabulous, this archaism was merely a literary convention required by art rather than by religion or reason. While these men and others were insisting on the existence of the traditional and monstrous, there was a wealth of opportunity, for those who would take advantage of it, to acquire a better quality of ethnological information.

For the mental torpor which is said to have cloaked the Western mind for so long during the Middle Ages, and which led in matters germane to social theory, anthropogeography, and ethnology to the acceptance of legend rather than unencumbered observation, two explanations may be offered. One of these was geographical ignorance, or better, perhaps, the refusal to accept obvious geographical facts. The other was the prolonged struggle against the Saracens.

Geographical knowledge, that ground and scaffolding of all successful social inquiry, was either so lacking in the ranks of official scholarship, or so clouded with theological controversy that sound ethnological observations were impossible.[1] Indeed, the ideas which an intelligent man in these early days harbored concerning the shape and regional habitability of the earth were often less in harmony with the facts even than his anthropological conceptions. Though many scholars still entertained the Pythagorean theory of the sphericity of the earth, with its several zones or climates, some Churchmen were uneasy or opposed. The Venerable Bede stoutly defended the doctrine. St. Augustine, confused by what he took to be contradictions between Holy Writ and Greek geographical thought, was hesitant and noncommittal. Lactantius and other Fathers came out for a flat earth. But whatever shape the dwelling place of man was said to have, whether it was regarded as a flattened disc riding aloft in the empyrean or a sphere divisible into several zones or climates, it was everywhere unorthodox to suggest that the sons of Adam and the progeny of Noah had ever, or could have ever, lived everywhere on its surface.

Those who believed that the earth was flat scoffed at the idea of antipodean man on the other side of the disk. They derided the notion of a human breed living upside down, foot to foot with European Christians, or falling off into space. Said Lactantius, while many applauded, "Is there anyone so stupid as to believe that there are men whose feet are higher than their heads; that it rains, snows, and hails upwards; that the roofs and spires of cities point at the sky beneath them; that the rivers flow into the air out of their channels?" On the other hand, among geographers and map-makers, influenced by one or another of the zonal theories of a spherical earth, the problem of antipodean man took another form. Given a division into climates, such as *septrionalis frigida, temperata nostra, torrida, temperata antipodum,* and *australia frigida,* it was inferred that the equatorial zone not only was uninhabited but had imposed a fiery barrier to the movement of any representatives of mankind into the south. The progeny of Adam had never been able to cross it.[2]

Unless Christian Europe was prepared to espouse an intolerably heretical polygenetic theory of the origin of mankind, it was necessary to regard the southern zone as destitute of colonies of human beings. If any wavered they were called upon to explain how such austral races could be descended from Adam, described in the Book of Genesis as the father of all mankind. They were compelled to demonstrate how it could be maintained that Christ had died to save all men, and the Word preached to every people, if half of them were cut off from communication with the other half. "Whereas they fable," said St. Augustine, "of a people that inhabit that land where the sunne riseth, when it setteth with us, and goe with their feete towards ours, it is incredible. . . . It were too absurd to say, that men might sayle over that huge Ocean, and goe inhabite there : that the progenie of the first man might people that part also." And, significantly enough, this discussion of the antipodes in the *City of God* follows closely on Augustine's response to another moot question in the Middle Ages, namely, whether Adam's or Noah's sons had begotten any of the monstrous kinds of men reported in legend and story, any dog-headed, or umbrella-footed, or flap-eared beings, such as some authors were wont to locate on the fringes of the human world or in the antipodes. Here again Augustine's answer was orthodox and monogenetic : "To close this question uppe with a sure locke," he said, "either the stories of such monsters are plaine lies, or if there be such, they are either no men, or if they be men, they are the progeny of Adam."[3] For these reasons, the Church Fathers, though obviously in repeated contact with uncivil man through commercial and missionary endeavor, displayed far less interest in barbarian types of culture than had the Greeks and Romans.

It also seems not unlikely that the prolonged struggle against the Saracens, and the ceaseless effort to implant Christianity among the barbarians, which lasted in some European regions for ten centuries, tended to make all the gentile tribes look more or less alike, even to those who knew better, and choked off any passing interest in differentiating among them. At all events, while these great European movements were taking place, knowledge of the great geographers and ethnologists of antiquity—Herodotus, Strabo, Ptolemy, Hipparchus—passed almost wholly from Christian memory. Whatever anthropological data were introduced into the literature of the period were culled almost exclusively from the epitomes of Pliny, Solinus, and Mela. As Francis Bacon was to lament in another connection, everything of value seemed to sink, and only light and worthless rubbish came floating down the stream of time. If occasionally, in the interest of religion or entertainment, ventures in descriptive ethnography were undertaken, they were shaped to lend substance to the slender Scriptural account of the dispersion from the Ark, to put before the weaker brethren the moral inspiration of the supposedly exemplary peoples, or to retell old tales of the terrors of the barbarian frontier, aided by ancient traditions of the culturally monstrous. In actual practice, each people—European, Asian, African, or the tribal components of each—was submitted to description, but the description was formalized and repetitious, the shorter the better; and included value judgments contrasting national virtues and iniquities. Each people thus described became a familiar entity in the iconography of the Middle Ages : arrested types of human beings, represented over the passing centuries as performing unvarying ceremonies, in unvarying costumes, and with unvarying characteristics. Medieval anthropogeography in this sense was tough mental stuff, so often repeated, so durable, so satisfying, that by the time of the Renaissance many of its preconceptions had been accepted as received experience, and were employed, to the confusion of thought, in the interpretation of the new peoples of the New World.

While these and other probable causes of intellectual inflexibility or decline during the Middle Ages are too many, too intricate, and too subtle to be captured either in a paragraph or in a volume, their results are not hard to find. They appeared in that brood of Pliny : Mela and Solinus, and the medieval encyclopedists; in the work of Isidore, Bishop of Seville, in the seventh century; in Bartholomew's *De proprietatibus rerum* in the thirteenth; in *Li livres dou tresor* by Brunetto Latini, counselor of Dante; in Albertus Magnus; in the *Speculum historiale* of Vincent of Beauvais; in the *Ymage du monde;* in Sir John Mandeville; in the *Polychronicon* of Ranulph Higden, and in many other lesser-known works.

The first of this long line of Christian encyclopedias was

Isidore's *Etymologies,*[4] written between 622 and 623, or before the Saracens had swept over Western Europe. The need for such a book had been long remarked. Said Augustine, Bishop of Hippo in the fourth century, "I think it would well if someone would compile a description of unknown places, animals, plants, minerals, and other things mentioned in Scripture," to parallel in form and purpose the already collected vocabularies of Hebrew or Syrian words found in the Bible. Isidore's work was the delayed response, designed to educate Spain's new Visigothic rulers in the culture of Christendom. The *Etymologies* or *Origins* was derived from both classical and patristic sources. Intended to be brief and definitive, a summary of the whole body of knowledge available to men of learning in the seventh century, it was cast in the form of a dictionary, in which the etymology of words and the epitomization of thought were central features. It brought together a large collection of excerpts from many previous works, grouped under appropriate headings: arithmetic, geometry, music, astronomy; law and chronology; theology; human anatomy and physiology; zoology; cosmography and physical geography; architecture and surveying; mineralogy, agriculture, and military science.[5]

Broad as was his general plan, Isidore's interest in ethnological phenomena, like that of his contemporaries, was small. The work contains no chapter or section specifically on manners and customs. If mentioned at all, such matters were scattered about in Book VIII, "On the Church and Different Sects"; in Book IX, "On Languages, Races, Empires, Warfare, Citizens, Relationships"; in Book XI, "On Men and Monsters"; and in Book XIX, "On Ships, Buildings, and Garments." Here, however, and within the limitations of his etymological scheme of presentation, the author had something to say on various relevant subjects: on the languages and races of mankind; on the monstrous peoples; on certain religions and the origin of idolatry or of the heathen gods; and also on that perennial and never omitted interest, the diversities of costume.

As might well be expected of a man living in Spain in the seventh century, the world view of the Bishop of Seville was severely circumscribed. Except for a slight knowledge of islands such as Britain, Ireland, and Taprobane—or of such distant peoples as the Seres—it was bounded geographically by the shores of the Mediterranean. His idea of the distribution of lands and waters appears in the statement that "the circle of lands is so-called from its roundness, which is like that of a wheel," with the ocean flowing about on all sides, and the lands divided into three parts: Europe, Asia, Africa. Indeed, this ancient conception, so fundamental to medieval thinking, was broadened a bit in the *Etymologies,* for Isidore showed some toleration for what were considered troublesome ideas. He admitted, at least on the basis of the reasoning of the poets, the possible existence of a fourth part of the earth "across the ocean to the south," and of a people "called Antipodes," whose footsteps were opposed to those of Europeans.

Concerning the tribes of mankind, the *Etymologies* was completely orthodox. They had been separated one from another by that partition of tongues which fell so tragically upon unilingual and culturally homogeneous mankind after the Deluge, at the time of the erection of the Tower of Babel. Of the seventy-three nations which emerged, fifteen were the descendants of Japheth, thirty-one of Ham, and twenty-seven of Shem. If national characteristics were mentioned at all, they were epitomized in as few words as possible, and then for only a few peoples. The Germans, for example, were so called because their bodies were of great size; the tribes of the Saxons were "brave and active"; the customs of the Franks were "uncouth" and accompanied by a "natural fierceness of spirit"; and the Britons were "stupid." According to Isidore, climatic influences were powerful. For this reason, the Romans were dignified, the Greeks unstable, the Africans crafty, the Gauls fierce by nature, with some "headlong in their disposition."

In Book IX, the Bishop of the primary see of Spain also offered the usual observations on abnormal births and monstrous races, accompanied by remnants of the classical sciences of human anatomy and physiology. He and his fellow spiritual leaders in the Middle Ages were as diverted as the lowliest peasant by anatomical novelties, provided these were simple and startling. Indeed, as every journalist or showman well knows, the births of omphalopagus or connected twins, of monstrous calves or geese, are subjects of perennial curiosity. But Isidore believed, as did many other Christian doctors, that just as there were abnormal individuals within the several "nations," so also there were abnormal "nations" within the totality of mankind. These included the fabulous peoples of classical anthropology : the giants, the pigmies, the cyclops, the dog-faced men, and the hermaphrodites. On this subject Isidore quoted Solinus two hundred times, and through Solinus reached back into the rich stores of the monstrous in Mela, Pliny, and Herodotus. Needless to say, all that remained of Herodotus was teratology. According to the *Etymologies,* the Anthropophagi lived near the Seres, the Cynocephali were born in India in company with the Cyclops; and the Blemmys, headless with mouths and eyes in their chests, were born in Libya. Races displaying even more abnormal characteristics were described as residents of the remoter East. Some of these were noseless; others enjoyed a protruding lower lip under which they took shelter while they dozed; and still others had mouths so tiny that the only nourishment they could receive had to be sucked through a straw of wheat. There were also Satyrs and Sciopods : the former notable for their turned-up noses, the latter for one outsize foot under which its fortunate owner could rest in the shade during torrid weather.[6]

Isidore reported that there were multiple religions in the seventh-century world, divided into two categories: one involved the worship of idols and included the heathen or gentile peoples; the other was composed of Christians. Among alien deities mentioned in the *Etymologies* were Isis in Egypt, Jove in Crete, Juba among the Moors, Faunus in Italy, and Quirinus among the Romans. Adopting a theory that had been proposed in Greece by Euhemerus, Isidore ascribed the origin of idol worship to the common experience of bereavement, or to that longing for the loved and lost which leads men to create likenesses of them. But error had so insinuated itself that the persons whom the bereft had sought merely to keep in remembrance came to be deified and worshiped as gods.[7]

The section on the costumes of mankind contains some descriptions of the attire of the priesthood, the garments of the ancients, and the dress of the peoples of Phoenicia, Spain, Phrygia, Syria, Egypt, Gaul, and Germany. There are also references to the fibers and materials out of which various textiles were made, including wool, linen, and silk; to the colors used by dyers and their sources; to the process of weaving; and to varying habits of ornamentation. The main interest of the section lies in its inclusiveness rather than its content. It may be one of the first efforts to assemble data on the apparel of peoples, a category of cultural description that was seldom to be omitted thereafter.

Like all medieval encyclopedias, Isidore's *Etymologies* was intended to cover the current knowledge of his time, doctrinal as well as secular. But, according to critics, his organization of the field of secular science, including ethnology or anthropo-geography, "amounted to no more than the laying out of a corpse." By reason of his habits of study and the qualities of the patristic mind, he was led "to select the palpable, the foolish, and the mechanically correlated." Consequently, the book is little more than a collection of terms and definitions, a conglomerate of miscellaneous knowledge, a compilation of compilations. A phrase in which he spoke of "culling the opinions of the Fathers like flowers from diverse meadows," occurs hundreds of times. Yet, as Professor Thorndike has pointed out, this is all to the good. It makes Isidore a valuable representative of his period and shows how scanty was the information of the early Middle Ages even among men of learning. At the same time, Isidore's influence upon those who followed him was very great. There was scarcely a library in chapter house or abbey whose catalogue failed to carry his name. The *Etymologies* continued to be cited as an authority until the thirteenth century.[8]

Between 1240 and 1260,[9] or about six hundred years after Isidore's *magnum opus* had brought the traditional ideas of pagan cosmography and anthropogeography into some sort of subordination to the dogmas of Christendom, another encyclopedia was introduced to the European public. This was the *De proprietatibus rerum,* compiled by the Franciscan Bartholomaeus Anglicus. It not only achieved instant popularity but remained a favorite book in Europe for over three hundred years, securing a wider audience than did Vincent of Beauvais, Albertus Magnus, Alexander Neckham, or even the *Ymage du Monde,* other encyclopedists or encyclopedias for which the thirteenth century became famous.

By this time, eighteen generations after the publication of Isidore's *Etymologies,* curiosity about the world and man had stirred again, not only in the ranks of the learned but also among the unlearned. Accordingly, although Bartholomew's book was written ostensibly for the common people *(simplices et rudes)*[10]—for the simple man who might not in "endelesse many bokes" be able to "seke and fynde all the properties of things, of which the holy writte maketh mencion"—it was read by all. This may account for the rapid multiplication of manuscript copies and their wide distribution among Continental libraries. In the fourteenth and fifteenth centuries, *De proprietatibus rerum* was translated into six European languages[11]—English, French, Spanish, Provençal, Dutch, and Italian[12]; and with the coming of the printing press it reached forty-six editions.

Despite its later compilation than the *Etymologies* and its immediate popularity, however, it was in no sense modern. Though its natural history and geography were more up to date than that found in most available sources, and though the book was the standard authority in Shakespeare's youth, it still represented a state of knowledge concerning the breeds of mankind already superceded in the twelfth-century Renaissance. And how could it be otherwise?

Bartholomew, like Isidore, relied on the epitomizers. Many sections ended with a deferential "So saith Solinus" or "So saith Pliny,"—dead a thousand years when Bartholomew took up his pen. Elsewhere, indebtedness was expressed to Martianus Capella (c. 400), to Macrobius (c. 409), to Boethius (480?-524?), and to Cassiodorus (c. 540), all of whose works were new at least half a millennium before. Otherwise, Bartholomew's well of information was Isidore. The Bishop of Seville was cited in approximately 660 chapters. Many quotations from the Bible and from the ancient poets were copied from the *Etymologies* rather than from the originals. Though Aristotle was frequently mentioned as an authority for certain statements, the old word-monger of the seventh century still comes out far ahead. With such models, or in spite of them, Bartholomew enjoyed a high academic standing. During the very decades when the Vatican was sending out emissaries to report on the ethnological characteristics of the Mongols, and the Polos were making their celebrated journeys to the Far East, this stale encyclopedia was one of the principal works of reference in the University of Paris. Essentially a textbook on

full of glewe, and of the dounge of Oxen and Kine dried and burned . . . they forsake dignitie and knighthood, and suffer none to rise and to be greater among them. . . . They love well chastitie, and punish all the unchaste, right grievously : and they keepe their Children chaste, unto the time they are of full age, and so when they be wedded, they get manly children and strong.

Whenever, on the other hand, Bartholomew was called upon to deal with lands and nations on the margins of Europe or far beyond, he followed in the well-worn footsteps of his predecessors, and immediately resorted to the traditional and fabulous. Here Isidore was constantly cited as an authority, even for those peoples of the thirteenth century whom he could not well have known, or, together with Pliny and Solinus, for marginal African or Eastern folk. Albania was said to be a province "of ye more Asia, and hath that name of the colour of men. For they be borne with white haire. . . . Plinius sheweth. . . . And . . . have eien painted, and yeolowe in the blacke, that they see better by night then by daye, as he saith, and Isidore also. . . . And Solinus telleth the same for mervaile." The Amazons were located by Bartholomew toward the east, and were equally fabulous. In Africa, or "Negros lande," many nations were reported with divers faces wonderfully and horribly shapen. Then come many old friends, met first in the pages of Herodotus. Among them were the Garamantes, who dwelt with women without law; the Troglodites, who "dug them dens" and ate serpents; the Satyrs, who had the shape of men but none of their manners; the Ethiopians, who lived only "by honey suckles dried in smoake."[15] Nor is Inde, a country of East Asia, omitted. Here there were men of dyed color, and great elephants, popinjays, and trees called cinnamon and pepper, and a reed with a sweet fragrance. Here, some of the Indians tilled the soil, some engaged in chivalry, some used merchandise to lead out

chaffer, some ruled and governed.[16] Leaning on obvious sources,
Bartholomew told of "their Philosophers that they call
Gymnophistae," who could "stande in most hot gravell from
the morning till even"; of men "with the soles of the feete
turned backward, and the foote also, with eight toes on one
foote"; of some with hounds' heads; of women "that bear
never a child but once"; of men without mouths, "cloathed in
mosse, and in rough hairy things, which they gather of trees";
and of those "hore in youth, and black in age." And, he says,
it was Pliny who rehearsed "these wonders and many other
moe."[17]

But Pliny can hardly be held
material drummed up by
much closer resemblance
detail lifted by Bartholo
purposely or inadvertentl
in his text. It is not unus
said by Pliny of one pec
to describe another, citin
Discrimination among des
important to the author c_____ ,.. .p...... .., ...gs. Indeed
after the p's were reached in his alphabetical recapitulation of
places and people, a sudden and irrational shift to a new
authority occurred—someone named Herodotus, who thereafter bore the burden for whatever was said concerning
Pannonia (Hungary), Perinea (the Pyrenees), Pictavia (Poitou),
Picardia (Picardy), Saxony, and Sitia. That neither Bartholomew nor his readers showed the slightest inclination to check
the accuracy of his stories, and that no one attempted to relate
Bartholomew's descriptions of peoples to facts which must have
come to their attention, reveals one difference between the
medieval and modern scientific practice. In regard to man, as
in regard to history and nature, legend was accepted as fact
and always in preference to accurate observation and reporting.

But when all of this has been said concerning the mental habits of Bartholomew and other medieval encyclopedists, the same insistent question again thrusts itself into the discussion. Why was it that Isidore and Bartholomew, two men who were scholars in the Middle Ages, knew so little about their fellow human beings? Why were they content with their ignorance? Why their absorption, ethnologically speaking, in the abnormal, monstrous, or trivial? Why their compulsive and tiresome reiteration of stale descriptions of fabulous peoples cribbed from predecessors, who in turn had cribbed from precursors all the way back to Roman and Hellenistic antiquity?

Plainly, it was a state of mind which reached far beyond these two men. The same, or at least similar, compulsive anthropogeographical conventions appear in many other encyclopedias: in the *Speculum naturale* and *Speculum historiale* of Vincent of Beauvais (1190–1264); in the works of Albert the Great of Bollstadt (1193?-1280), reckoned as second only to Aquinas; in the *Polychronicon* of Ranulph Higden (d. 1364); in Alexander Neckham's *De naturis rerum;* in Caxton's *Mirror of the world*. Both before and after the introduction of the printing press, new collections of geographical, historical, ethnological and other materials, treated in the encyclopedic manner, constantly appeared or reappeared. Of the twelve best sellers among incunabula in the fourteenth and fifteenth centuries, four—*De mirabilis mundi, Liber aggregationis, Secreta mulierum,* and Mandeville—dealt with marvels. According to George Sarton in his *Introduction to the history of science,* there was "not a single great work in the lot, nor a single great personality." Among all medieval collectors of books respect and admiration for Pliny persisted. His *Natural history* was given a place on the shelves of private libraries by the side of the *Etymologies* of Isidore, "who was the most favored of humanists." Petrarch relates that a copy of Isidore's work was given him by his father, and that he treasured it all his life. Through these and other media, the anthropo-geography of antiquity, the tales of wild men, and the marvels of the East enjoyed a vitality and longevity impossible to exaggerate.[18] Ethnographical knowledge was choked by a blanket of luxuriant superstition, and erroneous beliefs of a classical origin were joined to others of a Germanic, Celtic, or Oriental provenance. Sheer magic, incantation, divination, and witchcraft, abetted by alchemy and astrology, all flourished and mingled, overshadowing whatever sound knowledge there was of nature, man. ˈ   ˈ ˈ ure. The medieval injunction to " .   ˈ   . sted to you" was followed . that are almost incalculable. . and Sir John Mandeville . d in the fourteenth century, are . range submission to ethnological . else, they were alike in their literary . ioning commitment to geographical . gma. Despite the contact of European . counterparts as far to the east as China, . king journeys by missionaries which had . hey were born, neither the poet nor the travelogue writer had shaken loose from the old system of ideas in which they, their fathers, and their father's fathers, had been nurtured; nor did they feel any need to be shaken.

Dante's knowledge of mankind, outside of the narrow European range of his own experience, was limited to what he had learned from Orosius, Isidore, Albertus Magnus, and other writers who had prepared this "antique pabulum for the medieval stomach." His tutor, Brunetto Latini, had been a cosmographer, a compiler of *Li livres dou tresor,* and a notorious plagiarizer of Solinus Polyhistor. Dante the poet, a man otherwise of great intellectual attainment, faithfully and uncritically shared many of Latini's misconceptions. One, referring to the relative sizes of the continents, made Asia (including

Egypt) equal in extent to Europe and Africa. The western half of the world was thought of as divided by the inlet of the Mediterranean into two approximately equal land masses, with Jerusalem in the center. Rejecting the idea of an antipodal race on the usual ground that a Christian could not accept the underlying assumption of a polygenetic origin of mankind, Dante had little to say that was of ethnological interest, and certainly nothing that was new. The only inhabitants of tropical Africa he appears to have heard of were the Garamantes, already mentioned by every medieval encyclopedist and cosmographer. They lived, said the poet, under the equator and were so tortured by the excessive heat that they were compelled to eschew clothing. Then again in the northeastern part of the habitable zone he mentioned the equally venerable Scythians, who, exposed to the extreme inequality of day and night, suffered from intolerable cold.[19]

As for Mandeville, if such a man ever lived, his name has rightfully become synonymous with the legendary, the monstrous, the prodigious, and the mysterious. The purpose of his *Travels* (1356), written after the closure of the Mediterranean to commercial and pilgrim traffic by the Saracens, was first, to entertain, and second, to communicate with the members of a generation which had not only been cut off from the Holy Land and from the rest of their European and Asiatic coreligionists but which still possessed a desire to travel and "to see mervailes and customs of countries, and diversities of folkys and diverse shap of man and beistis."[20] A mixture of the serious and jocose, the book belongs to the history of literature rather than to that of exploration. Consequently, and appropriately enough considering the times, it is divided into two parts : the first, purporting to take the form of a guide book for pilgrims to the Levant, offers much information, both good and bad, concerning roads, seaways, and sights along the way; the second transports the reader to the Far East, and there plunges him so deeply into the fantastic and incredible that the edge of criticism is blunted.

If antiquity confers respectability, some of Mandeville's stories came from the most impeccable sources, the cream of the flamboyant anthropogeography of Pliny, Solinus, Mela, and Isidore; the Alexander romances and the bestiaries. Consequently, the reader finds himself at once at home and with boon companions. There are the Albanians, who made their first bow to the European reading public in the pages of Herodotus. They appear again in the *Travels* and are still whiter in aspect than anybody else.[21] There also are those old reliables among mythical peoples, the Amazons, in the Land of Feminy. On the Isle of Lamary lived another people, somewhat newer to the literature of medieval anthropogeography, but destined in the future to appear again and again, even in Shakespeare, Montaigne, and some of the Utopians. The habits of these people were said to be the opposite of those that prevailed in medieval Europe. Men and women went "all naked," and practiced cannibalism. They "married them no wives"—for all the women, like other forms of property, were held in common, "one man being as rich as another." As the author made his way eastward to the Isles of Ind, his tales became more and more extravagant and the customs of the people more outlandish. The King of Ceylon had a thousand wives, hundreds of children, and a thousand elephants. On the Island of Caffolos, approached over the Sea of Ocean, the natives hung their sick friends and kinsfolk to the branches of trees in order to spare them pain, and later devoured them. On still another island were a people of immense stature, like giants, with but one eye in the middle of their foreheads, and consequently even more hideous to look upon than their neighbors, who were merely headless and carried their eyes in their chests.

In more sober moments, Mandeville was much interested in

the diversity of religion, and, whether by accident or design, presented an account of a succession of the less orthodox faiths, beginning with the Greeks and ending with the purely "natural" religion of the Brahmins.[22] In India some of the people worshiped the sun, some the moon, some fire, some serpents, and some the first thing they met of a morning. Mandeville also attempted to deal with the problem of idolatry, or to distinguish between those who venerated "similacres," to which as mere likenesses of men no divinity was attributable, and "idols," which were the products of an inflamed and distorted imagination.

Writing in a literary genre which includes the *Odyssey* and all other great books of travel and romance, the account of Mandeville's romantic journeyings achieved immediate popularity. "Of about 250 surviving manuscripts," says Professor Bennett, "73 are in German and Dutch, 37 in French, about 50 in Latin, and about 40 in English. The rest are in Spanish, Italian, Danish, Czech, and old Irish. Over three times as many manuscripts of Mandeville's *Travels* survive as of either Odoric's or Marco Polo's." Written for the entertainment of laymen, the book was "popular" in the sense of being 'non-learned." But it was popular in another sense also. "It appealed to the many. Most of the manuscripts were inexpensive ones, often on paper, seldom illuminated," written by amateur copyists in a cursive hand that was cheaper than the book hand.

As Europe lingered in this twilight of the mind, even the greater geographers and cosmographers of the sixteenth century, Mercator and Ortelius, were slow to subject Mandeville to drastic criticism. They knew that most of what he had to say about many of the peoples of the world was unreliable, but they refused to condemn him. They doubted his stories, and "yet they could not do without him." This was true even of Sebastian Muenster, whose *Cosmographia,* published in

1544 and intended to supplant the *Travels,* took over all of Mandeville's marvels without mentioning any indebtedness, and whose publishers used the same woodcut illustrations.[23] Active ethnological curiosity and inquiry, if it existed at all, was conducted in pockets of learning, where men of intellectual stature were few and sealed off from one another by geographical isolation or other obstacles to communication. Some historians point out that news traveled so slowly that it took seven weeks to find its way from Rome to Canterbury, and four months from Asia to Europe.[24] Then, when its destination was finally reached, it was not always believed. The inland character of the Caspian Sea, discovered by William Rubruck in 1253, was not acknowledged in Europe until more than half a century later. Professional map-makers failed to embody new facts on their maps, preferring as ethnological decorations the human monsters made familiar by the popular encyclopedias. Their *mappa mundi* teem with Anthropophagi, Monuculi, Troglodites, earless people, tongueless people, noseless people, headless races, gorgons, and sea monsters. Nor was plagiarism rebuked. In c. 1280 the draftsman of the celebrated Hereford map copied blunders made by Orosius in the fifth century, eight hundred years before, even though some of these referred to the British Isles, where for a Briton the means of correction were patent to any average intelligence. Owing to intellectual stratification and noncommunicating groups in many medieval societies, information, even when tardily received, was not necessarily accessible to all comers.

On the other hand, there are historians who tell us that there may have been too much communication, or too much communication of the wrong kind, for the quiet prosecution of reflection and investigation. For while the writers of encyclopedias unblushingly copied one another, the peoples of Europe, during the first thousand years of Christendom, were torn asunder by antipathies and conflicts, both physical and idealogical. No sooner had the unfortunate inhabitants of civilized Roman areas met the encroachments of the barbarian tribes, and solved that problem as best they could by either surrender, infiltration, or accommodation, than the followers of Mohamet advanced from another direction. And then. when that threat had been reduced by similar expedients, the Tartars approached from still another quarter. It was a prolonged interlude of continual anxiety, affecting even the lesser folk on the margins of the contested areas. So great was the dread of the Mongols in Western Europe, says Matthew Paris, that in 1238 the people of Gothland and Friesland refused to go even as far as Yarmouth for the annual herring fishery.

Nor was this all. The succession of anti-Christian, anti-European movements may have prolonged the backward outlook of the West in yet a subtler way. For through them Christendom sustained a double exposure to the non-Christian. On the one hand there was classical paganism, which, transmitted by written and oral tradition, caused the Fathers much concern on doctrinal grounds. On the other, there was the primitive barbarism of the oncoming tribes from the north and east which surrounded and crowded in upon the young Church as it tried to extend its boundaries.

It is well known that the mission of converting the barbarians proceeded at a sluggish pace. "With all the aid given by secular rulers, and despite the zeal of the hundreds of ardent missionaries, even the superficial conversion of the Northern European peoples required most of the thousand years between the fifth and the sixteenth centuries. Clovis was baptised . . . toward the end of the fifth century. Yet it was two hundred and fifty years more before the majority of the Germans of the Rhine Valley became even nominally Christians." Not until the end of the twelfth century was the conversion of the Scandinavian peoples substantially completed.[25]

As the frontier of the young Church was pushed further and

further out into the barbarian hinterland, compromises had to be made with barbarian and pagan beliefs. The heathen religion to be supplanted was not one consolidated faith. It was a diversified miscellany of obscure cults, maintained chiefly among lowly folk by means of rude worship near springs or groves of trees, or in rustic sanctuaries. Though the Church made many attempts to discourage the practice of old rites, it was usually only the superstructure which yielded. Under a fragile ecclesiastical veneer, elemental paganism continued to survive in the loyalties, the rituals, the customs, and the beliefs of rustic folk. As for many of the pagan gods, the orthodox still believed in them under the guise of devils. To the multitude it mattered little what they were called; they were realities still.[25]

The problem of the missionary in all regions in the fifth and later centuries was therefore much the same that it continues to be in the twentieth. Through him, the Church may make itself intelligible to nonliterate, non-Christian people only by speaking in more or less non-Christian terms. Though among first- and second-generation converts he may hope to wean away a few from their devotion to local deities, he can hardly expect to eradicate an innate polytheism. Out of this dilemma emerged the medieval habit of dividing mankind into two categories, the heathen and the saved, a dichotomy that was destined long to retain its utility and to exercise considerable influence upon the method and techniques employed in the subsequent formal study of man. The Church, believing that the barbarian world as well as the secular, was worthless and corrupt, maintained an attitude of indifference towards the heathen, except as candidates for conversion. What their ideas were, what their practices had been before they began to call themselves Christians, was of no theological or intellectual moment. It was not until the twelfth century that the Church discovered a need to record them for posterity.

BIBLIOGRAPHY AND NOTES

1. "The word *Geography* . . . is not very common in the writers of the Middle Ages; the term *Geometry* (applied to one part of the Quadrivium) was used in exactly the same sense, but with the express inclusion of what is now called Ethnology or Anthropo-Geography; and among other medieval expressions for this study we have the common *De Natura rerum, De Natura Locorum, De mensura Orbis Terrae,* the equally common *Cosmographia,* and the rarer *Cosmimetria.*" (Beazley, *Dawn of geography,* II, 515.)

2. See Wright, *Geographical lore, passim;* Beazley, *op. cit., passim;* Armand Rainaud: *Le continent austral, hypothèses et découvertes* (Paris: A. Colin, 1893), *passim.*

3. Aurelius Augustinus; *Of the citie of God: with the learned comments of Io. Lod. Vives, Englished by J. H.* (London: Printed by George Eld. 1610), sig. Ddd 3 v.

4. Isidore of Seville, *Isidori Hispalensis episcopi, Etymologiarum sive originum libri xx; recognovit brevique adnotatione critica instruxit,* W. M. Lindsay (Oxford: Clarendon Press, 1911).

5. Ernest Brehaut, *An encyclopedist of the dark ages: Isidore of Seville* (New York: Columbia University Press, 1912), 32.

6. *Ibid.,* 244–47; 203–4; 17; 207–21. According to Thorndike, Isidore attributed racial and temperamental differences to the forces of the stars and the diversity of the sky, which suggests a belief in astrological influences. (Thorndike, *Magic and experimental science,* I, 633).

7. Brehaut, *op. cit.,* 203–4.

8. Thorndike, *op. cit.,* I, 623.

9. Robert Steele, ed., *Medieval lore: an epitome of the science, geography, animal and plant folk-lore and myth of the Middle Ages . . .* (London: Elliot Stock, 1893), 5; see also Jean Ferdinand Denis, *Le monde enchanté, cosmographie et histoire naturelle fantastiques du moyen age* (Paris: Vattier, 1843).

10. Sarton, *History of science,* vol. II, pt. ii, 586–88.

11. The first English translation was made by John de Trevisa, "the father of English prose," in 1397 before Chaucer's death; the second in 1592, during Shakespeare's lifetime, by Stephen Batman under the title *Batman uppon Bartholomew.*

12. Gerald E. SeBoyar, "Bartholomaeus Anglicus and his Encyclopedia," *Journal of English and Germanic Philology,* 19 (1920), 168–89; Kester Svendsen, "Milton and the encyclopedias of science," *Studies in Philology,* 39 (1942), 303–327; *Milton and science* (Cambridge: Harvard University Press, 1956), 14.

13. Sarton, *op. cit.,* vol. II, pt. ii, 586–88.

75

14. *Batman uppon Bartholomew, his booke De proprietatibus rerum, newly corrected, enlarged and amended: with such additions as are requisite, unto every severall booke: taken foorth of the most approved authors, the like heretofore not translated in English* (London: Imprinted by Thomas East, dwelling by Paules wharfe, 1582), sig, Rr v v.

15. *Ibid.,* Pp v r; Qq iii v; Tt iii r; Tt iv v; Oo v r; Qq iv r; Oo iii r.

16. For a fuller treatment of this literature, see Rudolph Wittkower, "Marvels of the East: a study in the history of monsters," *Journal of the Warburg and Courtauld Institutes,* 5 (1942), 159–97.

17. Batman, *op cit., sig.* Qq vi v. Other important medieval encyclopedias which at least touch on the cultural differences among mankind are: *Polychronicon Ranulphi Higden monachi cestrensis: together with the English translation of John Trevisa* . . . (London: Longmans, 1865–86); *Li Livres dou tresor de Brunetto Latini. Edition critique par Francis J. Carmody* (Berkeley: University of California, 1948).

18. Vincent's encyclopedia, like all others, is a compilation from other works. According to Sarton, it contains nothing new or original, but represents the knowledge accessible to the educated people of Western Christendom in the third quarter of the thirteenth century, not the people of genius, but the good, steady people. (Sarton, *op. cit.,* II, pt. ii, 929–32). It was Vincent also who included the reports of the most recent explorations in the Far East by Carpini (1245–47), as Roger Bacon included those of William of Rubruck in the same Tartar Empire (1253–55). See also Richard Bernheimer, *Wild men in the middle ages: a study in art, sentiment, and demonology* (Cambridge: Harvard University Press, 1952); George Sarton. "The scientific literature transmitted through the incunabula," *Osiris* V (1938), 191; Kibre, "Libraries of the fourteenth and fifteenth centuries," as cited, 284.

19. Edward Moore, *Studies in Dante. Third series. Miscellaneous essays* (Oxford: Clarendon Press, 1903), 109–13; 124, 142; Félix Archemède Pouchet, *Historie des sciences naturelles au moyen age; ou, Albert le Grand et son epoque consideres comme point de départ de l'école expérimentale* (Paris: J. B. Baillière, 1853), 488–89; Paget Toynbee, "Brunetto Latini's obligations to Solinus," *Romania,* 23 (1894), 62 *et seq.*

20. "Atiya suggests that the purpose of the *Travels* was to promote a crusade . . . Leonardo Olschki says that the purpose was entertainment . . . Letts says 'he was concerned only with the needs of pilgrims and the preservation of Holy Places' . . . A. C. Baugh . . . that he set out 'to write a mere guide book,' but continued it with an account of his travels in Asia." (Josephine Waters Bennett, *The rediscovery of Sir John Mandeville* [New York: The Modern Language Association of America, 1954], 69, note 1). See also Malcolm Letts, *Mandeville's travels: texts and translations* (London: Hakluyt Society, 1949), *passim.*

21. *Early travels in Palestine, comprising the narratives of Arculf, Willibald, Bernard, Saewulf, Sigurd, Benjamin of Tudela, Sir John Maundeville, De La Brocquière, and Maundrell,* edited, with notes, by Thomas Wright (London: Henry G. Bohn, 1848), 201.

22. *Ibid.,* 218–19; 225; 226; 228; Bennett, *op. cit.,* 72–75.

23. Bennett, *op. cit.,* 219–20; 240–41.

24. Charles Homer Haskins, *Studies in medieval culture* (Oxford: Clarendon Press, 1929), 101; see also James Westfall Thompson, *An economic and social history of the middle ages* (New York: Century, 1928), 575.

25. Kenneth Scott Latourette, *A history of the expansion of Christianity* (New York, Harper and Brothers, 1937–45), II, 20.

26. George Gordon Coulton, *Five centuries of religion* (Cambridge: Cambridge University Press, 1923–36), I, 179.

CHAPTER III

Ethnology, Trade, and Missionary Endeavor

"I will fetch you a tooth-picker now from the furthest inch of Asia; bring you the length of Prester John's foot; fetch you a hair off the great Cham's beard; do you any embassage to the Pigmies."—WILLIAM SHAKESPEARE, *Much Ado About Nothing.*

THOUGH THE COMPLEX RECORDS of European thought seem at times to lend themselves to a portrayal of the Middle Ages as confused, geographically ignorant, and wedded ethnologically to immemorial and fabulous tradition, another body of evidence suggests a somewhat different conclusion. For obviously, if those old mixers of the human family—trade and religion—be given their due, and if to these be added the migrations of the barbarians, the pilgrimages to holy places, and the movements of armies over both the European peninsula and the Eurasian landmass, the period was certainly not one of uninterrupted isolation and introversion. Due to contact with other lands and other peoples, some European travelers in a few occupational categories enjoyed a less distorted and more balanced knowledge of the facts of cultural diversity. Can there be any question, in this connection, that merchants, dependent upon the favors of tribal buyers and sellers from the far west of Scotland to the far east of China, knew in intimate detail their effective wants, their economic preferences, and some of the elements of the cultural systems of which these elements were parts? Can there be any doubt that the mission-

ary vocation of the higher and lower clergy, which led them
into the unchristianized areas of Europe, Asia, and Africa,
conferred similar insights upon the Church which received their
reports?

Merchandizing, evangelization, war—one or all of these
undertakings must have repeatedly summoned at least a few
members of countless little European communities into the
great world, where the observation of peoples different from
themselves and different from the fables concerning them was
not only possible but unavoidable. Who will refuse to believe
that traders and missionaries met the members of many tribal
and national groups at boundaries and markets; that all were
aware of the practice by others of different customs; that in
some degree cultural mingling took place? Who will deny the
probability that, when commercial and religious travelers returned home experiences were recounted, stories of alien
customs exchanged, and varying tactics devised for the
extension of markets and the propagation of the faith; and all
this in a realistic spirit wholly at variance with ethnological
fable. If this be so, few village communities, princely courts, or
aggregations of learned men could have been wholly or
permanently isolated from the news carried by traders, from
the commodities fashioned by strangers, or from information
concerning the lives and habits of faraway contributors to
European convenience and luxury. In a like manner, the
experiences and opinions of missionaries must have been
repeated in monastery, Church council, and Vatican, conferring upon those who listened a more vivid and sounder image
of the barbarian or savage. If descriptions of the fabled
Arimaspi, Troglodites, and Cynocephali of Pomponius Mela,
Solinus, Isidore, and Mandeville were reiterated by cosmographer after cosmographer, and if their fantastic likenesses
were drafted by cartographers on map after map, it cannot
have been because other data of a superior type were wholly

lacking. Nor can it have been wholly due, as Olschki suggests, to the barrier of language between trader and trader, missionary and missionary. After all, Jewish merchants in the Near and Far East were skillful linguists; the records show that they spoke Arabic, Persian, Latin, Greek, Frankish, Spanish, and Slavonic. Moreover, to facilitate exchanges in ports and inland centers, interpreters were maintained. Buyers and sellers must have been visible to one another, except under the rare conditions imposed by the silent trade, and from the fineness of their wares, it must have been apparent to Westerners that other lands, Eastern lands, were the sites of normal human beings as well as monsters.

Reasons for the failure to disseminate this superior knowledge over the whole of the European community may now be hard to come at, but the superior information was there, paralleling the fabulous, either in the memories of the traders and bankers, in the records of Churchmen, or in the minds of military men and pilgrims. One of the problems for the historian of European ideas is to account for the backwardness of ethnological thought despite sustained contact with non-Europeans.

It is well to remember that historians of commercial relationships between the continents of Europe, Asia, and Africa have wisely refrained from trying to guess when the merchant first began to carry on his joint functions of distributing goods and mediating intellectually among far-flung customers. But it must have been seen very early, as early perhaps as the Hallstatt settlements of huddled huts, or during the First Iron Age, when periodical fairs facilitated the work of itinerant peddlers and hucksters. It is established that in the Second Iron Age, new tools from the Mediterannean region were introduced among the barbarian populations north of the Alps and that traders followed regular routes under the protection of powerful tribes. The Greeks, of course, were well acquainted with Northern China, whose silks were carried westward by Central

Asian trading peoples. Under the later Roman Empire, a colony of Greek merchants was maintained in Cordoba and in Merida. In the seventh century, Byzantine ships may have reached England; and in Provence during these same years, when the stagnation of medieval thought was most complete, Marseilles and Arles enjoyed relations by sea with Italy, Spain, Africa, and the Levant, the goods received from Inner Asia being forwarded into the interior of Merovingian France by road and river. When a Frankish king made entrance into Orléans, he was cheered by a motley crowd speaking Latin, Syrian, and Hebrew.[1]

Additional evidence, though relatively scanty, clearly indicates that Jewish merchants, especially in the ninth century, surpassed both their Christian and Muslim colleagues in the geographical range of their endeavors. "In the more backward regions of Western Europe, such as the interior provinces of France and Germany, they seem to have held almost a monopoly of international commerce." The Arabic *Book of routes and kingdoms,* referring to economic conditions between 846 and 886, states that Hebrew merchants embarked in the land of the Franks on the Western Sea, sailing toward Al-Farana. There they loaded their merchandise on the backs of camels and proceeded to Sind, to Hind, and to China. Under the Byzantine emperors, Syrian merchants secured wares from Persia in the East and sold them in the West; and when access to the Urals was restored, traders of all nations met at Itil, the Khazar capital on the lower Volga, where silks from China were received and redistributed, along with Indian and Malayan goods, which were carried there through Afganistan and Persia.[2] In the tenth century, Venetian traders traveled goods in their own ships and maintained a regular passenger and mail service, which ultimately impaired the economic position of Constantinople. Nevertheless, when Benjamin Tudela, a perceptive Jewish merchant from Spain, entered that

Byzantine mart two hundred years later, in the twelfth century, it still seemed fantastically prosperous. "Great stir and bustle prevails," he said, "in consequence of the confluence of many merchants, who resort thither, both by land and sea, from all parts of the world," including Babylon and Mesopotamia, Egypt and Palestine, Russia, Hungary, Patzinakia, Budia, Lombardy, and Spain.[3]

Meanwhile, as early as the fifth and sixth centuries, traders from Northern Europe brought goods to Byzantium and returned home to their snow-clad forests with the exotic commodities of the Far East. Later, merchants from Germany, Flanders, Scandinavia, and France mingled regularly in the Empire; and, though transport was slow and cumbersome, the wants of Italy were satisfied by merchants who moved within an area extending "from the Scottish Lowland to the Euphrates and from the Black Sea to the Atlas Mountains" or beyond. One of the legacies of the Roman Empire to early medieval Europe was a commercial economy centered on the Mediterranean but dominated by Oriental merchants. The coastal trade between the merchants of Arabic lands and India, or even farther east, is of the highest antiquity; and there is a Mohametan literature pertaining to their Indian, African, and Chinese exploits.[4] In the sixth century, not long before Isidore wrote his *Etymologies,* southern Spain resumed trade with the Byzantine Empire, thus forging commercial relationships between the nations of the eastern Mediterranean and the Atlantic. At about the same time the marts of Central Europe were filled with Italians who carried a variety of Levantine and Oriental wares.

The geographical range of the medieval trader is all the more remarkable when considered in the light of the impediments to travel which had to be overcome. For tolls were heavy, routes difficult, transport primitive. Whenever possible the carrier followed navigable waterways or ancient roads.

Many of them were of Roman construction; but within the limits of topographical conditions older roads were often duplicated by others, until medieval Europe was a network of paralleling or alternative routes.

The missionary movement, another potential channel of improved ethnological information, also began early, although in the nature of things the expansion of Christianity was a far later phenomenon of inter-group communication than the exchange of goods. Though little is known of the *modus operandi* by which the barbarian tribes were earliest converted into Christian communities,[5] a few place-names and dates will suggest the range and times of the effort. From Edessa in northern Mesopotamia, where the faith was firmly established by A.D. 150, Christianity was propagated in the Persian kingdom; Hindustan, or at least Arabia, was reached by about 180; Armenia at the end of the third century; "Scythia" and the Crimea by about 311; and Britain in the same century, if not earlier. By about 330 the Abyssinian Church had been founded, as the result of the labors of communicants from Alexandria; and even before this, the tribes of North Africa were Christianized, including the Blemmys of classical fame, the Saharans, and the Soudanese. In Asia, in the fourth century, the line of the metropolitans of "Babylon" began; a Syrian mission was sent to Malabar in India; and, according to Arnobius, a mission to the "Seres," or Chinese, may have been undertaken. Certainly after the expulsion of Nestorius from the Church in 431, Christianity had reached China in Nestorian form. Before 540 their bishops were received at Samarcand and Herat; and sepulchral evidence, commemmorating Christian clergy and laymen, has been found as far east as the Balkash basin. A little later, while collecting evidence of the results of the mission of St. Thomas in Madras, Gregory of Tours (538-593) found that Nestorianism had already begun to exert some influence there upon an even earlier Indian form of Christianity.[6]

With Italy, Mesopotamia, Persia, Hindustan, Scythia, Abyssinia, Sahara, Syria, Malabar, China, Samarcand, Herat, Madras, and Britain all scenes of missionary endeavor before 540, together with Spain, Provence, and the chief Roman colonies of Gaul (such as Lyons, Trèves, and Cologne), who can doubt that the representatives of many tribal and national groups met at boundaries and markets? that all were aware of the practice by others of different customs? that, at least to some degree, cultural mingling took place? Can there be any doubt that when the missionary clergy returned to Rome and there related their experiences, information concerning alien customs was exchanged, and varying tactics debated for the propagation of the faith among strangers? As the frontiers of Christendom were pushed farther and farther into the territories of the barbarian tribes, and into Eastern lands, can there be any question that the strange cultures of these different folk received some consideration at the hands of Churchmen, and in a realistic spirit wholly at variance with the fabulous ethnology of tradition?

Though the trader and missionary may be regarded as the most effective agents for the dissemination of knowledge concerning distant peoples to the home-land of Europe, neither the pilgrim nor the crusader should be overlooked. For the pilgrimage, either to local shrines or to Jerusalem, was an incessant observance among Christians in all walks of life, commoners, princes, kings, and prelates; while the crusades took thousands of men out of Europe into the Near East.

England, like other lands in the Western world, was full of holy places from end to end. One of the most famous shrines was that of St. Thomas à Becket in Canterbury. Though the saint's relics were scattered everywhere (Bury cherished his

boots, and Verona one of his teeth), this old town had everything else to please the pilgrim. In the cathedral itself there
were monks to show the treasures of the sanctuary; in Mercery
Lane there were shops full of souvenirs to take home to those
who could not make the journey.

Some pilgrims traveled independently, some in groups led by
a bishop, some en masse. Whatever the choice, the Holy Land
could be approached by several routes. Crusading armies were
accompanied by guides or interpreters conversant with the
languages of the peoples among whom they found themselves.
The ordinary pilgrim was often less fortunate. He or she
walked across Europe, usually barefoot, weaponless, exposed
to inclement weather and the dangers of the road. After a first
or overland route, he or she usually took ship for Syria, there
to be huddled in a small, rickety craft, suffering, with crowds
of others, discomforts which would appall a modern tourist.
After only a few short days or weeks in the Holy Land, the
return journey had to be undertaken. All of the same miseries
had to be borne again; yet the Wife of Bath "was an old hand
at pilgrimages"; she had been to Rome, to Bologna, to Cologne,
to the shrine of St. James in Galicia, and three times to
Jerusalem.[7]

The motives of pilgrims varied from individual to individual,
and from time to time. The journey might be undertaken to
fulfill a vow, to expiate a sin, to wrest a Christian shrine from
the infidel, or more often in response to love of travel and
adventure. Certainly some went like gypsies to a fair, to enjoy
the pleasures of the road, to see new faces, to be diverted by
constant movement. In any case, the number of those who
made the journey, whether in piety or frivolity, was immense;
increasing "to such an extent in the fourteenth century that
the maritime Republic of St. Mark found it a paying proposition to establish a semi-regular 'ferry' service for the pilgrim
traffic to the Holy Places beyond the sea."[8] Thousands from

every nation of Europe, year after year, century after century, were thus brought into some sort of communication with those of alien customs and behavior—European, Levantine, North African, Egyptian. Whether they reported these experiences or not, they knew that such human beings existed, and knew much about them.

It is not impossible, indeed, that the mental outlook of these travelers is a better index to the general level of ethnological curiosity before the Renaissance than that of either the missionaries or the merchants, preoccupied as were the latter with the extirpation of heathenism or the details of buying and selling. Moreover, the pilgrims left behind them an immense literature of peregrination, written by priests, warriors, and laity, telling why they undertook their travels and what they saw. Yet in all this literature, issuing from a situation involving the mingling of peoples, they expressed little or no curiosity about their fellows, little interest in alien ways, little reaction to cultural diversities. Their minds and thoughts were elsewhere. True, Felix Faber, who made two voyages to the Holy Land, in 1480 and 1484, surveyed the nations represented in Jerusalem, and wrote a brief account of their creeds and characteristics. The separate headings under which it was arranged included the Saracens, Greeks, Syrian Christians, Jacobites, Abyssinians, Nestorians, Armenians, Georgians, Maronites, Turcomans, Bedouins, Assassins, Muslims, Mamelukes, Jews, and Latin Christians.[9] True also, when Bertrandon de la Brocquière reached Armenia sometime in 1432 and there encountered Turcomans, he took the time to say that they were a handsome race and excellent archers; that their dwellings were round, like pavilions covered with felt; that they lived on the open plain and obeyed a chief. He described their bathing habits, their breadmaking, meat-dressing, and customs of purification before prayer. But, in sum, these remarks claimed only a few paragraphs out of a hundred-odd pages devoted to other subject matter.[10] For the most part, the pilgrim literature is composed of guidebooks and itineraries, containing information concerning mileage from point to point; rates of exchange; food prices in differing localities; the comfort, or lack of it, on the journey; and the shrines themselves. Apart from quaint vocabularies designed to help weary travelers choose their foods and find a bed (not unlike those included in modern tourist guides), there was little information even about the Islamic religion, or the culture and characteristics of the Saracens.[11] Writers of devotional literature had little sympathy with geographical exploration as such, or with exploration for the sake of obtaining ethnological knowledge. De la Brocquière's comments on the Turks, if not unique, are unusual. These, and the similar comment to be found in the *Travels of Benjamin of Tudela in A.D. 1160–1173*, stand almost alone in a literature fashioned by the encyclopedists and the Mandevilles, full of pseudo-anthropological lore bearing little relation to any group of human beings living or dead. Were it not for the undeniable presence of traders and missionaries—men whose success in their callings must have borne some relation to their practical knowledge of the real cultures of their customers and converts—historians would be compelled to assume that the ethnologically fabulous was all any medieval European ever came to know.

Despite the labors of merchants or missionaries and the indefatigable tourism of pilgrims, little was known at the time of the First Crusade in the eleventh century concerning the Near Eastern peoples. Indeed the followers of Mohamet were looked upon not only as infidels but as heathen devils about whom no invention was too far-fetched to be believed. Usually they were crudely and systematically libeled. In the *Chansons de geste* they were portrayed as physical monsters, some of them giants, some with horns on their heads, some as demons who rushed into battle making noises like the barking of dogs. They were denounced as perpetrators of the foulest practices : they kept slaves, they ate their prisoners, they bought and sold their women. When an effort is made to fix responsibility for these unflattering imputations they seem to be traceable not to those who knew most about Islam, or to merchants and missionaries, but to official ecclesiastical propaganda. In the struggle with the infidel, theological policy made no distinction among unbelievers. Saracens, Persians, Saxons, Scythians, and what not were all lumped together as heathen and therefore monstrous. It seemed to be the purpose of those who guided the public relations of the Church to distort all alien beliefs and customs. This conventional caricature was drawn upon by everyone who wielded a pen. It was reproduced everywhere in almost identical wording and with the same repetitious episodes.[12]

In the thirteenth century, however, Western European thought on ethnological problems was tempered by a breath of fresh air. This seemed to come about as the result of the Mongolian conquest of a larger part of Asia and southern Russia, and its resultant challenge to Christendom. The Mongol and Tartar tribes who resided in the eastern portion of Central Asia to the northwest of China, having formed a confederacy, launched repeated attacks upon the West, a siege which struck terror into the hearts of both Christians and Muslims. To Christians, the prophecy of the coming of the anti-Christ with the destruction of the universe seemed to be on the verge of fulfillment; and fantastic stories concerning the Tartars were disseminated throughout Europe. By ordinary folk they were believed to be cannibals or even messengers from hell, for, according to a current pun, their deeds resembled those of fiends from Tartarus.

When in the course of time the Mongols were repulsed, leaving the Muslims staggering under their blows, it seemed a good time to the Western Church to bring both of its former adversaries under the banner of Christianity. As a gesture of goodwill, therefore, and as a result of closer acquaintance with the doctrines of the followers of Mohamet, the charge of idolatry was dropped. A few discerning Christians began to realize that the worshipers of Allah were heretics rather than heathen.[13] In this more relaxed attitude, proselytizing activity on a more modern plan was initiated. St. Francis made a journey to the East to look over the possibilities. To break the spell of bitterness, and to prepare missionaries more adequately for their labors, it was proposed that Arabic be taught in the University of Paris. Raymond Lull (1235?-1315) was a leader in this movement. After learning the Muslim tongue himself, he not only founded the College of Miramar on the island of Majorca, in 1276, but proposed the establishment of missionary training schools, and the inclusion of Arabic, Hebrew, and "Chaldee" in the curriculum of the European universities.[14] More than this, it was only a little later that three of the best observers of the thirteenth century found their way into Mongolia. Two of these were emissaries of the Pope and the French crown : Friar John de Plano Carpini (1182? or 1200?-1252) and Friar William Rubruck (1220?-1293). The third was an independent trader, Marco Polo (1254?-1324). Not to be outdone, Kublai Khan also invited the Pontiff to send him one hundred intelligent Westerners acquainted with the seven arts, and equipped to explain (if they could) why he and his people should abstain from idolatry and embrace Christianity. With these exchanges, the atmosphere between the West and East began to clear. To Westerners, Cathay seemed ripe for conversion and for the revival of commerce. This land, said Ibn Battuta in the fourteenth century is "the most secure of all lands and the best . . . for the travelers." Protected by the Pax Tartarica, Italian friars said mass, Italian merchants "chaffered" there or "moved unhampered with their caravans on the great silk route across Asia," passing through Persia to take ship on the long sea road.[15]

The Tartars with their tents and carts.

The reports of the two Franciscan friars, Carpini and Rubruck, and the manuscript finally compiled by the Italian merchant, Marco Polo, were so specific, so detailed, and so objective that they leave little doubt of the presence in Europe of readers ready to use them, especially among the higher clergy and the business men.[16] Carpini is a case in point. Understanding that his mission "ad Tartaros" had been organized to give the Pope and other leaders of the Church a first-hand account of the kind of people who had twice attacked Christendom, and also to establish, if possible, friendlier relations with them, Carpini's *Historia Mongolorum* is both an itinerary for subsequent travelers, and an analytical description of the Tartar civilization at its height, or during the dynasty of Genghis Khan. The report thus opens with a short geographical section surveying the lands of Tartars, followed by a description of the inhabitants—their religion and customs, their origin and history—and a careful statement of the military and political organization which supported so large and powerful an empire.

"The Mongols or Tartars, in outward shape," said Carpini, "are unlike to all other people. For they are broader betweene the eyes, and the balles of their cheekes, then men of other nations bee. They have flat and small noses, little eyes, and eye liddes standing streight upright. . . ." Then, always in meticulous detail, he considered "their habits . . . their tabernacles . . . their cattell, their chastity . . . their insolencie against strangers . . . lawes of matrimonie . . . ridiculous traditions . . . their worship of the moone . . . and their custome of purifying." In short, under four rubrics—*Of their forme, habite, and maner of living; Of their manners both good and bad; Of their lawes and customes; and Of their superstitious traditions*—the reader of Friar John will find that, in effect, he asked himself and his informants certain very definite questions concerning the customs and major institutions of his Asiatic hosts. What did the Tartars look like? What kinds of garments did they wear? How did they do their hair? Of what materials and on what plan did they construct their dwellings? What did they eat, and how was their food prepared? How did they make a living? As farmers? pastoralists? traders? artisans? What relationships obtained between the sexes? Were the women chaste? How many wives could a man possess? Within what kinship categories might a wife be chosen? Did widows remarry? What were the lines of inheritance? What religious beliefs were entertained and what rituals were practiced?

From the answers given to this unusually detailed and well-arranged questionnaire, it appears in part that the Tartar habitations were "rounde and cunningly made with wickers and staves in the manner of a tent. But in the middest of the toppes thereof," they had a window open to convey the light in and the smoke out. These felt "tabernacles" could be easily disassembled and carried elsewhere on the backs of horses, or in carts. As for food, they drank "milke in great quantitie, but especially mares milke." Their manners were "partly prayse-worthie, and partly detestable." Their women were chaste, neither was there "so much as a word uttered concerning their dishonestie"; but the men were "joyned in matrimony to all in generall, yea, even to their neare kinsfolkes except their mother, daughter, and sister by the mothers side, and also the wife of the father after his decease." The younger brother also, or some other of his kindred, was "bound to marry the wife of his eldest brother deceased." In religion, they knew nothing of eternal life and everlasting damnation, and yet, strange to say, they believed that after death they would live in another world, there multiplying their herds, eating and drinking as they had on earth. They worshiped the new moon upon their knees, and all men who abode in their tabernacles were compelled to be purified by fire.[17]

In 1253-55, several years after Friar John de Plano Carpini had returned home to Europe, Louis IX of France made another attempt on behalf of the West to open friendly negotiations with the Mongols. This time the emissary to the Tartar Emperor was William of Rubruck, and this time the mission was at least partly evangelical. It was believed that Sartach, a Mongol chief, was already a Christian and would be willing to aid Friar William in his work of conversion. To lend dignity to the celebration of Mass under these strange conditions, William's party carried with them a beautifully illuminated psalter, a Bible, church vestments, a cross, a censer, and other articles of sacred use.

These two good observers traveled much the same route and met representatives of the same peoples. Consequently their narratives not only touch upon many of the same items of ethnological interest, thus completing and corroborating one another, but also they differ in interest and emphasis, thus together giving a clearer picture of the culture of the Mongol East of their time. Like Carpini, Rubruck commented upon the nomadic habits of the Tartars, but paused also to tell of their customs of transhumance, a feature omitted by his predecessor.[18] Like Carpini, he told also of the elaborate preparation of mare's milk, of plural marriages, of the degrees of consanguinity within which marriages were permissible. But, since the purpose of his mission was predominantly religious in character, Friar William was far more informative on the varying aspects of Asiatic sects and creeds than Friar John. He may have failed to penetrate deeply into their spiritual and doctrinal ideas, but he at least came home with a vivid and reliable description of their temples and external rites.[19]

On reaching the country of the Iurgurs, where there were Shamanists and Buddhists, this European Christian exclaimed, "Here I first saw idolaters!" In the city of Cailac were three idol temples, "two of which I entered to see their foolishness." It may be that, viewing this in the only way he could, or through eyes which had observed Christian practices only, Friar William was naturally struck by the likenesses between Western religious symbolism and that observable in these heathen temples. Or it may be, as seems more probable, that in order to make his observations intelligible to European readers, he was compelled to call attention to similarities. Wherever they go, he said, "they have in their hands a string of one or two hundred beads, like our rosaries." In one temple, behind a chest which served as an "altar," was "a winged image like Saint Michel, and other images like bishops holding their fingers as if in blessing"; while in still another, the priests were robed in "sacerdotal vestments," and offered "the oblations of bread and fruit of the people." Then, attempting to organize what he had seen, William noted that a long pole was set up in front of all idol temples; that all idolaters commonly worshiped toward the north with joined hands, prostrating themselves "to the ground with bended knees," placing their foreheads on their hands; that they oriented their temples to the east and west, while on the north side they made an alcove projecting out like a "choir"; that to the south they placed the chief idol, a colossal Buddha, sometimes so large that it could be seen "from two days off." All the priests shaved their heads, were dressed in saffron color, observed chastity, and lived in congregations of one or two hundred. To one European onlooker they seemed "to be Franks, but they had barbarian mitres on their heads."

Apparently as a matter of regular usage in describing an alien folk, William also observed and recorded the burial customs of several Asiatic nations. Though the Tartars were thought to believe in one God, William acknowledged regretfully that they nevertheless made "images of their dead in felt"; and then, dressing them in the richest stuffs, "put them in one or two carts . . . under the care of soothsayers." On the march, the tribe was led by soothsayers as the pillar of cloud led the Children of Israel. But beyond, in Tibet, lived a people "in the habit of eating their dead parents, so that for piety's sake they should not give their parents any other sepulchre than their bowels."[20]

A few years after the return of William to Europe, or in 1260-69, the Polos of Venice, father and uncle of Marco, made their first trading expedition to the Far East, arriving at the court of Kublai Khan on the borders of Cathay by way of the Crimea, the Volga, Bokhara, and Samarcand. This venture was followed a few years later in 1271-75 by a second which included young Marco. Having reached Ormuz from Acre in part by sea, the three travelers turned north, traversed Kerman and Khorosan, Balkh and Badakhshan, continued to Kashgar via the upper Oxus and the Pamir highlands, and finally worked their way across the Gobi Desert to the court of the Khan north of the Great Wall near Kalgan.

It was thus in China, land of perennial wonder, that Marco Polo found himself as an impressionable youth of twenty-one. Possessing tact, charm, and a useful knowledge of several languages of the region, he was soon called upon to serve the Khan on distant missions and in the administration of the realm. His first journey carried him through the provinces of Shan-si, Shen-si, and Sze-ch'wan; into the wilder country east of Tibet, and also into the remote province of Yun-nan. For three years he was in charge of the provincial government of Yang-chau. On another occasion he passed a year at Kan-chau in Tangut. He visited Kara Korum and Cochin China, and finally several of the southern states of India.[21]

"He was discreet and prudent in every way," said Marco of himself, "insomuch that the Emperor held him in great esteem." Mindful that his royal employer was often bored by the dull reports of some commissioners, but took delight in hearing about the odd manners of the lesser-known peoples in his realm, Marco formed the habit on his journeys of taking notes on *mirabilia*. Consequently, the manuscript which he dictated in prison at the end of his life became a *Liber diversorum*. This conception of his work as a *Book of diversities,* his occasional departure from objectivity, and his bias toward the odd or unusual in human behavior render what he wrote somewhat less rewarding to the careful ethnologist than the reports of Friar John or Friar William. Moreover, he was always a businessman. Alive to the value of money and the potentiality in Asia for the expansion of commercial profit, the items first and most often reported were the products of each country and the skills of its artisans. Apart, therefore, from a few relatively long descriptions of the customs of the Tartars, the Chinese, and the people of the Coromandel coast of India,

Marco's total body of anthropological information is to be found only by assembling bits and pieces buried in geographical descriptions, or in comments on trading conditions, commodities, or natural resources. Sometimes, indeed, even when a people is rather generously described, the description will be in terms which reflect, more than anything else, Marco's estimate of their commercial morality. His relative indifference to cultural data other than that related to buying and selling, shown so clearly in the *Liber diversorum,* may partially explain why other merchants traveling back and forth over the East and West failed for so many centuries to lead European ethnological thought out of its morass of superstition.

Marco's almost exclusive interest in the commodities of Asia and the problems of marketing them began at once. In the account of the first leg of his journey from Italy to Cathay, or from lesser Armenia to the court of the Great Khan, the first city mentioned is Laya (Ayas), which, situated on the sea, was reputed to enjoy a great trade in spicery, cloths of silk and gold, and other valuable wares from the interior. Concerning the life of the people in this port, Marco characteristically says nothing. In the third chapter of the book, a city called Azinga was reached by the travelers. Here, the best buckrams were made, and in Georgia to the north a fountain of oil gushed forth to fill the holds of many ships. Likewise in Georgia, where the people lived by handicraft, textiles were produced in great abundance including silks and cloths of gold. Next was the kingdom of Mosul, where again cloths of gold and silk, called Mosolins, were made, and where merchants carried away quantities of spicery, pearls, and cloths of silk and gold.[22] On the culture of the people, there is still nothing said.

In the course of the first four chapters and in the midst of an abundance of detail invaluable to the merchant and trader, there are only three comments which can be considered ethnological, all referring to one culture, that of the Turcomans.

These people were said to be worshipers of Mohamet; they were rude and uncultivated; and they spoke an uncouth language.[23] Such scantiness of cultural detail is all the more to be regretted since in the use of the term Turcomania, Marco may have embraced a great part of Asia Minor.[24] To be sure, many other peoples were mentioned to whom he gave a word or phrase of description. There were the Persians, who were fire worshipers. There were the inhabitants of Ormuz, who sowed their wheat, rice, and other grains in December and harvested them in March, but lived chiefly on dates and salted fish and who also employed professional mourners at times of bereavement. There was an unnamed folk beyond Taican who drank to excess, bound their heads with a cord "ten palms long," and wore nothing but the skins of animals killed in the chase. There was the province of Pein, where, if a husband absented himself from his home for more than twenty days, his wife was free to marry whom she chose. And so on. In short, there is more than enough to prove that Marco knew what to observe. The pity is that he failed to set it down.

On the Tartars, however, the very magnitude of the subject encouraged comment. "Now, that we have begun to speak of the Tartars, I have plenty to tell you." And what he told parallels very closely the reports of his missionary predecessors. It also contains much that had been available in the literature since the time of Herodotus and his description of the Scythians.[25] There is the usual reference to the nomadic habits of the Tartars, their customs of transhumance, and their circular felt-covered dwellings, which on being disassembled could be loaded on carts and transported to another pasturage. Facts are noted with reference to the division of labor between the sexes; the diet of meat and mare's milk; marriage customs; tactics in warfare. But Marco's description of the Tartars' religion, as compared to Rubruck's, is slight. Perhaps because of his long separation from Christendom, and his want of a firm knowledge of the rites and doctrines of at least one high religion, this was something he was not prepared to grasp. In any event, all that he had to say was that "there is a Most High God of Heaven, whom they worship daily with thurible and incense, but they pray only for health of mind and body." Of other practices, we are told that "every man hath a figure of him in his house, made of felt and cloth. . . . When they eat, they take the fat of the meat and grease the god's mouth withal. . . . Then they take the broth and sprinkle it before the doors. . . ."[26]

When the province of Tangut was reached, the subject of religion was again broached, together with a discussion of customs for the disposal of the dead—this time in more detail. These people, said Marco, were idolaters, by which he meant Buddhists.[27] "They have a great many abbeys and minsters full of idols of sundry fashions, to which they pay great honour and reverence." When a sheep was sacrificed, they took the flesh home and, calling together all their kindred, ate it with them in great festivity. "And you must know," he continues,

that all idolaters in the world burn their dead. And when they are going to carry a body to the burning, the kinsfolk build a wooden house on the way to the spot, and drape it with cloths of silk and gold. When the body is going past this building they call a halt and set before it wine and meat and other eatables. . . . All the minstrelsy of the town goes playing before the body; and when it reaches the burning place, the kinsfolk are prepared with figures cut out of parchment and paper in the shape of men and horses and camels, and also with round pieces of paper like gold coins, and all these they burn along with the corpse. For they say that in the other world, the defunct will be provided with slaves and cattle and money, just in proportion to the amount of such pieces of paper that has been burnt along with him.

Since the appropriate time for cremation had to be determined by astrologers, the body was sometimes kept as long as six months. Polo relates in some detail how this was acomplished.

In Campichu, a city in the province of Tangut, Polo came with surprise upon something still to be seen in Siam, Burma, and Ceylon, namely a great recumbent figure of Sakya Buddha, symbolizing his entrance into Nirvana. "The people," he said, "are Idolaters, Saracens, and Christians, and the latter have three fine churches in the city, whilst the Idolaters have many minsters and abbeys after their fashion. In these, they have an enormous number of idols, both small and great, certain of the latter being a good ten paces in stature. . . ." Here, a man could take thirty wives, but the first wife was always held in highest esteem. Husbands endowed their wives with cattle, slaves, and money, according to their ability. Divorce was easy : if a man disliked a spouse, he turned her out and took another.[28]

Marco Polo visited many of the ancient cities of China—Nanking, Soochow, Hang-chau—and admired them all for their wealth, commercial acumen, ingenious artisans, beautiful women, distinguished physicians, and philosophers. He had much to say about their material well-being, their fine silks, their tissues of silver and gold, their fleets of river- and ocean-going vessels with rich cargoes, their canals and bridges, their charming gardens and enchanting buildings of exotic architectural design. But it was only after he reached Hang-chau (or Kinsay) that he dwelt even briefly upon the customs and institutions of the Chinese : birth registration; the influence of astrology; the freedom of association between men and women; the hereditary character of some trades, and their concentration, by craft, in certain streets; and certain burial customs which differed in a slight degree from those seen elsewhere.[29]

For all other Chinese cities, almost without exception, Marco Polo fell back on stereotyped statements, such as : "The people have paper money, and are Idolaters, and burn their dead." This, according to Yule, constituted a formula which was repeated "with wearisome iteration." It was, in fact, Polo's final definition of the Chinese people, for whom he seemed to lack a comprehensive name.[30]

So far in his *Book of diversities,* the author maintained an objectivity not only unusual for his time, but unsurpassed except by Carpini and Rubruck. Despite hasty generalizations and overcompression—especially through the unification in one description of several regions, races, or customs—most of his reports were from firsthand observation or from the testimony of reliable eyewitnesses. As he moved into remoter regions, however—southward into Indo-China, northward into Siberia, eastward into Japan, or southwestward into India—it plainly became more and more difficult for him to distinguish between experience and hearsay. Or else, despite his hard-headed common sense which for so long had kept it in check, Marco Polo finally succumbed to the medieval propensity for indulging in the marvelous when distant and little-known peoples were under discussion. Anyhow, this great traveler, whose reports for a time had been almost as free of the fabulous as those of Friar John and Friar William, finally yielded to the temptation to draw on the wells of legend and his own imagination.

This relapse began most conspicuously with a six-day journey southeast of Hang-chau, where the people were said to "eat all manner of unclean things, even the flesh of man." On doubtful evidence, or none at all, cannibalism is also ascribed to other faraway and little-known people in Tibet, Sumatra, the islands off India, the Andaman Islands, and Japan, where prisoners were cooked and eaten.[31] Other rude folk were endowed by Marco with strange matrimonial practices, some of which may have had merely a legendary sanction. In Tibet, according to his story, want of chastity in brides was considered a merit. In Coilum in southern India, the kinship barriers to matrimony considered proper in Europe failed to prevail. Instead, inhabitants were permitted to marry their cousins germane, and a man was allowed to take his brother's wife after she was widowed. In Indo-China, the *droit du seigneur* was maintained.[32] Few birth customs were mentioned anywhere by Polo, except the couvade in Zardandan, a region northeast of Bhamo in Burma, where the people were decorated with tattooing and gold teeth, and the temple towers with myriads of tinkling bells.[33] The people of Kashmir in northern India, whom Marco Polo never saw with his own eyes, were said to be "the original source from which all Idolatry spread about." They had an astonishing intimacy with the devilries of enchantment, and could make "their idols to speak."[34]

However, by the time he had reached the province of Malabar on the Coromandel coast of India, he had abandoned nearly all the legendary baggage with which ancient and patristic fantasy had filled that region. In its place is a refreshing if meager account of the king's household in this "best of all the Indies"; the jewels and fine horses of the realm; its collectively administered justice, which compelled a criminal's kinsfolk to supervise his self-execution; the nakedness of the people as they went into battle; their ablutions twice daily; their abstention from wine and maintenance of strict dietary rules; and the consecration of some of their young girls to idols.[35] As for the Brahmins, Marco seemed to be entirely unaware of the heavy incrustation of fabulous material which for so long had obscured their real characteristics from European readers.[36] To him, their chief excellence lay in their activities as merchants, rather than in their supposed renunciation of the world and its fleshpots. He mentioned their refusal to take the life of living things, their daily fasts, and their longevity. But disregarding widely publicized virtues, which may have seemed to him without foundation, he asserted that they were such "cruel and perfidious Idolaters that it is very devilry."[37]

Thus the *Book of diversities,* enlightened as it was for its day and generation, was still not free from anthropological legend. Though with the good sense of a practical trader Marco Polo concluded that the "pygmies" of Sumatra were purely hearsay, asserting that such creatures had never been seen on land or sea, in another breath he recounted the old, old story of "tailed men," and provided a place on his Islands of Males and Females, for a modified version of the Amazons.[38]

In some respects, all three of these men—Carpini, Rubruck, and Polo—deserve to be compared with Herodotus. They were not mere compilers or copyists. They were not true believers in the strange creatures, physically deformed and culturally repellent, with which medieval ignorance had peopled the margins of the world outside the narrow confines of Christendom. Each of them was to some degree an intellectual innovator, a breaker of the spell of ethnological tradition, with its abundance of oral or written reiteration and repetition. What they lacked most was the old Greek's detachment and fundamental humor. Certain practices among Asian or barbarian folk were utterly repugnant to the two friars. They were regarded as breaches of Christian morals even among those who knew not Christianity. Absent also was the moral, philosophical, and historical breadth of Herodotus' horizon; his recognition of the questions raised by any collection of cultural data; his regard for the value of comparison; his insight into some of the meanings of similarities and differences. The accounts of the two missionaries were not motivated by scientific curiosity. They were practical intelligence reports, made at the behest of an ecclesiastical superior, in order to obtain quick but essentially superficial information concerning the manners of a potentially hostile adversary. The Polo report, though livelier in literary tone, also had its limitations.

It was written by a trader in the interest of traders. Marco
possessed curiosity, but it lacked the scientific impulse to find
out, if possible, why people were as they were.

Strange to say, and significant as were the reports of the
three intrepid travelers for the history of European thought,
they were all but forgotten in the West during the centuries
that followed. The relatively truthful account written by
Marco Polo attracted far less attention in the later Middle Ages
than the mendacious romance which appeared under the name
of Sir John Mandeville. A fellow Italian and man of learning,
such as Dante, who lived for twenty-three years after the *Book
of diversities* had been written and who touched on many
things in the world, seen and unseen, makes no reference to the
Venetian merchant, to Cathay, or to anything connected with
Polo's experiences. In the fourteenth century, the situation was
only a little better. During that period, the literature contains
only five references to the book. But in the fifteenth century, a
Latin edition was known to Columbus; and this copy of the
Liber diversorum, now treasured in the *Columbina* in Seville,
bears evidence in the Admiral's own handwriting of its frequent
use.[39]

Outside the Vatican, the reception given to the work of
Friar John was somewhat warmer but not enthusiastic.
Knowledge of a portion of Carpini's *Historia mongolorum* was
transmitted to later generations by the author of the *Speculum
historiale,* Vincent of Beauvais (c. 1190-c. 1264).[40] Since
the latter work was one of the first books to come off the
newly invented printing press in the fifteenth century, Carpini's
description of the Tartars was carried with it into nine editions
and into the hands of countless readers. The fame of William
of Rubruck was far less permanent. Nevertheless, influenced
no doubt by William, Roger Bacon advocated the study of the
manners and customs of peoples, especially by the missionary
clergy. Missionaries, said he, "should know the rites and condi-

tions of all nations. . . . For very many have been foiled in the important interests of Christianity because they were ignorant of the distinctions in regions. . . . They have also encountered countless dangers, because they did not know when they entered the regions of believers or of schismatics, Saracens, Tartars, Tyrants, of men of peace, barbarians, or men of unreasonable minds." The "doctor admirabilis" not only examined Rubruck's account of the Tartars, but, after holding a conference with him, included portions of his report in his own great work. But between the date of the writing of *Opus majus* in 1264 and the middle of the nineteenth century, William and his work were lost to memory except for those who chanced to read Roger Bacon in the original Latin.[41]

BIBLIOGRAPHY AND NOTES

1. Michael Postan, "The trade of medieval Europe, the north," in *The Cambridge Economic History,* II, 119.

That fine scholar, Leonardo Olschki, takes another point of view: "Commercial exchange contributed but little towards a practical knowledge of so many lands known only by more or less fantastic names. . . . Merchants journeyed . . . either across the China seas, India, the Persian Gulf, and Mesopotamia, or else by the continental routes to Persia, . . . through western Turkestan. This commercial intercourse, however, was always indirect and was brought about by intermediaries of diverse origin who spoke many different languages. Hence it would be a mistake to suppose . . . that exchange of goods implied the exchange of culture. . . . The acquisition of exotic goods did not at all imply an attainment of geographical knowledge or a broadening of cultural horizons. . . . The extensive commercial activity of these traders was not equaled by a corresponding alertness and fruitful curiosity as to the nature of the countries and peoples who provided them with merchandise. Certainly not one of them felt the need of relating to his contemporaries what he knew. . . . Thus we may believe that the medieval traders contributed rather to the tenacious persistence than to the supression of these fabulous reports." (Leonardo Olschki, *Marco Polo's precursors* [Baltimore: The Johns Hopkins Press, 1943], 1–8. See also Lopez and Raymond, *op. cit.* 31–33, 342; I. A. Augus, "Control of the roads by Jews in pre-Crusade Europe," *Jewish Quarterly Review,* 48 [1957], 93–98.)

2. V. Gordon Childe, "Trade and industry in barbarian Europe until Roman times," in *The Cambridge economic history of Europe planned by the late Sir John Clapham and the late Eileen Power,* edited by M. Postan and E. E. Rich (Cambridge: Cambridge University Press, 1952), II, 27, 29–30; Robert S. Lopez, "The trade of medieval Europe, the south," in *The Cambridge Economic History,* II, 270–71. It is said that the Greek words *serikos* for silk and *Seres* for the Chinese were both derived from *ser,* the Chinese for silk. (Steven Runciman, "Byzantine trade and industry" in *ibid.,* 90–92; Lopez, *op. cit.,* 287; Robert S. Lopez and Irving W. Raymond, *Medieval trade in the Mediterranean world* [New York: Columbia University Press, 1955], 29, 31; Walter J. Fischel, "The region of the Persian Gulf and its Jewish settlements in Islamic times," in *Alexander Marx Jubilee Volume* [New York: The Jewish Theological Seminary of America, 1950]; "The Jews of Central Asia [Khorasan] in medieval Jewish and Islamic literature," *Historia Judaica,* 7 [1945], 29–50; Thompson, *op. cit., passim;* Henri Pirenne, *Mohammed and Charlemagne* [London: Allen and Unwin, 1939], 255, 258.)

3. "Early travels in Palestine," 74.

4. Thompson, *op. cit.*, 375–77; see also Bala-Krishna, *Commercial relations between India and England 1601 to 1757* (London: Routledge, 1924), *passim.*

5. Latourette, *op. cit.*, I, 15–18.

6. Sir Charles Raymond Beazley, "Missions," in *Encyclopedia of Religion and Ethics,* edited by James Hastings (New York:Scribner, 1926), VIII, 705–13.

7. Jean Jules Jusserand, *English wayfaring life in the middle ages (XIVth Century)* (London: Unwin, 1892), 338–402; Marchette Chute, *Geoffrey Chaucer of England* (New York: E. P. Dutton, 1946), 247, 254; Beazley, *Dawn of modern geography, passim.*

8. Aziz Suryal Atiya, *The crusade in the later middle ages* (London: Methuen, 1938), 41–42, 155–57; Jusserand, *op. cit.,* 350.

9. Atiya, *op. cit.,* 224.

10. "Early travels in Palestine," 316–18.

11. Dana Carleton Munro, "The western attitude toward Islam during the period of the Crusades," *Speculum,* VI (1931), 329.

12. C. Meredith Jones, "The conventional Saracen of the songs of geste," *Speculum,* 17 (1942), 201–25.

13. Munro, *op. cit.,* 329–43.

14. Atiya, *op. cit.,* 78, 83, 86, 89. Pierre Dubois also urged the study of Greek and Arabic for missionary work; and both Lull and Ricold de Montecroix preached in Arabic (*ibid.,* 52, 160).

15. Eileen Power, "The opening of the land routes to Cathay," in *Travel and travellers in the Middle Ages,* edited by Arthur Percival Newton (New York: Knopf, 1926), 124–25.

16. Latourette, *op. cit.,* II, 276–78.
Other missionary travelers to the Far East a little later in the fourteenth century were Ricold de Montecroix (d. 1309) and Friar Jordanus (c. 1330). Montecroix, a Dominican, is known for his *Peregrinatio,* written on his travels in Asia at the request of the Pope, and for his treatise *On the oriental nations,* found in Pico's library. Jordanus was the author of *Mirabilia descripta,* which deals with India with considerable objectivity. (Kibre, *Library of Pico della Mirandola,* 109; Catalani Jordanus, Bishop of Columbum, *Mirabilia descripta. The wonders of the east* [London: Hakluyt Society, 1863].)

17. *The texts and versions of John de Plano Carpini and William de Rubruquis, as printed for the first time by Hakluyt in 1598 together with some shorter pieces,* edited by C. Raymond Beazley (London: Hakluyt Society, 1903), 109–13.

18. *The journey of William of Rubruck to the eastern parts of the world,* 1253–55, *as narrated by himself, with two accounts of the earlier journey of John of Pian de Carpine,* translated from the Latin, and edited, with an introductory notice, by William Woodville Rockhill (London: Hakluyt Society, 1900), 53.

19. Olschki, *Marco Polo's precursors,* 55–56.

20. *The journey of William of Rubruck,* 141–51.

21. *The book of Ser Marco Polo, the Venetian, concerning the kingdoms and marvels of the East,* translated and edited with notes by Colonel

Sir Henry Yule. Third edition, revised throughout in the light of recent discoveries by Henri Cordier of Paris (London: Murray, 1921), I, 21–22.

22. *Ibid.,* I, 43, 46, 50–52, 60.

23. *Ibid.,* I, 43.

24. *Ibid.,* I, 44, note 2.

25. Herodotus, *op. cit.,* IV, 46–47.

26. *Marco Polo,* I, 251–69.

27. *Ibid.,* I, 168, note 1.

28. *Ibid.,* I, 203–204; 219–20.

29. *Ibid.,* II, 185–218.

30. *Ibid.,* II, 133, note 2.

31. *Ibid.,* I, 311, note 9; II, 225, 264.

32. *Ibid.,* II, 44–45; 268, 376.

33. *Ibid.,* II, 84–88; Beazley, *Dawn of modern Geography,* III, 109–10.

34. *Marco Polo,* I, 166; Beazley, *Dawn of modern Geography,* III, 66.

35. *Marco Polo,* II, 338–46.

36. *Ibid.,* II, 113–16.

37. *Ibid.,* II, 365–68.

38. *Ibid.,* II, 285–86; 299, 301, note 2; 404–05.

39. Beazley, *Dawn of modern Geography,* III, 20, 27; Sarton, *History of Science,* II, pt. ii, 1058–59.

40. Vincent, who died before 1264, was librarian to St. Louis, King of France, and tutor to the royal children. His vast encyclopedia was called *Speculum maius,* or sometimes *Speculum quadruplex,* because it contained four *speculae: naturale, doctrinale, morale,* and *historiale.* The whole work was essentially a compilation made between 1244 and 1254. It consists largely of direct quotations from previous writers pieced together in a certain order; and it represents the knowledge accessible to the people of western Christendom in the third quarter of the thirteenth century, (Sarton, *History of Science,* II, pt. ii, 929.)

41. Roger Bacon, *The Opus Majus of Roger Bacon; a translation by Robert Bells Burke* (Philadelphia: University of Pennsylvania Press, 1928), I, 321.

The Sixteenth and Seventeenth Centuries

CHAPTER IV

The Fardle of Façions: or the Cabinet of Curios

"We are much beholden to Machiavelli and other writers of that class who openly and unfeignedly declare or describe what men do and not what they ought to do."—FRANCIS BACON.

WHEN CHRISTOPHER COLUMBUS dropped anchor in the Tagus River at the port of Lisbon on that fateful day of his return to the Old World, he brought with him seven kidnapped Indians of the so-called Taino culture of the Arawack linguistic group. The Admiral and his charges were received with great interest by King John. His caravel "became the Mecca for the idle and curious who flocked to see the Indians and the popinjays." Nevertheless, astonishment was expressed that these aborigines were not Negroes such as the Portuguese mariners had been wont to import into Europe for upwards of forty years. Their hair, it was remarked, was not kinky but loose and coarse like horsehair.[1] Later, on Palm Sunday, the sailors and their captives made another sensational entry into Seville.[2] The citizens of Barcelona were also treated to a triumphal procession led by Red Men decked out in headdresses of bright feathers, with their faces painted and their arms covered with gold bracelets.[3] During the years which followed, Indians captured by other explorers were exhibited in other capitals of Europe. In 1494 six hundred were sent home as slaves; in 1496, thirty; in 1499, two-hundred and thirty-two; while Vespucci's first voyage netted two hundred and twenty-two.

In England, Sebastian Cabot appears to have been the pioneer showman. Stow records that in 1502 three natives from "an Iland founde by merchaunts from Bristoll farre beyong Ireland" were brought before Henry VII clad in beasts' skins, eating raw meat, and speaking an unintelligible language.[4] The first Indians to appear in France were brought by Thomas Aubert in 1506. Taken to Rouen, they were described in a Paris chronicle as sooty in color, black-haired, possessing speech but no religion.[5] In 1550, the citizens of the same city, desiring to surpass all others in the splendor of a royal visitation, presented Henry III with "un spectacle magnifique," in which a contingent of natives from Brazil were given a leading role. Four years later, in 1554, they were exhibited again when Charles IX made entry into the town of Troyes. In 1565, during a festival in Bordeaux, 300 men at arms conducted a showing of captives from twelve nations, including Greece, Turkey, Arabia, Egypt, America, Taprobane, the Canaries, and Ethiopia. Outside the city wall, in the midst of an imitation Brazilian landscape, a veritable savage village was erected with several hundred residents, many of whom had been freshly abducted from South America.[6]

With so many opportunities to examine these representatives of the population of the New World, it is no wonder that Indian characters almost immediately found their way into sixteenth-century English drama;[7] or that Montaigne made it his business to study the savage. To add to this body of knowledge available to the citizens of many European cities, John White's magnificent drawings of Indian life were printed in 1590 and became a notable publishing success. Copies of the book were soon issued in four languages—Latin, English, French, and German; and from 1590 to 1620, the year the Pilgrims made their landing in Massachusetts, it went through at least seventeen reissues.[8]

But despite all these more or less isolated instances of

publicity and showmanship, despite the exploration before 1502 of more than three thousand miles of coastal South America, the discovery of the New World made relatively little impression on Europe. Though the news of the new lands traveled everywhere, the rate of its transmission was slow. Moreover, the unlearned, if they heard at all, were loath to believe; while readers, if they knew their Pliny, Solinus, Isidore, and Mandeville, were hard to surprise. Neither Africa nor America was considered any more remarkable than the Cathay of the medieval travelers; and both were too far away, in miles and experience, to command sustained attention. Even the voyagers were something less than profoundly interested in the peoples of the New World; and if they described alien manners, their reports were seldom "scientific" in the sense that they were consciously organized to give readers at home systematic expositions of human phenomena. They dwelt above all on the hazardous episodes of their voyages, on their shipwrecks, battles with the savages, and near escapes from death. If, on occasion, descriptions of New World topography, flora, fauna, or people crept into their narratives, the strange and bizarre was emphasized at the expense of the prosaic and carefully examined.

For these reasons, it was all of fifteen years after the first Columbian adventure before a book describing it in the English vernacular found its way into print. And in sixteenth-century France, there were twice as many publications on Muslim ways and wives as on all the tribes of Africa and the Americas put together.[9] To be sure, such a man as Montaigne did seek out Indian informants, and such poets as Spenser and dramatists such as Shakespeare did utilize significant bits of New World cultural lore from the travel accounts. But this was unusual many years after the discoveries began. Jean Bodin, one of the most learned men of the sixteenth century and the author in 1577 *Of the lawes and customes of a commonweale,* shows by scarcely a syllable that he knew anything of the new forms of society which existed in non-European parts of the globe. Nor was he aware that a new age had dawned in the study of the ways of mankind.[10] In a world that still sought its future in the past and accepted mentally the existence of human monsters, as described by the earlier epitomizers and encyclopedists, there was at first little occasion for amazement at a few samples of Black and Red Men, much less an immediate impulse to formulate a newer type of ethnological investigation.

It is significant, however, that the Revival of Learning was accompanied by an infectious enthusiasm for the collection of curios, which came in due course to include the culturally curious as well. Perhaps this enthusiasm was kindled by the commercial promise of the New World and the need for information concerning the wants of potential customers among the savages. Perhaps there was some theological uncertainty concerning the moral condition of the Americans and Africans, a desire to know more about their religious beliefs or the lack of them, before engaging in missionary ventures. Perhaps an interest in human behavior was part of the Renaissance revival of interest in man, the individual. Perhaps, at last, it was just plain curiosity about their fellow men in other lands, long overdue but finally expressed. Whatever its cause, that multifarious and ubiquitous genus, the collector, made his appearance on the European scene, and with him a new kind of shopkeeper, who was described by John Evelyn as maintaining a Noah's Ark, where "all curiosities naturall or artificiall" were sold, including human artifacts.[11]

Serious vocation or amiable hobby, Renaissance collection took innumerable forms, depending upon changing fashion or the movement of ideas. It found expression, for example, at the early date of 1599 in the establishment near the Tower of

London of a zoo composed of six lions, one lean wolf, one tiger, and a porcupine;[12] at a later date in the following century, in the assembly of anatomical specimens in a first-floor room on the south side of the Bodleian Quadrangle in Oxford;[13] in the compilation in 1595 of a list of common sins and rascalities, entitled *The world of wonders;*[14] and in the publication in 1620 of Francis Bacon's *Parasceve,* with its advocacy of a giant assembly of facts large enough to give man "command of all avenues to the secrets of nature."[15]

Without question, the antiquarians who collected books, manuscripts, card-games, coins, giants' bones, fossils, or zoological and botanical specimens—the "curieux," as the French called them—performed a noteworthy service for scholarship by putting them together in little museums of odds and ends, called "cabinets de curiosités." To many of these men, some of whom were members of the newly formed scientific societies in Italy, France, and England, their collections possessed a serious scientific purpose. They were intended to goad the universities out of their sterility, to supplement inadequate curricula, and to help in resisting the conservatism of official scholarship. To the less bemused beholder, however, the collector often appeared eccentric, or even a little cracked, paralleling as a figure of fun today's longhair or egghead. In English plays of the period, an older type of beloved comic, the astrologer, was replaced by the antiquarian, "a vague and peevish type," who was easily gulled into buying trash, or busied himself studying "the nature of Eels in Vinegar, Mites in Cheese, and the Blue of Plums." Sometimes these critics were very harsh. According to lines given to one character, he "would rather be a Trumpeter to a Monster, and call the Rabble to see a Calf with six Legs, than such a blockhead." Samuel Butler in *Hudibras,* Shadwell in the *Virtuoso,* Nedward in the *London Spy,* and many others held their sides at the very thought of the magpie antics of the virtuosi.[16] The same breed was made the butt of ridicule by Jonathan Swift. Plagued during his Brobdingnagian adventures by wasps as large as partridges, he resolved after exhibiting some of them in several parts of Europe, to send three to Gresham College.[17]

The earliest of the collectors in the Renaissance were classicists, admirers of all that was representative of the civilizations of Greek and Latin antiquity. Between 1450 and 1550, when the ruins of ancient Rome were unearthed, many pieces of statuary or architectural ornament found their way into the palaces of Italian merchants, princes, and clerics.[18] When the Italian Renaissance reached England, movable remnants of Roman antiquity began to arrive in English homes and museums. About 1612, Thomas Howard, second Earl of Arundel, made a long visit to Italy, accompanied by Inigo Jones and his physician, William Harvey. There, as a collector, he laid the foundation of the Arundel marbles. Other amateur antiquarians searched out Roman coins and medals, of which there are said to have been 200 collections in the Low Countries, 175 in Germany, and more than 380 in Italy.[19]

While some men collected globes, mathematical instruments, or gems, others favored geological specimens and fossils. The study of the petrified remains of marine life was first pursued in Italy, where the foothills skirting the Apennines are singularly rich in deposits. Leonardo da Vinci, who died in 1519, was one of the first to realize that these peculiar formations, as the imprints of real shells, were evidence of the one-time presence of the sea in the vine-clad valleys. Having begun to collect fossils to decorate a grotto, Antonio Vallisneri decided to preserve the best of them "as a notable diversion for the curious." The museum of Calceolarius was another collection celebrated for similar relics. Catalogues published in the sixteenth and seventeenth centuries indicate the existence of many others. Thus the work of Gesner, *De rerum fossilium, lapidum, et gemmarum figuris,* written in 1565, contains a list of the petrifications to be found in the cabinet of John Kentman.[20]

But students of fauna and flora were no less active as collectors than their colleagues among the antiquarians and geologists. As early as the fifteenth century, menageries were regarded as among the proper appointments of a court, and were assembled by many princes. Louis XIII kept animals at Versailles; his son founded the famous "Ménagerie du Parc," which, maintained over a century, received many exotic creatures from Cairo and other African or Asian sources.[21] In the middle of the sixteenth century, when botany became separable as a discipline from medicine, the making of herbaria of dried plant specimens was encouraged by the universities; and collections of living plants, out of doors or under glass, were begun. During the twenty-five-year period from 1543 to 1568, five botanical gardens were founded in Italy alone : one in Pisa, another in Padua, and others in Florence, Bologna, and Rome. Meanwhile, the herbalists began to cultivate private gardens and museums. As Conrad Gesner's (1516-1565) open beds and glasshouses grew into a living assemblage of flora, his home became a museum. One room was dedicated to the arrangement of dried plants, metals, and fossils, others to stuffed animals and pictures of natural objects sent from every corner of the world.[22] In a like spirit John Ray (1627-1705), realizing the need for precise and ordered knowledge of the flora of the world, first studied and collated existing literature, then turned to the accumulation of examples of mammals, birds, fishes, cryptogams, and all known plants. Nor was any effort too great in the enlargement of his botanical collection. Distant friends, "skilful in Herbary," were called upon to ransack their neighborhoods. Many plants and flowers, having once been dried and sewed to large sheets of paper, went into his *Hortus siccus,* a work of twenty volumes.[23] Despite the difficulties of preserving the soft parts of flora and fauna, botanists and zoologists were as unwearied in collection as their fellows who worked with coins or books.

With collections of curios scattered all over Europe, men of letters and science made it their business to examine as many as possible. It was the fashionable and most intellectually respectable reason for going abroad. What could be pleasanter, said Joseph Addison, "than to see a circle . . . of virtuosos about a cabinet of medals, descanting upon the value, rarity, and authenticalness of the several pieces that lay before them," although he was less enthusiastic about the "curious observations made on spiders, lobsters, and cockle shells," or on whalebone and crocodile skin.[24] Assisted by informative catalogues—the first of which was compiled by Maistre Pierre Borel (1614-1671), a biographer of Descartes and himself a collector—serious students and self-improvers journeyed from cabinet to cabinet, gallery to gallery, and repository to repository, in their tours of the Continent.[25]

Such a pilgrimage may be followed day by day in the diary of John Evelyn (1620-1706), numismatist, architect, landscape-gardener, member of the Royal Society, and author of many books on painting and politics. In Leyden, he was shown the repository of the anatomy school well furnished with skeletons "from the whale and eliphant to the fly and spider," which last was "a very delicate piece of art." In Rome, his "sightsman" took him to "the museum of Fulvius Ursinos repleate with innumerable collections." In Milan, there was nothing "better worth seeing" than the collection of Signor Septalla. There, among other things, was a piece of an Indian wood that had the perfect scent of a civet; "divers chrystals" that had water moving in them; "much amber full of insects, and divers things of woven amianthus." In Paris, in 1644, he visited the library of the Duke of Orléans and saw his six cabinets "of Medails, and an excellent collection of shells and achates, whereof some are prodigiously rich." A day or so later

Evelyn was led by a friend through the garden of Monsieur Morine, "who from being an ordinary gardner is become one of ye most skillful & curious persons in France for his rare collections of shells, flowers, and insects. His collection of butterflies is most curious; these he spreads and so medicates that no corruption invading them, he keepes them in drawers, so plac'd as to represent a beautifull piece of tapissry." But in Evelyn's judgment, the collection belonging to Mr. Charlton of the Middle Temple in London surpassed anything seen abroad "either of private gentlemen or princes." Its content, reminiscent of a version of Pliny, "consisted of miniatures, drawings, shells, insects, medailes, natural things, animals (of which divers, I think 100, were kept in glasses of spirits of wine), minerals, precious stones, vessells, curiosities in amber, christal, achat, &c; all being very perfect and rare of their kind, especially his books of birds, flowers, and shells, drawn and miniatur'd to the life."[26]

The botanist John Ray was another traveler. In Verona, where he mentioned the existence of three notable assemblages of curiosities, he visited those of Mapheus Cusanus and Signor Muscardo. Cusanus, an apothecary, seems to have awarded places of honor to "Egyptian Idols, taken out of the Mummies, divers sorts of petrified shells, petrified cheese, cinnamon, spunge, and Mushromes." Muscardo, on the other hand, was a fancier of ancient Roman medals, lachrymal urns, and lamps. In Bologna, through the courtesy of one of the professors, Ray was conducted through the famous museum assembled by Ulisse Aldrovandi (1527-1605). Here, among the "many natural and artificial rarities therein preserved," he noted with special interest "10 Volumes of the pictures of Plants, and 6 of Birds, Beasts, and Fishes, drawn exactly in colours by the hand."[27]

All collectors and their patrons were profoundly interested in the practical problems of preserving, classifying, and arrang-

Ole Worm's Museum in Leyden, 1588–1685, containing human artifacts.

ing their treasures, an aspect of the vogue of collecting that
had an important bearing on the history of ethnological
thought. The care of collections took several forms. The larger
items were usually placed in halls of curiosities, "chambres de
raretés," "closets," or other "repositories" of one kind or
another, not unlike the rooms envisioned by Francis Bacon in
his plans for "Solomon's House," where patterns or examples
"of all manner of the more rare and excellent inventions" were
to be exhibited in two long galleries.[28] The Medici collection,
according to John Ray in 1663, was situated in the "Great
Duke's gallery . . . in the old palace, a handsome pile of
buildings . . . with a fair portico to walk in."[29] To attract
the public to the early museums, specimens were often
arranged on a plan borrowed from the apothecary's shop. Thus
the walls and ceiling of Tradescant's Ark in London, later to
become the Ashmolean Museum in Oxford, were hung with
chameleons, squirrels, shellfish, a natural dragon, a sea horse's
head, a mermaid's hand, and every conceivable kind of stuffed
animal and bird.[30]

Smaller objects, however, such as coins, fossils, thunderstones,
minerals, gems, bits of human skin, and the like were usually
placed in cabinets or cupboards, cunningly designed by skillful
artisans, and equipped with small drawers, trays, and pigeonholes, to make their contents readily accessible. In Vienna "the
first Cupboard or Case" in "the most Noble Treasury or
Repository of his Imperial Majesty" contained many vessels
turned or shaped out of ivory, cups of amber, spoons and
vessels of mother of pearl. In another was an elephant with a
castle on his back; and in still another watches and clockwork,
a globe and a sphere in silver."[31] Most cabinets were of fine
woods, simply constructed. Others, in princely surroundings,
were made of ebony, inlaid with lazuli and jasper, decorated
with columns of alabaster, and covered with canopies "so

richly set with precious stones, that they resembled a firmament of stars."

But few collections were really large. The famous one of shells, of which a catalogue was sent by John Kentman to Conrad Gesner, contained only 1600 items and could be accommodated in a cabinet of only thirteen drawers, each divided lengthwise by two partitions, for the proper display of the contents. Another, composed of geological specimens given by Dr. John Woodward to Cambridge University, was contained in five handsome, five-foot cabinets, each having thirty drawers in two tiers enclosed by two pairs of doors.[32]

It goes without saying that many of the "curiosi" or "virtuosi" were interested in ethnology, or at least in the assemblage of human artifacts from parts of the world remote from the capitals of Europe. At first these items were not separated from finds in other fields, such as those of classical antiquity, crystallography, geology, paleobotany, or conchology. Some were exhibited merely to confirm faith in the marvelous.[33] For this reason, the catalogue "of the cheifist Rarities of the Public Theatre and Anatomie-Hall of the University of Leyden" makes strange reading. For along with the usual miscellany to be seen in such an exhibit, there was also a Norway house built of beams without mortar or stone; there were shoes and sandals from Russia, Siam, and Egypt; the skin of a man dressed as parchment; a drinking cup made out of the skull of a Moor killed in the beleaguering of Haarlem; warlike arms used in China; Chinese gongs, paper, and books; Egyptian mummies and idols; a petrified toadstool; and "a mallet or hammer that the savages in New Yorke kill with."[34] And the same was true in the museum assembled by the great Aldrovandi to describe and illustrate external nature. There, man-made objects, stone tools and flint arrowheads, were placed side by side, or in the same categories, with rocks and earths, fossil plants, shells, and fish. In dealing with metals, however, this collector distinguished between those in a native state and those in a manufactured condition, describing the uses to which they had been put in the making of weapons and utensils.

By the seventeenth century, items of human handicraft began to find places of their own. One room of the Copenhagen Museum was given over to examples of the wearing apparel of various peoples : the arms and utensils of Indians, Greenlanders, and Turks, which entertained the eye with "a very agreeable pleasure." The collection of Ole Worm (1588-1654), a Danish physician and one of the founders of what was later to become prehistoric archeology, was divided into two sections : first, natural objects, including fossils, plants, and animals; and second, artificial rarities, classified according to the substances of which they were formed, and including many man-made artifacts such as vessels, utensils, tools, weapons, coins, and other articles of clay, amber, gold, silver, bronze, iron, glass, and wood.[35] Later on in Oxford, a similar attempt at classification was in evidence. While visiting the "bibliothecarius of ye Bodleian Library," John Evelyn was shown "in ye closet of the tower" Indian weapons, urns, and lamps; and, in his opinion, the chief rarities to be seen in Tradescant's museum were "the ancient Roman, Indian, and other nations' armour, shields, and weapons; some habits of curiously-colour'd and wrought feathers, one from ye phoenix wing as tradition goes."[36]

But obviously not all collections, ethnological or otherwise, lent themselves to containment in "closets," in the shallow trays and narrow pigeonholes of cabinets, or even to suspension from the ceilings and walls of galleries. The collecting impulse, wayward as it was, began early to spread into areas of interest for which the printed page in the bound book was the only conceivable means of record and safekeeping. Thus, it was none other than Francis Bacon who counseled the collection of all

conceivable facts or "instances" in "histories" or "calendars,"
as a first methodological step toward obtaining insight into the
processes of nature and thought. This procedure, variously
interpreted, and aimed significantly at doing for the inner life
of the mind what was already begun for the external world,
became for many the ideal of seventeenth-century inquiry. It
was adopted by Anthony Wood when he called his collection
of rarities "Britannica Baconia"; by Robert Boyle, and by those
interested in compiling "histories" of the trades; by Leibniz in
making "calendars" of all facts.[37] The original conception of a
bound book of descriptions of technologies appeared in the
*Parasceve, or preparative toward a natural and experimental
history,* attached to the *Novum organum.* Here a new kind of
natural history, a "History of Nature Wrought or Mechanical,"
was proposed. In conformity with this plan, William Petty, a
member of the Royal Society, later read papers on clothmaking,
dyeing, and shipping, Robert Boyle told what he knew about
varnish, and Henry Oldenburg, about making steel and latten
plates.[38]

Still earlier, anticipating by a generation or two the spirit of
Bacon's advice, there were also other bound book or manuscript
collections in the fields of literature, philology, and folklore.
One was a catalogue of six hundred literary men, *Commentarii
de scriptoribus Britannicis,* made by John Leland about 1545;
another was a *Summarium* of similar figures by John Bale in
1548 and 1557; and these were followed a century later by
Thomas Fuller's *Worthies of England,* a collection of literary
biographies, based upon a topographical plan.[39] A linkage
appears to have existed, at least in the minds of some scholars,
between the study of flora and fauna and the study of language
or folklore. Conrad Gesner, whose first love was certainly
botany, was also a linguist, and the author of a *Universal
dictionary* (1545), or alphabetical catalogue of authors, famous
and obscure, ancient and modern, with information concerning

Medieval monsters.

their writings and arguments. Among the works of botanist John Ray were several books of linguistic interest. One, a *Collection of English proverbs,* written in 1670, embodied the homely wisdom of hearthside and farm; another, a *Collection of English words* (1673), was a pioneer attempt to preserve the elements of local speech, a kind of *herbarium* of dialects. Nor was Ray the first in England to collect proverbs. He was preceded by John Heywood in 1546, and William Camden in 1614.[40]

Earlier still, and continuing well into the seventeenth century, the literature of the curious, the rare, the prodigious, and the improbable was further expanded by a large company of collectors of the physically abnormal or monstrous, as manifested among human individuals, races, plants, and animals. Although discussed already to the point of exhaustion by Solinus and Isidore, Brunetto Latini and Vincent, the subject still cast a spell upon many minds. Even members of the Royal Society and the Continental scientific organizations were not immune to the infection, for the need to ascertain the causes of morbid bodily conditions turned investigation much earlier to abnormal anatomy than to the structure of the ordinary human being. And here, during the 16th and 17th centuries the hagiology and demonology of medieval folklore lingered on unresisted.[41]

Among the innumerable compilers of works on the monstrous or grotesque only five need be noted. These were Obsequens, Boaistuau, Lycosthenes, Paré, and Bulwer. Aldus Manutius, a printer of Venice, who more than anyone else of his time was responsible for the dissemination of examples of the best classical scholarship, was also the publisher, in 1508, of a collection of prodigies made in the fourth century by Julius Obsequens. Thereafter, this work of the Latin literary twilight, which purported to establish a correlation between monstrous births and the incidence of personal or national disaster, was issued in 12 editions before Lycosthenes sent it forth on a new career, bound with the *De prodigiis* of Polydore Vergil. *Lycosthenes* (the Greek pseudonym taken by Conrad Wolff-hart, 1518-1561) was a grammarian of Basel and a lecturer on dialectics. In 1557 his large volume entitled *Prodigiorum ac ostentorum chronicon* appeared, and twenty years later was translated into English by Stephen Batman as *The doome warning all men to judgemente (1581)*. Like Pierre Boaistuau (d. 1556), the author of *Certaine secrete wonders of nature* (1557),[42] Lycosthenes was not only a collector but an exponent of the belief, widely and anxiously entertained, that God possessed the plastic power to alter the usual course of nature in the physical formation of man and beast, and that these deviations, properly read, were auguries of catastrophe. The book,

Barbarians, savages, and monsters are included by Muenster in the same category (1554).

richly illustrated, was prepared as a handbook of omens, or as a universal chronicle of the human monstrosities which were held customarily to foreshadow the coming of famine, fire, flood, or war. Sebastian Muenster (1489-1552), another Basel professor and author of the *Cosmographia* (1544), a book which enjoyed tremendous popularity, introduced similar notions into geography and ethnography. Muenster not only acceded without question to the existence of monstrous races, but by deriving the "cannibals" of the New World from the Anthropophagi of the ancients, drew all savage and barbarian peoples into the same frame of reference, and confirmed in the minds of many readers the opinion that this was the right place for them. The work of Ambroise Paré (1517-1590), like that of other medical men, was on a somewhat higher level. He and they were primarily concerned with the systematic study of abnormal births, that branch of natural science which has come to be known as teratology.[43] But their technique, usually that of the undiscriminating collector, was to pile together much of the same old material from classical and post-classical sources, so that the scientific aspects of their work was overwhelmed with discussions of mythological and medieval monsters which had never existed except in some overwrought imagination. Moreover, illustrations of these creatures, which had long been standardized in the old books on prodigies and portents, were still employed to "inform" the scientific reader.

As ethnological knowledge increased in the sixteenth and seventeenth centuries, confusion between the teratological, known to myth or story, and the monstrous, associated by some explorers with savagery, took issue in another collection of materials. This was John Bulwer's (fl. 1654) *Anthropometamorphosis: man transform'd or, the artificiall changling* (1650),[44] which presented neither the monstrous nor the savage alone, but rather that great world-wide array of cosmetic customs which have led many peoples deliberately to refashion their faces and figures away "from the mould intended by nature." In subject matter the book is comprehensive, and seems to be unique. The fruit of wide reading and "diligent looking not only into Civill Societies, but prying also into ruder crowds and silvestrous hordes," it contains chapters on

"Certaine fashions of the Haire . . . more derogating to the honour of Nature"; "Eye-brow rites, or the Eye-brows abused contrary to Nature"; "Certaine formes and strange shapes of the Nose much affected and artificially contrived"; and so on, progressing anatomically from the heads to the heels of many nations. To be sure, like many other collectors of the humanly curious, rare, and grotesque, Bulwer readily accepted the existence of the so-called fabulous races of mankind, but perceiving clearly the compulsive obedience exacted by custom among all peoples, he explained these deviations from the normal, as he did deviant hair styles or ear ornamentation, as voluntary and self-inflicted. There is no creature "but Man," he said with some insight, "that degenerates willingly from his Naturall dignitie."

Plainly, the whole great company of collectors, whether gatherers of shells, coins, fossils, proverbs, monsters, dialects, or artificial deformities, were good Baconians—some of them indeed Baconians before Bacon. For, as put by the *Advancement of learning* in 1605, the divisions of the "history" of nature are three in number. They summon inquiry to the study, first, "of nature in course"; second, to "nature erring and varying"; and third, to "nature altered or wrought; that is, history of Creatures, history of Marvels, and history of Arts." The collection of the wanderings of errant nature, said the author, was still insufficient, incompetent, and neglected. While books containing "fabulous experiences" or "frivolous impostures" abounded, a "substantial and severe collection of Heteroclites or Irregulars" was still wanting. Wanting also was a collector of false notions or mistaken ideas. Since the mind of man was "rather like an enchanted glass," full of superstition and imposture, long-cherished error should be sorted out and exposed. A calendar of popular errors should be compiled "such as pass in speech and conceit; and are nevertheless detected and convicted of untruth."[45]

Here again Bacon was not so much an original as a spokes-
man of the more advanced opinion of his time. Already as he
wrote, a collection of "vulgar errors" had been made at least
once in the field of medicine by one Dr. Laurence Joubert.
Appearing in several editions, this volume was followed by
others in medicine, religion, and superstition. But the best
known of all is that assembled by an English physician and
antiquary, Sir Thomas Browne of Norwich (1605-1682),
entitled *Pseudodoxia epidemica, or inquiries into many
received tenets and commonly presumed truths,* first published
in 1646. "To purchase a clear and unwarrentable body of
Truth," said the doctor by way of preface, "we must forget and
part with much that we know"; we must refuse to believe "at
first ear, what is delivered by others"; and refrain from
"prostration unto Antiquity."[46] The *Pseudodoxia* is thus a
printed collection or a printed repository of curiosities of
thought and belief, put together at the cost of a lifetime of
effort. Having made professional sojourns in Padua, Mont-
pellier, and Leyden, where collections of curios abounded, the
doctor became a collector himself. According to Evelyn's *Diary,*
"His whole house and garden" became "a paradise and cabinet
of rarities," composed of the best among "medails, books,
plants, and natural things."[47] Since no memory could have
retained the flood of facts, oddities, and strangenesses that were
poured into his hands by his son, by traveling friends, and by
his own voluminous reading, he maintained for 46 years a
system of Commonplace Books. Upon these rests the *Pseudodoxia* with its compendia of errors "concerning mineral and
vegetable bodies," its "received tenets concerning animals,"
and its popular notions concerning man, geography, history,
and the Scriptures. If, at times, Dr. Browne seems "fain to
wander in the America and untraveled parts of Truth,"[48] the
book is nevertheless a serious work, designed to destroy by logic

and ridicule countless errors and false theories still stubbornly held by the commonalty of men, both unlearned and learned.

The first, or at least one of the first, Renaissance collections of manners and customs (preserved necessarily between the covers of a little book) was amassed even earlier than many of the earliest or most famous collections of coins, gems, and fossils. The author was one Johann Boemus (fl. 1520); the book, vest-pocket size, was called *Omnium gentium mores, leges, & ritus ex multis clarissimis rerum scriptoribus.*[49] The date was 1520. Born in Aub in Franconia, Boemus was an obscure German Hebraist and a younger contemporary of those better-known students of Hebrew, Johann Reuchlin (1445–1552) and Conrad Pellikan (1478-?1556). He was also a contemporary of Machiavelli, Copernicus, and Sir Thomas More; an elder member of the generation of Jean Bodin and Giovanni Botero; and, if still living in the sixth decade of the sixteenth century, an old man when Bacon and Shakespeare were born. Little more than this—a date and the place of his birth—are known.

Johann Boemus made his simple purposes very clear. There were two of them. He wished, first, to make accessible to the ordinary reader an already not inconsiderable body of knowledge concerning the variety of human behavior, to arrange it on a broad geographical plan, with the geographical features subordinated to the ethnological, and to use the printed page, as others had employed the "cabinet de curiosités," for assembling and exhibiting the range of human custom, ritual, and ceremony. Second, in the interest of improved political morality, he desired to inform his readers concerning the laws and governments of other nations. Such a project, he was sure, would fill a real need and receive favorable reception. "I have . . . collected, abridged, digested, and compacted together," he said, "the manners and façions, the Lawes,

Customes and Rites" that hitherto "ware Skatered, & by piece meale, set furthe to posteritie. Those I saie have I sought out, gathered together, and . . . digested into this little packe. Not for the hongre of gaine, or the ticklyng desire of the peoples vaine brute, and unskilfulle commendacion : but partly moved with . . . the wondrefulle profite and pleasure, that I conceived in this kinde of studie my selfe, and partly that other . . . might with little labour, finde easely when thei would, the somme of thynges compiled in one Booke, that thei were wonte with tediousnes to sieke in many."[50]

These "histories" or descriptions, written at about the same time as Machiavelli's *Prince,* were intended not only to instruct his readers concerning the laws and governments of other nations, but to make it possible for them to form intelligent judgments as to "what orders and institutions" were "fittest to be ordayned" in their own lands for the establishment of perfect peace. With the ancient customs of the classical peoples spread out for contemplation and comparison, together with those of more recent practice, Boemus felt certain that Europeans could readily decide between the socially good and socially bad. They might, indeed, come to realize that they lived in a good age. They might perceive how man had advanced "in what perfection we now live at this day, and how simply, rudely, and uncivilly our forefathers lived, from the Creation to the Generall Flood, and for many ages after."

His timing was excellent. He was right about the need for the little book. It was an instant success, and was widely consulted for well over a hundred years. Some measure of its interest to the reading public of the sixteenth and seventeenth centuries may be inferred from the number of its reissues, revisions, and translations. A few years after its first appearance, or in 1536, a revised and expanded Latin edition was published. Following that or from 1536 to 1611 there were no less than 23 other re-issues in five languages—9 in Latin, 5 in

Italian, 4 in French, 3 or 4 in English, and 1 in Spanish. It was translated into French twenty years after its first Latin publication in 1520. Twenty-two years later there was an Italian edition; and it was received by the vernacular reading public of England, first as *The fardle of façions, conteining the aunciente maners, customes, and lawes, of the peoples enhabiting the two partes of the earth, called Affrike and Asie* (1555), then later in two or three other translations, the most complete of which was *The manners, lawes, and customes of all nations* published in 1611.[51]

The work was known to Jean Bodin, who cited Boemus as a pre-eminent authority, along with Diodorus Siculus, Pomponius Mela, Strabo, Leo Africanus, and Alvarez. It was used by Stephen Batman, the translator of Bartholomeus Anglicus and the author of *The golden booke of the leaden gods* (1577), said to be the first attempt in English to construct a pantheon of heathen deities. It was read by Edmund Spenser while writing his *View of the present state of Ireland* in 1596. Through Belleforest, the French popularizer of the *Omnium gentium mores* and Sebastian Muenster's *Cosmographia,* Boemus was read by Montaigne, and may have helped to shape his ideas on the diversity of custom. He was mentioned by Robert Burton and by Edward Brerewood, the antiquary, mathematician, and seventeenth-century student of languages and religions; by Alexander Ross, the author of *Pansebia: or, a view of all the religions of the world* (1653); by Samuel Purchas in *Purchas his pilgrimage* (1613); and by William Strachey, seventeenth-century promoter of colonization and possibly a member of Shakespeare's literary circle.

Moreover, as a collector of customs, Boemus initiated a literary and ethnological genre which has lived on vigorously until the present day. Within a few years after the publication of the first edition of the *Omnium gentium mores* in 1520, and continuously thereafter for more than two centuries, similar collections of customs were brought out by other hands, many of them to be printed and reprinted for upwards of two hundred years. One of these, entitled *Genialium dierum libri sex,* was written in 1522 by Alessandro Alessandri, a jurist of Naples. This book contained, among other things, 30 chapters on religious matters, 13 on social customs, and 10 on history.[52] Another was *De moribus et ritibus gentium libri iii* (1557) by Alessandro Sardi (c. 1520-1588),[53] an assemblage of rather commonplace Greek, Roman, and barbarian materials reminiscent of Herodotus. The works of Boemus' successors or imitators were in some sense cosmographies, a type of publication devoted to geography, history, manners, and science. One early example of these was the *Chronica, zëyt-büch ünd geschychtbibel,* published in 1531 by Sebastian Franck (1499-1543), a work of considerable originality, later expanded and frequently translated.[54] Another was Sebastian Muenster's vast *Cosmographia,*[55] later abridged for French readers and combined with substantial borrowings from Boemus by François Belleforest (1530-1583).[56] Still others in the sixteenth and seventeenth centuries were the cosmographies of Ortelius, Thevet, William Cuningham, and George Abbot, Robert Stafforde, Pierre d'Avity, Peter Heylyn, Nathanael Carpenter, Samuel Clark, Bernhardt Varen, and Pierre Duval. The moral encyclodepdias of Pedro Mexia and Pierre La Primaudaye contained similar cultural material, as did the works of Jean Bodin, a collector of historical documents, statutes, legal customs, and changes in states.

But the time was early. The year 1520, in which the little book *Omnium gentium mores* was first published by Boemus, was a scant generation after the first landing of Columbus in the New World. Avenues of communication were few and uncertain. Consequently, while the existence of lands to the west, different from India or Cathay, may have been surmised by better-informed men in Europe, the presence of other continents was unsuspected by most of the population. Nor was there any intimation by Boemus himself, except in a later and revised edition, that he was aware of human beings on or near a North or South American continent. Though it is well-nigh certain that he was associated with scholars who were responsible for the geographical renaissance in Germany, and may even have known Sebastian Muenster, the latter's *Cosmographia* (1544) had not yet been published. The works of Vesalius (1514-1564) and Copernicus (1473-1543), destined to shatter tradition in the fields of anatomy and astronomy, were still two decades in the future. Richard Eden (1521?-1626), Richard Hakluyt (1552?-1616), and Samuel Purchas (1575?-1626), those great compilers of voyages, were yet to be born. *The Advancement of learning* would not be written for eight decades; the great scientific societies would be founded still later. In fact, the content of the *Fardle of façions,* though published after the Columbian adventures, and the voyages of John and Sebastian Cabot, was in many respects pre-Columbian and medieval in character, or at most transitional. Among the few new features of the little book was the role of the author as a collector of cultural descriptions, "shocked up" together, "as well those of aunciente tyme, as of later years." Paralleling, as it did, similar collections in botany, zoology, and geology, the "shocking up," in the field of the study of man was very new indeed, and suggests a number of questions.

If Johann Boemus, in the *Fardle of façions,* was bent on assembling the manners and customs of many nations, "having never (himself) by traveling into those partes, beene eye-witnesse of them," which of all the nations were included in his "fardle"? On whom did he rely for information? Having found his information, how did he arrange and order it? To what traits, customs, institutions, did he direct his descriptive attention?

The world, for this German scholar, was still divided

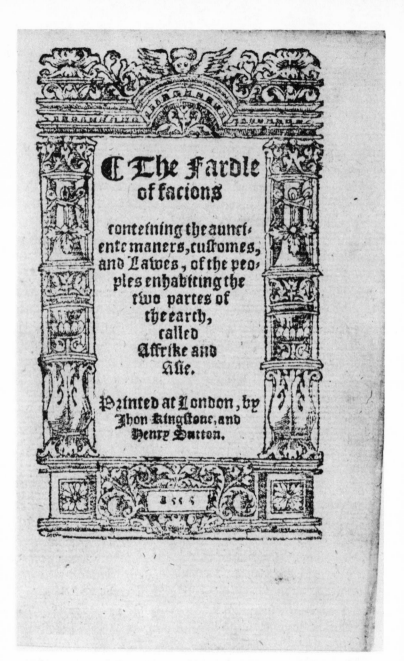

¶ The Fardle
of facions

conteining the aunci-
ente maners, customes,
and Lawes, of the peo-
ples enhabiting the
two partes of
the earth,
called
Affrike and
Asie.

Printed at London, by
Jhon Kingstone, and
Henry Sutton.

1555

One of the earliest Renaissance collections of manners and
customs, published by Johann Boemus, first in Latin in 1520
and then in English as The Fardle of Facions, 1555.

"according to thaunciente divisions of the earth," prescribed by Orosius in the fourth century. It was composed of only three continents, or "thre partes, Affrique, Asie, and Europe"; and his collection of ethnological descriptions begins in Africa, or rather in Ethiopia, which, according to the best medieval opinion, possessed an "Indian" or Asian component as well as an African. The African discoveries made by the Portuguese mariners in the fifteenth century were apparently unknown to Boemus. At any rate he omits reference to them, and to the Negro peoples with whom they established contact. Hence, his description of cultural diversities in this southern continent was limited geographically to regions on the Mediterranean littoral, or to nations known to antiquity, such as Ethiopia, Egypt, and Carthaginia. Later, when he turned to the manners and customs of Asiatic and European peoples, the geographical stage becomes broader, and the cultural panorama wider and more familiar. In Asia, it was the ten "most famous" nations which received his attention: Panchaia, a region of Arabia; Assyria and Babylonia; Medea and Parthia, Persia, Scythia, India, Tartaria, and Turkey. In Europe, working from east to west by north, he described twenty-nine areas, many of them neighbors of his own Germanic home: Greece, Russia, Lithuania, Livonia, Prussia, Poland, Hungary, Bohemia, Saxony, Westphalia, Italy, France, Spain, Portugal, and Britain. Moreover, the sources upon which he drew, his wells of ethnological material, were not the reports of recent travelers either in Europe or in the New World. In harmony with Renaissance devotion to the classics and with the collector's predilection for the antique, the "historiographers" and learned men of the elder world were called on, some forty-two of them: Thucydides, Diodorus, Ptolemy, Josephus, Pomponius Mela, Solinus, Orosius, and the like. Herodotus is mentioned nine times; Sabellicus, "out of whose history we have taken most matters," six times; Pliny, four; and the others once or twice. It should be noted, however, that Boemus had also read Carpini, either in the original or in Vincent's version, and cites that work in the course of his description of the Tartars. Other than this, the most modern of his sources were four fifteenth-century writers: Aeneas Silvius, Sabellicus, Volaterranus, and Martinus Segonius.

But selected as they were from a scattered body of cultural observations in many ancient sources, this collection of ethnological traits, rituals, and ceremonies found in the *Omnium gentium mores* throws a revealing light not only upon the concept of culture entertained by Boemus and his contemporaries but upon his idea of the classes or categories into which the traits of peoples might conceivably and usefully be assembled for closer analysis. With the clear intention of isolating the major social institutions for inspection, and with some degree of orderliness, Boemus placed special emphasis on divergences in marriage and the family, divergences in social organization, in religions, funeral rites, weapons, warfare, justice, diet, and apparel. Out of about twenty-five peoples to whom he gave his most detailed attention, he described the institution of marriage (including the morality of women and child care) for twenty-three; religion for eighteen; funeral rites for seventeen; weapons and warfare for fourteen; diet for twelve, and so on.

Like Bodin, who was to write his *Republic* two generations later, Boemus regarded the family as the cornerstone of society. In describing various marital systems, he distinguished between exogamous and endogamous peoples, though without using these terms; and between polygyny and polyandry. Approval was unquestionably given to marrying-in, with astonished interest in all forms of plural alliances. The Saxons, who took every care to avoid "doing anything that should be a touch or debasement to their stockes," held it to be "a stain and pollution to their bloud to marry with women of other nations."[57] Among the Medes, it was customary for the kings to have many wives. "Which thynge was aftrewarde also taken up of the communes : so that at lengthe it was thought unmiete to have feawer wives then seven. It was also a goodlie thyng for a woman to have many husbandes : and to be without five at ones, was compted a miserable state."[58] Nor were the Persians far behind, holding "many concubines also beside, for the encrease of issue."[59] Dowries, the position of women, provisions for divorce, penalties for adultery, betrothal and marriage ceremonies were also reported for many nations. Boemus noted that "the ordre of Mariage emong the Egiptians" was not uniform, "for the priests might mary but one onely wife. All other have as many as they wille, acording to their substaunce." So also no child was reckoned illegitimate, "though it be borne of a bought women slave." For they "onely compte the father to be the authour of his kynde; and the mother onely but to geve place and nourishment to the childe."[60]

Similar approval was expressed for forms of social organization taken to be old, firmly established, and by this token, invariable; while disapprobation was visited upon the unorganized, nonsocial herd "not distinguished into companies." Following a description of the Egyptians in which husbandmen, breeders of cattle, and craftsmen are distinguished as the three sorts of people composing the realm, a similar analysis was made of Athens, dividing its population into "societies, trybes, or wards, according to the estimation and valuation of every ones substance." In Italy, it is related, there were three companies or quires. The Germans consisted of "foure sortes of people" : the first being the clergy; the second, the nobility; the third, the citizens, composed of gentlemen and plebeians; and the fourth, subordinated to all others, the villagers and husbandmen. In this northern country, which Boemus knew so well at first hand, social structure became the organizing framework upon which the description of all other aspects of the culture was hung.[61]

In the matter of religion, the problem of the origin of idolatry was raised; sun worship was recognized and described; monotheists were distinguished from polytheists. True to tradition, the Ethiopians, as "the fyrst of all men," were made the discoverers of "the first waie of worshippyng God . . . with the maners and ceremonies there to appertinent."[62] Among their priests, he was accounted holiest who was most troubled by visions.[63] Concerning the Egyptians, certain beasts were worshiped "not onely whilest they be onlive, but also when they are dead. As the Catte, the Icneumon, the dagge, the hauke, the woulfe, the Cocodrille, and many other like. . . . And they go about on procession with the propre Images of them, from citie, to citie, and from place, to place."[64] The Tartars, whose dwellings were neither "in tounes ne Bouroughes, but in the fieldes abrode, aftre the maner of thauncient Scithians in tentes," believed in one God, the maker of all things, and Him they honored; "but not with any maner of Sacrifice or ceremonie." As Carpini, Rubruck, and after them Vincent, had related, they made little puppets of silk or felt, "like unto menne," which they set up on each side of their tents, doing them much reverence. Mohametanism, though so long a threat to Christendom, had not yet revealed itself clearly as a religious system to this northern European scholar; or else, the danger having passed, he chose rather to deal with instances of idolatry or with several varieties of Reformation dissent. Accordingly, the religion of the Saracens or Turks was dismissed as merely "the brainesicke wickednesse of a countrefeicte prophete," who had loosed a contagious evil into innumerable countries.[65] But the Saxons, upright in condition, sincere in life, and otherwise of irreproachable manners, were charged with once having been "great Idolaters, worshipping trees, and fountains of water."

The nations most fully described by Boemus were those at the farthest remove from sixteenth-century Europe, in both space and time: India, Ethiopia, Tartary, Egypt, Sparta, Scythia. The cultures receiving lesser attention were the homelands of Europeans, particularly the Slavs, the Poles, the Lithuanians, and the Bohemians. Not only was far-off India favored with an amplitude of detail, but his descriptions, reflecting admiration not unmixed with incredulity, reflect also, as in a mirror, the contemporary standard of the socially good, the ultimate criterion of true civility.

This Eastern country, said he, was so vast that it was thought to form a third part of the whole world. It contained "sundry sorts" of people and five thousand cities. Referring to the ever-recurring and always interesting theme of foreign habits of dress, he described the Indians as "greate deckers and trimmers of themselves" with precious stones, silks, linens, and wool, "to, to, gaude glorious." In social organization "the commune wealthe . . . was some tyme devided into seven states or degrees": sages, husbandmen, breeders and feeders, artificers, handicraftsmen, men of war, surveyors or masters of report, presidents, and heads of the common councils. The caste system was rigid. A man could not marry out of his calling or change his trade. "For neither maie the souldiour occupie housebandrie thoughe he woulde: ne the artificers intremedle with the doctrine of the sages." Among the Indian philosophers were sages called Gymnosophists, inhabiting the uttermost and shadowy parts of the realm; and among these were the Brahmins, beloved of medieval legend and true people of the Golden Age, who lived a pure and simple life, led with "no likerous lustes of other mennes vanities." They longed for no more than nature "requyreth naturallye." They were content with such food as came to hand, "desiryng no suche as other menne tourne the worlde almost upside downe to have, leaving no element unransaked to gette a gowbin for their glotenous gorge."[66]

Within the spacious reaches of the Indian subcontinent Boemus also noted other "sundry people" who existed in an uncivil condition. Some, whose literary lineage is traceable to Pliny or beyond, lived on marshy ground, fed themselves on fish, went out in boats made of cane, and wore reed garments. Some, like the Padae, were cattle-raisers, who killed their old or diseased parents and ate them. Some, the story goes, killed no living thing, nor planted, nor sowed, nor built houses, but lived only on herbs. Another people, the Catheians, burnt their widows on the sepulchers of their husbands; while a dog-headed folk, voiceless but for snarling and barking, resided in the hills.

Concerning other Asian peoples, Boemus relied on sources ready to hand: for the Scythians, on Herodotus; for the Mongols, on John de Plano Carpini, of the 13th century A.D., as transmitted by the *Speculum historiale* of Vincent of Beauvais; for the Chinese, on that dim, nameless contributor to legendary ethnology who first dismissed them as courteously withdrawn from the rest of mankind. In writing of the Land of the Seres, that "debonair people," Boemus tells of the practice of the silent trade: how merchants "passe their outmost floude toward them [their boundary river], but . . . may come no nigher"; how the Seretines set their goods in order on the banks of the river, "as thei judge them in price"; and how "the buyer cometh, and as he judgeth them by his eye to be worthe . . . so laieth he doune," without further fellowship or communication. There was no need among such people to enforce injunctions against adultery or theft, "for the feare of their lawes" was of more force upon them than the constellation of their nativities. So chaste were they that they dwelt "as it ware in the beginnyng, or entryng of the worlde." Like other exemplary peoples of tradition, they were "neither skourged

with Blastynges, ne Haile, ne Pestilence, ne such other evilles,"
but continued long in life and died without grief.[67]

But the *Omnium gentium mores* by the long-forgotten
German Hebraist was not the only expression of Renaissance
interest in the collection of human customs. There was also
the cosmography, sometimes described as a mixed kind of
history and geography. Persisting from the Middle Ages, when
it was used to accommodate a miscellany of pseudo-scientific
lore and *mappa mundi*,[68] it became, in the judgment of Francis
Bacon, a compound of "natural history, in respect to the
regions themselves; of history civil, in respect to the inhabita-
tions, regiments, and manners of the people; and the mathematics, in respect of the climates and configurations towards
the heavens."[69]

As the first modern description of man's earthly habitat,
Sebastian Muenster's *Cosmographia: beschreibung aller lander,*
published in Basel in 1544, was planned not only to inform but
to entertain, thus perpetuating one of the chief characteristics
of the medieval encyclopedia. The initial German edition was
followed immediately by two others in 1545 and 1550; these
in turn by a Latin version in 1550, and then by versions in
French, Bohemian, and Italian in 1552, 1554, and 1558
respectively. The English translation of Books IV and V by
Richard Eden appeared in 1553 and 1572.[70] So well, indeed,
did this cosmography fit the needs of the time that it remained
in use for over one hundred years, or until 1650, and went
through 46 editions in 6 languages.

Meanwhile, many other cosmographies were in the making.
Several of these were sumptuous publications containing
beautifully drafted, colored maps along with the text. All
extended ethnological information or misinformation to their
readers. Two of the greatest were published before the end of
the sixteenth century: that by Abraham Ortelius entitled

Theatrum orbis terrarum, in 1570, and the other by Gerardus
Mercator, *Atlas, sive cosmographicae meditationis de fabrica
mundi,* in 1585-95. At about the same time in England,
William Cuningham, Doctor in Physicke, had become the
author of *The cosmographical glasse, conteinyng the pleasant
principles of cosmographie* in 1559, and André Thevet in
France had brought out his *Cosmographie universelle* (1571).
Later on in the seventeenth century, the large, luxurious atlas-
type of cosmography was supplemented by books of another,
more modest sort. *A briefe description of the whole worlde*
(1599), written by George Abbot, one-time Archbishop of
Canterbury, was one of these. It was small enough and cheap
enough to fit into anybody's pocket; and so also was Peter
Heylyn's *Microcosmus, or a little description of the great world*
(1621), though with a succession of later expansions it finally
grew into a folio. Pierre d'Avity's *Les états, empires, et
principautez du monde,* published in France in 1614, and
translated into English the year following, began its career as
a large volume. But Robert Stafforde's *Geographicall and
anthological description of all the empires and kingdomes*
(1607), Nathanael Carpenter's *Geography delineated* (1625),
and Samuel Clarke's *A geographicall and anthologicall
description of all the empires and kingdomes both of continent
and ilands in this terrestriall globe* . . . (1618) were all small
books.

Born in 1489, Sebastian Muenster appeared on the scene a
little too early for complete accommodation to all of the new
ideas which were to flow into European thought from the post-
Columbian voyagers. Consequently, the medley of materials
displayed in the thousand-odd pages of the *Cosmographia* is
nothing if not arresting. At first glance, the book seems to have
been compiled without benefit of plan, and with no core of
organizing ideas. The proper subjects of cosmography, if such
there ever were, are jumbled together with the extravagances

of medieval fantasy. There are innumerable digressions: turning the pages one sees, for example, a section on "A Mountain Always Casting Forth Flame and Smoke"; another on a "Monster Born Nigh unto Worms in . . . 1495"; another "Of Wild Bulls in Prussia"; and still others on "A Straunge History of a King Devoured of Mice," and "Of the Cocatrice." On second reading, however, certain elements in the miscellany begin to coalesce and to take shape around a few major geographical and ethnological principles.

"In dealing with manners and customs, Muenster starts with the Britons in the far west, and then moves eastward across Europe, stopping first to describe the Spaniards, the French, and the Italians, then turning to Germany and Germany's northern and eastern neighbors, the Scandinavians and Slavs. The next cultures considered are those of the Near East— Turkey, Asia Minor and Palestine—followed by the ancient empires of Assyria, Medea, and Persia and the Scythians, Tartarians, and Seres. Finally, as legend overtakes fact, Muenster turns to Africa and the American 'newe found landes and Islandes'."

In this piece of collective cultural portraiture, the reader is informed concerning the boundaries of each country, the derivation of its name, its topographical and political divisions, its rivers and mountains, its fertility and agricultural products, its flora and fauna, and its cities. To this is added for good measure a list of its crowned heads, princely houses, and great lords, illustrious individuals, bishoprics, and universities. When occasionally the exposition begins to drag, Muenster introduces a salty story, and the attention of the reader is immediately recaptured.

But who were the peoples described by Muenster? How did he select them? And who were his authorities?

"I have written here," he says in the conclusion of his great volume, "of the peoples and nations of the whole world, with their attainments, laws, customs, manners, religions, ceremonies, kingdoms, principalities, trades, antiquities, lands, animals, mountains, rivers, seas, lakes, and other features."[11] Throughout the book he speaks frequently of the manners and customs of *mankind*. He evidently thought, or intended his readers to think, "that he had covered the subject for all peoples. This was hardly true. The sum of cultures described by Muenster fell far short of those known to intelligent men even in the sixteenth century, while the traits, customs, and institutions chosen to portray the daily lives of these folk left much to be desired."

As he moved from west to east across Europe, Asia, and the New World, the manners and customs of barely forty peoples received scrutiny, a number which corresponds closely with that achieved in the *Omnium gentium mores* published by Johann Boemus only twenty-four years before. More than that, his ethnological descriptions in many cases are very brief. The Irish, for example, as first entrants on the scene, were presented in a few words as "voyed of hospitalitie . . . uncivill and cruel, & therefore unapt for war-like affrayes," while the Carmanians followed the customs of the Medes and Persians and were compelled to ride asses into battle until after each man had presented his king with the head of an enemy.[12]

To his own people Muenster was more generous, allotting the whole of Book III to Germany—its geographical situation, its government and history—an organization of materials which anticipated in intent, if not in completeness, William Camden's *Britannia* (1586), and earned for his *Cosmography* the title of *Germanography* from Jean Bodin. But here again, in this longest book of over five hundred pages, the strictly ethnological section, entitled "The Laws and Customs of the Germans of Our Day," is very short, a little over two pages in length, and its content is limited to a recapitulation in Teutonic terms of the medieval concept of society as divided into four estates, with a meager description of German habits of dress, diet, and shelter. The remainder of Book III is given over to matters of geographical interest, including descriptions of notable towns or cities, with a few items here and there of interest to the anthropologist.

Strangely enough, it was the Turks and the Tartars, rather than the Germans who seemed at this time to call for the most extended ethnological analysis. Or perhaps it was not so strange after all. For in the world as known to Europeans in the sixteenth century, the fear of the Mongol hordes and the peril of the Turk still overshadowed almost all other claims on attention, even including that made by the more exotic inhabitants of the New World. Thus Muenster's description of the Turks covers over four folio pages, and is the longest in the book.[73]

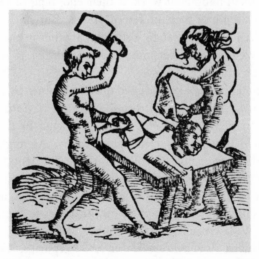

"Canibali antropophagi," from Muenster (1554).

Moreover, Muenster was not intolerant of medieval ethnological fantasy. His reading of the ancients and his preparation of editions of Pomponius Mela and Solinus Polyhistor had no doubt taught him to be astonished at nothing. At all events, some sections of the *Cosmographia,* notably Books V and VI on the Seres, the Scythians, the Budini, and the peoples of India, Africa, and America, teem with stories of fabulous folk. Though denounced by the author, these gentry, the Cynocephali, the Anthropophagi, the Acridophagi and their like, appear in his pages, their claims being upheld by their portraits. Concerning the Seres and the Brahmins, the same stories were told by Muenster which graced the pages of Solinus and the *Roman d'Alexandre* twelve hundred years before; and so slowly did news travel, so resistant were Muenster and his contemporaries to the acceptance of the real facts concerning the American Indians, that fifty years after their discovery they were still being described as cannibals—a verbal description which is reinforced in the *Cosmographia* with illustrations showing them happily at work at their chopping blocks, maintaining a supply of their preferred viands. But since medieval and modern ideas appear to jostle one another in the pages of the *Cosmographia,* it becomes of some interest to determine Muenster's sources.

Fortunately, he makes this pedantic task easier by including a *Catalogus, Doctorum Virorum Quorum Scriptis & Ope Sumus Usi & Aduiti in Hoc Opere,* or what in these latter days would be called a select bibliography. As might be expected, this *Catalogus* is a roll call of the "ancients," already made familiar in medieval historical and geographical literature. But to these are added a few medieval names, and those also of many recent geographers and travelers to the North of Europe—Volaterranus, Vartomannus, Nauclerus, Beatus, Olaus, Lazius, Jovius, Aeneas Silvius, Vespucius, Columbus.

As for Muenster's originality, it will have to be acknowledged that he possessed none. For whatever the sources of the *Cosmographia,* and however widely he may have read in the process of compiling his *Catalogus,* there can be little doubt of his profound indebtedness to one contemporary. This was

One of the earliest illustrations of the natives of the New World, issued perhaps in Augsburg in 1497–1504.

Johann Boemus. "A comparison of the ethnological sections in the two works suggests with a conclusiveness akin to certainty that when Muenster needed a model description of the way of life of some specific group of people, he turned first to his copy of the *Omnium gentium mores,* and if a description was there available he copied it, sometimes in whole, sometimes in part." The array of peoples chosen for descriptive treatment in the *Cosmographia* is almost identical with that to be found in the *Omnium gentium mores,* with the difference that Muenster elected to deal with Africa and the Africans last, Boemus first; Muenster included the inhabitants of the island of Iceland, Guiana, and Zanzibar, whereas Boemus excluded them; Muenster at least mentioned some of the peoples of the

Americas whereas Boemus ignored them. "But what Muenster has to say about each people, and the order of the saying, is almost identical with the relevant parts of the *Omnium gentium mores.* This is true not only for the briefer ethnological descriptions in the *Cosmographia* such as that on the Chinese or Seres, but also of the longest—those on the Turks and Tartars."

When the *Cosmographia* was first issued in 1544, the literature available on the Turks, in addition to the *Omnium gentium mores,* included Teodoro Spandugino, *De vita et moribus Turcarum* (1509); Sebastian Franck, *Cronica, abconterfayung . . . der Türckey, mit yren begriffe, inhalt, provintien* (1530); Antoine Geuffroy, *Briefve description de la court de Grant Turc* (1542); and finally, Bartholomew Georgiewitz, *Epitome de Turcarum ritu, moribus, et caeremonius* (1544), who is mentioned by name in Muenster's text.[14] But Muenster's section on the Turks, though the longest and most detailed in the *Cosmographia,* shows little evidence of the use of these sources. At a time when plagiarism was respectable, he turned, in the first part of his description of "these peoples, to his old stand-by, Boemus." On the military organization of the Turks, on their religious beliefs, on their laws and the administration of justice, on their rites of marriage and manner of dress, the account in the *Omnium gentium mores* is followed very closely. It is only in the latter part of the section, and in subjects which receive the headings, *On the Opinion of the Turks on the World to Come; Of Fasting and Meats of the Turks; Of the Circumcision of the Turks;* and *Of the Burialls of the Turks* that another source, probably Georgiewitz, is employed. In fact, in the possible confusion incident to the use of more than one source, Muenster seems to have been led into repetition. The busy compiler, transcribing rapidly without stopping to check, failed to note that he had already copied data from Boemus referring to the veiling of women, the abstention from swine's flesh, and ceremonial bathing,[75] for he then copied the same again from Georgiewitz.

In his treatment of the Tartars, Muenster's reliance upon Boemus is even more unmistakable. The history of communication during the Middle Ages between Mongolia and modern Christendom began with John de Plano Carpini and William Rubruck, predecessors of Marco Polo, who had made notable contributions to the ethnology of the Tartar tribes. Johann Boemus had unquestionably read Carpini, if not in the original, then in the version which appeared in the *Speculum historiale*.[76] He gives Vincent of Beauvais as his authority for the content of his chapter on Tartaria; and that chapter indeed consists of excerpts chosen from Vincent's version of Carpini. Muenster's account of the Tartarians, on the other hand, seems to have been based wholly upon that in the *Omnium gentium mores,* without an independent reading of either Carpini or Vincent. The proof of this statement lies in the fact that Muenster varies from Boemus in only a few respects, namely, in the order in which the customs and manners of the Mongols are discussed and in an occasional omission of some item included in the Boemus account. It is notable further that neither Vincent's name nor that of Carpini appears in Muenster's *Catalogus Doctorum* or in his text; that although Vincent's version of Carpini's *Historia mongolorum* is fuller than that in the *Omnium gentium mores,* Muenster's version is less full and contains no items which, absent from Boemus, could be referred to Carpini, or to Vincent's version of Carpini.

As for the several later cosmographers, such as Cuningham, Abbot, Stafforde, and Clarke, their claims to fame as collectors of manners and customs are slight. Despite their well-deserved distinction as geographers, the same might also be suggested for both Abraham Ortelius (1527-1593) and Gerardus Mercator (1512-1594), who took as their first obligation the trans-

ference to maps of the immense flood of geographical information poured into Europe by voyagers and travelers. Neither
found time to add greatly, either in content or procedure, to
the cultural descriptions which had already been made available. Nevertheless, the two Flemish geographers, with their
lesser English and French successors—Peter Heylyn and Pierre
d'Avity—were agreed on at least two things : first, that the
moral foundations of cosmography called for the study of
man's behavior in relation to his "station" on the earth's
surface; and second, that if mankind in all of his diversity were
to be understood, a firm case must be made for the integration
of geography, history, and manners. A geography without
history, said Heylyn, "hath life and motion, but at randome,
and unstable : so Historie without Geography like a dead
carkasse hath neither life nor motion at all." Seen together
they "crowne our happinesse : but parted asunder . . . are
like two sisters entirely loving each other and not without great
pittie . . . to be divided.'" If all these men were weighed
down by what they had undertaken, and treated the task of
describing man's cultures in a perfunctory manner, it should
occasion no surprise. The size of the project, in its geographical
aspects alone, was overwhelming. The need for some rational
division of the field as between geographer and ethnologist had
yet to be realized.

The celebrated *Theatrum orbis terrarum* by Ortelius, first
issued in 1570, and centered on the assembly of a collection of
maps which, when reduced to atlas size, could "easily and well
be seene and discern'd," was prefaced with a brightly colored
title page, at the top of which was Europa, scepter in right hand
and globe under her left. In the center, on either side, was Asia
adorned with jewels, and Africa, a naked woman. At the
bottom was another woman, a savage, representing America,
holding a club and a man's bleeding head. This geographer
was usually brief in his references to the habits and customs of

the peoples of the world. In Scotland, for example, the inhabitants of the southern part were said to be "more civill and humaine." Those who dwelt in the north were a rougher, harder kind of people, wearing mantles and skirts dyed with saffron after the Irish fashion. The people of Ireland wore "course blacke mantles or rugges." In riding they used no saddles, boots, nor spurs. Following a well-worn tradition, it was asserted that they were "wild and very uncivill." Of Moscovy and China, on the other hand, Ortelius' descriptions were lively and full of color. They refer not only to the general characteristics of these peoples but to their several institutions, sending the reader for more information to Siegmund von Heberstein.

Ortelius makes certain observations concerning the institution of marriage among the Russians. They tolerated bigamy, or allowed a man to have two wives, but they raised the question whether or not plural marriage was lawful. They granted divorces, and the state of women was declared to be most miserable, for

they thinke, except shee like a snaile do carry her house over her head, and be continually mewed up in her closet, or so watched, that by no meanes she may start out of doores, none possibly can be honest. It is a wilie and deceitfull people, and is rather delighted to live in servitude and slavery, than at large and in libertie. All of them do acknowledge themselves to be the Princes servants. . . . They weare long cliet gownes, without any pleits, with straite sleeves after the Hungarian fashion : bootes also, for the most part red and short, such as scarce come to their knees, and shoes or clogges clouted and hobbed with iron nailes. They tie their girdles not about their waists, but beneath their bellies as low as their hippes. . . .[78]

Apart from his maps and his measurements, Mercator's first interest was in what he took to be the fundamental geographical task of the cosmographer, namely, to state "the name, then

the Site, the Largenesse, the Bounds, the Fertilitie, the chiefe
Citties, Townes, Castles, Forts, Villages, Rivers, Mountains,"
and finally "the Religion, Customes, Manners, Conditions, and
Qualities of the Sundry Nations of the Earth." In this
"portraiture of the universall earth," he promised to offer
"lively descriptions, clad in new robes."[79] But the result ethnologically is disappointing. Confronted with so large a task, he
added little in the way of new material to the descriptions
composed by his predecessors. Like Ortelius, he made some
mention of the Russians, saying that it was the fashion for
women to love that husband best who beat them most, and to
think themselves neither loved nor regarded unless they were
"two or three times a day well swadled." But concerning
Europeans in general he reverted to a rhythmical recitative of
national vices, straight out of some medieval encyclopedia.
Nor was the first edition of Peter Heylyn's cosmography an
improvement, that little book which appeared first in 1621
bearing the promising and resounding title *Microcosmus, or a
little description of the great world. A treatise, historicall,
geographical, politicall, theologicall.* Both Ortelius and Heylyn
contain bibliographies indicating their knowledge of the
existence of modern writers. Heylyn even inserts their names
as references in page margins. But concerning the characteristics of the peoples described the conventions of borrowed
phraseology are largely retained. It was only when Pierre
d'Avity's *Les états, empires et principautez du monde* appeared
in 1614, and as the *Microcosmus* grew, edition by edition, into
a folio, that the worn currency of habitual usage, so long
passed from hand to hand, came at length to be reconsidered,
revised, and supplemented.

BIBLIOGRAPHY AND NOTES

1. Morison, *Admiral of the Ocean Sea*, I, 302; Madariaga, *Columbus*, 219. According to Azurara, Dinis Diaz brought the first Negroes to Portugal about 1447. Here, too, in Portugal the African voyages were first talked about "in a mocking manner." But opinion changed after the households of voyagers were seen to be full to overflowing with male and female slaves. (Gomes Eannes de Azurara, *The chronicle of the discovery and conquest of Guinea,* translated by C. R. Beazley and Edgar Prestage [London: Hakluyt Society, 1896–99], I, 61, 99–100, 115.)

2. Madariaga, *op. cit.,* 238, 243.

3. Carolyn Thomas Foreman, *Indians abroad, 1493–1938* (Norman: University of Oklahoma, 1943), 4.

4. Robert Ralston Cawley, *The voyagers and Elizabethan drama* (Boston: Heath, 1938), 357.

5. Foreman, *op. cit.,* 8–9.

6. Gilbert Chinard, *L'exotisme américain dans la littérature française au XVIe siècle* . . . (Paris: Hachete et Cie., 1911), 105–6.

7. Cawley, *op. cit.,* 357.

8. Stefan Lorant, *The new world; the first pictures of America, made by John White and Jacques le Moyne* . . . (New York: Duell, Sloan and Pearce, 1946), 182.

9. Geoffroy Atkinson, *Les nouveaux horizons de le renaissance français* (Paris: Droz, 1935), 10; Charles-André Julien, *Les voyages de decouverte et le premiers établissements (XVe–XVIe siècles)* (Paris: Presses Universitaires de France, 1948), 320; François de Dainville, *La géographie des humanists* (Paris: Beauchesne et ses fils, 1940), 5.

10. John Linton Myres, *The influence of anthropology on the course of political science* (Berkeley: University of California Press, 1916), 13.

11. John Evelyn, *Diary of John Evelyn, Esq., F.R.S., to which are added a selection from his familiar letters* . . . edited by William Bray . . . with a life of the author by Henry B. Wheatley (London: Bickers and Son, 1879), I, 51.

12. Thomas Platter, *Thomas Platter's travels in England 1599,* rendered into English from the German, and with introductory matter by Clare Williams (London: Jonathan Cape, 1937), 163.

13. Robert William Theodore Gunther, *Early science in Oxford, Vol. III, part I: The biological sciences; Part II: The biological collections* (Oxford: Oxford University Press, 1925), III, 252.

14. *A world of wonders. A masse of murthers. A covie of cosonages. Containing many of the moste notablest wonders, horrible murthers and detestable cosonages that have beene within this land. Not imagined falso to delight vaine heads ociose, nor practised trans mare to breed*

155

trueth cum ambiguitate, but committed even at home re vera, and may be proved cum honestate (London: William Barley, 1595). Another of the same kind was Robert Basset, *Curiosities: or the cabinet of nature. Containing phylosophical, naturall, and morall questions fully answered and resolved. Translated out of Latin, French, and Italian authors* (London: N. and I. Okes, 1637).

15. Francis Bacon, "Preface to the Parasceve" in *The works of Francis Bacon*, collected and edited by James Spedding (London: Longman and Co., 1857), I, 376. See also Emile Callot, *La renaissance des sciences de la vie au XVIe siècle* (Paris: Presses Universitaires de France, 1951), *passim*.

16. C. S. Duncan, "The scientist as a comic type," *Modern Philology*, 14 (1916–1917), 89–99; Claude Lloyd, "Shadwell and the virtuosi," *Publications of the Modern Language Association*, 44 (1929), 472–94; Marjorie Hope Nicolson and Nora M. Mohler, "The scientific background of Swift's 'Voyage to Laputa'," *Annals of science*, II (1937), 305. For other titles on the virtuosi, see M. F. Ashley Montague, *Edward Tyson*, M.D., F.R.S., 1650–1708 . . . (Philadelphia: American Philosophical Society, 1943), 320, note 38.

17. Johnathan Swift, *Gulliver's travels, the tale of a tub, and the battle of the books* (Oxford: Oxford University Press, 1919), 127.

18. David Murray, *Museums, their history and their uses* (Glasgow: MacLehose, 1904), I, 13–15.

19. Other historians place the beginning of the appreciation of classical antiquities at an earlier date in the twelfth century. See, for example, James Bruce Ross, "A study of twelfth century interest in the antiquities of Rome" in *Medieval and historiographical essays in honor of James Westfall Thompson*, edited by James Lea Cate and Eugene N. Anderson (Chicago: University of Chicago Press, 1938), 302–21.

20. William Whewell, *History of the inductive sciences from the earliest to the present time* (New York: Appleton, 1901), II, 507–508.

21. "Zoological gardens," *Encyclopedia Britannica*, 14th Edition (London, New York: Encyclopedia Britannica Co., 1929), XXIII, 962–63. Even human menageries were not wanting. One of the Medici family kept a troop of barbarians who talked as many as twenty different languages. (Jakob Christoph Burckhardt: *The civilization of the renaissance in Italy* [London: Harrap, 1929], 290–91.)

22. Henry Morley, "Conrad Gesner," in *Clement Marot and other studies* (London: Chapman and Hall, 1871), II, 127.

23. Charles E. Raven, *John Ray, naturalist: his life and works* (Cambridge: Cambridge University Press, 1942), 111, 140.

24. Joseph Addison, *The works of the Right Honorable Joseph Addison, with notes by Richard Hurd . . . A new edition, with additions unpublished, collected and edited by Harry G. Bohn* (London: Bohn, 1846), I, 256, 262, 292. See also George Bruner Parks, "Travel as education," in Richard Foster Jones, *The seventeenth century: studies in the history of English thought and literature from Bacon to Pope* (Stanford: Stanford University Press, 1951), 264–90.

25. Murray, *op. cit.*, I, 28–33; Walter Edwards Houghton, "The

English virtuoso in the seventeenth century," *Journal of the History of Ideas*, 3 (1942), 51–73, 190–219. Strange to say, the Royal Society was something less than interested in the collection of "curiosities," on the ground that since nature "still goes on in a steady Rode," the atypical or unusual was not natural. It was held also that the blindness of former ages having vanished away, men now, in the seventeenth century, were "weary of the Relicks of Antiquity." Though mariners were given instructions for making observations in new lands, these usually referred to natural resources or to natural events such as eclipses of the sun or moon. Except in the most general sense, the "New Philosophy" failed to include cultural behavior in its program of investigation. (Thomas Sprat, *The history of the Royal-Society of London, for the improving of natural knowledge* [London: T.R. for J. Martyn, 1667], 90, 152, 156.)

26. Evelyn, *op. cit.*, I, 69, 72, 25, 118, 275; III, 29.

27. John Ray, *Observations topographical, moral, and physiological; made in a journey through part of the Low-Countries, Germany, Italy, and France: With a catalogue of plants not native of England, found spontaneously growing in those parts, and their virtues* (London: Printed for John Martyn, Printer to the Royal Society, at the Bell in St. Paul's Churchyard, 1673), 218–19, 234.

28. Bacon, *Works,* III, 165.

29. Ray, *op. cit.*, 332.

30. Gunther, *op. cit.*, III, 279–97.

31. Edward Browne, "A brief account of some travels in divers parts of Europe," (1627) quoted in Alma S. Wittlin, *The museum: its history and its task in education* (London: Kegan Paul, 1949), 227.

32. Gunther, *Early science in Cambridge,* III, 424–33; Johann Beckmann, *A history of inventions, discoveries, and origins* (London: Bohn, 1846) I, 292.

33. Thorndike, *op. cit.,* VI, 269.

34. Murray, *op. cit.,* I, 29–31. Michele Mercati of San Miniato (1541–1593), the keeper of the botanical garden of Pope Pius V, was an industrious collector, and the founder of the Vatican Museum. A good observer, and a man of independent judgment, he was among the first to establish that flint arrowheads were man-made. Appealing to history, he also called attention to the use of flint knives among the Jews, and to stone tools and weapons by the American Indians. It was his opinion that the early inhabitants of Italy also used stone tools for similar purposes, adopting iron only when it was introduced by commerce. (*Ibid.,* I, 28, 82.)

35. *Ibid.,* I, 78–80, 103–105, 215.

36. Evelyn, *op. cit.,* II, 56, 93–94; see also Gunther, *op. cit.,* III, 423–31.

37. Martha Ornstein, *The rôle of scientific societies in the seventeenth century* (Chicago: University of Chicago Press, 1928), 42, note 65.

38. Walter Edwards Houghton Jr., "The history of trades: its relation to seventeenth century thought as seen in Bacon, Petty, Evelyn, and Boyle," *Journal of the History of Ideas,* II (1941), 33–60.

39. René Wellek, *The rise of English literary history* (Chapel Hill: University of North Carolina Press, 1941), 4–5, 16.

40. Archer Taylor mentions a Dutch collection of proverbs published c. 1485 and used as a school book (Archer Taylor, *Problems in German literary history of the fifteenth and sixteenth centuries* [New York: Modern Language Association of America, 1939], 84–85); Erasmus published a collection of Latin proverbs in 1500, designed to be useful to those who wished to write Latin elegantly; and John Aubrey's *Remaines of gentilisme and judaisme . . .* was a late seventeenth-century expression of the same passion for collecting folklore.

41. Wittkower, "Marvels of the East," 159–97.

42. More than ten editions of this richly illustrated book appeared, as well as translations into Spanish, Dutch, and English.

43. John William Ballantyne, *Teratogenesis: an inquiry into the causes of monstrosities. History of theories of the past* (Edinburgh: Oliver and Boyd, 1897).

44. John Bulwer, *Anthropometamorphosis: man transform'd: or, the artificiall changling, historically presented, in the mad and cruell gallantry, foolish bravery, ridiculous beauty, filthy finenesse, and loathsome loveliness of most nations, fashioning and altering their bodies from the mould intended by nature; with figures of those transfigurations. To which artificiall and affected deformations are added, all the native and nationall monstrosities that have appeared to disfigure the humane fabrick. With a vindication of the regular beauty and honesty of nature. And an appendix of the pedigree of the English gallant. Scripsit J. B. cognomento chirosophus M.D.* (London: William Hunt, Anno Dom. 1653); H. J. Norman, "John Bulwer and his *Anthropometamorphosis,*" in *Science, medicine and history: essays in the evolution of scientific thought and medical practice written in honour of Charles Singer* (Oxford: Oxford University Press, 1935), II, 82–97.

45. Bacon, *Works,* III, 330–31; Ornstein, *op. cit.,* 41–42.

46. Sir Thomas Browne, *Works,* edited by Geoffrey Keynes (London: Faber and Gwyer, 1928–31), II, 3, 38, 50. See also Robert Ralston Cawley, "Sir Thomas Browne and his reading," *Publications of the Modern Language Association, XLVIII* (1933), 426–70.

47. Evelyn, *op. cit.,* II, 270.

48. Sir Thomas Browne, *op. cit.,* II, 5.

49. Joannes Boemus, *Omnium gentium mores, leges, et ritus ex multis clarissimis rerum scriptoribus . . .* (Augustae Vindelicorum: S. Grimm & Wirsung, 1520).

50. Johann Boemus, *The fardle of façions conteining the aunciente maners, customes, and Lawes, of the peoples enhabiting the two partes of the earth, called Affrike and Asie.* (London: Jhon Kingstone and Henry Sutton, 1555), sig, A i r.

51. The word *anthropology* in its older usage embraced the science of the nature of man, including human physiology and psychology, or their mutual relationships. The word *ethnology* seems to have been adopted in the nineteenth century; other forms, such as *ethnic,* spring from a Greek root meaning heathen, and are constantly employed in this sense

in European literature to refer disparagingly to the non-Christian or Jewish nations. (See New English Dictionary and Thomas Bendysche, "The history of anthropology," in *Memoirs read before the Anthropological Society of London* 1863–64 [London: Trübner and Co., 1865].)

52. Thorndike, *op. cit.*, V, 142–3. See also Andrew Boorde, *The fyrste boke of the introduction of knowledge* (London: Wyllyam Copland, 1562?).

53. Alessandro Sardi of Ferrara (1520–1588) was an Italian savant, historian, critic, and numismatist. His *De moribus ac ritibus* was published by Zilletus in Venice in 1557. Another book, written in imitation of Polydore Vergil, was entitled *De rerum inventoribus libri octo,* and was translated into French by Gabriel Chapuis in 1584.

54. Sebastian Franck, *Chronica, zeyt-bück und geschycht-bibel von anbegyn biss inn diss gegenwertig MDXXXJ jar. Darin beide Gottes und der welt lauff, hendel, art, wort, wërck, thün, lassen, kriegen, wesen und leben ersehen un begriffen wirt,* etc. (Strassburg; Balthassar Beck 1531); translated into French as *Cosmographie, miroir et tableau de tout le globe (Tübingen,* 1534, 1542); reprinted with the works of Schmidt on the same subject in Frankfort in 1567; translated into Dutch in 1649. Franck established a press in Ulm, where Boemus made his home.

55. On Muenster see: Sebastian Muenster, *Cosmographiae universalis lib. VI. in quibus iuxta certioris fidei scriptorum traditionem describuntur, Omnium habitabilis orbis partium situs; propriaeque dotes. Regionum topographicae effigies. Terrae ingenia, quibus sit ut tam differentes & uarias specie res, & animates, & inanimatas, ferat. Animalium peregrinorum naturae & picturae. Nobiliorum ciuitatum icones & descriptiones. Regnorum initia, incrementa & translationes. Regnum & principum genealogiae. Item omnium gentium mores, leges, religio, mutationes: atque memorabilium in hunc usque annum* 1554. *gestarum rerum Historia* (Basileae: apud Henrichum Petri, M.D.LIIII. [1554]); Viktor Hantsch, "Sebastian Münster, leben, werk, wissenschaftliche bedeutung," *Abhandlungen (der philologisch-historischen Classe) der königlich Sächsischen Gesellschaft der Wissenschaften* (Leipzig), Bd. 18, No. 3; C. R. Beazley, "Sebastian Munster," *Geographical Journal,* 17 (1901), 423–25; Lucien Gallois, *Les géographes allemands de la renaissance* (Paris: E. Leroux, 1890); Margaret Trabue Hodgen, "Sebastian Muenster (1489–1552): a sixteenth century ethnographer," *Osiris,* II (1954), 504–29.

56. François de Belleforest, *L'histoire universelle du monde, contenant l'entière de description et situation des quartre parties de la terre . . .* (Paris: G. Mallot, 1570).

57. Joannus Boemus, *The manners, lawes, and customes of all nations. Collected out of the best writers: by Joannus Boemus Aubanus, a Dutchman. with many other things of the same argument, gathered out of the historie of Nicholas Damascen. The like also out of the history of America, or Brasill, written by John Lerius. The faith, religion and manners of the Aethiopians, and the deploration of the people of Lappia, compiled by Damianus à Goes. With a short discourse of the Aethiopians, taken out of Joseph Scaliger his seventh booke, De Emendatione Tem-*

porum. Written in Latin, and now newly translated into English by Ed. Aston (London: Eld and Burton, 1611), 264; see also Margaret T. Hodgen. "Johannus Boemus (fl. 1500); an early anthropologist," *American Anthropologist*, 55 (1953), 284–94.

58. Johann Boemus, *Fardle of façions*, sig. J viii v.

59. *Ibid.*, sig. K v v.

60. *Ibid.*, sig. E ii v.

61. Boemus, *Manners, lawes, and customes* (1611), 26, 181, 318, 253–63.

62. Boemus, *Fardle of façions* (1555), sig. C ii r.

63. *Ibid.*, sig. C ii v.

64. *Ibid.*, sig. E iii v–E iiii r.

65. *Ibid.*, sig. O ii r, P v v.

66. *Ibid.*, sig. L i r–L viii v.

67. *Ibid.*, sig. N iii r–N iii v. For other early references to the silent trade see "The silent barter" in Duarte Pacheco Pereira, *Esmeraldo de situ orbis*, translated and edited by George H. T. Kimble (London: Hakluyt Society, 1937), Appendix III, 176–78; André Thevet, *The new found worlde, or antarctike, wherin is contained wonderful and strange things, as well of humaine creatures, as beastes, fishes, foules, and serpents, trees, plants, mines of golde and silver* . . . (London: Henrie Bynneman for Thomas Hacket, 1568), sig. C iii r; Samuel Purchas, *Purchas his pilgrimage, or relations of the world and the religions observed in all ages and places discovered* . . . (London: William Stansby for Henrie Fetherstone, 1613), sig. Aaa 3 v, Hhh 3 r; P. J. Hamilton-Grierson, "Gifts (primitive and savage)" in Hastings, *Encyclopedia of Religion and Ethics*, VI, 197–209.

68. The best source on medieval cosmographies is Manuel Francisco de Barros Santarem, *Essai sur i'historie de la cosmographie et de la cartographie pendant le moyen-âge* (Paris: Maulde et Renou, 1849–52).

69. Bacon, *Works*, III, 340.

70. Richard Eden, *A treatyse of the newe India, with other new founde landes and Ilandes* . . . *Translated out of the Latin into Englishe* (1553), in Edward Arber, ed., *The first three English books on America* (?[1511]–1555 A.D.) (Birmingham [Edinburgh: Turnbull and Spears], 1885), 3–42; *A briefe collection and compendious extract of straunge and memorable thinges gathered out of the Cosmographie of Sebastian Munster* (London: T. Marshe, 1574). See also "A briefe description of Moscovia, after . . . Sebastian Munster, and Iacobus Gasteldus," in *The history of travayle in the west and east Indies . . . Gathered in parte, and done into Englyshe by Richarde Eden* (London: Richarde Iugge, 1577); and George North, *The description of Swedland, Gotland and Finland . . . Collected . . . out of sundry laten Aucthours, but chieflye out of Sebastian Munster* (London: John Awdely, 1561).

71. Muenster, *op. cit.*, 1163.

72. Eden, *Briefe collection*, sig. A 5 v; D 3 r.

73. Atkinson, *op. cit.*, 10; Dainville, *op. cit.*, 5; Julien, *op. cit.*, 320.

74. See Samuel C. Chew, *The crescent and the rose; Islam and England during the renaissance* (New York: Oxford Press, 1937); and

Clarence Dana Rouillard, *The Turk in French history, thought and literature* (1520–1660) (Paris: Boivin & Cie, 1940).

75. Eden, *op. cit.*, sig. F 6 v, F 7 r, F 3 r, G 1 v; Hodgen, *Muenster*, 510, 514, 525–27.

76. Beazley, *Dawn of geography*, III, 504.

77. Peter Heylyn, *Microcosmus, or a little description of the great worlde. A treatise historicall, geographicall, politicall, theologicall* (Oxford: John Lichfield and James Short, 1621), sig. B 2 r.

78. Abraham Ortelius, *Theatrum orbis terrarum* . . . (London: John Norton and John Ball, 1606), sig. 11 r, 14 v, 104 r.

79. Gerardus Mercator, *Atlas, or a geographicke description of the regions, . . . of the world . . . Translated by Henry Hexham* (Amsterdam: Henry Hondius and John Johnson, 1636), Preface, * * i, v.

CHAPTER V

Collections of Customs:
Modes of Classification and Description

"Even physics began with cabinets of curiosities, and the elves of antiquarianism have cut capers about the cradle of more than one serious study."—MARC BLOCH.

THOUGH THE questing spirit of the Renaissance was displayed in the multiplication of collections in all the capitals of Europe, most of the collectors themselves were unaware of their importance. Few, relatively speaking, attempted by classification or other scientific procedures to ferret out the meaning of their treasures. The addition of new items as quickly as possible, the expansion of their stores of "curios," was about all they asked.

It was more or less clearly recognized, however, that collections of customs were a little different. These might divert and entertain, but they also possessed an utilitarian value. Did the theologian wish to interpret the Bible with great topographical accuracy? Did the Bible reader desire more certain knowledge of the sacred land of Palestine, its place names and its peoples, ancient and modern? If so, then the cosmographer stood ready to give him all this plus a chapter on the Creation, brought somewhat up to date with sections on the divisions of the seas, the sources of rivers, a history of the Jews, and the geography of the Holy Land. Did the physician desire inform-

162

ation on weather phenomena and their relation to disease, or the properties of exotic herbs and drugs? Then such could be found in Muenster's pages. Did the moral philosopher seek to view his own people, their customs and their ceremonies, in contrast with others? Then it became the function of the cosmographer to engage in social inquiry; to consider the locations of various peoples; to collect information concerning marriage rites, food preferences, differences in customs, and the diversity of religions—which latter, usually misunderstood and misrepresented, disconcerted the learned and disturbed the devout.

Muenster's great work, and those of all the other cosmographers who followed him so rapidly, were designed to disseminate knowledge. In these pages, said Richard Eden, who converted a part of the *Cosmographia* into English, the fortunate reader was at liberty to wander throughout the whole world, and fill his head with the strange properties of divers beasts, fowls, and fishes, and the "straunge rites and Lawes of far distant nations." Nor was this all. Trade and exploration were also served. These compendia of geographical and cultural information "entreated" not only "of Trumpington a vyllage within a myle" of Cambridge town, but of the great commercial cities as well. So much was this the case that Eden considered his small venture in translation "a little glasse" for merchants and travelers. In it they were enabled to "see some cleare light . . . how to behave them selves and direct theyr viage to theyr most commoditie" and customers.[1]

But Johann Boemus, his colleagues the geographers, and that host of other students of manners and customs who came after him, confronted a problem relatively unknown to collectors of other curios—coins, butterflies, or shells. For coins, butterflies, and shells were substantial things. As such, neither the numismatist, nor the entomologist, nor the conchologist, was called upon at once to envisage the members of their several arrays of specimens in conceptual or verbal form. They dealt with material objects—objects, which, having been looked at, handled, turned this way and that, and scrutinized from every angle, could be readily consigned, without haste or much thought, to specific places in their cabinets, drawers, or pigeonholes. As long as the owners of such collections remained content with the simple joys of accumulation, as long as they remained content merely to look at their treasures, as long as they refrained from asking difficult questions of their *cabinets de curiosités,* there was no need for classification, conceptualization, or an appeal to the verbal devices of description. The steady addition of new rarities to their hoards, their neat placement in appropriate trays or compartments, was enough. If an overly inquisitive visitor raised questions, the items in the collection could again be displayed; they could be handled and rehandled, turned this way and that, or even placed elsewhere, until the difficulty seemed to be removed.

But the accumulation of manners and customs, their filing and arrangement, introduced unsuspected problems. From the very outset classification of some kind seemed to be imperative, and verbalization was unavoidable. For it began very early to be realized that man's distinguishing trait was not technology alone, nor the capacity to fabricate tangible artifacts, which eluding the tooth of time, found themselves at length on the shelves of some collector's cupboard. On the contrary, the unique creation of the human spirit was the array of cultures, those complex wholes which, including technology, included also much else—metaphysics, science, art; the social institutions of religion, the family, and state, and all their multitudinous rites, ceremonies, beliefs, and folklore. As Thomas Hobbes once said : "By manners, I mean not here, decency of behaviour; as how one should salute another, or how a man should wash his mouth, or pick his teeth before company, and such points of small morals; but those qualities of mankind, that concern their living together in peace and unity."[2]

The initial problem of the collector of manners and customs thus came to be found in the realm of concepts or ideas. To assemble a collection at all, he had first to distinguish between different cultural "wholes," often called "nations," and then to analyze these into their institutional or other component parts. It was necessary for him to grasp conceptually salient cultural themes, categories, and structures—themes which prevailed not only within the behavioral system of one people, but among all peoples; and then having done this for himself, to convey his findings descriptively to others. Whether the people or peoples under consideration lived in Europe, Asia, Africa, or the Americas, the strange had to be converted into the familiar by the magic of verbalization. The common styles of their daily lives had to be discerned and made explicit (no small task), the common forms of their activities and ideas communicated. Unless these cultural themes, categories, orders, or structures were perceived, unless they and their logically subordinate elements were made flesh in familiar words, ideas or images, manners and customs remained "curios" indeed.

To make the task still more difficult the sheer number of separable and sortable elements in any one culture, not to speak of the total in all, opposed an almost insurmountable obstacle to exhaustive description. A principle of choice was necessary, based upon some criterion of importance or universality. If themes, categories, and structures remained locked in an unanalyzed mass of cultural particulars, if the collector of "rarities" in human behavior was unable to discern likenesses or uniformities in his materials, if he failed to verbalize their associations with or similarities to one another, if he was unable to convey to others his conceptual organization of alien ways of living, then, despite all his labor in getting them together, he had no collection.

To put the matter in another way, every would-be collector of the manners of mankind, whether he realized it or not, was confronted at the outset with a similar set of questions: How were the ways of life of other peoples to be described? What items in their behavior were to be regarded as worthy of description and incorporation in a collection? What, in short, *was* a "manner" or a "custom"? And what words or images were to be called up by the members of a describing culture to communicate their views of the cultures under description?

Ideally speaking, scientific insight always attempts the representation of the things in nature, or in human behavior, as they are. But how are they? This problem confronted the natural scientist, Nehemiah Grew in 1681, as he set about the task of cataloguing and discussing the natural and artificial rarities belonging to the Royal Society of London. "As to the following catalogue," he remarked in his preface, "I have something to say, of the Order, Names, Descriptions, Figures, and Uses of Particulars. . . . As to the first, I like not the reason which Aldrovanus gives for his beginning the History of Quadrupeds with the Horse. . . . Much less would I choose Gesner, to go by the Alphabet. The very Scale of Creation is a matter of high speculation." Furthermore, how is one to judge what is rare and strange? It depends in a measure on locality. "What is common in one country, is rare in another." All of which yields "a great abundance of matter for any man's Reason to work upon." Especially was this the case in the Royal Society's miscellaneous collection of human rarities, including, as it did, an Egyptian mummy, a Greenland canoe, a gun, an Indian poisoned dagger, a tomahawk, a Brazilian fighting club, an Indian target, bows, arrows and quiver, a pot of poison, a Siam drum, and similar articles, many of which were from India.

In this dilemma, Grew realized that "things," whether natural or cultural, are not necessarily seen as they are. They appear as our minds make them. Montaigne once said, "Human eyes cannot perceive things but in the shape they know them by." Thus in meeting the problems of classification, verbalization, or description, the collectors of manners and customs in the sixteenth and seventeenth centuries had two options: they could call up familiar adjectives and imagery, as these had been applied time out of mind by their predecessors; or they could elect to find new ones. Unfortunately, they allowed the burden of decision and discrimination to be taken off their shoulders by tradition. To them, the cultural themes, styles, and categories, the structural elements of the several cultures of the world, the choice of the manners, customs, and institutions to be pricked out of their settings in surrounding phenomena by the perceptive use of language, were already ordained.

When Johan Boemus began to gather together his "fardle of façions," when Sebastian Muenster had fixed upon the general design of his *Cosmographia,* and when later collectors and cosmographers undertook the same task, they all found, not without relief, that the peoples to be described and the items of human behavior that each book was to contain had already been settled. Or so it was taken for granted. For to scholars of the time, the range of human customs were very nearly as obvious in their kinds and range as the fossils of Calceolarius or the floral specimens in John Ray's *hortus siccus.* As in thought generally, so in early ethnology, innovation had seldom occurred. The selection and description of the manners and customs of man had become formalized. When the great Varenius composed his *Geographia generalis* in 1650, the formula had already hardened. Those things, he said, which deserve to be considered in every country "seem to be of a triple kind, to wit, celestial, terrestrial, and human." To cover the subject of culture, or the humane properties of every country of the world, he urged the consideration of ten features: "(1) the stature of the Natives, as to their shape, colour, length of life, Original, Meat, and Drink, &c. (2) Their Trafficks and Arts in which the Inhabitants are employed. (3) Their Vertues, Vices, Learning, Wit, &c. (4) Their Customs in Marriage, Christenings, and Burials, &c. (5) Their Speech and Language. (6) Their State-Government. (7) Their Religion and Church-Government. (8) Their Cities and most renowned Places. (9) Their memorable Histories. And (10) their famous Men, Artificers, and Inventions of the Natives of all Countries."[3] Said Heylyn diffidently but significantly, when he felt compelled to make a personal judgment concerning the Swedes, [it is] "mine opinion (if it be lawful for me to insert mine owne)." Renaissance scholars who attempted to deal with the kaleidoscopic elements of human behavior found it easier to repeat than to reexamine and reformulate; to echo old judgments rather than to make new ones. Then, too, those who were faithful to tradition were cushioned from criticism.

The force of the operation of these processes of tradition may be easily observed in the taxonomic activities of collectors of manners or in the classification of social institutions. When, in the last quarter of the sixteenth century, a different and more specialized type of ethnological collection began to make its appearance, it was composed not of a miscellaneous assortment of strange practices, and not of "all" the customs of "all" men, but of certain groups or categories, such as the rites, ceremonies, and beliefs associated with religion; the rites and regulations associated with marriage and caring for a family; the ceremonies and beliefs accompanying the disposition of the dead; the customs of political organization; the customs of dress, shelter, and diet.

Naturally, considering the temper of the times, it should occasion no surprise to find that the first of these great con-

The false gods of the Muscovites before their Christianization, from Theophilus Warmundus, La religion ancienne et moderne des Muscovites *(1698).*

stellations of ceremonial and belief to receive attention, in both European and non-European lands, was religion. Shaken by the creedal differences which had emerged so stormily in pre-Reformation Christendom, shocked by face-to-face contact with the followers of Mohamet and the idol-worshipers of Mongolia, Africa, and the Americas, disconcerted by the newly apprehended elaboration of the classical pantheon of gods and goddesses, European scholars and theologians were forced reluctantly to suspect that God must have revealed Himself, not once only in Judea, but in varying forms in diverse lands. Something of this kind may be noted as early as the thirteenth century in the pages of Roger Bacon's *Opus Majus*. Here, to the best of his ability, this scholar not only observed that travelers and missionaries had encountered unbelievers and schismatics but attempted himself to indicate their kinds. The first, he said, was composed of the pagans who had no priests, but worshiped whatever they pleased and sacrificed at will. Then came the idolaters, who possessed "priests and synagogues and huge bells like those of the Christians." The Tartars were third. They worshiped one god as omnipotent, venerated fire, and caused the effects of the dead to be passed through flame. In the fourth group were the Jews. And last of all came the followers of the anti-Christ, who subverted all that Christendom held sacred.[4]

In the presence of this plurality, many early collectors of religious materials concerned themselves with the gods of the ancients. Such was Boccaccio's *Genealogia deorum,* written in Latin in 1472 and destined to be republished a dozen times before 1552.[5] Boccaccio's followers and imitators were very numerous, including Buccardo, Stamler, Pictorius, Giraldi, Comes, Cartari, Batman, and others. Often little more than manuals of classical mythology for those who had been newly introduced to Greek and Roman literature or were interested in its influence on contemporary belles-lettres, these handbooks were later expanded to include descriptions of a few Oriental cults or even Celtic, Germanic, or savage deities.[6] The second edition of Cartari's *I imagini de gli dei nelle antichi,* published in 1626, for example, contained information concerning not only the old high gods of the Mediterranean but also the "barbarous and butcherly" religions of the South American Indians, the Egyptians, the East Indians, Filipinos, and other peoples of the Far East.

In short, an interest in comparative religions, or the description and comparison of religions, so often ascribed to the influence of deism, began not in the seventeenth century with the works of Lord Herbert of Cherbury, but much earlier. Deism was one of its results. In Bodin's *Colloquium hepta-plomeres,* written about 1593 though not printed in its entirety until 1857, a debate was conducted by a Catholic, a Lutheran, a Calvinist, a Mohametan, and two or three others representing some kind of theism.[7] In 1613, six-score years after the first Columbian voyage, the Reverend Samuel Purchas published *Purchas his pilgrimage.* This, in his own words, was a "peram-bulation" over the whole world to trace "the footsteps" of religion: an enterprise never yet "by any, in any language attempted." Incidentally, Purchas fancied himself another Aristotle. Just as Alexander had furnished the old Greek phil-osopher "with Husbandmen and Observers of Creatures, to acquaint him with their diversified kinds and natures," so this intrepid country clergyman proposed to be of service to those whom he called "Universall Speculators" on the faiths of mankind. The book, he informed all who had the hardihood to read its title, declared "the ancient religions before the flood, the heathenish, the Saracenicall . . . with their several opinions, idols, oracles, temples, priests, fasts, feasts, sacrifices, and rites . . . their beginnings, proceedings, alterations, sects, orders, and successions. With brief descriptions of the countries, nations, states, discoveries, private and publike customes, and the most remarkable rareties of nature." Here and there Purchas may have inadvertently left out a deity or a detail; but he allowed himself no escape clause, in his formal preamble, for the omission of any form of worship, any idolatry, any fetishism, anywhere or at any time.[8] Nor was Alexander Ross (1590–1654), the author of *Pansebia* (1653), another monumental collection of religious phenomena, any less dauntless.[9] Such sixteenth- and seventeenth-century descriptions of the religions of the whole world were followed in the eighteenth century by universal histories of religion; universal histories, by diction-aries of religion; and dictionaries of religion, by yet more dictionaries, histories, and world-wide collections. Before long the literature which had been provoked by the effort of collectors to subdue this one category of cultural subject matter, man's way with his gods, became almost unmanageable.[10]

Marriage and the disposition of the dead, those two great "rites de passage" solemnized in every culture, were also singled out by the collector for comparative treatment at this early time, either in general discussions of human culture, in association with descriptions of religions, or in separate collections. In the second half of the sixteenth century Mexia and La Primaudaye, editors of two extremely popular encyclopedias, mentioned the marriage and burial customs of peoples such as the ancient Britons and French, the Babylonians, Assyrians, Greeks, Romans, and Arabians, occasionally citing Strabo or some other classical writer. These mentions were unquestionably responses to general interest in the two subjects, and their content may well have rested on still earlier collections, such as that compiled by Polydore Vergil (1470?–?1555), published in 1499. At all events, in the *Works* of this famous antiquary, printed in English in 1663, the reader was instructed first concerning the "originall of the heathen gods," then on the origin of the diversity of tongues, and then on the "beginnings of marriage" and sundry marriage rites among the Numidians, the Egyptians, Indians, Hebrews, Persians, Parthians, Scythians, Athenians, Arabians, Assyrians, Babylonians, and Saracens. A few years later, in the seventies of the sixteenth century, John Barston, an English student of politics, and Jean Bodin, the great French jurist and author of *Les six livres de la république,* made the family and marriage central among the institutions of the body politic. Barston's comments appeared in a little book on political morality entitled *The safeguards of societie* (1576). Here, he dwelt at some length on the distribution among nations of polygyny and polyandry. The nations chosen for discussion were largely ancient, though Muenster is cited occasionally. Bodin opened the first chapter of the *République* with the statement that "a common weale, is a lawfull government of many families," and a family is "the right government of many subjects . . . under one and the same head," a true seminary and beginning of every political unit."

One hundred years later, or in the seventeenth century, collections of matrimonial ceremonies of a more or less organized character began to appear under separate covers. In these, the customs of many nations were included as "curios." Apparently one of the earliest, a little book of seventy-two pages, was compiled in France by Louis de Gaya in 1681 and translated two decades later into English." Here, in *Les céré-monies nuptiales de toutes les nations du monde,* marriage rites were classified by religion and nation. In a short paragraph or two for each, De Gaya spoke first of the Jews; then of Roman Catholic peoples such as the Italians, French, German, Poles, Slavonians, and Flemings; then of Protestant Lutherans and Evangelical Protestants; and finally of the ancients and the idolaters, a category which included not only the Greeks, Persians, and Egyptians but the Negroes of Guinea, the East Indians, and the Red Indians of North and South America.

In the eighteenth century, as titles increased, the quality of performance cheapened. One of these was Thomas Salmon's *A critical essay concerning marriage, shewing, I. The preference of marriage to a single life. II. The arguments for and against a plurality of wives and concubines. III. The authority of parents and governors, in regulating or restraining marriage. IV. The power of husbands, and the privileges of wives. V. The nature of divorce. VI. The reasons for prohibiting marriage within certain degrees. VII. The manner of contracting espousals, and what engagements and promises of marriage are binding. VIII. The penalties incurred by forcible and clandestine marriages, and the consequences attending marriages solemnized by Dissenters. To which is added, An historical account of the marriage rites and ceremonies of the Greeks and Romans, and our Saxon ancestors, and most nations of the world at this day* (1724). The title tells all. Salmon's description of marriage rites referred very briefly to those of the Greeks and Romans, to the Muscovites, Poles, and Swedes, together with a long list of other peoples in Turkey, Persia, East India, Ceylon, Ethiopia, Brazil, Paraguay, and so on. By Salmon the largeness of the world, at least, was appreciated. Another, but anonymous, author in the seventies of the same century presented *An accurate description of the marriage ceremonies used by many nations* (1782), including the Jews, the Church of Rome, the natives of Hudson Bay, the Mexicans, Persians, Japanese, Greeks, Mohametans, Hottentots, and English.[13] In the meantime, a coterie of scholars was solemnly weighing the pros and cons of introducing polygamy into the European scene as a means of increasing the population.[14]

Since death is the one event in human experience which creates more disquiet than any other, and since Herodotus had set the pattern by emphasizing that category of manners with his detailed description of the obsequies of the Scythians, the funeral rites of mankind inevitably became of interest to the makers of collections. One of the first of these appeared as early as 1539 when the Italian Lilio Gregorio Giraldi published his *De sepulchris et vario sepeliendi ritu, libellus.* Another printed in 1574, written by Tommaso Porcacchi, was entitled *Funerali antichi di diversi populi e nationi, con la forma, pompa e maniera de sepolture, di essequie, di consecrazione antichi.* This was followed seven years later in 1581 by Claude Guichard's *Funérailles, et diverses manières d'ensevelir des Romaines, Grecs, et autres nations, tant anciennes que modernes,* and in 1639 by Francesco Perucci's *Pompe funebri di tutte le nationi del mondo; racolte dalle storie sagre et profane.*[15] Nearly all of these collections were concerned

Funeral rites of the Scyths, from Francesco Perucci, Pompe funebri di tutte le nationi (1639).

primarily with the funeral customs of the ancients, those published later being copied freely from their predecessors. Guichard alone was an exception to this rule. Relying not only on Herodotus, Diodorus, and Strabo but on such later cosmographers or travelers as Boemus, Georgiewitz, Thevet, Belleforest, Pigafetta, Muenster, Gomara, and Le Roy, he dealt also with the Turks, the tribes of Africa, and the Americans. As for more recent materials on the rites of death, no traveler in the Old World or the New, no missionary or trader, ever failed to observe and report on this phase of the lives of the peoples visited. The anthropological literature on the disposal of the dead from the seventeenth to the twentieth century is very large.

Another large literature of ethnological import relates to costume. No less interesting to the Renaissance mind than the religious beliefs of men, their matrimonial ceremonies and death rites, were the clothes they wore and the diversity thereof. "Good God," said Louis Le Roy in 1576, "how much paine hath bin procured unto men by their insatiable gluttonie. . . . But their curiositie in apparell hath not bin lesse . . . with change from Countrie to Countrie." The attire of the peoples they encountered, or their lack of it, was unfailingly mentioned by voyagers, missionaries, traders, and collectors. Sometimes it was the only observation reported. Consequently for about half a century, from 1560 to 1600, some dozen or more costume books were printed, and this interest swelled into a stream of titles which even now is growing.

The earliest collection in book form appears to have been that of François Deserpz. In his *Recueil de la diversité des habits qui sont de présent en usage tant és pays d'Europe, Asie, Affrique et Illes sauvages, le tout fait après le natural* (1567), the costumes range from those of rural France to those typical of other European and Asiatic countries. The book went through several editions. The next was compiled by

Abraham de Bruyn, a Flemish painter and engraver, and was entitled *Omnium pene Europae, Asiae, Aphricae atque Americae gentium habitus. Habits de diverses nations* . . . (1581). Filling it with portraits illustrating his hobby, De Bruyn told his readers that "Plusieurs savants personnages se sont employez à curieusement recerchez & descrire la situation des quatre principales parties du monde, avec l'origine, moeurs & conditions des peuples qui y sont : de sorte qu'ils ont donné contentment singulier aux bons esprits & amateurs de science en cests part. Restroit de représenter au vray la forme & façons diverses le leurs vestements : ce que i'ay taché de faire le plus fidèlment qu'il mea esté possible, ayant recouvré par le moyen de quelques miens amis certaines figures rares & non encores cognues par l'art de graveure ou d'Imprimerie. . . ." Though most of the space in the book was devoted to engravings of European costume, there is also a short section on the attire of the Turks, Americans, and Africans. Other writers on the same subject at about the same time were Jean Jacques Boissard and Pietro Bertelli.[16]

The influence of this taxonomic tradition among those who sought to deal descriptively with collections of cultural phenomena extended to the Utopias, especially that envisioned by Sir Thomas More. Indeed, his use of the same categories in 1516 testifies to their Renaissance, or more probably pre-Renaissance, currency. Whatever may have been More's purpose in writing the *Utopia*—social reform, satire, or entertainment—his comments on the culture of the Utopians were expressed in familiar categories. More's informant, the traveler Raphael Hythlodaye, was importuned by a circle of enraptured auditors to tell them something of the people of the strange island. What was he to say? How was he to communicate with them, or perchance keep them interested? He responded, as all cosmographers and travelers before him were wont to do, by describing the Utopians' religion, their institution of marriage and the family (with some emphasis on the propriety of monogamy), their betrothal customs, the rites celebrated over their dead, their dwellings, and their apparel, as well as sundry other customs. Hytholodaye's preparation for this undertaking is unmistakable. "When I determined to entre into my iiii. voyage," he says, "I caste into the shippe in the steade of marchandise a prety fardel of bookes." These included Thucydides and Herodotus; and More himself is known to have read Vespucci, Waldenseemüller, Peter Martyr, the *Germania* of Tacitus, Caesar, and Pliny, all of which contributed to the hardening in his mind of the familiar and traditional scheme of cultural classification."

Whenever, in conjunction with the acceptance of old institutional formulae, the description of culture in general was regarded as desirable, tradition again was operative. But this time there were three options. The reporter could choose that prototype which had been transmitted by medieval scholarship; he could rely upon the legacy of Herodotus; or, adopting a strongly Europocentric position, he could make use of comparison for the purpose of establishing similarities or correspondence, dissimilitudes or negations.

Wherever scholastic ideals prevailed, there brevity was the hallmark; and the medieval encyclopedia with its capsule epitomes, its stereotypes and typologies, became the model. In response to a deep human need for brief formulae which would express the characteristics of things and peoples in dichotomies of black and white, virtue and vice, these general cultural descriptions were short, terse, and apothegmatic. As stereotypes, they called attention first to physical differences —to the statures of men, to their complexions, to their eyes, hair-color and its quality; and second, to their "dispositions"— their peaceableness or bellicosity, their goodness or badness. Emanating presumably from an even earlier and vaguer astrological or environmental ethnological theory, these opposed qualities, decreed by celestial or terrestrial forces,[18] were construed as clues to the habitual behavior of peoples, and were transposed, when occasion arose, either into warm nationalistic approval or bitter racial invective.

There was much of this kind of thing in Muenster, just as there had been in Bartholomew's *De proprietatibus rerum* three hundred years before. In typical descriptive passages, the Scots were said to possess fine figures and to be prompt to seek vengeance; the Suevi were large in stature and bellicose in disposition. Moreover, the author of the *Cosmographia* took occasion to repeat that stereotype of all stereotypes, that distilled essence of all polar typologies, the medieval catalogue of the "divers vices and deformities of Nations," paralleled with its opposite, a list of their "divers vertues and honest properties." In the nationalistic inventory devoted to cultural or ethnical infamy, envy was allotted to the Jews, "Disloyaltye and unfaithfulnes to the Persians. Craftines to the Egiptians. Deceitfulnes to the Grecians. Cruelty to the Saracens. Levitie and Lightness to ye Caldeans. Unmerciful severitye to the Hungarians," and so on to "The unclenness & filthines of the Suevians. The foolishnes of the Saxons. The hardines of the Picts. The Luxurye of the Scots. The dronkennes and violency of the Spaniards. The anger of the Britaines. The rapacity and greediness of the Normans."

But this was not all. When the cosmographer turned to the other side of the ledger, or to the virtues of nations, there prudence was attributed "to the Hebricians. Stedfastnes to the Persians. Stabilitie & wittines to the Egiptians. Wisdome to ye Grecians. Gravity to ye Romans. Sagacitie to the Caldeans. Witte to the Affricans. Strength and fortitude to the Frenchmen. Faithfulnesse to the Scots. Subtile sophistrie to the Spaniards. Hospitalitie to the Britons. Mutuall participation to the Normans." Just as flowers and birds in the Middle Ages were studied not for their own sakes but as symbols of moral and metaphysical principles, so the differing breeds of men assumed an emblematic quality.[19]

Repetitious echoes of this medieval catalogue are to be found everywhere in sixteenth- and seventeenth-century literature—in Agrippa, in Boemus, in Mercator, in Heylyn. It was the easy and accepted formula for dealing with the alien and the stranger. Said Agrippa in about 1527 :

Some Nations are so planted by Heaven, that they appear eminent for the unity and singularity of their Customs. The Scythians were always infamous for Savageness and Cruelty. The Italians were always eminent for their Magnanimity. The Gaules were reproached for Stupidity. The Sicilians were always Subtile. The Asiaticks Luxurious, the Spaniards Jealous, and great Boasters. Besides, several Nations have some particular Marks of distinction, which are the more immediate marks of Heaven; so that a man may easily discern of what Nation such or such stranger may be, by his Voice, Speech, Tone, Designe, Conversation, Diet, Love or Hatred, Anger and Malice, and the like. For who that sees a man marching in more state than a Dung-hill-Cock, in gate like a Fencer, a confident Look, a deep Tone, grave Speech, severe in his Carriage, and tatter'd in Habit, that will not straight judge him to be a German? Do we not know the French by their moderate Gate, effeminate Carriage, smiling Countenance, pleasing Voice, courteous Speech, modest Behaviour, and careless Habit? The Italians we behold more slow in Gate, their Carriage grave, their Countenances varying, of few words, captious in Discourse, in their Behaviour magnificent, and decent in their Habit. In Singing also the Italians bleat, the Spaniards Whine, the Germans Howl, and the French Quaver.[20]

Said Boemus in the 1611 edition of the *Omnium gentium mores*:

Thereof ariseth this Proverbe, that Suevia onely is able to yeeld whores inough for all Germany, as well as Franconia affordeth good store of theeves and beggars, Boemia heretics, Barvaria pilferers and slaves, Helvetia Butchers and Bawdes, Drunkards in Saxonie, perjurers in Frisia and Westphalia, and gluttons about the Rheine.[21]

Said Mercator in 1585 :

The *Francons* are simple, blockish, & furious; the *Barvarians* sumptuous, gluttons, and brazen-faced; the *Sweeds* light, bablers and boasters; the *Thuringeans* distrustfull, slovens, and quarrelsome; the *Saxons* dissemblers, double-hearted, and opinionative; the *Belgians* good horsemen, tender, docible, and delicate; the *Italians* proud, revengeful, and ingenious; the *Spaniard* disdainfull, cautious and greedie; the *Gaules* proper, intemperate, rashheaded; the *Cimbrians* high-minded, seditious, and terrible; the *Saramates* gluttons, proud, and theeves; the *Bohemians* cruell, lovers of novelties, filtchers; the *Illyricks* variable, malicious, and ryotous; the *Pannonians* rude, superstitious; the *Grecians* miserable.[22]

Said Heylyn in 1621 :

If we believe the proverbiall speech . . . the Spaniards are said to seeme wise and are fooles; the French to seeme fooles and are wise; the Italians to seeme & be wise; the Portugalls are affirmed neither to be wise, nor so much as to seeme so; and not much different from this the Spaniards have a proverbe, which telleth us that the Portugalls are Pocus y locus, few and foolish.[23]

As substitutes for thought, or for the expression of hatred or of fellow-feeling, many of these stereotypes are in active service today.

At other times or by other men, adherence to tradition was expressed by continued use in cultural description of themes and categories first used by Herodotus in the fifth century B.C., or perhaps by his forgotten predecessors. These formulae, the familiar categories of marital customs, funeral and religious rites, dress, dwellings, diet, and the like, with their equally compulsory sub-themes and sub-categories, were legion. Their use often involved curiously anachronistic reasoning. For since

Old Testament chronology, as interpreted by medieval and Renaissance thought, usually allowed no more than six thousand years both for the Creation and for the enactment of subsequent historical periods, an awareness of greater distance in time was seldom present. Hence, the empires of antiquity, to which Renaissance scholarship gave unstinted admiration, were thought of as almost contemporaneous, not as separated from Renaissance Europe by fifteen hundred or two thousand years. When, therefore, in the sixteenth and seventeenth centuries, existing Mediterranean cultures were chosen for description, their characteristics were not ascertained by independent contemporary investigation or re-appraisal. On the contrary, they were described as though these earlier empires were still in existence. Descriptions of Roman culture, of Greek culture, of the cultures of Babylonia, Persia, or Chaldea, composed over a millennium before, were resurrected to describe the peoples currently inhabiting those same regions. For Africa a like procedure was followed. In dealing with the tribes on the southern shores of the Mediterranean or around the Black Sea, many Renaissance collectors merely took down their copies of Herodotus, or reverted to dimly remembered passages in other ancient authors. Despite intervening centuries of trade with Mediterranean ports, despite recent revelations by Portuguese and other explorers of the characteristics of living Africans, these peoples were called by their ancient names; and they were reported as conducting themselves in A.D. 1520 or 1620, or 1720, exactly as they had been portrayed in the fifth century B.C. Boemus, Muenster, Heylyn, and many other seventeenth-century cosmographers are notably confusing on this score. Dealing with Media or Persia in the present tense, they describe the cultures of these realms as if their ancient high civilizations were still in being; and the authorities cited range all the way from Herodotus and Pliny to Sir Walter Ralegh.

The tenacity with which old formulae of description held

their own among the educated classes is a phenomenon of
more than passing interest in the history of social and ethnological thought. For the collectors and cosmographers were
not ignorant men. They were often among the most learned of
their times. And the old formulae were not the only ones at
hand. Alternative modes of description were being made available by overseas voyagers and by the constant travel of the
virtuosi and their associates from capital to capital in Europe.
A list of titles on geography and travel from 1480 to 1600, in
English alone, numbers well over one hundred.[24] After the first
lull in geographical adventure, the printing presses from
Cracow to Seville were unresting in the publication in many
languages of the epochal letters of Christopher Columbus and
Amerigo Vespucci, the history of the discoveries by Peter
Martyr, and the travel accounts of many seafarers. Long before
Muenster, Ortelius, or Mercator had been translated into the
vernacular of the several nations, many a man, unused to the
sound of bells other than his own, could easily read himself into
the farthest corners of the globe in the company of the
greatest explorers.

It is sometimes said that the persistence of traditional
descriptive cultural formulae was due to the untutored
traveler who knew no other. In part this was true. Any sailor
home from the sea, any sea captain, trader, or adventurer,
could find an audience in some tavern or by some fireside.
Nor need he cling too closely to the unvarnished truth. The
more he demanded from the imaginations of his hearers, the
better his reputation as a storyteller. Ben Jonson accused the
voyagers of lying like beggars. Robert Burton, lashing out at
their mendacities, proposed to put their preposterous tales to
the test, to determine "whether Marcus Polus the Venetian's
narration be true or false"; whether "as Riccius the Jesuit has
written, China and Cataia be all one, the great Cham of
Tartary and the King of China be the same"; whether in

Muscovy men "lie fast asleep as dead all winter. . . . I would censure," he said, "the lies of all the Plinies, Solinuses, and Mandevilles. I would see those inner parts of America, whether there be any such great city of Manoa or Eldorado in that golden empire . . . any such Amazons . . . or gigantic Patagones in Chica."[25] Thus both Jonson and Burton pointed out that the travelers clung too stubbornly to tradition: either to that transmitted to them from antiquity, or to that later version employed in the Middle Ages. In almost every report of newly found marvels there were reminders of these habitual and overworked concepts.

But the sea captains and sailors who undertook overseas voyages, the urbane young men who with their tutors moved sedately along the highways of Europe, were not willful frauds, attempting in folly to gull their homebound fellows. They were members of the European community; they drew upon a stock of ideas common to all. If at times they fancied that they had encountered the outlandish or incredible, it was not that they were unredeemed charlatans. It was rather that their minds, like the minds of their forefathers, had been nourished on a commonly cherished blend of fact, legend, and fable. When abroad, their eyes saw no more than their minds, shaped at home, were prepared to accept. If the pages of the travelers and cosmographers of the period are crammed full of "a fascinating amalgam of the new and the old," the true and the false; if poets and other literary men borrowed from them without qualm or misgiving; it was to embellish with well-known images that which might otherwise have been less colorful, less emotionally satisfying, or even less well understood. The better educated were often well aware that many traditional anecdotes were no longer to be regarded as fact. But the travelers, and the cosmographers dependent upon the travelers, gave them authority for continuing to think they might be fact. "The Ancients thus were substantiated by the

Moderns, who repeated their stories and their theories without bothering to question their truth."[26]

It should also be remembered, in defense of the travelers, that when finally a move was made to correct old formulae, it came either from them, or from those who advocated a plain and naked literary style rather than rhetorical flourishes, or from men such as Montaigne, who strove mightily really to understand the condition of savagery as it was then found in the New World.

These innovators made their contributions as early as the sixteenth century, when the travel guide first became popular as a literary genre. Restricted at an earlier period to the recitation of the comforts and discomforts to be encountered by pilgrims to the Holy Land, some authors began now to comment freely upon the peoples met. Others, conscious of an obligation to disseminate information concerning various forms of government and various manners and customs, not only published their own observations, but undertook to instruct subsequent travelers on what they should observe when they themselves went abroad. Their literature falls naturally into two groups: one contains information for the sojourner on the Continent, the other was designed for venturers overseas.

Those who make journeys, said Jerome Turler, around 1575, in a little book "necessarie unto all such as are minded to traveyll," should learn to mark down "suche things in strange Countries, as they shall have neede to use in the common trade of lyfe."[27] They should be steady men, said Bourne, in 1578, not attracted by "banketting, and play, and gaine, & dauncing and dalying with women."[28] Nothing is more conducive to true wisdom and sound discretion, said Lipsius, in 1592, in *A direction for travellers*, "than the sight, consideration and knowledge, of sundry rites, manners, pollycies and

11 The induſtrie, ſtudies, manners, honeſtie, humanitie, hoſpitalitie, loue, and other morall vertues
of the Inhabitantes, and wherein they chiefely ex-
cell.

12 The ſpeciall manuarie artificers, and handicraftes of
the place of greateſt perfection.

13 The anuuall fayres and markets, where they are kept,
and howe often, and what commodities do there
principally abound, with the priſes of each good
commoditie.

14 The money and coyne, with the value, bignes, ſtampe,
and mettall, eyther gold, ſiluer, or copper.

15 The waightes and meaſures, both in drie wares, and
liquid matters, with their names: whether yardes,
elles, quartes, gallons, buſhels, quarters, hundreds,
&c. and whether they be leſſe or greater than ours,
or of the ſame quantitie.

16 What offences are there moſt common, and moſt pu-
niſhed, or tolerated.

17 The kindes and varieties of puniſhmentes for malefa-
ctors.

18 The prerogatiues and priuileges of ſpeciall cities,
townes, portes, and hauens.

19 The ſubſidies, toules, impoſtes, cuſtomes, due, and
payd to the prince.

20 The diſpoſition and ſpirit of the people: whether war-
like and valiant, or faint hearted and effeminate :
their ſtore or want of militarie furniture, and pro-
uiſions : whether they, or their Anceſtors haue
beene famous for victories, or infamous for
cowardlineſſe and ouerthrowes, yea or no.

21 How the king or prince is allyed with his neighbour
Princes, and who are his confederates, and who
not.

22 The manners, rites, and ceremonies of *Eſpowſals*,
marriages, feaſtes and bankets.

23 The varietie and manner of their exerciſes for paſtime
and recreation.

24 The

---

*An example of the instructions given to merchants and travelers
for the collection of cultural materials. From Albrecht Meier's*
Certaine briefe and speciall instructions *(1589).*

governments," especially if they be compared together "perfectlie." [29]

As early as 1587, one Albrecht Meier published an important little book which within two years was translated into English, probably at the request of Richard Hakluyt. Its purpose, according to a flowery introductory statement, was to enroll every traveler abroad in the Catalogue of Homer as "Seers of many Regions, and of the manners of many Nations." With Germanic thoroughness, the author sought to organize an informal corps of reliable informants. Entitled *Certain briefe, and speciall instructions for gentlemen, merchants, students, souldiers, marriners etc.*, the book contained a syllabus of twenty-one pages, divided into twelve sections, each composed of serially numbered statements of what should be regularly observed and recorded. Though there was no section specifically entitled "manners and customs," these matters were fully covered. Meier instructed travelers to take note of how cities were governed; "the fare and dyet of the region"; "the habites and apparell of men, women, wives, Maidens, citizens, contrimen, Courtyers, noblemen, officers, Magistrates, Gentlemen, Marchants, Ministers, &c"; "the manners, rites, and ceremonies of Espousals, marriages, feastes and bankets"; religious practices, coinage, crimes, punishments; and innumerable other features. [30]

Somewhat later, similar injunctions were embodied in Bacon's essay *Of travel,* published in 1625. "It is a strange thing," said he, "that in sea voyages, where there is nothing to be seen but sky and sea, men should make diaries; but in land-travel, wherein so much is to be observed, for the most part they omit it. . . . Let diaries therefore be brought into use." [31] But the Lord Chancellor lacked a grasp of the wide range of customs and institutions possessed by Meier. The things to be observed, in his opinion, were political rather than broadly cultural. Among the English, Richard Hakluyt included in his *Divers voyages touching the discoverie of America* (1582), a few notes of advice to merchants sent out by the Muscovy Company, some of which called upon them for cultural information; and later John Locke was the compiler of an annotated bibliography, in which he recommended, as the proper reading for a gentleman, titles that might now be classed as ethnographical.

As for the scientists, their contribution to an improved study of the customs of peoples in the seventeenth century was, in view of their high reputation, rather small. In the first gathering of the members of the Royal Society in Oxford, there were few members who could be called students of man, politics, or culture; nor were there any collectors of manners, in the strictest sense of that word.[32] Later, in the first numbers of the *Philosophical transactions,* which appeared in 1665–67, twelve programs of research for travelers and navigators were published, entitled "General heads for the natural history of a country." Here, in addition to reports on the "ignobler" products of the new lands, such as flora, fauna, geological formations, and other natural resources, careful accounts of inhabitants were requested,

. . . both Native and Strangers. . . . And in particular, their Stature, Shape, Colour, Features, Strength, Agility, Beauty (or the want of it), Complexions, Hair, Dyet, Inclinations, and Customs that seem not due to Education. As to their Women (besides other things) may be observed their Fruitfulness, or Barrenness; their hard or easy Labour, etc. And both in Women and Men must be taken notice of what diseases they are subject to. . . . To these General Articles of Inquiry . . . should be added; (1) Inquiries about traditions concerning a particular thing, relating to that Country, as either peculiar to it, or at least, uncommon elsewhere. (2) Inquiries, that require Learning or Skill in the Anserer; to which should be subjoined Proposals of ways, to enable men to give answers to these more difficult inquiries. . . .[33]

Thus it is made abundantly clear that this group of able men was interested primarily in the material prospects of colonists—the improvement of agriculture, commerce, and industrial production—and not in the collection of day-to-day practices of strange and remote human beings. Indeed, the members of the Royal Society in the seventeenth century cared less about obtaining knowledge concerning the cultures of other peoples than did Albrecht Meier, over one hundred years before. Nor was the situation improved in 1692, when Robert Boyle brought these travelers' programs together in a little book entitled *General heads for the natural history of a country, great or small; drawn out for the use of travellers and navigators.* Scientists though they were, he and most of his colleagues were more absorbed in the study of natural rather than social phenomena. At the time of the founding of the Royal Society, they met together to practice the "new philosophy," by which they understood "Physick, Anatomy, Geometry, Astronomy, Navigation, Statisticks, Mechanicks, and Natural Experiments." Occasionally, travelers' reports were given a hearing. Occasionally, papers were read on archeological and historical subjects. But these were relatively few in number. In a time of strife such as this, said Thomas Sprat, "to have been eternally musing on Civil business . . . was too melancholy a reflexion"; while "the consideration of Man and humane affairs" would have affected the group "with a thousand various disquiets."[34] Consequently, although the first three volumes of the *Transactions* number some nine hundred pages, only about thirty-six of these report social material.[35] Nor in a strict sense was all of this material "ethnological." Quite the contrary. Too many readers of travel accounts before the Society were like Edward Brown who in 1673, opened his paper on Hungary with the remark that he would "pass by the observations made of Polity, Economy, Manners and Customs . . . as not belonging to our task; and observe only what is Physiological, and may contribute to the History of Nature."[36]

One exception to this rule seems to have been Sir William Petty, always an original. Not content with outlining "A Method of Enquiring into the State of any Country," he also drew up in 1686 a series of questions concerning "The Nature of the Indians of Pensylvania." Part of this was concerned with demography, the remainder was straight ethnology. His questions called for descriptions of the policy of the Indians, their languages, their habitations, religion, marriage customs, dwellings, diet, music, weapons, tools, money, ornament, knowledge of medicinal herbs, and honesty.[37] Though there was probably no connection, Petty's program of investigation was very similar to one which had actually been carried out by Roger Williams forty years earlier among the American Indians.[38]

While the serious study of manners and customs had no standing among natural scientists in the sixteenth and seventeenth centuries, some of the views entertained by physicians, naturalists, and mathematicians could not fail to rub off on their humbler admirers, the collectors. This was especially the case in matters of stylistic propriety when modes of description were under consideration. Among the early Baconians fine language, as the result of its association with medieval philosophy, was suspect. It was felt that it tended to obscure rather than to enlighten. Furthermore, to men such as Petty and Hobbes, the modes of description employed for the inclusion of culture traits in some sort of collection seemed only too often to hark back to the time when disputes were concerned with words rather than realities. With some "contempt for the superficial fineries of verbal dress," Petty consequently insisted on clearer definitions of ethnological entities and the curtailment of all superfluity in language; while Hobbes attacked the

Cambridge Platonists and listed the metaphorical use of words as among the abuses of scientific discourse.[39]

But without question, the man who did most to clarify the problems of cultural description, especially as they impinged upon savage societies, was the French philosopher and essayist Michel de Montaigne (1533–1592), whose ethnological sophistication, even at this early date, surpassed that of most men a century later. In writing the famous essay *Of the Caniballes* about 1580, Montaigne found himself confronted with two questions. One was clearly cultural in character and was prompted by reports on the customs of certain tribes near Rio de Janeiro, where French voyagers had recently attempted settlement. What manner of men were these Brazilians? The other was also ethnological, though perhaps less obviously so. To what, it was asked, was the partition of nations into civil and uncivil to be ascribed?

In approaching the task of describing the existing way of life of a far-away South American people, Montaigne deliberately broke both with scholastic epitomizations and with the type of cultural data to be found in classical literature. For him there were to be no capsule descriptions of vices and virtues; there were to be no wholesale cribbings of descriptions of marital customs, religious and funeral rites, apparel, dwellings, and diets from Herodotus or other ancient historians. On the contrary, there were to be comparisons and the detection of cultural similitudes.

Above all, knowing full well that the informant was the weakest element in the flow of ethnological knowledge from the New to the Old World, returned travelers who were both intelligent and trustworthy were to be sought and found. Montaigne had enjoyed unusual opportunities to inspect the booty of homecoming seamen. He had observed their "curios": the Indian hammocks, drums, bracelets, and other items. He had read the books on the New World by Thevet,

Léry, Benzoni, Gomara, and possibly Belleforest, whose work was in part a translation of Boemus and Muenster. But he still preferred oral testimony, especially when it could be obtained from commen men who had lived for some time among the people of France Antarctique. Such men, when they drifted into his neighborhood, he found to be "simple and rough hewen," hence more "fit to yeelde a true testimonie." Subtle men might be curious; they might take in more, but they might also be tempted to gloss over details. Subtle men, said Montaigne, "the better to perswade, and make their interpretations of more validitie . . . cannot chuse but somewhat alter the storie. They never represent things truely, but fashion and maske them according to the visage they saw them in; and to purchase credit to their judgment, and drawe you on to beleeve them, they commonly, adorne, enlarge, yea, and Hyperbolise the matter." There were two problems, as Montaigne saw it, for those who wished to understand the new tribes of the New World. One was to see them as they really were, to pierce the veil of traditional interpretation of distant peoples; to envision their activities without the intrusion of preconceived European legend. The other was that of communication : of conveying the facts to the homeland; of presenting a true and undistorted portrait of the savage. What was needed for this undertaking was "either a most sincere Reporter, or a man so simple that he . . . had no invention to builde-upon." The good informant wrote what he knew and no more. What Montaigne desired by way of description was to be framed in language that was "natural and unaffected. . . . not Pedanticall, nor Friar-like, nor Lawyer-like."

Moreover, if improvement were to be made in current canons of description, in which epithets were sometimes the only content, some stable touchstone of comparison had to be found. With this in mind, it seemed clear that the only known and useful standard was that of Europe. "We have no other ayme of truth or reason," said Montaigne, "then the example and *Idea* of the opinions and customes of the countrie we live-in." Hence no attempt was made in the short essay *Of the caniballes* to cover every feature of Brazilian life. The author chose rather to describe only those elements which seemed comparable in some way with what a sixteenth-century Frenchman knew as the way of life in sixteenth-century France. There was much left out. But Montaigne's longish paragraphs on the dwellings of the Brazilians, their diet, crafts, religion, practices in warfare, systems of consanguinity, customs of inheritance and marriage—all subjects of interest to Europeans—were new and fresh in spirit. They contained a wholesome attempt to adhere to facts, and to abstain from traditional moralizing or vituperation.

At the same time, the endeavor to be clear drove his informants not only to be Europocentric but to rely on comparisons and similitudes, those most natural and elemental aids to understanding. "Their buildings are very long," Montaigne was told,

and able to containe two or three hundred soules, covered with barkes of great trees, fastened in the ground at one end, enterlaced and joyned close together by the toppes, *after the manner of some of our Granges.* . . . Their beddes are of a kind of cotton cloth, fastened to the house-roofe, *as oure shippe-cabbanes.* . . . Their drinke is made of a certaine roote, and of the colour of *our Claret wines.* . . . Their yong men goe a hunting after wilde beastes with bowes and arrows. Their women busie themselves ther-whilst with warming of their drinke. . . . Some of their old men, in the morning before they goe to eating, preach in common to all the housholde. . . . They are shaven all-over, much more close and cleaner *than wee are,* with no other Razers than of wood or stone. They believe their soules to be eternall, and those that have deserved well of their Gods, to be placed in that part of *Heaven* where the Sunne riseth; the cursed toward the West in opposition. They have certaine *Prophets and Priests,* which commonly abide in the mountaines, & very seldom show themselves unto the people; but when they come downe, there-is a great feast prepared, and a solemne assembly of manie *townships* together.[40]

It would be unjust to expect from Montaigne more than a mood and illustrations. The illustrations of man's cultural variety, in the essays *Of the caniballes* and elsewhere in the *Essays,* are multiplied almost to weariness.

Other cosmographers, collectors, and commentators of the period were equally Europocentric. Like Montaigne they selected for description those features of other cultures which were familiar in their own; and they interpreted them, they communicated their verbal conceptions of them to others, in terms of their own experience and education. Their problem was akin to that confronted by the translators of the King James version of Scripture. In order to make their translation of the religious ideas and practices of an ancient Near Eastern Semitic people intelligible to Englishmen, they had to resort to the imagery current in seventeenth-century English speech and literature.

But, as many scholars were soon to find out, the use of European custom as a touchstone of communication was a double-edged instrument. It could lead either to a positive or to a negative mode of description. Alien peoples could be judged to be like Europeans, or unlike. It could be held that two cultural systems presented many or few similarities; it could also be said that they presented none at all. When similitudes were observed, the newer formula required that they be indicated; when they were absent, description was still feasible, but only by resort to negation, or by the observation of differences.

The alien customs which were found to be the most difficult

to convey to European readers, and hence the ones for which similitudes were most frequently invoked, were government and religion. And the results were often droll. In Calcutta, said Muenster as translated by Richard Eden, "the King hath in his Chappell [sic] the image of this devyl Deumi, sytting with a diademe or crowne on his head, much lyke unto the myter [sic] which the Romayne Bishoppes weare. . . ."[41] In Borneo, according to Heylyn, the people were ruled by "Counsellors of State" who convened in a "Senate House."[42] Johann Boemus, according to the translator of the earliest English edition of his book, described the land of Egypt as "divided into Shieres : and to every shiere was appointed a Presidente." The leader of religion in this ancient empire on the Nile was called "a Primate"; and certain political obligations were delegated to "the Pieres of the Realme."[43] Samuel Purchas (1575?–1626), the Sussex clergyman whose travels had never carried him more than two hundred miles from his birthplace but who was probably the first collector of religious rites on a world-wide scale, tried to communicate such matters to his readers, but with some self-consciousness. "These Rareties of Nature, I have sometime suted in differing phrase and figure of speech : not that I affect a fantasticall singularitie; but that these divine works might appear in Robes, if not fitting their Maiestie, yet such as our Wordrobe did . . . afford." In the throes of clarification, he noted that the Chinese pantheon contained many "hee and shee *saints.*" There were monasteries governed by *"Generalls"* or *"Provincialls";* and convents, by *"Abbesses."* When he turned to the religion of Mexico the same descriptive device was employed. Virgins, serving in the temple, "rose at midnight to the Idols *Mattins.* . . . They had their *Abbesses* . . . they did their *penance* at midnight." There was a "cloyster or Monasterie" for the young men "which they called *Religious.* Their crowns were shaven, as the *Friars* in these parts, their haire a little longer. . . . Touching their

Priests in Mexico, there were some *High Priests* or *Popes,* even under the same name."⁴⁴ (Italics added.)

The cosmography written by Pierre d'Avity entitled *The estates, empires, & principallities of the world,* published in 1614 and translated into English in the year following, is full of the same sort of thing. The priests of Cyprus wore headdresses like Bishops' miters; religious services in Calcutta were conducted in oratories and chapels: "masses" were "celebrated," and the "clergy" included members whose function were like those of the "Pope." To the Chinese gods d'Avity added "angels" and "apostles"; and he described the religion of Mexico much as did Purchas, noting in it practices regarded as similitudes to Christian ritual and organization.

On the whole, however, it was the failure to find similitudes, due to what were taken to be radical divergences from the European norm, which often attracted most attention; and it was then that the negative mode of attack was invoked. In such instances, Europocentrism was not banished. Far from it. But its function as a criterion of description was inverted. Instead of serving conceptually as a means of bringing alien cultures into some degree of rapport with that of Europe, it emphasized their cleavage and separation. In some uses, it segregated and classified as barbarians any people who failed to fit into the European scheme of things. In others, the denial of likeness was endowed with historical implications. By virtue of undeclared assumptions, the cultures thus submitted to negative description were assumed to be in an aboriginal, a natural, or a prelapsarian condition of either purity and goodness or corruption and lawlessness.

It would be ill -advised to try to assemble all instances of the use of this negative formula prior to Montaigne. Eventually the search would lead back to those lines in the *Works and days* of Hesiod which recounted the myth of Prometheus, that initial speculation in Western literature con-

cerning the original condition of mankind. There the first men
were thought of as devoid of the rudiments of culture, or, as
Plato was later to put it in the *Protagoras,* "naked, unshod,
unbedded, and unarmed." It is significant that in writing of
the Brazilians, Montaigne employed a similar and typical form
of negative description, declaring them to form "a nation,—
that hathe *no* kinde of traffike, *no* knowledge of Letters, *no*
intelligence of numbers, *no* name of magistrate, *nor* of politike
superioritie; *no* use of service, of riches, or of poverty; *no*
contracts, *no* successions, *no* dividences, *no* occupation but
idle; *no* respect of kindred, but common, *no* apparell but
naturall, *no* manuring of lands, *no* use of wine, corne, or
mettle."[45] (Italics added.)

It has been thought that Shakespeare borrowed Gonzalo's
lines in *The Tempest* from this section of the essay *Of the
caniballes.* And it must be granted that the resemblance is
there. But similar modes of negative description are to be
found throughout the literature of the sixteenth and seventeenth centuries, and certainly in the works of the collectors
and cosmographers. They were on the tips of many pens whenever New World peoples were under discussion, or when it
became necessary to deal descriptively with the qualities and
behavior of barbarous, uncivil, or primitive man. The convention appeared in the *Omnium gentium mores* to indicate
a condition of incivility, though not among New World
savages. It was employed by Boemus to make clear "the rude
simplicitie of the first worlde, from Adam to the floud," and
the like condition of several contemporary groups, such as the
Libyans, the Ichthiophagi, and the Brahmins. From Adam to
the flood, said he, men lived "skateryng on the earthe, *without*
knowledge of money . . . or Merchauntes trade, *no* manner of
exchange (other than barter) . . . *no* man claimed aught for his
severalle, but lande and water were as commune to al, as
Ayer and Skie . . . thei gaped *not* for honour, *ne* hunted after

richesse, but eche man contented with a little, passes his daies in the wilde fielde. . . . *Not* then environed with walles, *ne* pente up with rampers and diches of deapthe, but walking at free scope . . . *without* knowledge of evillesy . . . *without* lawe or rule, or facion of life, roiling and rowmying . . . *without* place of abode." (Italics added.) The Libyans lived a rude and savage kind of life, using "neither swords nor knyves nor any other weapons," and observed "neither lawe nor equitie toward strangers." While the Brahmins, beloved of medieval legend and regarded as true people of the Golden Age, by reason of their omissions rather than their commissions, lived "a pure and simple life, led with no likerous lustes." They longed

for no more then nature requyreth naturallye . . . desiryng no suche as other menne tourne the worlde almost upside downe to have . . . but suche as the earth unploughed, or undolven, yeldeth of herself. And because thei acqueinte not their table with surfet, in dede thei know not so many kindes of sicknesses, ne so many names of diseases as we doe. . . . Thei have no neide to crave one anothers helpe and reliefe, wher no manne maketh clayme by (thine) and by (myne) but every manne taketh what he lusteth and lusteth no more than he niedeth. . . . Thei have no officers of Justice among them. . . . Ther can no lawe appiere, because none offence appeareth. . . . Neither is there any kinde of bonde knowen amonge them : . . . For the building of their houses, they sende not over sea for stone . . . but either make them caves in the earthe, or take suche as thei finde ready made in the sides of the mounteines and hilles. . . . Ther is no glittering apparell, no rattelinge in sylkes, no rusteling in velvettes, but a little brieche of brawded rushes. . . . The women are not sette out to allure, ne pinched in to please, ne garnished to gase at. No heare died, no lockes outelated, no face painted, no skinne slicked, no countre-feicte countenaunce, nor mynsing of paste. . . . Thei builde no toumbes for the deade : more like unto chirches then graves. Thei bewry not up their ashes in pottes dalmed full of pearle and precious stone. . . .[46]

The negative mode of description appeared once again in that learned work, *De la vicissitude ou variété des choses en l'univers,* published in 1575 by Louis Le Roy (c. 1510–77), called Regius, just five years before Montaigne published his *Essays,* though possibly not before the actual writing of *Of the caniballes.* Concerning the savages of the New World, Le Roy sets forth in words very like those of Montaigne that "they which have navigated thither, have found many people living yet as the first men, without letters, without Lawes, without Kings, without common wealthes, without arts; but yet not without religion. . . ." Again, describing the backward Northern and Southern peoples of the old European world, somewhat after the manner adopted by Bodin, he says that they too "are not civil by nature, nor governed by discipline, nor conjoined in habitations, neither do they sowe nor plant; helpe themselves little or nothing with manury trades; exchange in their bargaining one thing for another, not knowing the use of money; but living without houses, townes, cities . . . dwelling in fields or Champaignes infinitely large . . . without waies or bounds. . . ."[47]

Here, in *De la vicissitude,* one finds the acultural condition, or barbarism, expressed by a slightly different choice of non-existent customary or ceremonial activities from that of Montaigne or Boemus, with the result that if all three are combined, one emerges with a fairly complete list of all the conventional elements in this negative formula, or certainly with those most frequently invoked, such as "no (or without) letters; no (or without) laws; no (or without) kings or magistrate, government, commonwealth, rule, commanders; no arts (or occupation); no traffic (or shipping, navigation); no husbandry (or agriculture, tillage, tilth, vineyards, sowing, or planting); no money (or no exchange, gold, riches); no weapons (no war, knives, pikes, swords, etc.); no clothes (naked); no marrying (no wedding, no respect of kindred); no bourne or bound (without waies or bounds)."

The negative mode of description was also utilized in the cosmographical, ethnographical, and geographical works of the seventeenth century : in George Abbot in 1599, Samuel Purchas in 1613, Pierre d'Avity in 1614, Peter Heylyn in 1621, Nathanael Carpenter in 1625, and Thomas Hobbes in 1651. When George Abbot, Master of University College at Oxford and later Archbishop of Canterbury, prepared *A briefe description of the whole world* (1599) for his students of geography, it seemed necessary to acquaint them with the cultural condition of the native tribes in America. His mode of expression is familiar. "At the first ariving of the Spaniardes, . . . they founde in those parts nothing shewing trafique or knowledge of any other Nation, but the people naked, uncivill, some of them devourers of mans flesh, ignorant of shipping, without all kinde of learning, having no remembrance of history or writing . . . never having heard of any such religion as in other places of the world is knowne : but being utterly ignorant of Scripture, or Christ, or Moyses, or any God. . . ."[48] Writing in 1613 of the peoples recently discovered "in the last Age of the World," Samuel Purchas describes them as "they which never wore clothes on their bodies, never furnished their mindes with Arts, never knew any Law . . . or Magistrate, but their Fathers." Speaking of the Albanians, and echoing Strabo, Purchas asserted that "these men were so simple, that they neither had use of money, nor did they number above an hundred; ignorant of weights, measures, warre, civility, husbandrie : there were in use amongst them sixe and twentie languages." Speaking of the Numidians : "Very rarely is a judge found among them. . . . As for Letters, Arts, Vertue, they dwell not in these deserts." Speaking of Negro-land : "They live . . . without King, Lord, Commonwealth, or any government, scarce knowing to sow their grounds : . . . not having any peculiar wife. . . ."[49] In 1614, in *Les états, empires, et principautez du monde,* Pierre d'Avity (1573–1635) fitted the same conventional description to Mexico and Peru by remarking that, among the peoples of the New World, those leading a savage and brutish life were "without commanders, without lawes, without any forme of civilitie, or policie." D'Avity also makes an effort, almost unique in his generation, to give greater precision to the concept of barbarism. In so doing, he distinguished five degrees of cultural lack or privation. There were first those who had no knowledge of religion; those "who sow not, nor have any tillage"; those who go in nakedness; those without habitation, having no dwellings but caves and hollow trees; and those, the most brutish, deprived of government. "For some being altogether barbarous, live without lawes or a commaunder, either in peace or warre."[50] Nor should Thomas Hobbes (1588–1679) be omitted from among these seventeenth-century figures, for when he wrote of the earliest condition of mankind in the *Leviathan,* published in 1651, the same Europocentric but negative mode of description was unforgettably employed.

During the time men live without a common power to keep them all in awe, they are in that condition which is called war. . . . In such condition, there is no place for industry; because the fruit thereof is uncertain : and consequently no culture of the earth; no navigation; nor use of the commodities that may be imported by sea; no commodious building; no instruments of moving, and removing, such things as require much force; no knowledge of the face of the earth; no account of time; no arts; no letters; no society; and which is worst of all, continual fear, and danger of violent death; and the life of man, solitary, poor, nasty, brutish, and short.[51]

BIBLIOGRAPHY AND NOTES

1. Eden, "Treatyse of the newe India," 5–6.

2. Thomas Hobbes, *The English works of Thomas Hobbes of Malmsbury, now first collected and edited by Sir William Molesworth* (London: J. Bohn, 1839–45), III, 85.

3. Bernhardt Varen, *Cosmography and geography in two parts* . . . (London: S. Roycroft for Richard Blome, 1682), 3.

4. Roger Bacon, *Opus majus,* I, 321; II, 790–91.

5. Frank L. Shoell, "Les mythologistes Italiens de la renaissance et la poèsie Elizabéthaine," *Revue de littérature comparée,* 4 (1924), 8. See also Douglas Bush, *Mythology and the renaissance tradition in English poetry* (Minneapolis: University of Minnesota Press, 1932); Giovanni Boccaccio, *Genealogia deorum* (after 1500); Johann Stamler, *Dyalogus de diversarum gencium sectis et mundi religionibus* (1508); George Pictorius, *Theologia mythologica ex doctiss, virorum promptuario* . . . (1532); Lilio Gregorio Giraldi, *De deis gentium* . . . (1548); Natal Conti, *Mythologiae sive explicationum fabularum* . . . (1551); Vincenzo Cartari, *Le imagini, con la spositione de i dei de gli antichi* . . . (1556); Stephen Batman, *The golden booke of the leaden goddes* . . . (1577).

6. Jean Seznec, *The survival of the pagan gods; the mythological tradition and its place in renaissance humanism and art,* translated from the French by Barbara F. Sessions (New York: Pantheon Books, 1953), 238; see also Ernest H. Wilkins, "Descriptions of pagan divinities from Petrarch to Chaucer," *Speculum,* 32 (1957), 511–22.

7. Edward Herbert, Lord Cherbury, *De religione gentilium, errorum que apud eos causis* (Amstelaedami: Typis Blaeviorum, 1663), translated into English by William Lewis as *The ancient religion of the gentiles, and the causes of their errors considered* (London: John Nutt, 1705). The deistic standpoint "had already been foreshadowed to some extent by Averroists, by Italian writers like Boccaccio and Petrarch, in More's *Utopia* (1515), and by French writers like Montaigne, Charron, and Bodin." It is not difficult to see how a critical spirit could develop very early, for the claims of Christian doctrine were challenged from the very first day "by the spirit of secular philosophy." There were also educated Jews in every large European community "who clung tenaciously to their own religion and philosophy, and in the thirteenth century Europe had forced upon it a new respect for the Mohammedans and their religion, partly because of contact . . . during the Crusades, and partly because the Arabs were the possessors of great treasures of ancient learning, especially the true Aristotle." A new tolerance toward these enemies of the Church eventually led to a comparative view of religions, implying "that there was falsehood as well as truth in all religions." The dissemination of such religious liberalism "first in Italy, then in France

and England, explains a large part of the pagan spirit of Renaissance literature." (Louis I. Bredvold, "Deism before Lord Herbert," *Papers of the Michigan Academy of Science, Arts, and Letters* (New York: Macmillan, 1925), 431, 434, 436–37. On Bodin's *Heptaplomeres*, see George H. Sabine, *The history of political theory* (New York: Holt, 1937), 401, note 2, and by the same author, "The colloquium heptaplomeres of Jean Bodin" in *Persecution and liberty* (New York: Century, 1931), 289–90.

8. Samuel Purchas, *Purchas his pilgrimage, or relations of the world and the religions observed in all ages and places discovered . . .* (London: William Stansby for Henrie Fetherstone, 1613).

9. *Alexander Ross*, ΠΑΝΣΕΒΕΙΑ *or, a view of all religions in the world* (London, 1653). On Ross, see Richard Foster Jones, *Ancients and moderns: a study of the background of the battle of the books* (St. Louis: Washington University Studies, 1936), 125–27.

10. For information on this early interest in comparative religions, see: Edward Herbert, Lord Cherbury, *op. cit.*; Bernard Picart, *Cérémonies et coutumes de tous peuples du monde* (1723–43); L'Abbé Antoine Banier, *Histoire générale des cérémonies, moeurs, et coutumes religieuses de tous les peuples du monde* (1741); Henri Pinard de la Boullaye, *L'étude comparée des religions* (1922).

11. Polydore Vergil, *The works of the famous antiquary, Polidore Virgil. Compendiously English'd by John Langley . . . Containing the original of all arts, sciences, mysteries, orders, rites and ceremonies, both ecclesiastical and civil. A work useful for all divines, historians, lawyers, and all artificers* (London: Simon Miller, 1663), sig. B 7 v–C 4 r; John Barston, *The safeguarde of societie: describing the institution of lawes and policies, to preserve every felowship of people by degrees of civill governemente: gathered of the moralles and policies of philosophie* (London: John Shepperde, 1576), *passim;* Jean Bodin, *The six bookes of a commonweale . . . out of the French and Latine copies, done into English by Richard Knolles* (London: G. Bishop, 1606).

12. Louis de Gaya. *Cérémonies nuptiales de toutes les nations du monde* (A Paris: Chez Estienne Michallet, rue Saint Iaques, à l'image Saint Paul, proche la Fontaine Saint Séverin, 1681); *Nuptial rites, or the several marriage ceremonies pracised amongst all the nations of the world,* by I.S.S. (London: Printed by T.S. for the Author, Anno Domini, 1685).

13. *An accurate description of the marriage ceremonies used by many nations; the oddity of some, the drollery of many; and the real or intended piety of all* (Edinburgh: Printing house in the West-bow, 1782), *passim;* see also Archer Taylor, "The history of marriage," in *Problems in German literary history,* 165–72.

14. Alfred Owen Aldridge, "Population and polygamy in eighteenth century thought," *Journal of the History of Medicine,* 4 (1949), 129–48; "Polygamy and deism," *Journal of English and Germanic Philology,* 48 (1949), 343–60.

15. Lilio Gregorio Giraldi, *De sepulchris et vario sepeliendi ritu, libellus* (1539); Tommaso Porcacchi, *Funerali antichi di diversi popoli,*

e nationi, con la forma, pompa e maniera di sepoltura, di essequie, di consecrazione antichi (1574); Claude Guichard, *Funerailles, et diverses manières d'ensevelir les Romaines, Grecs, et autres nations, tant anciennes que modernes* (1581); Francesco Perucci, *Pompe funebri di tutte le nationi del mondo: raccolte dalle storie sagre et profane* (1639). See also Pierre Muret, *Cérémonies funèbres de toutes les nations* (1677), an unoriginal volume translated into English as *Rites of funeral, ancient and modern,* by P. Lorrain (1683). In the articles on death customs and the disposal of the dead in the *Encyclopedia of the Social Sciences* and Hastings' *Encyclopedia of Religion and Ethics* the authors seem to be unaware of these sixteenth- and seventeenth-century contributions to the literature.

16. Louis Le Roy, *Of the interchangeable course, or variety of things in the whole world.* Written in French . . . : and translated into English by R.A. (London: C. Yetsweirt, 1594), sig. F 4 v–F 5 r; François Deserpz, *Receuil de la diversité des habits qui sont de présent en usage tant és pays d'Europe, Asie, Afrique, et isles sauvages, le tout fait après le natural* (1567); Abraham de Bruyn, *Omnium pene Europae, Asiae, Aphricae atque Americae gentium habitus. Habits de diverses nations . . .* (1581); Jean Boissard, *Habitus variarum orbis gentium. Habitz de nations estranges* (1581); Pietro Bertelli, *Diversarum nationem habitus . . .* (1594). See also Hilaire and Meyer Hiler, *Bibliography of costume, a dictionary catalogue of about eight thousand books and periodicals* (New York: H. W. Wilson, 1939).

17. Sir Thomas More, *Utopia with the 'Dialogue of comfort'* (London: Dent, 1928), 81–82; 53; 55, and 69; 60–66 and 84–86; 100; 103.

18. At times, especially in the fifteenth and sixteenth centuries, astrology took the form of a kind of psychology and was used to explain the differences in the customs of mankind. (Don Cameron Allen, *The star-crossed renaissance* [Durham, N.C., Duke University Press, 1941], 38, 62–63, 68.)

19. Eden, *Briefe collection,* sig. A 6 r.

20. Henry Cornelius Agrippa, *Of the vanitie and uncertaintie of artes and sciences* (London: J. C. for Samuel Speed, 1676), 147.

21. Boemus, *Manners, Lawes* (1611), 293.

22. Mercator, *Atlas,* 42.

23. Peter Heylyn, *Microcosmus. A little description of the great world. Augmented and revised* (Oxford: Printed by John Lichfield and William Turner, 1625), sig. D 7 v.

24. George Brunner Parks, *Richard Hakluyt and the English voyages* (New York: American Geographical Society, 1928), 269–77.

25. Robert Burton, *The anatomy of melancholy* (London: Everyman's Library, Dent and Sons, 1949; New York: E. P. Dutton), II, 35–39.

26. Robert Ralston Cawley, *Milton and the literature of travel* (Princeton: Princeton University Press, 1951), 117.

27. Jerome Turler, *The traveiler of Jerome Turler, divided into two bookes. The first conteining a notable discourse of the maner, and order of traveiling oversea, or into straunge and forrein countreys. The second comprehending an excellent description of the most delicious realme*

of Naples in Italy. *A woorke very pleasaunt for all persons to reade, and right profitable and necessarie unto all such as are minded to traveyll* (London: by William How, for Abraham Veale, 1575), sig. B 3 r.

28. William Bourne, *A booke called the treasure for traveilers, divided into five bookes or partes, contaynyng very necessary matters, for all sortes of travailers, eyther by sea or by lande* (Imprinted at London for Thomas Woodcocke, dwelling in Paules Churchyarde, at the syne of the black Beare, 1578) sig. * * 4 v.

29. Justus Lipsius, *A direction for travaillers* (Imprinted at London by R. B. for C. Burbie, 1592), sig. B i r.

30. Albertus Meierus, *Certaine briefe, and speciall instructions for gentlemen, merchants, students, souldiers, marriners, &c. Employed in services abrode, or in anie way occasioned to converse in the kingdomes, and governments of foreign princes* (London: Printed by John Wolfe, 1589), sig. A 2 r.

31. Bacon, *op. cit.,* VI, 417–18.

32. Gunther, *Early science in Oxford,* III, 168 ff.

33. *Philosophical transactions: giving some accompt of the present undertakings, studies, and labours of the ingenious in many considerable parts of the world* (London: T. N. for John Martyn and James Allestrey, 1665–66), I, 186–89.

34. Sprat, *Royal Society,* 56.

35. Parks, "Travel as education," 285–86.

36. *Philosophical Transactions,* VIII.

37. William Petty, *The Petty Papers: Some unpublished writings of Sir William Petty, edited from the Bowood Papers by the Marquis of Lansdowne* (London: Constable and Co., 1927), I, 175–78; II, 116–19.

38. Roger Williams, *A key into the language of America, or an help to the language of the natives in that part of America called New-England; together with briefe observations of the customes, manners, and worships, &c. of the aforesaid natives* . . . (London: Gregory Dexter, 1643).

39. Richard Foster Jones, "Science and English prose style in the third quarter of the seventeenth century," *Publications of the Modern Language Association of America,* 45 (1930), 980, 982; "Science and language in England of the mid-seventeenth century," *Journal of English and Germanic Philology,* 31 (1932), 316.

40. Michel de Montaigne, *The essayes or morall, politike and militarie discourses* . . . *First written by him in French. And now done into English by John Florio* (London: Val Sims for Edward Blount, 1603), sig. K 3 r– K 4 r. Purchas either had read Montaigne with approval, or independently took a similar position on printed informants. "I mention authors sometimes, of meane qualitie, for the meanest have sense to observe that which themselves see, more certainly then the contemplations and *Theorie* of the more learned." (Purchas: *Pilgrimage,* as cited, "To The Reader").

41. Eden, "Treatyse of the newe India," 17.

42. Peter Heylyn, *Cosmographie in foure bookes contayning the chorographie and historie of the whole world, and all the principall*

kingdomes, provinces, seas, and isles thereof (London : Henry Seile, 1652), sig. Xxx 5 v.

43. Boemus, *Fardle of façions* (1555), sig. D v r; D ii v.

44. Purchas, *Pilgrimage,* Kk 3 r–Kk 4 v, Mm 4 r–Mm 4 v.

45. Montaigne, *op. cit.,* sig. K 3 v.

46. Boemus, *Fardle of façions* (1555), sig. L vii v – M ii r.

47. Le Roy, *Of the interchangeable course,* sig. F iii v, C vi v – D i r.

48. George Abbot, *A briefe description of the whole worlde* . . . (At London : Printed by T. Hudson for John Browne, and are to be soulde at the signe of the Bible in Fleete – streete, 1599), G 4 r.

49. Purchas, *op. cit.,* Cc 4 r, Aaa i v, Aaa 3 r.

50. Pierre d'Avity, *The estates, empires, & principallities of the world* . . . Translated out of French by Edward Grimstone . . . (London : Printed by A. Islip, 1615), 252, 266–67.

51. Hobbes, *op. cit.,* III, 112–13. Hobbes continues : "The savage people in many places of America . . . live at this day in that brutish manner." (*Ibid.,* III, 114.)

CHAPTER VI

The Ark of Noah and the
Problem of Cultural Diversity

"How falls it out that the nations of the world, comming all of one father, Noe, doe varie so much from one another, both in bodie and minde?"—Du Bartas.

ONE OF THE major differences between the thought of the Middle Ages and that of the Renaissance was the value attached to the trait of curiosity. During the earlier and longer period, this spring of scientific inquiry was profoundly distrusted as meddlesome and impertinent. It was spoken of as *turpis curiositas*. To encourage the mind to play wantonly with its own powers was denounced as self-indulgence; to seek learning outside the accustomed categories of medieval logic and information was to invite scandal. The Renaissance, on the other hand, was a period of a restless search for knowledge. Why? Whence? What? Whither? Questioners gave no quarter and respected no boundaries. In a little book called *The foreste, or collection of histories,*[1] translated from the French in 1571 and repeatedly reissued in several languages, nearly every chapter heading posed a problem. Many of these were of ethnological intent. Why in the first ages did men live longer than at present? Who invented war, weapons, arms? Why did man walk upright? What speech was used in the beginning of the world, and how first began the diversity of tongues? How profitable was the invention of letters? What marriage customs were used by our elders? These questions, or ones like them, were repeatedly propounded by all the Renaissance encyclopedias.

In the midst of all this, the collectors—botanical, zoological, and cultural—could not long remain aloof; nor could their collections continue to be regarded merely as a source of entertainment. A common characteristic of their contents— multiformity and diversity—provoked insistent comment. This was notably true with respect to collections of manners. Every assemblage of artifacts, every fardel of fashions, disclosed to the impatient European viewer a disconcerting array, in the one family of the children of God, of diverse institutions, diverse types of shelter and diet, diverse customs of dress, diverse systems of betrothal and matrimony, diverse organizations of commonwealths, diverse gods. From one point of view or another no two "nations" conducted their lives along similar lines. Nowhere in the behavior of man, son of Adam and progeny of Noah, did there seem to be any tranquilizing uniformity. To any one who stopped to reflect, the facts were glaring. Collectors of ethnological materials in the sixteenth and seventeenth centuries, whether they willed it or not, were confronted with the problem of cultural difference; not, to be sure, for the first time in the history of thought, but with the added impact of more, newer, and more pressing evidence. As Montaigne remarked, with some perplexity, in his essay *Of coaches:*

Were my memory sufficientlye informed of them, I would not thinke my time lost, heere to set downe the infinite variety, which histories present unto us, of the use of coaches in the service of warre : divers according to nations and different according to ages. For there in nothing wherein the world differeth so much, as in customes and lawes. Somethings are here accompted abhominal, which in another place are esteemed commendable . . . There is nothing so extreame and horrible, but is found received and allowed by the custome of some nation. It is credible that there be naturall lawes; as may be seene in other creatures, but in us they are lost.[2]

Nor was this all—this absence of natural law, of uniformity, regularity, in human behavior. Difference in culture was observed to be paralleled by difference in living forms. Organic nature was shot through and through with bewildering variety. Diversity in biological and social phenomena was early and frequently remarked. "For even as we see a varietie in all sorts of beasts," said Jean Bodin, ". . . in a like sort we may say, there is in a manner as great difference in the nature and disposition of men."[3] Since the *Six bookes of a commonweale,* published in Latin in 1586, was soon translated and read everywhere in Europe, this observation awakened many echoes. Said Casaubon (1599-1671), putting the matter in more philosophical terms, "The consideration of this varietie [among men] affords, as unto Naturalists, matter of speculation." It shows "how even herein nature delights in *varietie* . . . What in the Heavens, the Sunne and the Moone, divers Starres and Planets are . . . to divide the day from the night . . . so varietie of fashions and customes, serve unto man for the Civill and politike distinction of the severall times and ages of the World. . . ."[4] It was a problem no less to missionaries than to philosophers. In its very organization, Father de Acosta's *Natural and moral history of the Indies,* which was published and republished, translated and retranslated, before the end of the sixteenth century, was one of the many acknowledgments of the diversification of phenomena. His consideration of the many kinds of idolatries observable among the Indians of Peru and Mexico was preceded by a detailed description of the varieties of flora and fauna.

Then as now, however, there was little interest, either among

Various peoples depicted on a pack of English playing cards, 1670.

naturalists or among students of man, in estimating the general dimensions of their problems, the total number of differing categories in either the zoological or cultural array. In recent biological literature, to be sure, occasional statements may be found suggesting the existence of 320,000 vegetable species and 2,000,000 animal species; 10,000 species of slime-forming microscopical algae, 4,000 of sea mosses and kelp, and 50,000 species of the fungi commonly called toadstools. It was conjectured by Alfred Russel Wallace, but only conjectured, that in the whole of the past history of extinct forms there must have been thirty or forty times as many species as now exist— a number he places at something like eighteen to twenty million.[5] Statistically speaking, no one has ventured to indicate how these astonishing figures were arrived at, or the degree of their reliability.

Concerning the number of diverse cultures, there has been even less information and less interest. Though the explorations may well have emphasized the facts of cultural unlikeness by the expansion of the category of savagery, subsequent years have seen almost no attempt to estimate the actual numbers involved, or the relative proportions of civil to uncivil groups. In ancient times, if his allusions to various peoples around the Mediterranean be counted, Herodotus referred to about half a hundred. With a Roman's appreciation of the almost limitless tribalization of mankind, Pliny's total was higher, especially for those many "nations" mentioned merely by name. Mela and Solinus, though they dealt purportedly with the wide, wide world, fell notably below their two predecessors.

Throughout the past, Europeans, or at least some of them, have known of the existence of far more differing peoples than have ever been mentioned or listed. Unquestionably the merchant-travelers of Greece, Rome, and medieval Europe, who moved with more or less ease over the Eurasian land mass, were intimately acquainted with the manners and customs of many more different peoples than were ever reported in the mediaeval encyclopedias or manuscripts. They had to be. This kind of information was a commercial necessity. Goods could be bought and sold only when buyers and sellers were aware of peoples to buy from and sell to. But for reasons which are still tantalizingly difficult to come at, this kind of cultural information was either of no interest to scholars and geographers, or was deliberately withheld from them. In both antiquity and the Middle Ages, the selection of the tribes, peoples, or nations to be included in scholarly discussion was controlled by tradition or by an ancient concept of the *oikoumene.* The latter differed markedly from the world known to experienced merchants, for it was composed merely of the peoples, or some of them, inhabiting the Mediterranean littoral, with occasional brief leaps into traditional ethnographies of India, China, and northern Europe. Nor was this cramped and narrow view of world demography observable only in the classical geographers and historians. It appears also in the list of savages and other folk known to St. Jerome in the fourth century,[6] in the encyclopedia of Bartholomeus Anglicus in the thirteenth, in the works of Johann Boemus and Abraham Ortelius in the sixteenth. Among these Bartholomew, even though he maintained that only God could number and name all the peoples, deserves special attention, for within that scholar's usual concept of the inhabited world, he presented the longest list of all. It was composed of 177 separate groupings. After the publication of *De proprietatibus rerum,* it was not until the seventeenth century that Peter Heylyn, in one of the later editions of his *Cosmographie,* freed himself and his readers still further from the strait jacket of geographical and ethnological tradition by introducing descriptions of northern Europeans, Asians, Africans, and Americans as well as the more ancient peoples.

In recent decades there have been at least two attempts by

anthropologists to deal with the numerical aspects of their own peculiar field of inquiry, namely, the savage cultures—a question different from but comparable to that which confronted these earlier students of cultural diversity. The first of these was made by Professors Hobhouse, Wheeler, and Ginsberg. Planing to make a study of existing "primitive" societies, but confining their attention solely to those "about which they happened to find information that was sufficiently full and sufficiently trustworthy for their purposes" (a qualification almost as narrow as the *oikoumenikos* of the ancients), they drew up a list of about 650, which was later used by Professor Toynbee in the discussion of "primitive" man in his *Study of history.*[7] In 1931, however, or three years before Toynbee's acceptance of the Hobhouse figure, Professor James G. Leyburn published his *Handbook of ethnology.* Here are listed "over 12,000 tribes, language groups, nations, clans, and other social divisions"—certainly, if not definitive, a more realistic estimate.[8]

In setting out upon an analysis of the problem of cultural diversity, as its solution was undertaken by sixteenth- and seventeenth-century inquiry, it should be said at once that cultural divisions were never associated with "racial" divisions. Any effort to distinguish among the "races" of mankind on either anatomical, physiological, or cultural grounds was relatively negligible. Racialism in the familiar nineteenth- and twentieth-century sense of the term was all but nonexistent. True, there were constant reiterations of some features of the medieval polar typologies which included national virtues as well as national vices.[9] True, also, one of the first cleavages among men to claim attention was that of pigmentation. But as long as all men were considered brethren in the family of God, *as long as no efforts were made to classify some men among the beasts,* as long as no political or economic interest called for a theoretical imputation of debasement with respect to any group of dependent people, neither skin color nor the natural anxiety caused by conflict with enemies such as the Muslims or the Tartars led to anything like what we now know as racial "tension."

The problem of pigmentation, already a very old one at the time of the Renaissance, was stilled somewhat as an element in intergroup relations by the confident Europocentric theory that variation in complexion was ascribable to difference in length of exposure of originally white skins to the rays of the sun. The popularity of this theory helped to keep the Negro and other darker-skinned peoples theoretically in the family of Adam, thus upholding their dignity as human beings. When flaws were inevitably discovered in the purportedly high correlation of color and climate, the controversy over pigmentation flared up anew.[10] But in these earlier days, the word "race," in its many linguistic forms and cultural applications, held little meaning. As for the Arabs, Europeans finally learned to know them during the crusades without any accompaniment of "racial" antipathy. Under medieval law, the Jews too were free from legal restrictions based on "racial" grounds.[11] Peoples were differentiated from one another as "nations,"[12] while the term "race" carried a zoological connotation properly applicable only to animals. As long as man— even pigmented man—was regarded as monogenetic in origin and homogeneous in descent, he could not be submitted to zoological divisions, or to the terms used to designate them.[13]

Owing to his Biblical inheritance and indoctrination, it was rather difference in language and religion which touched the Renaissance European to the quick: language, because of the efforts of scholars to establish a universally acceptable canon, text, and translation of the Bible by the comparison of Hebrew, Greek, and Latin with modern tongues; religion, because of Reformation pressure to abandon pagan and Catholic rites, because of the bewildering multiplication of Protestant heresies, and because, above all else, of the shocking practices of the natives of the New World and Africa. Each one of these categories of cultural diversity seemed at the time to divide man from man much more sharply than any physical difference.

Certainly the sum of religions, sects, rituals, gods, and idols known to any well-informed Christian during this period was disconcerting and overwhelming. "Oh sencelesse man, who cannot possibly make a worme," cried Montaigne, "and yet will make Gods by the dozen."[14] "The pagans," said Robert Burton, "paint God and mangle Him after a thousand fashions; our heretics, schismatics, and some schoolmen, come not far behind: some paint Him in the habit of an old man, and make maps of heaven, number the angels, tell their several names and offices; some deny God and His providence, some take His office out of His hand, will bind and loose in heaven, release, pardon, and be quarter-master with him; some call His Godhead in question, His power and attributes, His mercy, justice, providence."[15] Collectors, such as Johann Boemus, touched upon the strangeness of many beliefs, and so also did many of his imitators; while the voyage accounts were full of the strange practices of the Negroes and Red Indians. On the subject of the bizarre performances in Africa and the New World which some observers chose to call religious, others were almost incoherent. By many, the savage was said to have "no religion" at all.

Though much had already been written on some facets of the cultural problem of diversity in religion—on the gods of classical antiquity, on the continuity of Western theology across the centuries, and on some of the Asiatic and savage cults—a compilation of the whole body of descriptive material was long in coming. It was too formidable an undertaking, and awaited the quiet audacity of that prosy Sussex clergy-

The great religions of the world. Frontispiece from Johannes Stamler's Dyalogue de divisarum gencium sectis *(1508).*

man, Samuel Purchas, whose prolixity often outran his lucidity. But even he was aware of his burden. In the dedicatory homage to the Archbishop of Canterbury, he pointed to his work, *Purchas his pilgrimage* (1613), as a task "never yet . . . by anyone," in any language attempted; requiring "both an Atlas and a Hercules too." Nor was he far wrong. The *Pilgrimage,* long and widely perused, led the intrepid author (and his floundering readers) not only from Paradise to the Ark, but around the world, drawing upon seven hundred authorities and he knew not "how many hundreds of their Treatises, Epistles, Relations, and Histories." [16]

For those who weakly asked what profit there might be in so ambitious an undertaking, he had a ready answer. He called attention first to the example of the natural philosophers and the magnificent scope of their inquiries. Did not they observe "the different constitution and conmixtion of the Elements, their diverse workings in diverse places?" Did they hesitate to take the phenomena of the whole earth and the heavens above as their province? Was man less important than these? Was man's religion less important? If there were a million million stars in the night sky, was it not important that man had worshiped many gods?

Adonided amongst the Syrians; Adramelech amongst the Capernaites; Asiniae amongst the Emathites; Astarte with the Sidonians; Astaroth with the Palestines; Dagon with the Philistines; Tartary with the Hanaei; Milcom amongst the Ammonites; Bel, the Babylonians; Beelzebub and Baal with the Samaritans and Moabites; Apis, Isis, and Osiris amongst the Egyptians; Apollo, Pythius at Delphi, Colophon, Ancyra, Cumae, Erythrae; Jupiter in Crete, Venus at Cyprus, Juno at Carthage, Aesculapius at Epidaurus, Diana at Ephesus, Pallas at Athens, etc. And even in these our days, both in the East and the West Indies, in Tartary, China, and Japan, etc., what strange idols, in what prodigious forms, with what absurd ceremonies are they adored. [17]

Should anyone who pondered the behavior of mankind in the "varietie of States and Kingdomes, with their differing Lawes, Policies and Customes" quail before an investigation of varying creeds and rituals? The Reverend Samuel Purchas thought not. Neither he, nor any of his many followers, who plunged into the sea of religious materials for the purpose of bringing it into some sort of order, were ever dismayed by torrential detail, or doubted their powers to cope with it. Writing at a time when the explorations could still stir the dullest imagination, they were all in some degree geographers, absorbed in the minutiae of the distribution of man and his cultures on every continent and island of the world. All were conners of maps, disposed to think of the array of strange rituals, creeds, and theologies in spatial terms; as associated with certain already located peoples; as distributed geographically, sometimes with the aid of statistics.

Robert Brerewood (1565?–1613) was one of these, and so was Ephraim Pagitt (1575?–1647). Both relied upon the technique of geographical distribution to help them get under way, and one, Brerewood, was something of a social statistician as well. An antiquary and the first professor of astronomy in Gresham College, Brerewood was also probably the first man to apply mathematical analysis to cultural and religious phenomena, and this in conjunction with a similar treatment of the origin and diffusion of languages. In his *Enquiries touching the diversity of languages and religions in the cheife parts of the world,* published in 1614 just over one year after Purchas' *chef d'oeuvre,* he divided contemporary world faiths into four "sorts" : Christianity, Mohametanism, Judaism, and Idolatry. Then, after each of these had been properly allocated, all were considered statistically, or in terms of "the quantitie and proportion of the parts of the earth possessed by the several sorts." According to Brerewood's rough findings, the Christians occupied approximately one-sixth of the inhabited world, the

Mohametans one-fifth, the Idolaters almost two-thirds. Or, to put the matter as Brerewood did : if the known regions of the world were divided "into 30 equal parts," the Christian part was as five, the Mohametan as six, and the Idolatrous as nineteen,[18]—a bit of quantitative information which was to be repeated many times by other students. Then, having applied this technique of measurement to Christianity and declared its proportional relation to other major religions, Brerewood turned to the Christian sects. These were described and located more accurately for his readers, drawing meanwhile a blast from Robert Burton for his quiet toleration of variety within Christendom. "See how the devil rageth," shouted the latter. "A fifth part of the world, and hardly that, now professeth Christ, but so inlarded and interlaced with superstitions, that there is scarce a sound part to be found, or any agreement amongst them."[19] But Brerewood's little book was original and thoughtful, and it enjoyed a high reputation among scholars.

Ephraim Pagitt, more sanguine than the author of the *Anatomy of melancholy* or even the Gresham College professor of astronomy, agreed that heresy and factionalism had split Protestantism into a chaos of contentious groups, but he refused to concede that all that remained of Christianity was "so eclipsed with several schisms, heresies, and superstitions" that no one could find it. It was these very heresies, or at any rate the geographical locations of the non-Roman sects, which he took as a subject of investigation. On them he lavished his time, and of them, in 1635 and 1645, wrote two books, the first entitled *Christianographia,* the other, *Heresiography.* With reference to the former he said, "That which I intend in this treatise, is, to shew that there are many Christian Churches as well in Europe, as in other parts of the world. . . ."[20] Furthermore, he gave his readers a catalogue of Protestant congregations, and where Purchas had merely mentioned "a mappe of superstitions," Pagitt carried out the idea of present-

A distribution map of the non-Roman Christian groups in Eurasia in 1635.

ing religious phenomena in a visual distribution. This little
book thus contains something new under the sun : a series of
distribution maps showing the locations of the Protestant
branch of European religion at the early date of 1635.

It all came to this : if that brave new world of physical and
social phenomena, which the explorers had laid open before
the bemused eyes of European beholders, was to be understood
at all, then there were countless questions to be asked. Of these
Robert Burton in his "Digression on air," a part of the
Anatomy of Melancholy, was ready to suggest a few.

"As a long-winged hawk, when he is first whistled off the
fist mounts aloft," said he, "and for his pleasure fetcheth many
a circuit in the air . . . so will I." I will first see what be "the
true cause of the variation of the compass. . . . Whether the sea
be open and navigable by the Pole Arctic. . . . Whether Guinea
be an island or part of the continent . . . I would see those inner
parts of America. . . . I would know for a certain whether
there be any such men" as those described by the more imaginative voyagers. "I would examine the true seat of that
terrestrial paradise, and where Ophir was, whence Solomon
did fetch his gold." I would ask, "how come they to dig up
fish-bones, shells, beams, iron-works, many fathoms under-
ground, and anchors in mountains far remote from all seas?
. . . Came this from earthquakes, or from Noah's flood, as
Christians suppose? or is there a vicissitude of sea and land?"

Having stated a few of the problems put by the heavens, the
earth, the oceans, and the array of animal forms, Burton
turned then to that puzzle of puzzles, man himself. I would
try to find out, he continued, "whence proceed that variety of
manners, and a distinct character (as it were) to several
nations?" Borrowing the diction of Bartholomew, "some are
wise, subtile, witty; others dull, sad, heavy; . . . some soft, some
hardy, barbarous, civil, black, dun, white." Borrowing a query

from Montaigne, "How comes it to pass . . . that people separated only by a river or a mountain are dissimilar?" Who can give a reason for this strange diversity?[21]

Of course, the problem of ethnic differentiation which Burton, a physician to men's minds, formulated with such clarity and power, was hardly a new one. It had been stated and restated, solved and re-solved, since Palestinian and Greek antiquity. Renaissance scholarship was thus, as a result, the legatee of two hypotheses. One of these was Biblical, the other secular; and both, to a greater or lesser degree, were framed in accord with the universal respect always paid to historical or genetic types of explanation. That is to say, enlightenment concerning the unintelligible cultural composition of the present was to be sought by a long, hard look at the past, either under the guidance of the first eleven chapters of the Book of Genesis, or in the historico-environmental terms suggested by some of the classical philosophers, and restated by the French historian Jean Bodin.

The dilemma for both Christians and their critics was inseparable from the question of which solution had the greater validity; and out of that dilemma arose uncertainty and endless controversy.

Apart from the environmental explanation, of course, there could be but two general solutions to the problem posed by the recognition of cultural diversification, or by the observation of differences among the usages by which human groups, so like physically, had conducted their several lives. One was monogenetic, and to that extent in conformity with the historical position adopted by Moses. The other was polygenetic, heretical, and in conflict with Genesis.

According to the monogenetic hypothesis proposed in Genesis (and accepted knowingly or unknowingly by all anthropologists who latterly have espoused some form of cultural developmentalism or evolutionism). mankind in the beginning was the creature of a single creative act, at a single moment in time, and at a single spot on the earth's surface. Of one blood and one inheritance, he was therefore physically, ethnically, and socially homogeneous. Diversity, his present condition, was something that had come upon him. It had supervened, regrettably, at some moment or moments in time subsequent to his first terrestrial appearance. According to the polygenetic theory, on the other hand (out of bounds logically for the developmentalist or evolutionist), mankind was the outcome of plural creative acts, at plural moments in time, and at plural geographical stations. Conceivably, therefore, he might always have been as he was, or as observed and describable during the Renaissance—split physically and culturally into an unknown number of varieties. Or again, if changes had supervened in past time, one array of diversities might have been replaced by another, once, twice, or unnumbered times. At all events, according to this heretical hypothesis, diversity in manners had been the rule from the very beginning of things.

For many Renaissance scholars social theory at this point came to a dead stop. Once a side had been chosen in the controversy, there was little inclination to consider the possibility of alternative hypotheses, to weigh original assumptions, or to pursue logically remote and disconcerting consequences. For those who accepted the first eleven chapters of Genesis with childlike faith, and there were many of them, discussion was superfluous. One might elaborate reverently and imaginatively on the events related there, but they could not be questioned. For those, on the contrary, who took a critical course, an initial choice of the congenial, more orthodox hypothesis became merely a first step in the recognition of historical difficulties unsolved in the sacred text, and therefore the incentive for inferring events not included by its Mosaic author. For if the monogenetic theory were granted, if it were assumed out of hand that diversity had descended upon mankind after a primeval interval of cultural uniformity, then it still became imperative to explore the past and to indicate, with more precision than Moses had ever deemed necessary, just when and under what circumstances original uniformity had broken down into existing multiformity.

To those who chose the polygenetic solution, there were similar difficulties to be faced. For if it could be demonstrated that the existing array of cultural diversities differed from some other earlier array (thus indicating changes in past time) another intellectual predicament was begotten. It then became necessary, in order to spell out an explanation of such changes, first, to present descriptively for study a minimum of at least two universal arrays of differentiated cultures, one existing in the present (and thus forming the problem) and a preceding one (no small assignment); and second, to indicate at least theoretically, or by hypothesis, how and under what circumstances the later and present array came to be different from the earlier and preceding array. Although this partial inquiry, composed of only two arrays, would still be far from solving the problem statable as "How do cultural differences come to be what they are?", it would be a small start. Furthermore, it would give substance to the assertion that both monogenists and polygenists were compelled to appeal to the past, to find solutions of their problem in the past, to consult the historical record, to resort to historical documentation. Put baldly, the acceptability of either hypothesis, the Biblical or the secular, turned, during the Renaissance upon the fullness, antiquity, and reliability of the documentation employed; upon the legitimacy and precision of the intellectual devices or conceptual expedients adopted to overcome inevitable historical gaps; and upon the inevitable scantiness or absence of documentary evidence.

Opinion or belief being what it was, it need not be emphasized here that the Scriptural solution was the dominant one, both because it was orthodox and because, as the focus of critical, "atheistic" comment, it became the point of departure for presumably sounder alternatives. So universally accepted were the historical assumptions entertained by Moses and the details of his historical recovery, so strong was the traditional position of the account in Genesis, that even convinced environmentalists seldom failed to include some part of his reconstruction in their own explanations of how things came to be what they were. Divine will, said Jean Bodin respectfully, "led Moses to write about origins . . . that all men whom his story might reach should understand clearly that they are of the same blood and allied by the same bond of race."[22] All who concerned themselves intellectually with the manners and customs of mankind were in some measure defenders of the Judeo-Christian formula. The chilly logic of strict environmentalism had little to offer such men as Boemus, Purchas, and Heylyn, or even Ralegh. However much attention they gave to the new and popular science of geography, human destiny was regarded generally as the product, not of anonymous, blind natural forces, but of willing, acting individuals, known well by their names and deeds. For all, whether they were orthodox or fashionably heterodox, whether they were fighters for the faith or contenders in the lists of the critical "atheists," it was the Bible—and in the Bible the first eleven chapters of Genesis—that held the lost key to the lost lock of the cultural riddle.

As for the monogentic and Scriptural solution, it was plain to anyone who stopped to think about the matter that the substance and spirit of the Book of Genesis were historical. That is to say, the solution of the problem of human differences, as imparted by Moses, or other nameless historians, was not only monogenetic in intent but its monogenism was embedded in a genealogical context dictated by that extremely ancient and persistent form of explanatory thought. It was assumed that the world, as Moses knew it, with its array of differing peoples, tribes, nations, or cultures, could be best understood in terms of the past; if its past were recovered; and if the recovery were accomplished on the ancient conceptual model employed in genealogy. It was assumed that the members of the initial hexameral series of episodes, followed by the equally well-known series of subsequent Scriptural events (a succession which formed the backbone of the first eleven chapters of the sacred historical narrative), were related to one another as the human members of a succession of generations.[23] Concerned also with major demographic episodes, the monogenetic hypothesis was developed in part by means of a sequence of population phenomena : beginning with the origin of man, continuing with the first peopling of the world, its depopulation, and its re-peopling.

One of the greatest attractions of the earlier historical chapters of Genesis lay in the fact that they related what had happened in human and historical, or familiar genealogical, terms. Teeming with major and minor incidents and characters, terse in some spots, diffuse in others, Moses, in his role as historian, filled an aching void between an undecipherable past and a confusing present. Here in the familiar setting of an ancient conceptual model, and in a style at once austere, simple, and humane, the answer to the perplexing problem of mankind's diversity was written in precise, colorful, and above all dramatic detail. Some might disagree on the meaning of a word, a phrase, a verse—and they did. Some might add glosses and interpretations gleaned from an ever-growing library of Commentaries on the Bible—and they did. Indeed, by the time the first collection of manners had been made, Genesis meant not the Book alone, but the Book plus all its commentators.[24] Nevertheless, as shown by Purchas' *Pilgrimage,* Grafton's

Chronicles, Ralegh's *History of the world,* and every other inquiry which, at that time, took mankind as its object of interest, no one embarked upon a substantial piece of work in which the problem of cultural diversity was at issue without taking into account both Genesis and the commentators on Genesis. But with all its encrustations of Western legend and imagery incompatible with the Book's Near Eastern provenance, the Mosaic hypothesis still satisfied. It satisfied a craving to know something not only of man's earliest condition but of the conditions which followed. Within this familiar framework the first step in the historical solution of the problem of cultural differences was made in hexameral terms. The creation of the physical universe and the origin of man was delivered in a philosophy of history composed of six time units, designated as "days," the advent of each new condition, or "day," being contingent, like each new generation, upon the prior appearance and maturation of the one just preceding.

The second step in the solution, beginning with man's creation on the sixth "day," fell into a more conventional, but still genetic, mode of historical narration. "Days" were replaced by events, and events were consummated either by God or by human and willful actors. Actors, actions, and events were selected and combined to elucidate the earliest condition of man as he was set down in a garden planted with beautiful trees and watered by a river of four branches. Then after the Fall, a first essential element in the explanation of the onset of cultural diversity, came the narration of the first peopling of the world, its subsequent depopulation, and final repeopling. And accompanying these accounts were other hints or statements concerning the origin of the family, the institution of marriage, polygamy, agriculture, pastoralism, nomadism, the arts, the nations and cultures.

As for the demographic episodes[25] leading up to the final

diversification of mankind, the Mosaic account relates that the earth was stocked with human beings on two separate occasions, each time with the seed of Adam. But it also makes clear that the homogeneity of the original culture, due to its monogenetic heritage, was thrice breached : once by Cain and his posterity, again by the descendants of the sons of Noah, and once again at Babel; each episode being accompanied by periods of prolonged human migration, mingling, cultural diffusion, and degeneration.

That great demographic episode, the first peopling of the world, occurred after important preceding events, namely, the creation of Adam and Eve, the Fall, the expulsion from the garden (when, for the first time, the "Adamic culture" was carried or diffused outside its original precincts), the births of Cain and Abel, and the fratricide. In punishment for the fratricide, Cain was exiled by the Eternal to the Land of Nod east of Eden (still farther away from the original home of the first homogeneous or "Adamic culture"). There he became not only a cultureless wanderer and vagabond, but also (a break with the original monogamy) the husband of plural wives, the forefather of many generations of offspring for whom he built the first city, the ancestor of shepherds who lived in tents, the progenitor of musicians who played on the lyre and pipe and of inventors who forged the first bronze and iron tools.

The second peopling followed the Deluge and was the ultimate result of a dispersion after the recession of the waters. When Cain's posterity had multiplied all over the world, their wickedness increasing as their numbers mounted, the patience of the Eternal became exhausted. Noah was instructed to build an Ark. A Flood was sent to destroy the evildoers and all their works. When the waters receded, the only souls left on the soggy planet were a little company of eight—Noah, his wife, his three sons and their wives. In this demographic emergency, "God blessed Noah and his sons, bidding them,

'Be fruitful and multiply and replenish the earth . . . breed freely on earth and subdue it.' " According to Moses, in one of his more laconic genealogical passages, the nations descending from Japheth were the Cimmerians, Magog, the Medes, the Ionians, Tubal, Meshek, Tiras, and others; those from Ham, the Ethiopians, Egyptians, Put, Canaan, and their descendants; and those from Shem, the Elamites, the Assyrians, Apachshad, the Lydians, Aram, and their descendants.

But in the eleventh chapter of Genesis another narrative of the dispersion of mankind is offered, possibly to account for cleavages even wider and deeper than the national or tribal. For "when the whole earth was one language and one vocabulary," and when man, becoming presumptuous, proposed to build a city with a tower reaching into Heaven, the Lord was again displeased. "Down came the Eternal to see the city and the tower which human beings had built. 'They are one people,' said the Eternal, 'and they have one language; if this is what they do, to start with, nothing that they undertake will prove too hard for them. Come, let us go down and make a babble of their language on the spot, so that they cannot understand one another's speech.' " And forthwith the men, their languages, and their ambitions were scattered "all over the wide earth."

This, in essence, was the Scriptural solution of the problem of cultural differences. After two peoplings of the earth, after three ruptures of the uniformity of the original and uniform Adamic culture, after the migrations of founders of nations to their several geographical stations, diversity accompanied by degeneration supervened. Since the details vouchsafed by the author of Genesis are often meager, especially with reference to Cain's wanderings and marital adventures, and with reference also to the migrations of the progeny of Noah to their final homelands, and since diversity was directly ascribable to these neglected areas of the narrative, Renaissance authors and commentators exhausted themselves in filling in gaps or trying to infer what really happened. Much of what later became known as the theory of diffusion was evolved in the course of these imaginative flights. Meanwhile, despite Cain's exogamous alliances with the "daughters of men," cultural diversity was usually traced to one source, the sons of Noah and their experiences during the dispersion.

Though the account in the Book of Genesis was generally accepted among European men of learning in the sixteenth and seventeenth centuries, and with it the monogenetic hypothesis, there was some revision of the interpretation of its contemporary ethnological meaning. In the age of faith, or while the medieval population was small, cultural diversification, in so far as it was known to most men, had been restricted geographically to the shores of the Mediterranean, to the vaguely rumored tribes of northern Europe, and to a few of the inhabitants of the Near and Far East, known largely through Mandeville or other purveyors of legend and fable. To account for this small human sample, the Biblical story of the Noachian dispersion, with its short muster roll of tribes and empires mentioned as the posterity of the three brothers, seemed circumstantial enough. The list of nations said to have emerged here and there in this narrow geographical realm possessed the finality and certitude of the familiar.

But as geographical knowledge, combined with Biblical criticism, began its work upon the intimate fabric of the Book of Genesis, the unrevised sacred history no longer seemed inviolate or universally satisfying. There were not only the Commentaries to be reckoned with; there were also the "impudent atheists." The latter questioned everything: the universality of the Flood, the sources of the Flood waters, their final disposition, the numbers and kinds of animals on the Ark, the adequacy of their supply of food and water, the distribution of the progeny of Noah—everything which gave substance and certainty to this part of the sacred solution of the problem of differences.

Moreover, during these crucial years of the sixteenth and seventeenth centuries, the world no longer remained small or stable. Old and long-remembered peoples with their familiar national cultures had refused to stay put in old and well-known habitats. Uprooted by circumstances, they had chosen rather to creep or pour over ancient boundaries. Peoples new to Bible readers were discovered. Human behavior shocking to those acquainted with the Old Testament was revealed. By the time the crusades were over and the explorations under way, the sum of the national or cultural groups known to Christendom had increased several fold. Some of the newer "nations," such as the German, were extremely hard to fit into the select company of the posterity of Noah. Who was there to endow them with reputable Noachian forefathers? Where were sound genealogies to be found? Still more difficult were the savages of Africa and the Americas. For them, there seemed to be no conceivable Scriptural precedent, and many of the efforts to insert these newcomers into the Adamic lineage were ludicrous in the extreme.

Of course, as always when some breach in a conventional pattern of belief is threatened, Renaissance revisions of the Biblical tradition were met by different scholars in different ways. Some, the better to meet the enemy with a solid front, insisted upon the irrefutable validity of the older system of theology and ethnological explanation. There were others, however, who sought to ignore unpalatable alternatives. They acknowledged reasonable doubt but, preferring to shepherd their thoughts along comfortable channels, recoiled from the burdens of decision. Only a few, though always subjected to abuse and calumny, went out of their way to welcome critical activity and to attempt a reconciliation between the sacred history and recently available ethnological fact.

The details of this critical adjustment, on the part of those willing to make it, were extremely complex. To elucidate them completely, to deal with the reconciliation of all old ethnological ideas with new ones, would require a tedious review of the total literature of the period, theological, geographical, economic, and imaginative. Fortunately, some insight into the working of men's minds may be obtained by dealing with a few examples: with the early collector, Boemus; with the theologian and collector of religions, Purchas; with the historian, Grafton; with the geographer, Heylyn; and finally with that man of many parts, Sir Walter Ralegh, and his redoubtable contemporary, Bishop Stillingfleet.

As for Johann Boemus, the author of the *Omnium gentium mores* (1520), translated in 1555 as the *Fardle of façions,* one cannot read far without realizing that his collection of "the most famous and memorable lawes, customes, and manners" raised serious questions. Statements in the book make it evident that his security in the inerrancy of the Bible had been rudely shaken by prevailing criticism. It was impossible for him to collect the customs of mankind without being confounded by their diversity. It was impossible for him to consider the problem of ethnological diversity as though Genesis had never been written. Yet, it is plain throughout that the Biblical solution was not enough. He was a reader of the Commentaries. Materials from these, as well as from legendary sources, were used freely in his exposition.

Before he could get under way with the description of various groups of men and their customs, he was compelled to account for them genetically: to recover "mans originall"; to locate the "begynnyne" of mankind in historical time and geographical space; to surround him with a cosmography and ground him in history. For a churchman this was not hard.

With only momentary hesitation Boemus committed himself, at least formally, to monogenetic doctrine. And here his argument falls into the usual hexameral pattern, but the hexameral pattern submitted to modification. That is to say, with the appearance of man, the first series of six stages (or "days") is succeeded by three, a triadic concept of human history which was to serve as the basis of much later social theory, down to and including Auguste Comte, Karl Marx, and many other nineteenth- and twentieth-century sociologists. Beginning with Adam and Eve, man was said to have traversed three periods. The first was characterized by incivility but enjoyed in Paradise without "blemish of wo"; the second was a period of evil, corruption, and conflict; and the third, a period of civility.

Like all such philosophies of history, then and later, more ink was usually spilled on the description of the traditional and historically undocumented first or original stage than on either of the others. It was reconstructed by an appeal to Scripture and a floating stock of the fabulous. Improving on Genesis men were said to live

under the open heaven, the coverte of some shadowie tree, or slendre houselle, with such companion or companions as siemed them good, their diere babes and children aboute them. Sounde without carcke and in restfull quietnesse, eatyng the fruictes of the fielde, and the milke of the cattle, and drinking the waters of the christalline springes. First clad with the softe barcke of trees, or the faire broade leaves, & in processe with rawe felle and hide, full unworkemanly patched together . . . Mery at the fulle, as without knowledge of the evillesy.

But as the world grew older, ways were changed. Discontent entered Paradise. A rough pattern of towns and cities made its appearance "with divers inventions and handicraftes and science." Now also began an attempt "to transplante their progenie, and offspring into places unenhabited, and to enjoye the commodities of each others countrie, by mutuall traffique."[26]

Though Boemus approached the problem of diversity in a Biblical spirit, as one of the concomitants of the intrusion of evil, evil, in his view of things, intruded not twice or thrice, as is declared in Genesis, but only once, when the waters of the Flood had subsided, and when Noah "dispersed his yssue and kindredes," possessed of a common biological inheritance and a common culture, to "sondrie Coastes."[27] Moreover, according to his reworking of the Scriptural narrative, it was Ham, a son of Noah, not Cain, who severed the Adamic bond. It was he who vanished into Arabia, and there left "no trade of religion to his posteritie, because he had none learned of his father." Then, as time passed and the numbers of the people "increased to to many for that land," many other parties were sent out "swarme after swarme into other habitations"; some, like those who accompanied Ham, falling into error from which they never could "unsnarl" themselves. During these migrations, even the language was altered, "and knowledge of the true God and all godlie worshippe vanished out of mind"; so that in the end those who went to Egypt founded the worship of the sun and moon, while many others became so uncivil and barbarous "as hardly any difference be discerned between them and brute beasts." Boemus makes it clear that either historical accident or divine judgment— whichever had imposed the sentence of the Deluge—had also decreed the dispersion of plants, animals, and man over great distances after the recession of the waters. Distance, weakening the slender threads of memory and the process of transmission "of minde to minde without Letters," led to the decline of ancient institutions. With this process of degeneration, a state of barbarism descended upon the sons of Ham, and the culture of men was divided into two categories, the civil and the uncivil, the advanced and the barbarous. Shem and Japheth, on the other hand, having been lawfully instructed by their parents and elders, and content to stay put, or "to live on their own limits," handed on the Adamic tradition to their children and their children's children. They worshiped "according to the older way," a fact which explains, says Boemus, why the true God "remained hidden in one onely people untill the tyme of Messias."

But despite all this orthodoxy, there were moments when the monogenist in Johann Boemus yielded to an alternative doctrine. While he refrained from adopting a theory of multiple human creations, with its corollary of original cultural diversification, he allowed himself on more than one occasion to deviate radically from the Mosaic solution. For example, he can be discovered installing the "first men" in at least two different regions. In conformity with certain classical habits of thought, they were set down in Ethiopia, where the gods were "first honoured," and sacred ceremonies ordained. Then, in deference to Scriptural historiography, he tells us of a people who resided in Judea and who "onely of all other may challenge the honour of Auncientie . . . as beinge of all other firste . . . the people that was mother of letters, and sciences." In addition, China was also considered a possible site of the origination of mankind because people still dwelt there who were "as it ware in the beginnyng, or entryng of the world."[28]

Manifestly, in this dual or triple implantation of the race, Boemus appears less the advocate of a theory of plural creations than the victim of that intellectual conflict which afflicts any transitional generation. Or, since during the earlier Renaissance many men could not make up *their* minds on this and related questions, he stands as an example of that uncertainty. The alternatives are emphasized in the first two chapters of the *Fardle of façions,* entitled "The true opinion of Divines concerning mans originall," and the "The false opinion of the Ethnicks concerning mans originall."

When Samuel Purchas took up his pen, in 1613, to write

the concluding words of his monumental work on the diversity
of religions in the world, almost a century had passed since
Boemus had published the *Omnium gentium mores*. Meanwhile, much had changed in the intellectual environment of
European men of letters. The increase in geographical and
ethnological knowledge had been enormous. Consequently,
this chaplain to the Archbishop of Canterbury was a far more
sophisticated man than his German predecessor. He knew of
the existence in Europe, Asia, Africa, and the Americas, of
peoples Boemus had never heard of. Moreover, prosy though
he was, he possessed an erratic streak of originality. The task
undertaken in *Purchas his pilgrimage* was unusual to the point
of extravagance. No one before him had ever attempted anything like it. King James is said to have read it through seven
times. Nevertheless, the encyclopedic and world-historical plan
of the book, together with his calling as a divine, made certain
demands with respect to its setting and organization. From a
clergyman, it required without fail a conventional introduction, composed of a résumé of the events recounted in the first
eleven chapters of Genesis, similar to that appearing at the
time in nearly all historical enterprises of ecumenical dimensions. In addition, it was necessary to offer some explanation
for the existing and appalling diversity of religion which had
replaced its original and Adamic uniformity.

Purchas was not a man to break sharply with conventional
theology. His recapitulation of the first episodes of the Mosaic
story proceeds with prolixity, but without radical heterodoxy,
unless literary embroidery be considered un-Scriptural. In the
garden, where our first parents took their pleasure strolling
along "enamelled walkes," the rivers "ranne to present their
best offices to their new Lords, from which they were forced
by the backer streames, greedie of the sight and place which
they could not hold : The Trees stouped down to behold them,
offering their shadie mantle and varietie of fruits . . . each

creature in a silent gladnesse rejoyced in them." After this poetic amendment of Genesis 2, the author passed on to the crisis precipitated by the headstrong Cain. His versatility in the arts is mentioned, as is also the multiplication of his family "in numbers, sciences, and wickednes." There are also details about "the sons and daughters of men,"; about their fathering of giants, and their skill as makers of swords, weapons of war, and jewelry to adorn their women. When all had become as bad as it could be, the Lord intervened to acquaint Noah with His plan for the approaching end.

Concerning other details of the Mosaic narrative, however, Purchas was compelled, like Boemus, to confess difficulty. On the Ark and its dimensions, elementary arithmetic had already done its unnerving work. "Divers doubts have been moved," said he darkly, "through curiosity and unbeleefe" by those who have "lost their conscience and their Religion." But active curiosity and unbelief were not for him. He refused to engage in a controversy over a trivial matter which had already shed more heat than light. "I holde it not meete that a few conjectures should counterpoise the generall consent of all the ages." If the author of Genesis had erred, it could not have been on the major historical facts, but only in his mode of presentation. He might have been too concise.

On another important matter, however, the repeopling of the world after the Flood, Purchas found himself in more serious trouble. "To shew directly," he acknowledged with pain, which nation descended from which of the three sons of Noah "was a hard task : and now after this confusion of Nations by wars, leagues, and otherwise, impossible." What follows in the *Pilgrimage,* therefore, is a revised version of the Scriptural account, three pages long, derived from the Commentators. Of the origins or ancestors of peoples, said Purchas unhappily, "wee have probable conjectures, not certaine proofs, as appeareth by the difference of opinions of Authors concerning them." Nor could he find a way to let himself say that Moses had written "a Geographicall Historie of all the Nations of the World." For many of them known to Purchas had been "planted" after Moses' time. He could say much, he acknowledged, touching the several nations descended immediately from Noah's three sons, or near the point of dispersal, or touching the bounds of their habitations, "but the uncertainty maketh me unwilling to proceed in this argument further." To this extent, he was compelled patently against his will, to join with the so-called Renaissance "atheists" or higher critics.

On the problem of diversity in religion he was even less at ease. Reasonably clear for his day on the facts of religious difference, he either failed to sense the overarching importance of the problem or refused to grapple with it in carefully organized argument. Though religion, in his opinion, was written on the hearts of men, it had become corrupted by sin. But not by the sin of our first parents. Rather it was Cain who had initiated the first divisive impiety when he departed from "the visible society of the Church, cradled yet in his father's household."[29] Later, one of Noah's sons became a second source of disruption. Shem was a loyal propagator of the true religion; so also was Japhet. But Ham was the author of ruin, for it was he and his posterity who "began to divine by Starres, and to sacrifice children by Fire."

Both Richard Grafton (d. 1572) and Peter Heylyn (1599–1662)—to mention only one important sixteenth-century historian and one geographer-ethnologist—also made use of the Bible, but with the help of the Commentators, and to a certain extent in response to convention rather than firm belief. Their treatments of the Biblical episodes are formal, cursory, and attenuated, appearing in the introductions to their books as a thing customary and proper rather than as the result of logical or historical necessity; and they emphasize features of the Biblical account which reflect current economic interests.

In Grafton's *Chronicle* of England, written in 1559 and planned to run from the creation to "the firste yere of the reigne of our most deere and sovereigne Lady Queene Elizabeth," fourteen hundred pages were needed to complete the history of the one nation; less than thirty to lay out the conventional and Biblical history of the world. Like many historians of his time, furthermore, Grafton was susceptible to the charms of some of the more colorful legendary accretions to Scripture which had been made available by fable-mongers and the Commentaries—especially those which contained demographical or technological supplements to Genesis. Thus Cain and Abel were presented with twin sisters, and these feminine siblings became obvious historiographical assets when, with the purportedly concurrent relaxation of the laws relating to the marriage of near kindred, the peopling of the earth had to be accomplished within what Grafton regarded as a reasonable span of time. Cain's function as an originator of the arts, treated with so much reserve in Genesis, was also elaborated in the *Chronicle*. "This Cain," Grafton said, in tune with the Tudor awakening of interest in technological advancement,

Was a great toyler and moyler in the earth, but very covetous and full of malice withall, at the prosperitie of any other. . . . For that cause he . . . sought out by his wicked imagination the Mathematicall artes. And although he found in that travaile great vexation of mynd, and businesse, yet as the paine ceassed not, so did not his avaricious covetous and greedye desire cease, by rapyne, spoyle, or by any other wicked meane to attaine to treasure and ryches . . . Of the which mischiefes he was a most chiefe and principall doctor. Also he altered and chaunged the honest and simple doings that before tyme had bene used by honest and good men in their exchaunges and traffiques, and caused all things to be done by weyghts and measures, and brought in craft and corruption.[30]

Peter Heylyn's *Cosmographie* is notable for its orderly and businesslike construction, some of which may have been acquired by practice. For the book, first issued as a small volume, became larger and larger with many editions. Here again, as in the work of Grafton, the argument opens with an interpretation of the economic and commercial features of the Mosaic narrative. Responding, no doubt, to the influence of an expanding colonial economy, Heylyn dwelt at length upon the contrast between the first and second peoplings of the earth. During the episode of the first distribution of population, accomplished by Cain's posterity, man is presented as naturally destitute of all talents and capacities except the inward faculties of judgment, wit, and understanding. These, said Heylyn, he used to furnish himself with all that he needed in his new surroundings. "For hereunto the first original of all Manufacture and mechanic Arts is to be referred, as is most plain and evident in the Book of God." In the first division of labor, "Abel betooke himselfe into keeping sheepe, and Cain to husbandry; Jubal to handle the Harp, Organ, and such Musical Instruments; and Tubal-Cain to work upon brass and Iron, two metals very necessary to moste kinde of Trades. The like may be supposed in all Mysteries and Arts of living, though there be no express mention of them in those early dayes. . . . God made the World and fitted it with all things necessary for the life of man, leaving man to provide himself with such Additions, as rather serve for comforts and conveniencies in the way of his living. . . ." But for Heylyn and his readers, God, the Economist, also provided something else, namely "that most admirable intermixture of Want and Plenty," whereby he united all parts of the world in continual traffic and commerce. "Something there is," said Heylyn, "in every Countrey, which may be spared to supply the defect of others." Quoting from Du Bartas, he reminded his readers that

Hence come our Sugars from the Canary Isles,
From Candie, Currans, Muscadels, and Oyls.
From the Moluccoes, spices; Balsamum
From Egypt; Odours from Arabia come
Indique, Gums, rich Drugs, and Ivory.

Having thus imaginatively reconstructed pre-Flood trade and technology in the light of the mercantilist theory of economics, Heylyn then turned to a related subject, the growth of population, an interest which he shared with such men as Petty, Graunt, and Sir Matthew Hale. How large did the company of Cain's posterity become before the Flood? How densely was the earth peopled when the wrath of God descended? How quickly had the pre-Flood distribution of men, women and children, taken place in comparison with the post-Flood dispersion and repeopling? What were the comparative rates of migration? Every syllable in the few short verses in Genesis dealing with these matters, together with their inferences and implications, was pressed into service to yield the kind of information needed by seventeenth-century colonizers and entrepreneurs.

Heylyn took his stand on a theory of a fully peopled earth of five or six continents prior to the Deluge: else why the universality of the sea of waters? Besides (and here all sorts of "proofs" are offered), so great was the rate of increase in population that families were driven by necessity to seek out new dwellings for their children. What necessity had wrought in the Adamic period over a long tract of pre-Flood time was repeated in the second dispersion after the Deluge, but at an accelerated rate. Nevertheless, the remoter plantations were not made, nor were colonies founded, until population aggregates near the center had been completed. "It being in Plantations of Men, as in that of Bees, amongst whom one swarm sends out another, that begets a Castling, till the whole ground or Garden grow too small to hold them." The dis-person was also associated in Heylyn's mind with cultural change not unallied with geographical determinism. "It came to passe," said he, "that though they were all descended from one common Root, yet by the situations of their severall dwellings, they came to be of severall tempers and affections; in which they were so different from one another; that it might seem they had been made at first out of severall Principles, and not all derived from one common Parent."[31] Thus, though both Grafton and Heylyn occasionally used the framework of Scriptural history as a convenience in making known some of their own views of the history of economic phenomena, neither took issue with the major episodes related in Genesis. They resisted the inclusion of material that might have been considered outright atheism; and they included in their treatment of the problem of cultural differences the usual and repetitious lists of nations descended from the sons of Noah.

But all in all, Sir Walter Ralegh (1552–1618) and the Reverend Edward Stillingfleet (1635–1699) are probably better examples of the influence of Biblical ethnological theory upon Renaissance social thought, and the forces operating to liberalize it, than either Boemus or Purchas, Heylyn or Grafton. Both of these men were made of sterner stuff. They were more aware of the threat to Mosaic doctrine contained in the proliferation of secular expositions and interpretations. They were more on the defensive and more able controversialists. They were also both staunch defenders of orthodoxy, the one an Elizabethan adventurer and statesman, the other a bishop skilled in the polemics of theology and historiography. But the Bishop's faith was never questioned, whereas the adventurer was sometimes branded as an atheist.

One reason for the indictment of Ralegh's orthodoxy grew out of the very exploits which had sharpened his knowledge of the world and its inhabitants. His sea-faring experiences had left him prepared to form judgments on both geographical and ethnological questions in the Old Testament which were far more informed than many, and hence destined to startle the timid. The first five or six chapters of the *History* were also based on wide reading in secondary and tertiary materials certain to impress his readers with the vastness and complexity of these problems. Then, too, although many of his fellows considered the marginal datings in Genesis to be as sound and inviolable as the text itself, Ralegh chose to follow his historical bent wherever it led, even on to the quicksands of Biblical chronology; and when the compact style of Genesis, a book written by an ancient Hebrew for the ancient Hebrews, became an obstacle to the understanding of seventeenth-century Englishmen, when the laconic phrases of Moses failed to preserve important ancient detail, Ralegh turned to another avenue of documentation. This was the assumption of the uniformity of the human mind and the likeness therefore of past to present historical processes. Armed with the historiographical supposition that men in the earliest epochs of the sacred history, and men who were his European contemporaries in the seventeenth-century, were moved by similar motives to similar actions with similar results (or assuming that the unknown or scantily documented past, usually considered irrecoverable, could be partially reconstructed by observing the human present), Ralegh took the radical step of appealing to his conception of recent European experience to illuminate the past of the earliest Hebrews.

Ralegh's *History of the world* (1614) is especially instructive on questions relating to the history of ethnological ideas and their modifications because, as a universal history, the leading role in the cast of characters is taken by a collective person, man; and the author thus confronts the same geographical and demographic problems which had tried the powers of the author or authors of Genesis and all subsequent commentators. Before he could get under way as the biographer of the later career of all the people in the world, or World History, he was compelled to place this collective person, his hero, on the world stage; to increase his numbers and get his posterity spread about. With that accomplished, he had then to separate nation from nation, language from language, and culture from culture, in a way which accorded both with the earliest Hebrew records and with the existing seventeenth-century distribution.

Some estimate of his orthodoxy, his ethnological theory, and the influence on both of his interest in careful geographical discrimination may be formed by noting his concern over the true location of Paradise. Not, of course, that this element in monogenetic social theory had ever suffered from neglect. Far from it. The precise determination of the spot upon which man had first seen the light and enjoyed the first few years of human felicity—the locality from which Cain had wandered to found a city and father a brood; the region, according to some, from which the sons of Noah began their migrations— was far too important to have been overlooked by earlier Commentators.[32] But Ralegh chose to examine the matter again with unusual care. Desiring to make an end to ridiculous guesses he regarded it as necessary to discover the location of Eden. "For by knowing this place we shall be the better judge of the beginning of Nations, and of the worlds inhabitation : for neere unto this did the Sons of Noah also disperse them- selves after the floud, into all other remote regions and countries . . . from whence all the streames and branches of Mankind have followed and bin deduced."[33]

However, it was when the geographer joined with the historian in Ralegh that he became especially interesting. For it was then that he attempted to dispel some of the difficulties created by the stylistic reserve of the Mosaic account by calling upon documentation derived from contemporary geographical or human experience. One illustration of his reconstruction of the past by this means, or more technically by appealing to presently operating processes, may be found in his commentary on Genesis 4 : 17. Here the reader is informed without further amplification that "Cain built a town and called it after his son Hanok."

Note that the only Scriptural documentation for this pristine exhibition of civic enterprise, this Biblical theory of the origin of urbanization in human settlement is one short declarative sentence. But one short sentence was not enough to satisfy all minds. Even the apprentice skeptic took pleasure in asking how it was possible for Cain, with no assistance other than that of his son, "to performe such a Worke as the building of a City, seeing there is thereto required so many hands and so great a Masse of all sorts of Materials?" To which Ralegh made reply that if here the Hebrew historian was tight-lipped, if we find "that of Cain . . . Moses useth no ample declaration," that he had no impulse to record the births, the numbers, or the ages of Cain's other issue, and hence his helpers in city building—it was not to be marveled at. The old chronicler knew that he was writing for reasonable men. Reasonable men, had only to recall the existing facts of city building, to reckon up the probable length of time presently consumed in so large an undertaking, and to estimate, judging by contemporary experience, the number of workers, their fertility, and the volume of materials needed. Moses was blameless. No historian, even the oldest and greatest, could be expected to mention everything.[34]

But Ralegh relaxed at times in his effort to put the burden of interpretation of the Mosaic past wholly upon the shoulders of the readers of Genesis. For when he came later to a discussion of the Noachian dispersion, he himself showed a fine feeling for the tracts of time required for the completion of great historical processes, and a sensitive apprehension of the meaning in human experience of geographical distance. To him, as also to Peter Heylyn, the rates of demographic phen-

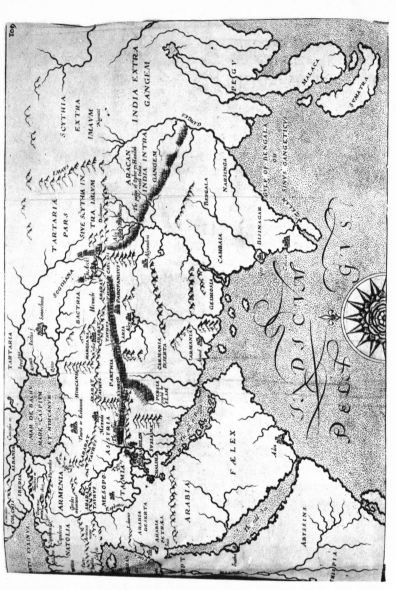

The dispersion from the Ark, according to The History of the World (1634) by Sir Walter Raleigh

omena were of absorbing interest. On a proper evaluation of
the time it took to people the world after the Deluge depended
the logical reliability of the Mosaic account. He suggested
therefore that in the newness of a world, just drying out, and
"wanting instruments and materials," the overland movements
of peoples would not only be controlled by geographical conditions but would be slow in pace. "The world after the Flood
was not planted by imagination," said he: "neither had the
children of Noah wings to flie from Shinaar to the uttermost
border of Europe, Africa, and Asia, in haste." Light believers
were advised to recall that post-Flood migrations covered
uncounted generations and traversed all kinds of terrain, rough
and smooth. Knowing what we do of the climates and topography of the world today, said he (recurring to his argument
from present processes), "we must call to minde and consider,
what manner of face the earth every where had in the 130.
yeere after the great inundation, and by comparing those
fruitfullest Vallies, with our own barren and cold ground,
informe ourselves thereby, what wonderful Desarts, what im-
passable fastnesse of woods, reeds, bryars, and rotten grasse,
what Lakes, and standing Pooles, and what Marishes, Fens,
and Bogs, all the face of the earth (excepting the Mountaines)
was pestered withall." It was over such exhausting terrain that
the migrations had to take place. "Let all men of judgement
weigh with themselves how impossible it was for a Nation or
Family of Men, with their Wives, and Children, and Cattell,
to travel 3000. miles through Woods, Bogs, and Desarts,
without any guide or conductor"; and they will find it "rather
a Worke of 100. years than of 100. dayes." Let reasonable men
try to imagine "what it was to travaile farre in such a forrest
as the Worlde was . . . and wherein there could hardly be
found either part or passage through which men were able to
creepe."[36] Drawing on his knowledge of the New World, the
routes taken by the migrants, said Ralegh, might well be like

those in the West Indies, "of which the Spaniards have the experience, in those places where they found neither Path nor Guide," and where they could not make ten miles in ten years. To clarify some of the conditions under which the Noachian migrations were conducted, Ralegh offered a map showing one train of colonists moving off west from the Ark on Ararat in Chaldea, and another moving east toward the Ganges. Then he turned to the accustomed enumeration of the posterity of Noah's sons and the lands allotted to them, with the reservation that he would deal with the first and second plantations only, or the first nations after the flood. As for the subderivations which came in after years, he said, "it were infinit to examine them." [36]

The pen which Ralegh laid down was picked up in 1662 by the good right hand of Edward Stillingfleet, Bishop of Worcester, another pertinacious defender of the monogenetic, Mosaic solution of the problem of human diversification. Moreover, the Bishop was no amateur. He was an accomplished historiographer and the possessor of untiring polemical powers. His *Origines sacrae, or a rational account of the grounds of Christian faith,* composed to scatter the "atheists," was full of elaborate and formidable arguments.

It was as critics of Genesis that "unbelievers" called forth his best effort. They alleged in and out of season that the accepted chronology of the Mosaic narrative, which made it purportedly the oldest of historical documents and a reflection of the earliest period of human experience, was incompatible with the claims of other Mediterranean historians. "The most popular pretenses of the Atheists of our Age," observed the Bishop, "have been the irreconcileableness of the account of Times in Scripture, with that of the learned and ancient Heathen Nations." To a degree Stillingfleet was in agreement with this contention. He too was aware of an inconsonance. But he stated it with an important difference. In his judgment, the claims of the classical historians were incompatible with Genesis not because Genesis was of later composition, but rather because the heathen works themselves had been written later. Written without the benefit of reading Genesis, they were full of defects not to be found in Genesis.

The Bishop's fluent and comprehensive discussion of these conflicts and deficiencies was carried on largely in the first six chapters of the *Origines sacrae,* where the historiographical practices of the Phoenicians and Egyptians, the Chaldeans and the Greeks, were dissected, line by line and phrase by phrase. In general, all the ancient historians were charged with "monstrous confusion, ambiguity, and uncertainty." Each was said to be partial to his own nation, or to be inconsistent with all others. Even more distressing, their documentation was imperfect.

And how could it be otherwise? How could these earliest secular historians be provided with the means of knowing, recording, and transmitting the past? Were they in a position to communicate with the past either by symbols, speech, or letters? Were there memorials of high antiquity enshrined in the recorded memories of their ancients? The Bishop's answer was a voluble "No." Symbols, speech, letters, took much time to invent; and each in its course of development was subject to imperfections which were later to color every historical judgment dependent upon it. It was the solemn custom of the Egyptians, for example, so "to wrap up all the knowledge they had" under such mystical representations (symbols) that historical inquiry "was clogg'd with two inconveniences very unsuitable to the propagation of knowledge, "which were obscurity and ambiguity. . . ." Similar inaccuracies were to be found in the other ancient historians. To be useful, language had to be "delivered down from Father to Son" with constancy of usage, or without serious modifications in meaning. Never, in heathen antiquity, had such an ideal been realized. Words, especially, were so perishable, and men's memories so weak in retaining them, that they ceased to be reliable agents of transmission. "By whomsoever they were first invented," we are certain they were but lately in use in the Nations, so that all the ancient historians, save only Moses, have been in "want of timely and early records to digest their own histories."

If this argument failed to convince, Stillingfleet had a second, with Moses as its subject. Was the historical work of the author of Genesis subject to the same flaws which marred the work of his colleagues? Was the Book narrated on the basis of a recent or corrupted tradition? Once again, his answer was "No." Plainly, this history of the early world and the Jewish people was dependent neither upon symbol nor upon prematurely used speech or letters. For a wise God would not "suffer the History of the world to lye still unrecorded, but made choice of such a person to record it, who gave abundant evidence . . . that he acted on no private design, but was peculiarly employed by God himself for the doing of it." As for reliable documentation Moses was very favorably situated. He was either an eyewitness to the events he related, or was helpfully provided with the memorials of "a certain unmixed lineal descent from Father to Son in the Jewish Nation," which was unavailable anywhere else.

The great cause of most of the confusion in the tradition of other Nations, was the frequent mixing of several families with another; now that God might as it were on purpose satisfie the world of the Isrealites capacity to preserve the tradition entire, he prohibited their mixture by marriages with the people of other Nations and families. So that in Moses his time it was a very easie matter to run up their lineal descent as far as the flood, nay up to Adam; for Adam conversed sometime with Noah; Sem his son was probably living in some part of Jacobs time, or Isaac's at least; and how easily and uninterruptedly might the general tradition of the ancient History be continued thence to the time of Moses. . . ."[37]

BIBLIOGRAPHY AND NOTES

1. Pedro Mexia, *The foreste or collection of histories, no lesse profitable, then pleasant and necessarie, dooen out of Frenche into Englishe by Thomas Fortescue* (London: John Kyngston, for William Jones, 1571).

2. Montaigne, *Essayes*, sig. Zz 2 r, Gg 1 r.

3. Bodin, *Commonweale,* sig. Aaa iii r.

4. Meric Casaubon, *A treatise of use and custome* . . . (London: John Legate II, 1638), sig. L 3 v – L 4 r.

5. Edward Clodd, *Pioneers of evolution from Thales to Huxley* (London: G. Richards, 1903), 55.

6. George Boas, *Essays on primitivism and related ideas in the Middle Ages. (Baltimore)*: The Johns Hopkins Press, 1948) 130–32.

7. Arnold Joseph Toynbee, *A study of history* (London: Oxford University Press, 1934–54), I, 148.

8. James Graham Leyburn, *Handbook of ethnography* (New Haven: Yale University Press, 1931), v.

9. See above, pp. 179, 180–81.

10. For characteristic comments on pigmentation, see Purchas, *Pilgrimage,* sig. Bbb i v, and Burton, *Anatomy,* II, 43–44.

11. Guido Kisch, *The Jews in medieval Germany; a study of their legal and social status* (Chicago: University of Chicago Press, 1949), 312–16.

12. "Nation," of course, is a difficult concept to define. "The Jews and the Greeks are the only peoples of antiquity whose characteristics emerge clearly." (Hans Kohn, *The idea of nationalism: a study in its origins and background* [New York: Macmillan, 1944], 29–30, 595, n. 24.)

13. Leo Spitzer, "Ratio and race," *American Journal of Philology,* 62 (1941), 129–43. The literature of the sixteenth and seventeenth centuries also made little effort to distinguish between the various tribes of Indians in the Americas (Cawley, *Voyagers,* 378).

14. Montaigne, *Essayes*, sig. Dd. 4 r.

15. Burton, *op. cit.,* II, 59.

16. Purchas, *Pilgrimage,* Dedication and To the Reader.

17. Burton, *op. cit., III,* 326.

18. Edward Brerewood, *Enquiries touching the diversity of languages, and religions through the cheife parts of the world* (London: John Bill, 1614), 118–19.

19. Burton, *op. cit., III,* 323.

20. Ephraim Pagitt, *Christianographie, or the description of the multitude and sundry sorts of Christians in the world not subject to the Pope. With their unitie, and how they agree with us in the principal points of difference betweene us and the church of Rome* (London: T. P. and W. J. for Matthew Costerden, 1635), sig. b 2 r; *Heresiography: or, a*

description of the heretickes and sectaries of these latter times (London: M. Okes, 1645).

21. Burton, *op. cit.,* II, 34–46. In referring to puzzling local differences Burton drew freely upon both Montaigne and Bodin.

22. Jean Bodin, *Method for the easy comprehension of history,* translated by Beatrice Reynolds (New York: Columbia University Press, 1945), 335.

23. Frederick John Teggart, *The theory of history* (New Haven: Yale University Press, 1925), 76–78.

24. Arnold Williams, *The common expositor: an account of the commentaries on Genesis 1527–1633* (Chapel Hill: University of North Carolina Press, 1948), 6.

25. The importance of the demographic problem appears clearly in many works of the period, including those of Richard Cumberland. He was concerned with "the possibility of a sufficient increase of men from the three sons of Noah, to a number "mention'd in the oldest credible histories: and that in the times assign'd to their foundation, agreeably with the Hebrew accounts." (Richard Cumberland, *Origines gentium antiquissimae, or, attempts for discovering the times of the first planting of the nations* . . . [London: W. B. for R. Wilkin, 1724], 142.)

26. Boemus, *Fardle of façions,* sig.A ii r – A iii r.

27. *Ibid.,* sig. B iii r.

28. *Ibid.,* sig. N iii v.

29. Purchas, *Pilgrimage,* sig. D 5 r; E iii v – E iv r; Eva Germaine Rivington Taylor, "Samuel Purchas," *Geographical Journal,* 75 (1930), 536–39.

30. Richard Grafton, *A chronicle at large and meere history of the affayres of Englande, and kinges of the same, deduced from the creation of the worlde, unto the first habitation of thys islande:* . . . (London: H. Denham, 1569), sig. A ii v.

31. Heylyn, *Cosmographie* (1652), sig. B ii v – B ii r; B 5 r; C 3 v.

32. Williams, *Common expositor,* 36, 140.

33. Sir Walter Ralegh, *The history of the world* (London: William Stansby for Walter Burre, 1614), sig. C 5 v.

34. *Ibid.,* sig. F 2 r.

35. *Ibid.,* sig. K 2 r, K 3 r.

36. *Ibid.,* sig. L 1 r.

37. Edward Stillingfleet, *Origines sacrae, or a rational account of the grounds of Christian faith* . . . (London: R. W. for Henry Mortlock, 1666), sig. b 2 v (preface), C 4 r, D 2 v – D 4 v, P 3 r, S 2 v – S 3 r.

CHAPTER VII

Diffusion, Degeneration, and Environmentalism

"The danger of man since his fall is more in sinking down then in climbing up, in dejecting then in raising himselfe to a better condition."—JOHN BULWER.

THE BIBLICAL SOLUTION of the problem of cultural differences was an European one, based upon a narrowly European system of ideas and beliefs. It was regarded by most men as the best that reason and faith could propose. To others, however, it was neither as simple nor as satisfying as it seemed. The first eleven chapters of Genesis, with their artless bias in favor of one people, with their historical or genealogical ideas, with their unaccountable reservations and condensations, became the source of labyrynthine inferences which led ethnological thought and allied inquiry down many a winding way.

A first inference, and one deeply to influence the study of man, was uncompromisingly moral. Resting flatly upon an hypothesis of original cultural uniformity,[1] a first infraction and each subsequent breach in conformity, even the processes of innovation or change themselves, were freighted with evil. Had the author of Genesis allowed man in his purportedly original condition to avoid these unfortunate changes in behavior, or failed as an historian to select these events as central, had non-conformity been made less important in the Scriptural account of man's first years on the planet—who knows? His ultimate destiny might have been different, and the inquiries devoted to his understanding different also. As it was, kaleidoscopic variety in his institutions, customs, and habits, were construed as evidences of a fate meted out to him for his transgressions.

A second inference laid the foundation of a theory of cultural diffusion. But in the sixteenth and seventeenth centuries, it too raised a moral issue. The transmission of traits from one people to another was not regarded as an ethically neutral inter-group phenomenon. It precipitated a process of cultural change associated with cultural decline; and it was allied with a philosophy of history which offered no escape from corruption and degeneration.

A third reaction to the Mosaic hypothesis came from the skeptic or infidel. Many of these critics subscribed to little of the usual argument resting on Genesis I–II, apart from an attenuated belief in degenerationism and a recognition of the facts of the transmission of traits across cultural boundaries. But in their recoil from dogma, they not only raised questions very difficult for the orthodox to answer but promoted the secularization of history and the revival of classical and medieval environmentalism.

During the Renaissance no one with any pretension to learning, or any knowledge of ancient history, was unaware of at least some of the facts of the diffusion of culture. Boemus, for example, drawing directly or indirectly from Herodotus, mentions that the Egyptians "were the first that fained the names of twelve gods . . . erected Altars, Idols, and Temples, and figured living creatures in stones, all which things doe plainely argue that they had their originall from the Æthiopians, who were the first Authors of all these things." Plato is quoted as asserting that the Lacedemonians and the ancient cities of Greece "derived their lawes and ordinances from

Crete"; while the colonizing Romans "receiving unto them many peoples out of those cragged and cold countries [of northern Europe] which naturally were barbarous, inhumaine, and unsociable, have so reclaimed them, by mingling them with other people, as they have learned those rude and savadge people to live soberly and civilly." The Hebrew relapse into paganism with the worship of the Golden Calf was often ascribed by expositors to "corruptions" learned from the Egyptians. Pointing to the Hebrews, Chaldeans, Syrians, Egyptians, Arabians, and others of the East, Nathanael Carpenter declared that from these fountains "have the Greeks and Latins derived those large streames, wherewith they have . . . watered all Europe"—an opinion adopted from Bodin, and restated again and again by many later social philosophers, including Hegel.[2] The change or fall of commonwealths was often ascribed to the incursion of strangers.[3] It was also Bodin's opinion that all religions had taken "their beginning from the south, and from thence had been dispersed over the whole earth"; while commonweals originated "from a Familie, by little and little increasing," or else arose out of migration.[4] Backwardness in culture, such as that observable among the native tribes of the Americas, was said to have supervened "when wandring farre from their first fountaine, and leaving no sufficient monument to instruct their posterity in their first originall, [they] came short of the other." They could not help but come short "as being most distant from the first head," where the original tradition was to be found in its greatest perfection.[5] All of which led Louis Le Roy (c. 1510–1577) to say that "there is in men some natural desire to chaunge their habitations and dwellings; having a mutable mind, impacient of rest, and desirous of novelties: By reason whereof, they cease not from going one to another, changing of maners, tongues, letters, lordships, and religions: Few countries are inhabited by the true originaries: almost all Nations are mingled."[6]

Many men were also aware of the existence of a two-way transmission of culture among human beings. One, spatially or geographically oriented, involved the recognition that traits had been and could be carried "laterally," or "transported" overland through the agency of moving, mingling peoples or their representatives. The other, derived from the observation of the operation of the processes of tradition, resulted in the temporal uniformity of customs and institutions, and was attained by the "vertical" handing on of ideas and practices from father to son, along the channels of genetically linked generations, or through the "Conduit of Nature."

It was here during the sixteenth and seventeenth centuries that the usual moral judgment was introduced in relation to the theory of diffusion. The vertical transmission of traits over "tracts" of time, the maintenance of tradition with its end product, temporal cultural uniformity, was regarded universally as good. To it such men as Boemus applied the term "home-bredness." It conserved the old in culture, and perhaps a few remnants of an ancient original. It was regarded as one of the best characteristics of the best peoples, the true source of their pre-eminence. The Athenians, said the author of the *Fardle of façions* in admiration, "were not strangers at the beginning, nor was their City first inhabited by any rabble of wandering people, but in the same soile they now inhabite, their were they borne, and the self same place which is now their seat and habitation, was also their original and foundation." Again, the Ethiopians, "being in that country naturally bred, continued free men, and were never subject to slavery." "Home-bredness" also adorned the Germans. Boemus described them eulogistically, with the added thought that while some people might have ascribed their virtues to inheritance from one of the sons of Noah, their country was actually populated in the beginning "by such as were bred and borne, and not by such as were brought from other places."[7]

On the other hand, diffusion proper, or the lateral, horizontal, or overland transmission of culture, was regarded as bad. It was linked, as from an obvious beginning, with the rupture of the original Adamic culture, followed by an unfortunate sequence of like events, all productive of evil. One group of these events, not reported in its entirety but always subject to the embellishments of the pious imagination, was composed of that multitude of willful acts by Adamic man which led to the exile of Cain and the endless wanderings of his posterity. In other words, given the monogenetic hypothesis, given a single center of creation and the need theoretically to explain how from it the wide, wide world had become populated and culturally diversified, the author of Genesis had no choice. He was logically compelled to assume human movement, and human movement outward from the original center. There was no other way to people the earth either before or after the Deluge; and then afterward to repeople it. But the process, or rather the incidents of which the process was composed, were never regarded as good. They were associated each time with sin, with the violation of God's original plan for mankind. When once the first disobedient step had been taken in the Garden, man's moral as well as cultural future was determined, St. Augustine's providential and semi-progressionist theory of social change notwithstanding. Subsequent events were represented as the unhappy but inevitable elements in a pessimistic philosophy of history.

Recognition of the process of diffusion, and its relation to cultural diversification, was widespread among Renaissance scholars, including some of the more confirmed environmentalists. Nearly all authors of the period assumed that difference in manners was in some sense a function of human movement, plus the influence of time and distance. Human movement, especially in its earlier or Noachian phases, received much attention from writers who tried to picture graphically for their readers what these migrations entailed for their unfortunate participants. Time, "passing from age to age," separated generation from generation; and distance, ever lengthened, divided fathers from sons and grandsons; while both acted as solvents of cultural homogeneity. With the element of time in mind, Boemus asserted that diversity was due to "that spedie and unripe puttyng forthe of children from their progenitours before they had thoroughly learned and enured themselves with their fathers fashions and manners"; while Ralegh was critical of Josephus because that historian took too little account of time, but gave "all Noah's children feathers, to carry them far away in haste."

Distance, in turn, broke down lines of communication between migrants and parental colonies. The links of a common culture were weakened by faulty or too little repetition of old practices and doctrines. Ralegh dwelt upon this difficulty in his discussion of the "Worlds Plantation after the Floud." When the sons of Noah had multiplied in great numbers, "and dispersed themselves into the next Countries . . . it was (at first) in such a manner as that they might repayre to each other, and keepe intelligence by River."[8] Diversity supervened when no such communication was possible : when families and clans, on the move, put too many miles between themselves and patriarchal hearths to recall the values of common descent and common history; when years piled upon years dimmed the memory of a father's ways; when tradition, that cement of the generations, at last failed; when the ideals and principles it had once carried had lost their meaning.

Diffusion, contact, mingling, the horizontal transmission of culture from one people to another was branded therefore as something less than desirable. People, in the English idiom,

were "meddled" with one another to the detriment of all concerned. The process was conducive to mixture and to all that
followed in its train. Travel was sometimes discouraged
because it brought about the same pernicious results. The
Muslims were felt to be culturally less happily endowed than
other peoples because Mohamet was the child of mixed paren-
tage or an exogamous marriage. His father was an "idolatre
after the maner of the heathen, his mother an Ismalite leaning
to the lawe of the Jewes." The outcome, to use the modern
psychological term, was "insecurity." Mohamet's mixed
ancestry "printed in hym suche a doubtful belief, ye when he
came to age he cleaved to neither," but "framed and invented
out of both of those laws, a religion most dangerous and pernicious to all mankind."[9]

The question of whether a culture was the handiwork of
forebears who were native to the soil of the country, or had
been carried in by outsiders, became a matter not lightly to be
passed over; and the same question found expression in early
biological reflection. Albertus Magnus noted that plants and
animals grew either larger or smaller as they were moved from
one climate to another. Making use of an analogy, Bodin
declared : "We see men as well as plants degenerate little by
little when the soil has been changed."[10] Said Heylyn : "As the
plants and trees loose much of the vertue, being transplanted
into another soyle," so also with men.[11] Said Carpenter :
"People suffer an alteration in respect to their several Plantations. . . . Colonies transplanted from one region to another
farre remote, retaine a long time their first disposition, though
by litle and litle they decline and suffer alteration."[12] There
were few to say a good word for the mixing or moving of men,
animals, or vegetables; and many to condemn it as bad.

The elements of this argument appear in countless contemporary discussions of cultural phenomena. Cultural diversity,
the inimitable Boemus wrote in 1520, was one of the con-

comitants of the intrusion of evil. It ensued upon the severance of the Adamic or Noachian tradition; upon "that short and untimely alienation of the children [of Noah] from their progenitors (of whose life and manners they had but little taste)"; or more specifically, upon that episode when Ham, as one son, planted himself in Arabia, "whereof it came to passe, that when in the processe of tyme they were increased to to many for that lande : being sent out . . . swarme aftre swarme into other habitations, and skatered at length into sondry partes of the worlde . . . some fel into errours."[13]

Movement of any kind, even for purposes of trade or war, was often frowned upon. According to *The French Academy,* that mid-sixteenth-century encyclopedia of ethics which was read everywhere in Europe, "the nature of man desirous of diversity and novelty, suffereth itself to be easily overcome . . . of naughtiness rather than goodness." Sedition, said La Primaudaye, "cometh to passe when the inhabitants of a place are not of the same nation, but many strangers are received into it."[14] In the morally indifferent matters of "eating and drinking; of cloathing, and civil implements and the likes," there might be a variety of fashions and customs in the world, according to differences in either place or time. But in questions of right and wrong, diversity gave wonder and offense.[15] For custom, habit, or long-standing practice not only was regarded as the cause for many marvelous or unusual achievements, but through use and exercise became "at last nature."

The whole thing was repeated again with reference to savagery in William Strachey's *Historie of travell into Virginia Britania* (1612), a work which not only "solved" the moot problem of the origin of the American Indians by tracing their descent from the wandering Ham but may have influenced Shakespeare in his composition of the *Tempest.* Strachey's text, known to many colonizers, is worth a few quotations. "Yt is observed that Cham, and his famely, were the only far Travellors, and Straglers into divers unknowne countries, searching, exploring and sitting downe in the same : as also yt is said of his famely, that what country soever the Children of Cham happened to possesse, there beganne both the Ignorance of true godliness . . . and that no inhabited Countryes cast forth greater multytudes, to raunge and stray into divers remote Regions." The unsatisfied wanderings of this one man and his offspring brought about "the Ignoraunce of the true worship of God . . . the Inventions of Hethenisme, and adoration of falce godes, and the Devill. . . ." It is not at all unlikely "that both in the travells and Idolatry of the famely of Cham, this portion of the world (west-ward from *Africa,* upon the Atlantique Sea) became both peopled, and instructed in the forme of prophane worshippe. . . . But how the vagabond Race of Cham might discend into this new world, without furniture . . . of shipping, and meanes to tempt the Seas," remained a mystery.[16]

A little later the same idea was given literary expression by John Dryden. "Truly I am apt to think," said he, "that the revealed religion, which was taught by Noah to all his sons, might continue for some ages in the whole posterity. That afterwards it was included wholly in the family of Shem, is manifest : but when the progenies of Cham and Japhet swarmed into colonies, and those colonies were subdivided into many others, in process of time their descendants lost, by little and little, the primitive and purer rites of divine worship."[17] In the middle of the eighteenth century, one hundred years later, the work of the French savant Goguet (1758) was informed with the same set of ideas. In the preface to the *De l'origine des lois, des arts, et des sciences* he entreated his readers never to forget that those colonies which "after the confusion of tonges and dispersion of families, did not settle soon, but led a wandering and vagabond life for a certain time," lost all traces of the arts and sciences, and "were under the necessity of inventing them anew. The case was different with those families which settled early, especially with such as continued to dwell in the same districts where Noah and his family fixed immediately after the Deluge. We cannot doubt but these families, on the contrary, preserved the fundamental principles of the arts and sciences, when we perceive all useful discoveries proceeding from the countries where they dwelt, as from a common centre. . . ."[18]

Between the evil reflected in cultural diversification and in that other tormenting anxiety of the Renaissance, the theory of the world's mutability and decay, the relationship was very close. It was hard to tell where one idea ended and the other began. They could be found either in Genesis and the hexameral literature, or in the "contemptus mundi" of the Hebrew prophets; in the verdict of some of the ancient Greeks that man was an altogether calamitous thing, or in the works of other pagan writers, who played with the notion that the world was old and tired, that its productivity in ideas and inventions was on the wane.

And now again, in the sixteenth century and in the presence of the conflicting philosophies to which the new learning had offered hospitality, it took a new lease on life. To an extent difficult fully to apprehend in the twentieth century, the fall of man from spiritual innocence had come to occupy a central place in secular reflection. Religious doubt and the inability to reconcile classical systems of philosophy with one another or with the Bible were partially responsible. Added to these confusions were those produced by the astronomical discoveries. For if few hearts were lifted up by the doctrine of the Fall, fewer still took comfort in the newer conceptions of the earth's position in the universe. Once the center of God's undivided attention, it had become merely one of many worlds, inhabited perhaps by a plurality of planetary colonies of God's children. To those who accepted the conventional Biblical limit to the longevity of the world and of man's life in it, the last days were at hand. Lamentations were to be heard on every side, from divines, poets, scholars, laymen. Like Rosalind they mourned that "the poor old world is almost six thousand years old," leaving scant time for old age to run a dignified course through decay to death. John Donne drew the universe into the net of his despair : *"This is Nature's nest of Boxes:* The Heavens containe the *Earth,* the *Earth, Cities, Men.* And all these are *Concentrique;* the common *center* to them all is *decay, ruine."* To all those in the sixteenth and seventeenth centuries who entertained this philosophy of history (and this meant as many as now accept the idea of progress), every change was for the worse. Corruption like a nauseous weed had "growne with speede." The world was "rotten," a "carkasse," "fragmentary rubbidge," senile, as good as dead.[19]

Inevitably, this almost universally entertained theory of natural decay found its way into ethnological and social reflection, becoming one of its dominant themes. Those who were interested in the staggering array of languages and religions in the world, or in the origin of idolatry, fell back upon it as the only rational envisagement of the process of change which had taken place since the creation. It became the refuge of students of politics, especially those who felt compelled to offer some explanation for the strange fate of many great states and empires no longer viable. And it was combined at times with the often congenial classical theory of cyclical change, becoming the "theoretical" base of each cycle's repetitive declining arm.

The two related wings of degeneration theory—that associated with Renaissance pessimism and that tied to ethnological phenomena—were brought together in 1614 in Edward

Brerewood's perceptive little book on the geographical distribution of languages and religions. To Brerewood as to many others of his time, the two terms *change* and *degeneration* were not indicators of separate and distinct ideas. They were interchangeable. The mere passage of time, day to day, year to year, was enough to ensure the maintenance of the process. "The general rust of the world," said he, "weareth, eateth, consumeth, and perforateth all things," reducing man to barbarism.

In examining the Greek tongue, as then currently known and spoken in Europe, Brerewood immediately came upon evidences of decay, "not onely as touching the largenesse and vulgarnesse of it, but also in the purenesse and elegancy." Nor was this corruption due wholly to the migrations and minglings of peoples. Decline and degradation in the tongues of men were inescapable because of the nature of the world; they were the way things worked, a law of nature. The same hypothesis was employed by other Renaissance philologists in dealing with the problem of the original language of mankind, and the process by which other tongues had emerged from it. Needless to say, this process "had no sodaine beginning, by the mixture of other forrain nations." It was due to "the ordinarie change which time and many common occasions that attend on time, are wont to bring to all languages in the world."[20] Most philologists regarded Hebrew as the speech of the first generations of mankind, and all other tongues as derivatives. Yet, whether modifications occurred as the result of the faulty pronunciation of unlearned men and infants, or as the outcome of migrations, wars, and colonizations, judgment as to the direction of change in language was always the same. Each tongue, in turn, was the descendant of some other, and all except one, the original Hebrew, were formed as the result of disintegration or degeneration.

When that other major problem, the diversity of religion,

was broached, there was the same envisagement of the process of change. The slender thread of social and historical theory which bound together the unwieldy mass of materials in Purchas' *Pilgrimage* was of this order. During the brief interval in the Garden, while Adam still maintained his good standing with the Almighty, "nature was his Schoolmaster, or if you will rather God's Usher, that taught him . . . all the rules of divine Learning." After that, the apostate was Cain; the first author of irreligion, Ham. From then on, infection spread among the nations, until the world became the scene of a great miscellany of idolatries and superstitions, all of them the outcome of the decay of the true faith. "The true Religion," said Purchas, "can be but one, and that which God himselfe teacheth . . . all other religions being but strayings from him, whereby men wander in the darke, and in labyrinthine errour." The same conviction was registered by Roger Williams in 1643 : "The wandering Generations of Adam's lost posteritie, having lost the true and living God their Maker, have created out of the Nothing of their own inventions many false and fained Gods and Creators."[21]

With the belief that the world was decaying, that man had reached the lowest point in his sinful history, that the end of everything was near at hand, it should occasion no surprise to find that in 1614, a year after the *Pilgrimage* was published, Sir Walter Ralegh painted a companion picture of the senility of nature and its expression in the diversification of religion. In the migrations and the geographical obstacles which retarded the movements of the progeny of Noah, time was again seen as an agent of inevitable and universal degeneration, not, as it had been for Bacon, the medium of progress. The vigor of the world, said Ralegh, had run down like a clock. Even the waters of the general Flood had not washed away the first fallings away from God, the first idolatrous corruptions; and the same defection had continued.

In the very generation and nature of mankinde. Yea, even among the few sonnes of Noah, there were found strong effects of the former poyson. For as the children of Sem did inherite the vertues of Seth, Enoch, and Noah; so the sonnes of Cham . . . began soone after the Floude to ascribe divine power and honour to the Creature, which was onely due to the Creatour. First, they worshipped the Sunne, and then the Fire. So the Egyptians and Phoenicians did not onely learne to leave the true God, but created twelve severall gods . . . whom they worshipped, and unto whom they built Altars and Temples. . . . But as men once fallen away from undoubted truth, doe then after wander for evermore in vices unknowne . . . so did these grosse and blinde Idolaters every Age after other descend lower and lower, and shrinke and slide downwards. . . .[22]

The theological source of this theory of the degeneration of the institution of religion, and its lack of relationship to careful historical investigation and the real world of religious differences, are well brought out by Robert Burton's solution, only seven years later, in 1621, of the same problem. "A lamentable thing it is to consider," said Burton in a long chapter on religious melancholy, "how many myriads of men this idolatry and superstition hath infatuated in all ages." For Burton, unlike Ralegh, decadence was not the product of time alone. It was the work of the devil and his human agents, the politicians, statesmen, priests, heretics, impostors, and pseudo-prophets. These gentry, widely experienced in the techniques of exercising power, had long since discovered that there was no better way to curb social disturbance or rebellion than to use religion for Machiavellian ends, "to terrify men's consciences, and to keep them in awe." According to Burton, their like was to be found in every age and every realm.

This was Zamolxis' strategem among the Thracians. . . . 'Twas for a politic end, and to this purpose, the old poets feigned the Elysian fields. . . . Pluto's kingdom, and the variety of torments

after death. . . . 'Tis this which Plato labours for in his *Phaedo*
. . . the Turks in their Alcoran, when they set down rewards and
several punishments for every particular virtue and vice. . . .
Many such tricks and impostures are acted by politicians in
China. . . . How many towns in every kingdom hath superstition
enriched. What a deal of money by musty relics, images, idolatry,
have their mass-priests engrossed. . . . This hath been the devil's
practice, and his informal ministers' in all ages.[23]

One hundred years later, in 1724, when Père Lafitau's
Moeurs des sauvages Amériquains was first published, the
solution to the problem of variation in religion remained orthodox and unchanged. Though God had inscribed the elementary truths of natural religion on the hearts of all men—
Christian, heathen, and savage—ignorance, that first penalty
for original sin, had enveloped it in the gloom of idolatry and
the horrors of magical practices. The religion of the Indians of
North America was thus the result of decay.

Nor was this all. Since both Churchmen and philosophers
were obsessed with what appeared to be the ephemeral and
retrogressive character of human experience, the same ideas
were applied to other social institutions. One of these was the
state. In Pedro Mexia's *Treasurie of auncient and moderne
times,* written in Spanish before the middle of the sixteenth
century and translated into English in 1613, commonwealths
were described as so unpredictable in their mutability as to
defy human wit to bring them to that perfect harmony "which
is requisite for the conservation of civill unity and amity."[24]
Nor was Mexia alone in his dejection. Political pessimism had
become a commonplace. *The French Academy,* La Primaudaye's compendium of knowledge published in English in 1618
declared that every commonwealth, after it had come to the
top of perfection, had "but a short time of continuance:
whether her overthrowe proceedeth from the violence of her
enemies . . . or whether shee waxe olde through long tract of

time . . . or whether she suddenly decay and fal downe with her owne weight by reason of some other hidden cause".[25]

Decline was also the fate of civilizations. In human affairs, said Heylyn's *Cosmography*—much read and followed by John Milton in his treatment of the evanescence of earthly glory—"there is nothing permanent, and much less of certainty. The greatest Monarchies of the world, the Babylonian, Persian, Grecian, Roman, have all had their periods, nothing remaining of them now but the name and memory. . . . And if it be so, as it is, with the greatest Monarchies, the most mighty Cities of the world, we must not think that smaller Kingdoms & Estates can either be so evenly ballanced, or so surely founded, as not to be obnoxious also to the same vicissitudes."[26] Even Purchas, not to be outdone, reminded his pilgrim that he might "at leisure look backe, and view the ruines" of many mighty monarchies, puissant kingdomes, stately cities, and renowned states, "which by the wise, just and provident hand of the *Disposer of Kingdomes,* have had their fatall Periods, and given place."[27]

The monogenetic theory of social origins, with its melancholy philosophy of history and its rejection of the positive values of human movement, cultural contact, borrowing, or diffusion, was the conventional Renaissance answer to the problem of cultural differences. There were as few to quarrel with it as with the Darwinism of today; few to plunge so far into infidelity as to attempt the formulation of alternative theories. Yet, as always, there were some. There were dissenting voices : revisionists, polygenists, and environmentalists.

Influenced more by the classics than by the Book of Genesis, some revisionists maintained that the general historical process, the process of change, was not unidirectional but rather rhythmical or pulsatory, with man living at the moment under the inhibitions of a declining arm of an historical cycle, but not doomed forever to increasing misery. La Primaudaye, Heylyn, Purchas, and others each recognized in his own way that the great states had had periods of ascendancy, only to give place, "some to Barbarisme, and some to their succeeding heires (springing out of their ashes) flourishing in greater glorie than their predecessours. . . ." Confronted by ruins, they took comfort in the thought that the history of empire had often involved periods of success; that what had been lost with one civilization was sometimes regained, or even surpassed, by another.

There can be little doubt that this type of revisionism, the revival during the Renaissance of the cyclical philosophy of history, was largely the handiwork of three men—Niccolò Machiavelli (1469–1527), Louis Le Roy (c. 1510–1577), and Jean Bodin (1530–1596)—whose lives, overlapping, covered the sixteenth century. All three were empiricists as well as secularists. They sought to avoid the pitfall of other Renaissance scholars, who, still working under the shadow of scholasticism, were without experience in the day-to-day affairs of human communities. Instead of relying on a tradition which cast man's destiny in a wholly pessimistic mold, they advocated a return to the record of human experience as found in the several histories of the several nations. Machiavelli's energies were poured into the political phase of the investigation; Le Roy's and Bodin's into social and economic aspects as well. "Herein," said Machiavelli at the end of his *Discourses on the first decade of Titus Livius* in 1516, "I have expressed what I know, and what I have learned by long experience and continual reading of the affairs of the world."[28] Applying the Greek theory of historical cycles to the careers of political states, as Plato and Polybius had done before him, he asserted that nations, as a rule, when making a change in their systems of government, "pass from order into confusion, and afterwards recur to a state of order again," because nature permits no stability in human affairs.[29] Degeneration was included in his theory of political change, but so also was advancement. In the *Discourses* and in the *Florentine history* (1525), with their treatment of all states as subject to a common cyclical process, Machiavelli tried to free the political career of mankind on earth from its inevitable association with decay, and did much to shift the method of the historian from that of an artist to that of a scientist.

Louis Le Roy in *De la vicissitude ou variété des choses*, a book which was reprinted four times between 1575 and 1583,[30] and translated into English in 1594, was also concerned with man's achievements and potentialities rather than with his defeats. Like Bodin's *Methodus*, it was a secular discussion of the use of an historical method of investigation and its possible results. Its argument was in praise of human learning and not, as were many others of the time, a glorification of God's power to humble and degrade his creatures. But the range of Le Roy's interests was wider than that of either Machiavelli or Bodin. The book is the seasoned work of an old scholar who not only had read much and traveled widely, but who employed his great store of learning in comparing the human past with the human present; in comparing the historical materials descriptive of the ancient empires not only with each other but with sixteenth-century European accomplishments and with the explorers' accounts of contemporary African, Asian, and American man as well. A long sentence in the "summarie of this worke" states his purpose. He proposed to lay before his readers "the successive, or rather alternative changes of the whole world, as well in the higher or superiour, as lower and inferiour part thereof : and how by the concurrence of Armes and Letters, thorough the most renowned Nations of the world all liberall Sciences, and Mechanical Arts have flourished together, fallen, and bin restored, divers times in proces of Ages . . . , and conferring of this our present, with the famousest former Ages, to know wherein it is either inferiour, superiour, or equall to any of them."[31]

Though Le Roy willingly acknowledged the presence of a general belief in universal decay, he ascribed it to the influence of the aged.[32] The belief that manners waxed every day worse and worse seemed to him to be without foundation : a worn-out, threadbare complaint. Had it been true, men would long since "have come to the height of iniquitie"; and there would now "be no integritie in them; which is not true."[33] His message to the sixteenth century was a hopeful one, and in the light of the history of conceptions of social change, prophetic. There is a vicissitude and an interchangeable course "in all humane affaires, armes, learning, languages, arts, estates, lawes, and maners. . . . They cease not to arise and fall : amending or empairing by turns."[34] Men were advised to take heed of these words, and of the fact that those who had suffered decline might, with effort and in conformity with a naturally cyclical process, redeem themselves, eventually entering another period of accomplishment and advancement.

Other dissenting views or hypotheses were those advanced by Isaac de la Peyrère (1594–1676), and Jean Bodin. One voice, Peyrère's, was frankly polygenetic in intent; the other, Bodin's, avoided commitment but led logically in that direction. One sought by criticism to break down the influence on thought of the Book of Genesis, the other by positive historical and geographical research to correlate cultural differences with difference in men's habitats.

Rational inquiry into the text and canon of the Scriptures, of which Isaac de la Peyrère's effort formed a part, was not wholly a Reformation phenomenon. It began much earlier, perhaps with the Church Fathers, in a desire to reconcile the reading of various manscripts of the canon in several languages. Indeed, the higher criticism of the Pentateuch may go as far back as the work of a great Jewish scholar Isaac ben Suleiman, who in the tenth century expressed some doubt concerning its Mosaic authorship.[35] In the sixteenth and seventeenth centuries, however, independence in Biblical interpretation was not often initiated by professional theologians, but rather by philosophers such as Paracelsus, Bruno, Hobbes, and Spinoza. Formulating a rationalistic principle of interpretation, Hobbes in the *Leviathan* (1651) implied that the Bible was not the veritable Word of God, but merely a record maintained by some men who were inspired by the Almighty; and he expressed doubt of the Mosaic authorship of the Pentateuch in its existing form. Spinoza favored an objective review of Scripture, particularly the Book of Genesis, for the purpose of eliciting historical contradictions and chronological difficulties. In order to grasp fully the thought and intention of the Bible, it was his belief that each book should be examined "exactly as the naturalist observes the phenomena of nature," for the purpose of extracting every possible bit of knowledge concerning the date of its composition, its author, and its purpose. To studies such as these, Renaissance scholarship brought the same skill and earnestness that it was accustomed to lavish on the profane works of Greek and Latin antiquity.

The writings of Isaac de la Peyrère, with their penetrating and highly disturbing polygenetic implications, appeared in the Low Countries in 1655, just a few years after Hobbes published the *Leviathan,* and just a few years before the *Tractatus theologico-politicus* (1670) by Spinoza; and they all embodied in cold type much that other skeptics had only suggested.[36] For example, the pamphlet *Praeadamitae* and the book *Systema theologicum ex prae-Adamitarum hypothesi* presented evidence intended to show not only that Moses could not have been the author of the Pentateuch, being already dead at the time it was written, but that these five books were "not Originals, but copied out by another."[37] Who was there to say that Moses was the first and only early historian of the Jews? Why could there not have been other historians before him? In all likelihood, he who had epitomized over a thousand years of Hebrew history in five meager chapters had derived his material from predecessors. Having expressed these doubts and made this point elsewhere in the *Systema,* La Peyrère enlarged upon other problems of great contemporary interest, namely, the historical priority of the Hebrew people to all others and the universality of the Flood. With reference to the unrivaled antiquity of the Hebrews, many doubts had already been expressed. The greater age of the Phoenicians, the Scythians, the Egyptians and Chaldeans, not to speak of historical peoples of other areas, had been argued by "the most ancient and best esteemed Philosophers and Historians" Herodotus, Diodorus, Plato, Strabo, and Cicero. Hence the Jews were adjudged to be much younger. As for the Flood, since there had been no need to punish the gentiles in China and America, since God's anger was directed solely and locally against the Jews, the extent of Deluge had been limited to Palestine. Obviously its local nature had been proved by the condition of the olive branch brought back to the Ark by the dove. If some parts of the world had not escaped inundation, a fresh, fully developed olive branch would have been unobtainable; if its leaves had been subjected to long immersion in flood waters, they would have lost their greenness and become sodden or covered with slime.[38] Nor was it credible that the whole postdiluvian, vacant earth had been divided solely between the three sons of Noah, or repeopled solely by their progeny. As indicated by unimpeachable place and tribal nomenclatures, their shares in the land were restricted to Palestine.[39]

There was all of this in the *Praeadamitae* and the *Systema* to cast doubt on the historical reliability of the Book of Genesis and upon any monogenetic theory based on Genesis; and there was also much more. For the fame of La Peyrère rests upon still another assertion, already suggested by Paracelsus and Bruno.[40] This was the claim that Adam was not the first man. On the contrary, there had been not one but at least two separate creative episodes. The first had produced the gentiles, the second Adam, the forefather of the Hebrews. The arguments to support this conclusion were ingenious and diverse, though often farfetched. Evidence that there had been men on earth before the appearance of Adam consisted of an hitherto enigmatic passage in Genesis referring to the marriage of the sons of God with the daughters of men. Plainly, it was insisted by La Peyrère and his brother skeptics, this could imply nothing other than the union between the sons of Adam and the daughters of previously created gentiles. There were also technological evidences of pre-Adamic generations. The fact that God had provided tunics of skins to cover the nakedness of Adam and Eve indicated that already in those days, in those presumably first days, there were "Curriers, Shoomakers, and Skinners," and a broader culture than that of Adam to support these skilled trades. Then again, if Cain was a husbandman, as Genesis implied, he must have needed tools. Therefore, there must have been artificers, or men other than those in the family of Adam to build the furnaces and the forges for fabricating hammers, hatchets, plows and harrows. Finally, where did Cain find a wife, and who helped him build a city? These and many other questions were solved on the general thesis that there were people in the world more ancient than the earliest Hebrews.[41] And from this it was assumed that existing diversities among men were ascribable to a plural rather than a single origin.

These arguments told against the simple faith that the Bible had solved all historical and ethnological problems. But the critic who did most to turn the minds of scholars away from Genesis as the final answer to these questions was not La

Peyrère with his bewildering harvest of heresies. It was his predecessor the French jurist Bodin, author of the *Methodus ad facilem historiarum cognitionem* (1565), the *Six livres de la république* (1576), the *Colloquium heptaplomeres* (1588), and several other important books.

Jurist Jean Bodin is best known as an environmentalist. Political and ethnic diversities were ascribable, in his judgment, not to plural human origins in the sense of "men before Adam", not to postdiluvian migrations, minglings, and diffusions, but to prior diversities in topography and climate. Each of his books in some degree gave currency to this hypothesis: the *Colloquium* as a series of dialogues on various religions; the *République* as a discussion of the rise, flourishing estate, and decline of commonwealths; and the *Methodus,* his earliest work, as the first statement of his argument and manner of thought. Obviously naturalistic, rationalistic, and heterodox, the *Methodus* found its sources in the humanist revival of the classics and was sustained at many points by the reassertion of medieval astrology. But Bodin avoided the charge of infidelity by bowing at critical phases of his argument to Biblical authority. For him, and for those who felt as he did, a sound solution of the problem of cultural diversification was not to be clouded by controversy over the early peoplings of the world, or by a theory of original sin, migration, or the breakdown of communication among the bearers of the Adamic tradition. Leaving all of this one side, he elected to take man as given, concentrating on the relation of the several cultures to land, to climate, and to the topographical features of the several geographical regions.

It is not without significance that Bodin was also a collector as well as a theorist. Long before Bacon, he had advocated the procedure of collection as the first step in the use of scientific method. But while others assembled the customs of human beings with no end in view other than the satisfaction of idle curiosity, Bodin assembled human histories with a well-defined philosophical or scientific purpose. Realizing, as a lawyer who had need for a practical grasp of the divergent juridical systems of mankind, that "the best part of universal law," the customs of peoples, and the beginnings, growth, changes, and declines of all states,[42] lay hidden in historical documents, history became his treasure trove. There, according to Bodin, in the recorded experience of past generations, already gathered materials had only to be rearranged in their correct order, compared with one another and the several environments of the peoples involved, in order to yield insight into the springs of human conduct. As part of his technique, and to facilitate analysis, Bodin advocated the compilation of a general historical chart "for all periods," containing the "origins of the world, the floods, the earliest beginnings of the states and of the religions which have become more famous, and their ends, if indeed they have come to an end."[43] To this was added the advice that a small map be kept close by, showing the continental divisions of the earth and their relation to the stars in the heavens. Since there appeared to be a greater disorder and obscurity in the affairs of man than in any other area of historical interest, divine or natural, the student was urged to search for principles of order, or "to concentrate upon the topical arrangement of human interests and actions." All of these matters were to be run through lightly at first, then examined with greater care; and as a last step, a collection of the chief teachings of all religions was to be made, with the authors of each, their beginnings and ends.[44]

Needless to say, Bodin's thought was informed by a heterodox bias, a predisposition which might well have thrown him into the arms of the "atheists," skeptics, and doubters. As a member of the school of Machiavelli, Le Roy, and Montaigne, all of whose work fell clearly in the sixteenth century, he was interested in facts, in what men were and did rather than what they ought to be. But to give his geographical determinism a traditionally acceptable substratum, his naturalism gracefully gave way, *ab initio,* to old-fashioned orthodoxy. In other words, if it was necessary as a first step to get mankind on the geographical scene as an originally homogeneous unit which later, when exposed to diverse external influences, was to exhibit heterogenous features, the most available and congenial source was Genesis. So Bodin, the companion of heretics, appealed at this point to the historian Moses, "that very wise man," whose writings had placed him "far ahead" of all philosophers. For the purpose in hand, the assumption of the original uniformity of mankind was derived from man's purportedly universal descent from the Chaldeans, "since in their country or certainly near it, came to rest that ship which served as the nursery of the human race. From there men scattered hither and thither and propagated their kind in the way in which Moses and the teachers of the Jews fully described."[45] But for the later and more important elements in his hypothesis, he turned back to other ancient literatures, to traditional physiological ideas, and to astrology.

It was also Bodin's conviction, in dealing with the problem of diversity in culture, that nothing was more indispensable for the correct interpretation of history and the art of government than an acquaintance with the nature of peoples. The physical constitution of men, or their humoral[46] make-up, determined their moral aptitudes or dispositions. Environment, climate, the conditions of place and time, did all the rest, reacting on men through their bodies.[47] "A wise governour of any Commonweale," said he, "must know their humours, before he attempt anything in the alteration of the state and lawes. For one of the greatest, and it may be the chiefest foundation of a Commonweale, is to accomodat the estate to the humor of the citizens; and the lawes and ordinances to the nature of the place, persons, and time."[48] The one secure basis for explaining diversities of human behavior was to be found in the correlation of culture with climate and topography, of human differences with historico-geographical differences. "For even as we see a great varietie in all sorts of beasts, and in every kind some notable alteration for the diversitie of regions; in a like sort we may say, that there is as great difference in the nature and disposition of men. . . ."[49]

As for history, Bodin's belief in its power to confer knowledge concerning the ways of mankind was unfaltering; and much of both the *Methodus* and the *République* is devoted to the assemblage of documentation to support this contention. Never before perhaps had a writer on politics or ethnography amassed so large a body of dated materials or laid so large a literature under tribute. He was well-read, not only in the law and the Bible, but in the Talmud and the Cabala; in the ancients, including Herodotus, Strabo, Cicero, Tacitus, and Caesar; in the modern historians, such as Joinville, Froissart, Monstrelet, Commines; and in the travelers, Marco Polo, Leo Africanus, and Las Casas. "As they err," said he, "who study the maps of regions before they have learned accurately the relation of the whole universe and the separate parts to each other and to the whole, so they are not less mistaken who think they can understand particular histories before they have judged the order and sequence of universal history and of all times, set forth as it were in a table."[50]

Dividing the northern hemisphere into three fundamental types of climate—hot, cold, and temperate—he noted in substance that the people of the south were

of a contrarie humour and disposition to them of the North: these are great and strong, they are little and weake; they of the north, hot and moyst, the others cold and dry; the one hath a big voyce and greene eyes, the other hath a weake voyce and black eyes; the one hath a flaxen haire and a faire skin, the other hath both haire and skin black; the one feareth cold, the other heate;

the one is joyfull and pleasant, the other sad; the one is fearefull
and peaceable, the other hardie and mutinous; the one is
sociable, the other solitaire; the one is given to drinke, the other
sober; the one is rude and grosse witted, the other advised and
ceremonious; the one is prodigall and greedie, the other is
covetous and holds fast; the one is a souldier, the other a philosopher; the one fit for armes and labour, the other for knowledge
and rest.[51]

And with these qualities were associated a multitude of traits,
customs, and institutions, which, in their several combinations
and permutations, determined the political and ethnological
destinies of nations.

It is often said that Bodin was not original either in his
emphasis on the problems of historiography or in his reasoning
on human diversification; that his absorption in secular history
was shared by others during the Renaissance; and that many
like him were trying to replace a theocentric view of man's
present and past condition with one that was geocentric. It
has also been asserted that his doctrine of climate, far from
constituting a new and modern contribution to the study of
man, was "little more than a borrowing from medieval astrology, whose last sighs have sometimes been mistaken for the
first breath of a geographical interpretation of history."[52] To a
certain extent these charges are well founded, but it still cannot be said that Bodin left history, geography, politics, and
ethnology exactly where he found them. By him, each of these
humane disciplines, full-fledged or still embryonic in the sixteenth century, was brought into touch with all the others, and
thus renewed and modified. The majority of scholars before
and during the early Renaissance, had viewed man above all
else as a moral being. The moment when he could be thought
of or studied in his social, economic, political, or ethnological
aspects, with these aspects disassociated mentally from value
judgments, had been slow in coming. Compare the works of

earlier scholars with the *Methodus* and the *République*. In these books, Bodin thrust man into the foreground of inquiry, linking the historian and the geographer into a single term, "geographistorian."[53] To Bodin's predecessors among the Schoolmen, geographical determinism, either in its terrestrial or astrological form, had been of interest only as a threat to free will, and then only as a philosophical and moral problem. When such matters were discussed, no illustrative material was used, or only bits and pieces worn threadbare by age and repetition. Compare these earlier attempts to win an argument by logic alone with Bodin's plan to achieve knowledge of man by using not only logic but evidence, both historical and geographical. Compare the absence of illustrative material with the mass which Bodin quarried from the rich stores of his reading. Note again his insistence upon the comparison of the histories, the religions, the languages, and the commonwealths of peoples; and note the absence of such comparisons in the Middle Ages.

With Bodin, moreover, the grim hold of Renaissance pessimism was loosened. "They are mistaken," said he with Le Roy, "who think that the race of men always deteriorates. When old men err in this respect, it is understandable . . . they sigh for the loss of the flower of youth . . . as though returning from a distant journey, they narrate the golden century."[54] His resistance to the morbid clichés of decline, corruption, and degeneration was shown in two ways : by his failure to use them, and by his hostility to the philosophies of history by which they had been spawned,—the Greek legend of the Golden Age and its Biblical parallel, the Fall of Man and his expulsion from Paradise. At the same time, he had much to say in the Renaissance manner about the world as the creature of incessant mutability and change. When he discussed the fortunes of various types of commonweals he acknowledged their mortality and mentioned recurrent periods of lessened vitality and accomplishment. But the declining phase was never stressed, nor was its melancholy outlook allowed to dominate his thinking. He was far more interested in distinguishing among the antecedents or possible causes of mutability than in subjecting changes to judgments of value as types of advance or deterioration. Nor does recourse to Genesis and the episodes of the Ark, the Deluge, and the Dispersion, lead him to regard diffusion as evil. Though the acknowledgment of cultural borrowing at any time in the past was not logically consistent with an environmental theory of differences, Bodin spoke frequently of mingling. "The fusion of peoples," said he at one point, "changes the customs and nature of men not a little"; at another, "all commonweales take their beginning either from a Familie, by little and little encreasing; or els arise at once, as when . . . a Colony drawne out of another Citie or Commonweale, doe as a young swarme of bees fly abroad unto another place."[55] Historical study had convinced him that the migrations of the human race had been constant. They had helped to lay the foundations of different types of civility, of new states and new cities.

Bodin's insistence upon the comparison of all historical materials and histories, as a central feature of social investigation, was notable. In the middle of the sixteenth century, "history" in the historian's sense rode the crest of the wave in various fields of intellectual endeavor. Consequently Bodin's books on historical method and on the inter-relation of history and geography were well received. Between 1566 and 1650 the *Methodus* was issued in thirteen Latin editions, the *République* translated into four languages and published frequently in abridged form. That the proud position of history was to be short-lived and that the Cartesians were to denounce it as unreliable—a collection of myths, and a conglomeration of errors—is relevant only on the Continent, where historical pyrrhonism rose to its highest level and where Bodin's name was seldom mentioned. In England the reception of his work was different. There, from 1580 to the end of the first quarter of the seventeenth century, the French scholar enjoyed a reputation for brilliance and high originality. He not only was known to all serious English students of history and geography but was admired, quoted, and imitated. William Harrison, the author of the *Description of England* in 1577, mentioned him, as did Holinshed, Sidney, Nash, Spenser, Bolton, Hobbes, Wheare, Heylyn, Burton, Carpenter, and Hakewill.[56] "You cannot stepp into a schollar's studye," said Gabriel Harvey, "but (ten to one) you shall litely finde open either Bodin *de Republica* or Le Royes *Exposition*. . . ."[57] Robert Burton, at one time a teacher of geography,[58] referred to him many times in the *Anatomy of melancholy* (1621), especially in that section entitled "Digression of air," which is frankly organized around the French jurist's climatic theory. "As the air is, so are the inhabitants, dull, heavy, witty, subtle, neat, cleanly, clownish, sick, sound." Said the doctor to those who would shake off their depressions, "The clime changes not so much customs, manners, wits, (. . . as Bodine . . . hath proved at large) as constitutions of their bodies, and temperature itself." He that loves his health "must often shift places, and make choice of such as are wholesome, pleasant, and convenient."[59]

It was on the geographers, or cosmographers, and through them upon the literary men of England, that Bodin exerted his greatest influence. For cosmography or geography, especially in its humanistic aspect, was read by all. In the sixteenth century it was included in the school curriculum; in the seventeenth, its study was advocated for every intelligent person. Said Lord Herbert of Cherbury: "It will be requisite to study geography with exactness, so much as may teach a man the situation of all countries in the whole world, together with . . . something concerning the governments, manners, religions, either ancient or new, as also the interests of states . . ." Since England was entering a nautical age, geography was the science of the future. There had been a time, said Richard Willes in his *History of travel,* when the art of grammar was esteemed, or when it was honorable to be a poet. That time was past. There had been a time when logic and astrology wearied the heads of young scholars. That time was also past. Not long since, "happy was he that had any skil in Greke language." But now all that was changed, and "all Christians, Jewes, Turkes, Moores, Infidels and Barbares be this day in love with Geographie."[60]

The number of foreign geographers known in England by an inveterate reader such as Robert Burton was amazingly large. "What greater pleasure can there now be," he asked,

than to view those elaborate Maps of Ortelius, Mercator, Hondius, etc. To peruse those books of Cities, put out by Braunus and Hohenbergius? To read those exquisite descriptions of Maginus, Munster, Herrera, Laet., Merula, Boterus, Leander, Albertus, Camden, Leo Afer, Adricomius, Nic. Gerbelius, etc.? Those famous expeditions of Christopher Columbus, Amerigo Vespucci, Marcus Polus, the Venetian, Lod. Vertomannus, Aloysius Cadamustus, etc.? Those accurate diaries of Portugals, Hollanders, of Bartison, Oliver à Nort, etc., Hakluyt's *Voyages,* Pet. Martyr's Decades, Benzo, Lerius, Linschoten's *Relations. . . .* What more pleasing studies can there be than the Mathematics, theoric or practic parts? as to survey land, make Maps, Models, Dials, etc., with which I have ever much delighted myself.[61]

Two books bearing the imprint of Bodin's theory, and destined to be read by people in every walk of life, were published in Britain in the first quarter of the seventeenth century. The first was by Peter Heylyn, a clergyman whose young manhood had been spent at Oxford, where his lectures on geography followed "a new Method not observed by others, by joyning History with Cosmography that made the work very delightful." The second was Nathanael Carpenter (1589–1628?), also an Oxford don, and a member of that unusual company of teachers of geography which included Robert Stafford, Joseph Prideaux, and others. Heylyn's *Microcosmus, or a little description of the great world,* published in 1621, was later expanded into a folio entitled *Cosmographie in four bookes. Conteining the chorographie and historie of the whole world and all the principall kingdomes, provinces, seas, and isles thereof,* and republished repeatedly throughout the seventeenth century. Carpenter's contribution appeared four years later, in 1625, and was entitled *Geography delineated forth in two bookes. Containing the sphericall and topicall parts thereof.*

Being carried "headlong" in the *Microcosmos* by the "swindge" of his own genius, Heylyn frankly acknowledged the influence of Bodin in his joint interest in geography and history. He promised that in his work "the long-parted sisters" would shake hands and kiss one another; while Purchas declared that geography without history was nothing more than a carcass.[62] Paraphrasing Bodin's preamble to the *Methodus,* Heylyn declared that history could not be ignored because it stirred men to virtue and deterred them from vice;[63] while geography delighted the reader by telling him something of the conditions under which men lived.[64]

Heylyn was more ingenious even than Bodin in relating Genesis to geographical determinism, monogenetic theory, and the plurality of races or cultures. At the time of the dispersion of the sons of Noah, "it came to pass that though they all descended from one common Root, yet by the situations of their severall dwellings they come to be of severall tempers and affections; in which they were so different from one another, that it might seem they had been made at first out of severall Principalls, and not at all derived from one common Parent." The ground or reason for this diversity was topographical— the differing conditions of the different countries in which the wanderers settled, and "the different influences of the Heavenly bodies."[65] Since Heylyn's Look belonged to the genre of cosmography, the author was "punctual and exact" in his descriptions not only of regions but of peoples. But with his absorption in history, his cultural descriptions differed markedly from many which had gone before. There are many which describe not only the existing conditions of manners, institutions, and morals, but at least one earlier period of the cultural past. He commonly wrote of a people as it had been "antiently" or in "olden times," and then of its culture as it existed in his own day.

The subject matter of Nathanael Carpenter's *Geography* was also unusual for his time. In a comprehensive and learned manner, it covered a wide range of geographical subjects: mathematical and theoretical aspects; the relation of the earth to the heavens; the magnetic qualities of the globe; longitude and latitude; descriptions of the seas, lands, rivers, mountains, animals, and men. He emphasized the necessity for using reason and evidence; the superiority of investigation to tradition, authority, or speculation. We should "rather stoop to Nature and observation," he said, "then Nature be squared to our own conceits."[66]

It was only in the last four chapters of the book, however, that mankind, or "the civil affections," received Carpenter's attention, and there only in response to a problem stated in terms similar to those employed by Bodin. That is to say, Carpenter resisted the study of the varying cultures of peoples. As phenomena which seemed to him less than primary or elemental, they were regarded as unstable, mutable, and transient. The stated object of the ethnological part of his inquiry was rather the description of the several "natural dispositions" of men. These were taken to be fundamental, immutable, and durable; though, to the confusion of the reader, such "dispositions" comprehended "Complexion, Manners, Actions, Languages, Lawes, Religion and Government," in short the very features he seemingly sought to avoid. "There is nothing," he declared, "more subject to admiration then the diversity of the naturall Dispositions in Nations. . . . For not to rove farther off than our neighbouring Nations Confines; what writer . . . hath not taxed pride and ambition in the Spaniard; levity, or rather (as Bodin would have it) temerity in the French; dangerous dissimulation in the Italian; Drunkennesse in the Dutch; Falshood in the Irish; and gluttony in the English? And however many means have bin put into practise . . . to curb such enormities . . . yet these markes are found to stick as close as the spots unto a Leopard." Then, attempting to classify the dispositions of nations, which are obviously of a medieval typological character, he came to the conclusion, under Bodin's influence, that the people of the northern hemisphere far surpassed those living in the south. "The extreame Inhabitants toward the Poles are naturally inclined to Mechanicall workes and martial endeavors; the extreame towards the Æquator to the work of Religion and Contemplation : The Middle to lawes and civility."

But despite this interest in human "dispositions," or in what he took to be psychologically and culturally immutable characters, Carpenter was often at his best and most discerning when he recorded his observations on cultural change, and its source, namely, migration and diffusion. Here, time and distance, so central in importance to the earlier monogenists, were again appealed to. Sudden changes in conduct Carpenter regarded as unlikely. "All mutation requires a certaine distance in time." Colonies transplanted from one region to another, for example, retained for a long period their original dispositions, though little by little they underwent alteration. "We reade that the Gothes . . . long after their first invasion of Spaine, France, Italy and other territories of Europe, retained their own *disposition* and *nature,* altogether disagreeing with the nations amongst whom they lived. . . . But in the process of time it came to passe, that putting off their harsh temper, they grew into one nation with the native Inhabitants." Historical instances of diffusion were frequently cited. "The footsteppes of Languages . . . proves nothing else but that civill Lawes, Arts, and Learning was derived to the Grecians from the Chaldeans, or the Nations neare adioyning."[67] Who can deny, he asked, with early insight into the westward course of civilizations, that the Greeks and Latins derived "those large streames, wherewith they have (as it were) watered all Europe," from the Hebrews, Syrians, Egyptians, and Arabians, as well as the Chaldeans?

Geography, with its large ingredient of ethnology, both ancient and modern, and its oft-repeated claim that human beings in their behavior were the creatures of their environment, made a profound impression upon the minds of other men in the sixteenth and seventeenth centuries. Said Meric Casaubon in 1638 : from the mutability and inconstancy of man's will, "wee may first deduce Varietie of fashions and customes. But secondly, differences of places and times cause differences of fashions and customes, and this of necessitie. For it is not possible . . . that men that live under different clymates should all live after one fashion."[68] Said Thomas Burnett in 1681 : "The mode and form, both of the Natural and Civil World changeth continuously more or less, but most remarkably at certain periods, when all Nature puts on another face

. . . For every new state of Nature doth introduce a new Civil Order, and a new face and Oeconomy of Humane affairs."[69] Men of letters, dramatists, essayists, philosophers, and poets pored over maps, and thumbed the closely printed pages of atlases or cosmographies to find the exotic bits of descriptions they wished to incorporate in essays, plays, and poetry. One was John Milton, whose mind was a crowded storehouse of geographical and historical facts, and whose *Brief history of Moscovia,* published in 1682, was a model description of a land and a people.[70] In *Paradise lost* and *Paradise regained,* geography was rivaled "in importance by none of the sciences except astronomy." Several times in those epic poems extensive panoramas of the world were evoked by the device of a rapid recitation of a succession of place names. Adam, standing with the angel on the hilltop, saw far in the distance, as a background to human history, the two Tartar cities of Samarcand and Cambalu. To the east lay Paguin, or Pekin. As his eyes moved southward and eastward, they fell upon India, Persia, Russia, Agra, Lahore, Ecbatana, Ispahan, and Moscow. Then gazing southward along the eastern coast of Africa, he saw Ercoco, Mombaza, Quiloa, Melinda, Sofala, and around the cape and western coast the Mediterranean states of Tunis, Morocco, Algeria, and Tremisen.[71] The poet knew the old geographers—Pliny, Mela, Strabo, Diodorus, Josephus—and the new ones as well. But Heylyn seems to have been the modern to whom he turned most often. The *Cosmographie* acted as a catalytic agent, bringing together the poet's knowledge of many other geographers.[72]

Milton and other literary men of his time were also familiar with the theory of climatic influence, especially as it seemed in some of its formulations to cast doubt upon the competence and future of English art. According to Bodin (and also to Botero the author of the widely read *Relations of the most famous kingdomes and commonwealths, thorowout the world,* translated from the Italian in 1601), the northern peoples, though strong of body and courageous, were retarded mentally and wanting in the understanding of beauty. This charge was often debated in Elizabethan England and even later, for English authors were not prepared to concede the inferiority which this geographical determinism seemed to impose. According to the heated reply of one opponent, "the wits our climate sends forth" were the equal of any. It was declared, furthermore, that the inhabitants of the north, the Flemings, the Scots, and the English "were ever equall, and rather deeper Schollars than either the Italians or the Spaniards."[73]

BIBLIOGRAPHY AND NOTES

1. This attitude was not peculiar to Christendom. Professor Hans Kohn is responsible for the statement that the Athenians "proudly believed themselves to have no admixture of barbarism or non-Athenian blood. When Thucydides, Euripides, or Isocrates, wished to bestow high praise upon the Athenians, they were called autochthonous. They were supposed not to have immigrated into Attica, a land never conquered nor inhabited by any people except the Athenians, who according to the legend had sprung from the soil." (Kohn, *Nationalism,* 54.)

2. Boemus, *Manners, lawes (1611),* 18, 178.

Thomas Godwyn, *Moses and Aaron. Civil and ecclesiastical rites used by the ancient Hebrewes . . . Herein likewise is shewed what customes the Hebrewes borrowed from heathen peoples. And that many heathenish customes, originally have beene unwarrentable imitations of the Hebrewes* (London: John Haviland, 1625), sig. Bb 4 r.

Nathanael Carpenter, *Geography delineated forth in two bookes. Containing the sphaericall and topicall parts thereof* (Oxford: John Lichfield and William Turner, 1625), Bk. II, sig. Ii * 3 v.

3. Peter de la Primaudaye, *The French Academie. . . .* (London: Thomas Adams, 1618), sig. Bb 3 v.

4. Bodin, *Commonweale,* Mm V v.

5. Carpenter, *op. cit.,* Bk. II, sig. Ii * 2 r.

6. Le Roy, *Of the interchangeable course,* sig. D 4 r.

7. Boemus, *op. cit.* (1611), 186, 11, 246.

8. Ralegh, *History,* sig. K 6 v.

9. Boemus, *Fardle* (1555), sig. P v r.

10. Marian J. Tooley, "Bodin and the medieval theory of climate," *Speculum,* 28 (1953), 76; Bodin, *Method, op. cit.* 87.

11. Heylyn, *Microcosmus,* 548.

12. Carpenter, *op. cit.,* Bk. II, sig. Mm * 2 v.

13. Boemus, *op. cit.* (1555), sig. B iii v – B iii r.

14. La Primaudaye, *op. cit.,* sig. Bb i v – Bb i r.

15. Pedro Mexia, *The treasurie of auncient and moderne times. Being the learned collections, judicious readings, and memorable observations: Not onely divine, morall and philosophicall; But also poeticall, martiall, politicall, historicall, astrologicall, etc. Translated out of that worthy Spanish gentleman, Pedro Mexia . . .* (London: W. Jaggard, 1613) sig. Qqq 3 r.

16. William Strachey, *The historie of travell into Virginia Britania* (1612) (London: Hakluyt Society, 1953), 54–55.

17. Don Cameron Allen, *The legend of Noah: renaissance rationalism in art, science, and letters* (Urbana, Illinois: University of Illinois

[Illinois Studies in Language and Literature, Vol. 33, Numbers 3–4, 1949], 116, note 13.)

18. Antoine Yves Goguet, *De l'origine des lois, des artes, et des sciences, et leurs progres chez les anciens peuples* (Paris: Desaint et Saillant, 1758). Translated into English as *The origin of laws, arts, and science, and their progress among the most ancient nations* (Edinburgh: Alexander Donalson and John Reid, 1761), I, xvi.

19. Victor Harris, *All coherence gone* (Chicago: University of Chicago Press, 1949), 127–28; Don Cameron Allen, "The degeneration of man and Renaissance pessimism," *Studies in Philology*, 35 (1938), 202–27.

20. Brerewood, *Diversity of languages*, 8.

21. Purchas, *Pilgrimage*, sig. C 4 v, D 4 r; Roger Williams, *Key into the language of America*, 118.

22. Ralegh, *op. cit.*, sig. F 6 r – F 6 v.

23. Burton, *Anatomy*, III, 325–39.

24. Mexia, *op. cit.*, sig. I, Qqq 3 r.

25. La Primaudaye, *op. cit.*, sig. Bb 2 r.

26. Heylyn, *Cosmographie* (1652), sig. A 5 v; Cawley, *Milton and the literature of travel, passim.*

27. Purchas, *op. cit.*, sig. Rr 5 r.

28. Quoted in Hiram Collins Haydn, *The counter-Renaissance* (New York: Charles Scribner's Sons, 1950), 216.

29. Niccolò Machiavelli, *The History of Florence* . . . (London: Bohn, 1847), 202.

30. Atkinson, *Nouveaux horizons*, 22.

31. Le Roy, *op. cit.*, sig. A 3 r.

32. *Ibid.*, sig. Y 5 r.

33. *Ibid.*, sig. Y 4 v.

34. *Ibid., sig.* Y 6 r.

35. Allen, *op. cit.*, 41, 60.

36. Samuel Terrien, "History of the interpretation of the Bible. III. Modern period," in *The interpreter's Bible* (New York: Abingdon–Cokesbury Press, 1951–57), I, 127–30.

37. David Rice McKee, "Isaac de la Peyrère; a precursor of eighteenth-century critical deists," *Publications of the Modern Language Association*, 59 (1944), 465; Allen, *op cit.*, 134.

38. McKee, *op. cit.*, 464.

39. Allen, *op. cit.*, 135.

40. *Ibid.*, 133.

41. McKee, *op. cit.*, 461–63.

42. Bodin, *Method*, 8; see also John Lackey Brown, *The Methodus ad facilem historiarum cognitionem of Jean Bodin: a critical study* (Washington: Catholic University of America Press, 1939), *passim.*

43. Bodin, *Method*, 21.

44. *Ibid.*, 24–25.

45. "It is evident," said Bodin, "that the Chaldeans were the most ancient of all peoples, by the weighty testimony not only of Moses but

also of Megasthenes, Herodotus, Ctesias, and Xenophon." (*Ibid.,* 335, 337.)

46. *Ibid.,* 85.

47. Tooley, "Bodin and the medieval theory of climate," 64–83.

48. Bodin, *Commonweale,* sig. Aaa iiii r.

49. *Ibid.,* sig. Aaa iii r.

50. Bodin, *Method,* 26.

51. Bodin, *Commonweale,* sig. Ccc ii r.

52. Lynn Thorndike, "The survival of medieval intellectual interests into modern times," *Speculum,* II (1927), 159; on medieval astrological ethnology, see Theodore Otto Wedel, *The medieval attitude toward astrology, particularly in England* (New Haven: Yale University Press, 1920), 71–73; Allen, *Star-crossed Renaissance,* 4; Ruth Leila Anderson, *Elizabethan psychology and Shakespeare's plays* (Iowa City, Iowa: The University, 1927); Tooley, *op. cit., passim.*

53. Bodin, *Method,* 367.

54. *Ibid,* 302.

55. Bodin, *Commonweale,* sig. Mm V v.

56. Leonard F. Dean, "Bodin's *Methodus* in England before 1625," *Studies in Philology,* 39 (1942), 160–66.

57. Gabriel Harvey, *Letter book of Gabriel Harvey, A.D. 1573–1580,* edited by E. J. L. Scott (Camden Society Publications, n.s., London: 1884), XXXIII, 79.

58. John Norman Leonard Baker, "Academic geography in the seventeenth and eighteenth centuries," *Scottish Geographical Magazine,* 51 (1935), 132.

59. Burton, *op. cit.,* II, 61–62.

60. Clive Staples Lewis, *English literature in the sixteenth century, excluding drama* (Oxford: Clarendon Press, 1954), 308.

61. Quoted in Foster Watson, *The beginnings of the teaching of modern subjects in England.* (London: Isaac Pitman and Sons, 1909), 109–10.

62. Purchas, *op. cit.,* sig. E 6 v.

63. Heylyn, *Cosmographie* (1652), sig, C 4 v.

64. *Ibid.,* sig. C 4 v – C 5 r.

65. *Ibid.,* sig. C 3 v – C 4 r.

66. Carpenter, *op. cit.,* Bk. II, sig. Ff * i r.

67. *Ibid.,* Bk. II, sig. Ee * i v, Ff * 4 v.

68. Casaubon, *Use and custome,* 80.

69. Thomas Burnet, *The theory of the earth: containing an account of the original of the earth, and of all the general changes which it hath already undergone, or is to undergo, till the consummation of all things* (London: R. Norton for Walter Kettilby, 1684–90), *passim.*

70. Robert Ralston Cawley, *Milton's literary craftsmanship; a study of A brief history of Moscovia, with an edition of the text* (Princeton: Princeton University Press, 1941), vii, 5; see also Cawley, *Milton and the literature of travel, passim.*

71. Elbert N. S. Thompson, "Milton's knowledge of geography," *Studies in Philology,* 16 (1919), 159–60.

72. Cawley, *Milton and the literature of travel*, 23.

73. Zera Silver Fink, "Milton and the theory of climatic influence," *Modern Language Quarterly*, 2 (1941), 70–71.

CHAPTER VIII

Similarities and Their Documentary Properties

"Man is an Object of greatest vicinity to himself, and hath thereby . . . the best opportunity to know and understand himself with the greatest certainty and evidence."—SIR MATTHEW HALE.

"Though man has always been a problem to himself, modern man has aggravated that problem by his too simple and premature solutions."—REINHOLD NIEBUHR.

IF DIVERSITIES IN CULTURE were puzzling to thoughtful men during the Renaissance, so also were similarities. For there are two types of mind among scholars. There are those who in their efforts to understand the world submit to the methodological principle of specification or particularization. When drawn into making comparisons, they resist assertions of likeness, similarity, analogy, unity. The phenomenon of differentness in culture prevails against even the most persuasive arguments from likeness. The other type adheres to the principle of homogeneity; to the fruitfulness in explanation of arguing from the similar, the corresponding, the parallel, or the identical. These latter inquirers, though their services to thought can scarcely be overpraised, have sometimes strained the facts in an effort to reduce divergent phenomena to some common denominator. In the study of man, rightly or wrongly, this common denominator has often taken the form of a common or original human nature, a common or natural body of laws, an universal series of species, orders or classes, or a common and natural historical origin.

Both habits of ratiocination were operative in Renaissance ethnological thought. Though the voyages of discovery and the travels of merchants and missionaries had brought the Europeans face to face with an astonishing and never-to-be-forgotten array of cultural diversities, they were thought also to have revealed an equally astonishing assortment of cultural likenesses. When the usual Europocentric comparisons were made, variance, dissimilarity, and difference were observed, it is true, but cultural correspondences also made themselves known and, to some observers and for some purposes, seemed actually to predominate.

With respect to time or history, the cultural similarities thus perceived fell generally into two categories. Some were contemporary. They were remarked between people such as living Europeans and living African Negroes; or between living Negroes and living American Indians; or between living East Indians and living Turks, the people of Cochin China and the desert nomads, living Christians and living pagans; or between innumerable other contemporary pairs and combinations. But this recognition of contemporary and coexisting correspondences failed to exhaust the matter. Bred upon the historism of Scripture and other forms of antique thought, accustomed to historicizing the whole range of natural and social phenomena, certain men of the Renaissance were even more conscious of historical parallels, or the similarity between some present peoples and some past peoples. The usual historical likenesses cited were those purportedly observable between contemporary Indian or African behavior and that of the Old Testament tribes; between the culture of contemporary savagery and that of the ancient Greeks or Romans; between contemporary savagery and the barbarism of northern

Europe in Roman or medieval times; between contemporary savagery and the rude, rustic peasantry of contemporary Europe, supposedly still untouched by civilizing influences.[1] Such likenesses were thought to have historiographical significance. They were thought to confer documentary properties upon the contemporary member of each pair of parallels, to make of it a present and accessible reflection of the past of some very early and otherwise undocumented cultural condition. Comparison leading to the disclosure of similitudes was thus regarded as an highly illuminating procedure, not only with respect to the existing array of disparate peoples, but also when applied in a temporal dimension to the reconstruction of the cultures of peoples living early in time.

This stress, this procedural reliance upon the observation of cultural correspondence, was far from new in European thought. It was a mental habit which was present, unquestioned and unexamined, in high antiquity and which persisted throughout the Renaissance, the Enlightenment, and well into the twentieth century. Long before the discovery of the New World, correspondences were mentioned by nearly every seafarer, land-traveler, or hearth-bound savant, from Herodotus to Mandeville, from Marco Polo to Samuel Purchas. They were utilized in the construction of conjectural histories, so-called in the eighteenth century by Dugald Stewart. They formed the substance of the Comparative Method so christened by Auguste Comte. They have been discussed with care by Sir Edward Burnett Tylor, and by many recent writers of textbooks on anthropology.

To a degree, the interest in similarities persisted because they possessed elements of surprise and amusement. It has been an unfailing source of entertainment to be reminded, now and again, that some feature of European culture is shared with the Hottentot or Cherokee. How in the world could this have happened? Similarities were also useful in description, especially when voyagers and others found themselves face to face with the almost impossible task of conveying to provincial European readers the bewildering customs of peoples living in non-European lands. Without cameras, without phonographs, without recording instruments with which to report accurately what had been seen and heard, with pens only or by word of mouth, these early and untutored reporters of ethnographical phenomena were compelled to resort to verbal and logical devices. It was believed, therefore, and not without foundation, that by finding points of agreement between the European, well known and long familiar, and the savage, recently discovered and strange, savagery could be interpreted or transformed into the relatively understood and commonplace.

Hence it was, as it has been mentioned before, that, when one of the Franciscan friars visited a Mongolian temple in the fourteenth century, the outlandish was clothed for his readers in the guise of the accustomed. He beheld there, or so he said, "a chapell" containing the image of a woman "with a Child hanging about her necke, and a Lampe burning before her." The Virgin, of course. There also he saw "a great Altar, after the Dutch fashion, that one may go around it." For the like purpose of communicating with his readers, Johann Boemus said that the Lacedemonians used "the same orders in their Kings Funeralles, as the barbarous peoples of Asia did," and in this agreed with the Persians; that the Moscovites shot "leaden bullets out of brazen peeces after the manner of the Almaines, and learned their music after the Greek manner."[2] Muenster, the great German author of the *Cosmographia,* engaged constantly in comparison. Time and again non-European cultures were contrasted with one another and correspondences elicited: the Lacedemonians, he said, "agree with Persians, that when the King is dead, he that succeedeth dischargeth from all debts whosoever oweth anye thing to the King"; or "the customs of the English and Scots are very similar."[3] But more often the touchstone by which all other cultures were judged and delineated was Europocentric. That is to say, they were compared with Continental peoples. To European eyes, with their limited vision of what was possible in the variability of religions and other practices, these were naturally more likely to appear similar to those of Europe, past or present, than to those of any other people. Accordingly, the Asiatic Scythians, who lived beyond Mt. Imaus, were thought to worship the Roman gods Vesta, Jupiter, Apollo, Hercules, and Venus[4]; while in Virginia, according to that English man of letters, William Strachey, the principal "temple" of the Indians was so holy that like the "Grecian Nigromancers," none but the priests and kings dared to come therein. And when Pierre d'Avity attempted a description of the religion of Cuzco in South America, he told of a pagan temple where the sacrament of confession was observed, the Trinity worshiped, and a certain cake made, composed of "maize and the bloude of white sheepe," like the bread of the Eucharist.[5]

In early ethnological reflection as well as in later, resemblance among peoples living contemporaneously in neighboring territories was taken more or less for granted. Day-to-day communication—trade, intermarriage, war—took care of that. It was only when parallels made their appearance in cultures widely separated from one another, in either time or space, that thought was brought to a pause. Then it was that similarities became something more than amusing; they became a problem calling for a solution.

Perplexity concerning widely separated cultural likenesses certainly existed in Renaissance Europe as early as the mid-sixteenth century. They were cited in the *Essayes* of Montaigne to convey to readers one of the more inexplicable oddities of human behavior. "I have divers times wondred," said he, "to see in so great a distance of times and places, the simpathy or jumping of so great a number of popular and wilde opinions, and of extravagant customes and beliefs." Speaking then in *spatial* terms of the peoples of the New World, he pointed out that nations had been found "which (as farre as we know) had never heard of us," yet "where our crosses were in severall waies in great esteeme." There also was found "a very expresse and lively image of our Penitentiaries : the use of Myters, the Priests single life; the Arte of Divination by the entrailes of sacrificed beasts; the abstinence from all sorts of flesh and fish, for their food; the order among Priests in saying of their divine service, to use, a not vulgar, but a particular tongue . . . There were places found, where they used the perswasion of the day of judgement," so that the people grew angry at the Spaniards who defiled their graves and dispersed their bones. They also "used traffike by exchange . . . and had Fairs and Markets for that purpose." There were those who adored but one God, "who heretofore lived man, in perfect Virginitie, fasting and penance, preaching the law of Nature, and the ceremonies of religion; and who vanished out of the world, without any naturall death."[6] On the other hand, in his *New found worlde or antarctike* (1556), André Thevet reported the existence of strange temporal correspondences. "These *Americanes,*" he said, "they make their haire grow as Monkes were wont to doe, the which passeth not their eares." Then, still dissatisfied with this exposition of the trait, he pushed his comparisons *further back in time.* "It would be thought, ye if these wilde men have frequented Asia, they should have learned this of the Abantes. . . . Also Plutarke sheweth in the like Theseus, that ye custome of the *Athenians* was, that they . . . were bounde to offer lockes of heare . . . to the God in the Iland of *Delphos.*"[7]

With observations such as these, mere wonder gave way to more or less organized investigation. Similarities, both spatial and temporal, became the stuff of ethnological problems not yet to this day solved or dismissed, namely: How had correspondences in cultures, in regions as far removed from one another as Europe, Asia, Africa, and the Americas, come to be at all? How had those as widely separated in time as Hebraic or classical antiquity and the savages of Renaissance discovery come to exist?

It was primarily in the contemplation of man's religions and his languages that the presence of conformities first challenged the interest of scholars at least in the sixteenth century. Given the plurality of religions in the world, past and present, together with the assumed uniqueness, historical priority, and superiority of the Judeo-Christian synthesis, how, it was asked, were the surprising similitudes between Christianity and other faiths to be accounted for; how especially the likenesses which seemed unaccountably to obtain between the religion of Christendom and the idolatries of the pagan, the heathen, and the savage? It was hard enough for Christians to acknowledge that their own faith, obviously the true one, could have competitors; it was still harder to understand how practices seemingly identical with those followed around Christian altars could have counterparts in the quagmires of heathendom, removed from Europe by weeks and months of travel. Given again the plurality of diverse languages among men and the assumed superiority and historical priority of the ancient Hebrew, how were similarities in words and grammatical structure to be explained?

In accounting for the similitudes observable among the religions of mankind, suggestions were naturally drawn from that safest of all sources, the sacred history. When similarities in Christian rites or beliefs were noted in non-Christian lands, especially among savage folk, the devil was charged with the responsibility. The widespread distribution of idolatry, that cunning device which separated man from God, said Viret

(1511–1571), was obviously his handiwork. He had arrogated to himself the power and might of God; he had uttered counterfeits of holy things.[8] From the time of William Rubruck onward, all travelers in Buddhist Tartary were struck by the resemblances between many features of this ecclesiastical system and the usages of the Roman Church. They were ascribed to "the manifest deceits of the devil," who had parodied the mysteries of the Christian faith. Although idol worship had been rooted out of the Christian West, the remoter parts of the world, to which the Evil One had fled, were still full of it. "There is scarce any thing," said Father Joseph de Acosta (c. 1539–1600) in his *Natural and moral history of the Indies* (1588), "instituted by Jesus Christ our Saviour in his Lawe and his Gospel, the which the Devil hath not counter-fieted in some sort and carried to his Gentiles."[9] Where God would have built a temple, said Robert Burton, the devil had put a chapel; where God had ordained sacrifices, the devil had established oblations; where God had planted religion, the devil had instilled superstition.[10] Moreover, his nefarious work had had its inception long before among the pagans. To steal away from antique man his belief in the Incarnation, he had "faigned" things like it : Bacchus was said to be twice-born; Erichthonius was "borne of Pallas a virgin."[11]

Closely akin to this common intellectual expedient, which attributed to God's adversary all religious parallelisms from which orthodox Christians shrank back in disapproval, was a concurrent tendency to deal with the problem of cultural similarities within the framework of the prevalent Renaissance pessimism. They were ascribed to a process of change, but a process of change in the direction of corruption, degradation, degeneration, or decline. By some observers, the plurality of religions in the world, or what was then taken to be a discon-certing loss of uniformity in belief, was thought to be the end product of this philosophy of history. Cited as unquestioned evidences of degeneration, were not only the religions of the Greeks, Romans, and other peoples of high antiquity, but the whole swarm of savage idolatries—all existing systems of belief, indeed, save only that of the Christians. All were regarded as the degenerate expressions of some earlier and purer faith, usually assumed to be that of the Hebrews, the ancestral matrix of Christianity; and all were thought to bear some attenuated resemblance to this common source, some slight "reminder," or "remainder," "remnant," or "survival" in reverse.[12]

The manifest corruption of classical creed and rite was often proclaimed. "We Christians now lyvinge in the cleare light of the Gospel," said Stephen Batman, "may evidently see, with what erroneous trumperies, Antiquitie hath been nozzled : in what foggy mystes they have long wandred : in what filthye puddles they have been myered."[13] Moved by a like conviction, and desiring to synchronize classical mythology with Old Testament history, Jean Bodin adopted the position that the myths were merely corrupt versions of prior Christian or Hebrew truths. Islam was held to be an heretical form of Christianity; Islamic principles and practices, degraded remnants of earlier Christian creed and rite. The identification of the gods and heroes of classical paganism with Biblical personages, followed by a declaration of their obvious degradation, became an established practice among Christian historical writers. Marsilio Ficino spoke of Plato as the Attic Moses. Noah was said to have been known among the pagans under the names of Prometheus, Saturn, Deucalion, or Janus; the identification with Saturn being more certain than any other because "both men divided the earth among their sons, both were described as the justest men of their age, both were associated with drunkenness, both were able to converse with beasts, both were 'men of the earth,' and both instructed the world in agriculture."[14] Said Bishop Stillingfleet : "The story of Saturn and Moses do much agree and many things concerning Moses are preserved in the story of Bacchus."[15] It was also thought that the memory of Jacob's long service with his uncle Laban was preserved in the story of Apollo and his banishment. Certain parallelisms in the nomenclature of the heathen gods were nothing but corruptions of the name of Jehovah, proceeding from classical misinterpretations of the earlier Hebrew Scripture.[16]

In the study of linguistic similarities, on the other hand, or whenever philological investigation was conducted under the commanding shadow of the Tower of Babel, the fundamental conditions of explanation were somewhat different. For variety had been decreed, that day on the Plain of Shinar, by the Eternal; and neither the plurality of tongues nor their similarities could well be imputed to the devil. There seemed to be nothing left for the scholar but to count diverse tongues or, when that failed to satisfy, to try to reach a decision as to which among them was the original, the first and earliest, out of which all others had arisen. The initial, or statistical, problem was greatly simplified by the tenacity of medieval legend. This declared that there were either seventy languages, or seventy-two, the slight difference providing substance for several centuries of enjoyable wrangling.[17] The question of the original language was more complex, and its answer awaited the prolonged deliberations of generations of philologists.

It is instructive in the latter connection to note that Abraham Mylius (1563–1637), a Dutch theologian and linguist, was among the first of his time to perceive the presence of an historical problem in linguistic correspondences.[18] They were due, said he, either to the natural congruence of name and thing, to common inheritance from an earlier tongue, or to borrowing induced by intertribal or international trade or mingling. Soon it was determined that the first possibility, natural congruity, fitted only a few cases, the other two—

inheritance, or the transmission of similar linguistic elements along the channels of tradition from a common source— became the favored explanation. Later, since the adoption of inheritance as an hypothesis raised the question of the original or common tongue, that problem became paramount, especially in the seventeenth century, when, with the Old Testament as the supreme guide, pre-Babel Hebrew became the favored candidate.

Meanwhile, the similarities detected between cultures existing at different dated levels introduced an important new element into linguistic discussion. They suggested either persistence or borrowing; they suggested historical or genetic relationships among peoples or groups. And it was here that a new and different question arose, namely, the question of documentation. For if, as it had often been said, similarities in language were ascribable to their derivation over long tracts of time from a common source in Hebrew, how was this hypothesis to be sustained? What kind of evidence was to be brought forward to confirm it?

In the presence of this new problem, similarities, similitudes, correspondences, likenesses, agreements, conformities, parallels, or whatever at one time or another they happened to be called, took on a new meaning and a new methodological function. They constituted a problem—yes. But they also possessed, or they came logically to be endowed with, properties which made them invaluable to students in *solving* problems. Resemblances, detected as existing at different dates, suggested to linguists and other students of cultural phenomena that like traits and like institutions might be more profoundly related than appeared on the surface. They might have been transmitted across time by successive generations, or across space by wandering peoples.

With something of this sort in mind, the procedure adopted among linguists to prove the primacy of the Hebrew tongue or original linguistic uniformity, took the form of compiling word lists in various languages and the comparing of vocabularies, present and past. Bodin, for example, in support of the thesis that the Jews were the oldest of mankind, attempted to trace current German words to the Celtic, French words to the Greek, and Greek words to the Hebrew. If words with equivalent meanings in current languages were spelled like their counterparts in the Hebrew—if, in that sense, similarities were elicited—then it was assumed that the existing language or languages in which such likenesses occurred were later and degenerated forms of the earlier and superior Hebrew tongue. Though many of these derivations were preposterous, the practice of comparing etymologies across historical time became an absorbing game among professional philologists. Among the names associated with the procedure in the sixteenth and seventeenth centuries were those of Postellus, Gesner, Lazius, Avenarius, Lamphaeus, Scaliger, Casaubonus, Grotius, Salmasius, Heinsius, Martinius, Vossius, Bochartus, Daviesius, and Lyscandrus.[19] But even more indicative of original linguistic uniformity was that type of "family relationship" among the tongues of men shown purportedly by correspondences in structure. And so flexible was the argument from similarities, considered as containing documentary import, that toward the middle of the sixteenth century new theories of origin began to compete with the old. Low German was proposed by Johannes Goropius Becanus as older than the language of the Jewish tribesmen, and therefore the original language; and in 1669 John Webb, a member of the Royal Society, asked for the acceptance of Chinese as the oldest language of all.

Mylius and others also stressed the process of borrowing or diffusion as a solution of the problem of language likenesses. Commerce and colonization had led to the use of like words for like objects and ideas. Time in its passage, said Louis Le

Roy, "maketh words to fall; and use maketh new to spring in their places. . . . But such change and varitie commeth ordinarily of the mingling of divers Nations, and of great faires, and armies. . . ." The Latin language, for example, followed the advance of Roman colonization. Its spread or, in another sense, the imposition of linguistic uniformity on colonies, was aided, according to Brerewood, by the fact that the business of the empire had to be conducted in Latin, that the laws were written in Latin, that the magistrates handed down their decisions in Latin, and that the schools, "erected in sundry Cities of the Provinces," allowed nothing to be taught but Latin.[20] The task of the scholar in dealing with this aspect of his subject, the delineation of the process of borrowing or diffusion, called for the power to distinguish between an earlier donating and a later receiving language, or between lender and borrower. In this matter, two generally accepted principles served as guides: first, an older language was usually regarded as the donor, a younger one the receiver; second, the oldest language was Hebrew, hence all others in some respect were genetically related to Hebrew. But to most men, depressed by the gloom of Renaissance pessimism, cultural borrowing could mean nothing better than copying, with an inevitable degeneration from the quality of the original. Only those customs and languages bearing the seal of original Adamic use, or of Mosaic ratification, were free from taint.[21]

But the effort to deal with cultural similarities as a problem was not all. It was paralleled in the sixteenth and seventeenth centuries by another even more complex, or an attempt to employ similarities in the solution of other problems. In general, such other problems were of an historical nature. They involved the recovery of historical periods usually deemed inaccessible by any procedure. That is to say, solutions involving the use of cultural correspondences followed the principle of ascribing to one thing all the qualities of its like. Thus, given a pair of similar traits—one from a contemporary but perhaps utterly history-less culture and another from an ancient but richly documented one—the age and evidential import of the ancient trait was imparted to its history-less contemporary, permitting the documentary use of the contemporary, despite its recency and historical emptiness.

With scarcely a dissenting voice and with all its frailties, this ingenious procedure was pressed into service in the presence of a wide range of problems—historical, sociological, ethnological. During the Renaissance, for example, it was called upon to solve at least three : first, the question of the origin of the native peoples in the Americas; second, the problem of replacing the chronology of the world based on Genesis with one more in conformity with historical fact; and third, the problem of bolstering up the hierarchical notion that savagery, as known to the sixteenth and seventeenth centuries, was antecedent to all other forms of human culture. Still later, and still unexamined, the same procedure became the mainstay of the Comparative Method, by sociologists and anthropologists in the developmental or evolutionary interest of "proving" the "primitive" origin of culture.

Apparently one of the earlier instances in which cultural similarities were called upon to perform their documentary magic was a direct result of the discoveries and in response to the problem of the origin of the American Indians. The difficulty sprang in part from natural curiosity, in part from the intellectual necessity for relating these strange people in some familiar way to the commonly accepted scheme of the universe and of man. Correspondences were therefore consulted either to "prove" their Noachian descent or to demonstrate that they were not autochtonous but migrant from some other region. Other problems arose in the field of religion or in those closely related to it. To confound the heretics, to refute the "atheistic" critics of the Scriptural account of man's history on this earth, it was regarded by the devout as necessary to bring both the ancient Hebrews and all other ancient peoples into the single orthodox chronology of six thousand years. To combat Popery, or so it seemed to the Reformers, it became necessary to expose the corruption of the Church by linking Roman rites with pagan practices. In both of these controversies, the contenders leaned heavily upon the documentary implications of correspondences. In the matter of chronology they were called upon to "prove" the greater antiquity of the Hebrews to the Greeks and Romans, and hence the greater reliability of the Mosiac history. In the quarrel with Romanism, the Reformers endeavored to show an historical connection between the religious practices of idolatrous classical antiquity and those of the Papists. The problem of savagery was kindled by the very existence of the savage himself, and the pressing need to bring him conceptually into some familiar and clearly defined relationship with other members of the human family. In harmony with the temper of the times, these questions and others could best be answered in genetic or historical terms, or on the assumption and then "proof" that one thing was prior to another, one people earlier or later than another, one culture older or younger than another. Hence, all of these problems were solved on the ground, sound or unsound, that cultural similarities were clothed with documentary import; that by finding similarities, and then using them as historical evidence, temporal relationships could be established, historical or genetic sequences determined.

One of the first questions to be asked after the Columbian voyages—or as soon as it became clear that the natives of the Americas were not Marco Polo's Cathayans but a brand new people—was ethnological. Who were they? Who were their forefathers? Were they autochthonous, or had there been more than one Adam? Were they the descendants of a special creation or were they the existing representatives of some ancient migration from Ararat: the great, great, grandchildren many times removed of one of the sons of Noah? General interest in the problem was very wide, and its implications for Biblical orthodoxy crucial.

With wide interest, solutions were legion. There were so many, indeed, and they were all so involuted, repetitious, and contradictory, that by the middle of the seventeenth century every conscientious geographer or cosmographer felt obliged to summarize and evaluate them. John Ogilby was a case in point. "About the Original of the Americans," said he in his *America, being the Latest, and Most Accurate Description of the New World* (1671),

> . . . the Learned Dispute so much, that they find nothing more difficult in Story . . . for whether inquiry be made after the time, when the Americans first settled themselves where they now inhabit, or after what manner they came thither, either by Shipping or by Land; on purpose, or accidentally; driven by Storm, or else forc'd by a more powerful People, to remove from their old Plantations, and seek for new? or if any one should be yet more curious, asking the way that directed them out of another Countrey to this New World? or else enquire for those People, from whom the Americans deriv'd themselves? He will find several Opinions. . . .[22]

Then, too, as might well have been expected, especially at this era in European thought when the historical meaning of the first eleven chapters of Genesis was in dispute, nearly all theories turned on the venerable alternatives of monogenism and polygenism, with the weight of opinion thrown to the former. Marc Lescarbot, a French explorer in Brazil, for example, was a monogenist. It was his belief that the newly discovered continents had been visited and peopled by Noah himself. Was it credible, he asked, that this man of many skills had failed to perfect himself in the art of shipbuilding? that during a post-Flood career of 350 years he had retired from active maritime life, refusing to carry out any more lofty enterprises? Certainly, it should have been no more difficult for him to have sailed from Gibraltar to New France, or from Cape Verde to Brazil, than for his children to have carried their families and impedimenta from Java to Japan.

Given a typical Noachian hypothesis such as this, the main tasks of the scholar were first, to indicate similarities between New World tribes and some Asian people deemed to be descendants of Noah; and second, to show how, or by what form of transportation and by what route, Noah or one of his progeny could have made his way first across the Eurasian land mass and then over the dividing ocean to the continents of the New World. In other words, the general outline of the theory of the peopling of the New World, now accepted by anthropologists, the theory of migration from Asia, was proposed and widely adopted as early as the seventeenth century, if not before.[23]

A little later, when a few dissenting souls undertook to defend variants of this orthodox position, or in the wake of La Peyrère to propose polygenetic solutions, Thomas Burnett spoke out for his anti-Noachian brethren by suggesting the presence in America of an autochthonous, prediluvian population unrelated by descent to either Shem, Ham, or Japheth. After the Flood, said he in his *Theory of the earth* (1681), when the earth was broken and the sea laid open, the same race might have continued in the New World, if settled there before. He saw no need for deducing all mankind from Noah. If America was peopled before, it might have so continued, for Providence, "we may reasonably suppose, made provision for a saving remnant in every Continent."[24] Others, influenced by classical humanism, identified America with the island of Atlantis in Plato's *Timaeus,* and its people with the purported remnants of another, but local, deluge which was said to have swept away the majority of the population. Something of the same kind may have been in the mind of Sir Francis Bacon when he wrote of the new continent,

. . . marvel you not at the thin population nor at the rudeness and ignorance of the people; for you must account your inhabitants of America as a young people; younger a thousand years, at the least, than the rest of the world; for that there was so much time between the universal flood and their particular inundation. For the poor remnant of human seed which remained in their mountains peopled the country again slowly, by little and little; and being simple and savage people, (not like Noah and his sons, which was the chief family of the earth), they were not able to leave letters, arts, and civility to their posterity.[25]

In due course, even the classical or Platonic theory of plural local floods, and the indigenous origin of the Indians, was challenged. For there were other heterodox proposals. Some of these derived the Red Indians from the Welsh, some from the Greeks and Romans, some from the Carthaginians, the Scythians, the Egyptians,[26] the Jews, the Ten Lost Tribes of Israel, the Africans, Ethiopians, French Kurlanders, or Phoenicians. "The Learned men of these later times," said Ogilby as he struggled to make a proper exposition of conflicting opinions, "jangle amongst themselves."[27]

But whatever the theory, monogenetic or polygenetic, orthodox or heterodox, its proof almost invariably rested upon documentation by similarities. That is to say, the procedure employed involved the comparison of the presently existing American Indian—physically, philologically, religiously, and culturally—with other peoples, either contemporaneous or antecedent, to determine which he most resembled. When resemblances were found, as they always were, consanguinity or a genetic cultural relationship was inferred. As Ogilby said, when the descent of the Red Men from the Phoenicians was in dispute : "We will search a little further to see whether the People Analogize, either in their Religion, Policy, Oeconomy, or Custome." This done, and the likenesses established, the American Indians, a contemporary people, were declared to be the descendants of some ancient European or Eurasian people. Somewhere in the back of the mind of every inquirer was the conviction, never analyzed and never questioned, that *a European or Eurasian culture was, and must be, older than an American culture.* Always the newly discovered world was considered to be historically the younger world. Never, in a Europocentric society, was it suggested that similarities, taken alone and without this unconscious historical presumption, might just as well suggest the priority of New World peoples to those of the Old, or a migration from the Americas to Europe. The recency of their discovery, or the tenacity of Biblical tradition, fixed upon the American Indians posteriority in time to the Noachian dispersion or to the events of ancient secular history.

To many minds after the discoveries, it was more or less unthinkable that the Indians could have had other than a Noachian origin, or could have been derived from any people other than the Hebrews. Consequently, the earlier literature usually assumed a long trek across Asia and a Bering landbridge, with supporting comparisons between the existing Indians and the Israelites of the ancient Near East. Some of these likenesses were particularized and quaint. In Father Joseph de Acosta's *Natural and moral history of the Indies* published in Latin in 1588-89,

There are great signes and arguments amongst the common sort of the Indians, to breed a beleefe that they are descended from the Jews; for, commonly you will see them fearfull, submisse, ceremonious, and subtill in lying. And, moreover . . . they weare a short coat or waste-coat, and a cloake imbroidered all around; they goe bare-footed, or with soles tied with latchets over the foot. . . . It appears by their Histories, as also by their ancient pictures, which represent them in this fashion, that this attire was the ancient habite of the Hebrewes, and that these two kinds of garments, which the Indians onely use, were used by Samson, which the Scripture calleth *Tunicam* and *Syndonem;* beeing the same which the Indians terme waste-coat and cloake.[28]

Later, in the seventeenth and eighteenth centuries, French explorers and missionaries developed other explanations of the presence of Indians in America. But here again comparisons and similarities were employed, similarities between Indian custom and the practices of the classical or other peoples of antiquity. The clothing which the Indians wore, said Lescarbot, was like that of the Greeks, seen "in the pictures of Hercules, who killed a lion, and put the skin on his back." No headgear was worn by the savages, and in this they were like all the ancients, the Hebrews, the Persians, and the Romans. "Indeed, Julius Caesar was wont to wear neither cap nor hat."[29] Again, Père Latfitau insisted that the religion of the Indians was basically the same as that of the ancients, and cited innumerable rites and practices which seemed to bear a striking resemblance to those of the Greeks at the time of Homer and the Hebrews at the time of Moses. Hugo Grotius, on the other hand, would have none of this. He preferred a Scandinavian theory of origins, and employed philological correspondence to shore up claims to blood relationship between the Norwegians and the native inhabitants of North America. According to Ogilby, the learned Grotius could see little difference "between Pagod and by-God, or like God: Guaira and Waeijer that is, A Fan; Llama, and Lam, in English Lamb; Peko, and Beke, a Brook and Rivulet. Both Customs and Constitutions have also great resemblance. The Mexicans relate, that their Predecessors only follow'd Hunting; that they divided and reckon'd the Time not by Days, but by Nights, and wash'd their Children as soon as they were born in cold Water." [30]

Controversialists differed widely, of course, on what they regarded as adequate proof of descent and in the thoroughness with which they exploited the evidence purportedly conveyed by similarities. Most of them were satisfied with the citation of only a few of the most obvious likenesses. Edward Brerewood, sometimes referred to as a pioneer in anthropology, defended his acceptance of a connection between the Americans and Asiatic Tartars with a mere handful of correspondences stated in the most general terms. He also resorted to "negative" correspondences, or the assumption that since likenesses had not been discerned, connection was not to be inferred. In his judgment, the Indians unquestionably came from Asia because they had "no rellish nor resemblance at all, of the Arts, or learning, or civility of Europe." Their coloring spoke against an African or Negroid descent. There was no token among them "of the arts or industry of China, or India, or Cataia, or any other civill region along all that border of Asia : But in their grosse ignorance of letters, and of arts, in their idolatrie . . . and many barbarous properties," they resembled the old and rude Tartars, above all nations of the earth. [31]

As early as the middle of the sixteenth century, to be sure, a few scholars began to assume a more critical posture. This was true even of Father de Acosta, who seemed to take the position that the detection of a few similarities between two peoples was not enough to demonstrate historical connection, antecedence, or succession. Unless it could be shown that two cultures were identical over a wide range of traits, the investigator was bound to consider the hypothesis unproved. Speaking of his own suggestion of an historical connection between the Hebrews and the Indians, the Father frankly acknowledged that "all these conjectures were light," and rather against the theory than for it. "For wee know well, that the Hebrewes used letters, whereof there is no shew among the Indians; they are great lovers of silver, these make no care of it; the Jews, if they were not circumcised, held not themselves for Jewes, and contrariwise the Indians are not at all, neyther did they use any ceremonie neere it as many in the East have done."[32] Many years later, John Ogilby voiced a similar warning. Though it be certain, he said, that "the ancient Phenicians liv'd in tents, and sometimes exchang'd eaten-up pastures for fresh," and though the Americans to this day do the same, what of it? Are the Americans thereby to be adjudged of Phoenician extraction? "But why not as well deriv'd from Numidia, Tartary, or the ancient Patriarchs, who all liv'd such an unsettl'd wandering Life? . . . As to their Religion, if it agreed with the Phenicians, it was the same that all the World profess'd at that time, and therefore may as well be extracted from any other, as them."[33]

But despite these procedural doubts, these admonitions, to beware of hasty generalizations, similarities, however incorrectly observed, continued to be cited as evidence. Broad and assured judgments were made on slender grounds. Differences, and the part they should have played in any such argument, were largely ignored. Missionaries, owing to protracted residence in the Americas, enjoyed an advantage over the explorers in their knowledge of some of the Indian languages. Unhappily, few of them were willing to stay strictly within the limits of their own competence. They were prone to hazard risky hypotheses on the grounds of conformities much too hastily established. It would be unnecessary to stress these points were it not for the fact that they reveal the weakness of the argument itself, the confusion between likeness and identity, between superficial analogies and sounder indications of historical dependence. It was for reasons such as these that one seventeenth-century scholar, Bishop Stillingfleet, refused to participate in the American Indian controversy. After a discussion of the origins of nations in general he closed his remarks with a plea for testimony of a more trustworthy character. On the peopling of the vast new continent of America, he said, "I cannot think we have yet sufficient information, either concerning the passages thither . . . or concerning any Records the Indians may have among themselves. . . . Only in the general it appears from the remaining tradition of the Flood and many Rites and Customes used among them, that they had the same original with us."[34]

Cultural similitudes in the sixteenth and seventeenth centuries were profoundly interesting to men in many fields of controversy; and their use as documentation, where documentation was otherwise scanty or absent, was all but irresistible. Thus comparisons came to be made, and correspondences were again employed in the context of two well-known controversies over religion. In one of these, the bone of contention was chronology. Argument revolved erratically around the opposition between a sacred and a secular computation of the world's age. In the other, a more sectarian quarrel, disagreement proceeded from a Protestant attempt to belittle the Roman communion by charging it with a pagan origin. Whatever the dispute, however, similarities were elicited between a contemporary religious condition and a past one. Likenesses were then endowed conceptually with documentary significance; and employed in making judgments on contested questions of historical priority or on the origin of contemporary religious practices.

For the orthodox Christian and Bible reader, there could never be any doubt that the true chronology of man's past was already known. The Book of Genesis contained the oldest human records; and Moses, the first historian, was the authority to be reckoned with by anyone who desired authentic information concerning the earliest peoples and the earliest episodes in human history.[35] There was also no doubt as to the length of the span of time covered by the historical books of the Old Testament, of the historical period, or of man's residence on the planet; nor was there any doubt concerning the age of the universe. After all, the life spans of the patriarchs were given. The total of these successive generations, together with the length of major episodes in the history of the first people, the Hebrews, could be computed. Their sum showed an interval of approximately four thousand years between the Creation and the birth of Christ, or, with the addition of the span of Christian European history, a total historical period of about six thousand years. The tact with which the commentators handled this problem in the first few chapters of Genesis indicated its gravity. It was agreed among them that these chapters constituted "the only reliable history of mankind for the first sixteen hundred years of its existence;" while the accounts of such classical historians as Herodotus, alleging the greater antiquity of the Egyptians and Babylonians, "were clearly post diluvian, or when presumed to be antediluvian, were fabulous."[36]

This sweeping claim found confirmation of a kind in a simple, conventional, congenial, and confusing piece of analogical reasoning. A day was a thousand years unto the Lord; Adam, a Hebrew, had come on the sixth day of Creation; Christ, the second Adam, had come among the Hebrew people in the sixth millennial epoch. What could be plainer? Though claims to greater antiquity might be made by nations which considered themselves older than the Jews, they need not be heeded. Their pretensions were unsupportd by the necessary Biblical evidence, even for that skeptical Frenchman Jean Bodin, whose book bore the English title of *Method for the easy comprehension of history.* "From all the writers of other nations," said Bodin during one of his more orthodox moments, "I see no one older than Moses. Herodotus the oldest, Ctesias, Hallicanus, and Xenophon, contemporaries, are younger than Moses by eighteen hundred years." [37] The tale told to Herodotus to the effect that "there had been a kingdom among the Egyptians for 13 thousand centuries" was not to be believed. Even more absurd was the assertion that these dwellers on the Nile had a history of 800,000 years hidden away in their records, and the Chaldeans one of 470,000. Since (according to the chronology of the sacred history) the origin of the pagan nations had taken place after that of the Hebrews, the testimony of pagan history to events allegedly occurring prior to Creation, and prior to the Flood, was to be rejected as irresponsible hearsay. The episodes referred to were obviously postdiluvian. By common orthodox consent, the genealogies of all nations were traceable from Adam through Noah to one of his sons, and thence perhaps to the Trojans, a favorite postdiluvian forebear. Both historians and divines felt themselves bound by this train of reasoning. Though often accused of skepticism or outright atheism, Sir Walter Ralegh composed his *History of the world* within the framework of the Mosaic chronology. When and if he cited profane historians, it was only for events after the Flood, or for manners and customs which, being of later origin, were unaffected by Flood conditions. Many other historians, national and universal, did the same. And even that great scientist, Sir Isaac Newton, as late as the year 1732, found time and inclination to publish a work on the *Chronology of the ancient nations amended*. His purpose was to rebuke atheism, to refute rationalist criticism of the Bible, and to make the chronology of human history "suit with the Course of Nature, with Astronomy, with Sacred History, with Herodotus the Father of History, and with itself." [38]

But meanwhile the critics were not silent. After a two-hundred-year quarrel over the canon, text, and inspiration of

Scripture, there were many intelligent and conscientious men who no longer regarded the Bible as infallible, or the method of computation beloved of theologians and their sympathizers as sound.[39] Scripture was filled with inconsistencies, textual variations, and scientific blunders. Historically and chronologically it deviated sharply from the correct annals of mankind. The problem of chronology was difficult and technical. It demanded for its solution the same kind of trained skill and objectivity that had been expended by scholars on the classical studies. Such men thought it was high time to take stock; to determine the true order of the appearance of nations, both Hebrew and Gentile; to settle upon a span of time and a correct temporal order in which all events in human history, both sacred and profane, could be rationally accommodated. "Those who think they can understand histories without chronology," said Bodin even though he sometimes lent uncritical concurrence to the orthodox position, "are as much in error as those who wish to escape the windings of a labyrinth without a guide."

With all of this in mind, there were thus certain pointed questions to be put to those who held inflexibly to traditional and Scriptural criteria for fixing dates. Was it really true that the Hebrews were the oldest of all the nations? Were there no other claimants? Should not other claimants be given a hearing? After all, on no less authority than Diodorus Siculus, Egyptian history was said to go back more than twenty-three thousand years; according to Pomponius Mela, thirteen thousand; Plato, eight thousand; Diogenes Laertius, forty-eight thousand. Could all of these ancient historians have been wrong, and only Moses right? Then again, there was a Babylonian claim to a record of over four hundred thousand years, reported by Alexander Polyhistor. There was mention of a Persian nation six thousand years before the alleged date of the Fall. While Aristotle had taught that the world had neither a beginning nor an end, but was eternal.[40] Was knowledge among the Egyptians of a "First Age of the world" due, as Ralegh thought, merely to the fact that they had come upon a few inscriptions remaining after the Flood and misinterpreted them? Or were they actually older as a nation than most conservative students of Genesis cared to admit? An unbiased comparison of other histories and dating systems from Homer to the present seemed to indicate that by Abraham's time all the known parts of the world had already been developed, and that Egypt, among others, possessed many great and famous cities. Which then was true: that Homer had read all of the previously written books of Moses and stolen bits here and there, as Ralegh suggested; or that the Greek people existed in pre-Mosaic, or even pre-Adamic times?[41] It was boldly urged in the interest of truth that the Hebrew Scriptures be fully and critically reviewed and that due weight be given to conflicting historical inferences and dates.

Attacks of this kind put the faithful upon their mettle. Those who presumed to question the superior antiquity of the Mosaic record had to be convinced of their error. The inaugural position of the Hebrew nation in the historical sequence of nations had to be reasserted and confirmed, once and for all.

But how? That was the question. And upon what kind of evidence? . . . The classics themselves provided a hint.

Impressed by similitudes and correspondences which they had happened to observe, certain Latin and anti-Christian authors had rudely asserted that the personnel of Genesis was nothing but a later and Hebrew version of an earlier pantheon of classical gods, demigods, and heroes. Since imitation obviously follows invention, the borrowing Hebrews were pronounced to be later arrivals on the scene than the creative Greeks and Romans. With this logical model in front of them, discomfited Christian scholarship decided to turn the tables on the heathen. A counterclaim was filed: The pagan gods and demigods were not older than Adam, Noah, Abraham, Isaac, or Jacob. Quite the reverse. They were nothing but later and "faulty" recollections of these very Hebrew patriarchs..

Nor was the use of the term "faulty" accidental. By combining two ideas—first, that the pagan gods were a memory, and second, that the memory was defective—Christian theologians not only gave the Hebrew patriarchs priority in historical time but also drew the whole controversy into the congenial territory of Renaissance pessimism. Again and again they insisted that the pagan gods were nothing but faded, decadent, corrupt, or degenerate copies of Hebrew originals. Again and again, they argued that since Christianity, through its Hebrew heritage, was the one original and universal faith, that fact carried with it the happy corollary that any self-styled religion, that had arisen since the founding of Judaism, even though it carried with it all the intellectual authority of the classics, was a bastard and debased offshoot of the true faith.

Received thus into Renaissance thought, not only by way of the Middle Ages and the doctrine of the Fall, but by way of what were intellectually the most reputable classical sources as well, the idea of decay and degeneration was easily synthesized with the study of religions and orthodox historiography. Indeed, on a more general level of discourse, all mutability, all change in religion, and the process of change itself, were deplored. On this, the ancients in both the Holy Land and in Greece were agreed. According to Moses, Paradise once lost was never regainable. According to Plato and many other Greek philosophers, the best condition ever enjoyed by man was in the past. Indeed, Renaissance dejection over the forfeiture of an original felicity was scarcely less profound than that of the medieval Christians or the pagans before them. For some Renaissance theologians the most disconcerting product of corruption was the existence of a plurality of religions in the world. All of these, including the religions of the Greeks, the Romans, and other civilizations of antiquity, were taken to be the degenerate expressions of an earlier, truer faith, usually described as that ancestral matrix of Christianity, Judaism.

So believing, and desiring to uphold the traditional Christian chronology, orthodox scholarship took refuge in that search for comparisons and similitudes which had been initiated by classical authors. The only difference between Christian and heathen scholarship was that instead of demonstrating the priority of the classical religious system to that of the Hebrews, all pagan myths, and all the pagan gods whose biographies were the subject matter of myth, were converted into corrupted versions of prior Biblical episodes or Bible personages.

How was this known?

The answer was simple. It was "known" because, in the orthodox view, pagan deities and heroes and their stories exhibited correspondences with the Biblical narrative its characters and its episodes. It was "known" because such correspondences were considered "proofs" of the priority of the Hebrew scripture and the Hebrew nation. How could it be otherwise? "The ancient poets," said Bodin, "transformed into stupid fables the truth of the matter they received from their elders." The identification of the purportedly earlier Hebrew patriarchs with the purportedly later gods of the Greeks and Romans became standard practice among historical writers. The procedure was used by Varrerius, Allatius, Albertus, Nauclerus, Lazius, Functius, Irenicus, Muenster, Podianus, Bolducus, Stillingfleet, Ralegh, Godwyn, Vossius, Huet, Vico, and countless others.[42] It was asserted that the classical god Janus received that name only because he "discovered" the vine which was already known to and named *iain* by the Hebrews. The story of Ham and his father, Noah, told for the first time in Genesis 9 : 22–24, later became attached to the Greek god Jove; while the earlier Biblical Nimrod was transformed into the later Greek Saturn.[43]

A general statement of the principle employed in this argument is to be found in Ralegh's *History,* where the author suggests that "in old corruptions we may find some signs of more ancient truth," borrowed or stolen from the Books of God. Thus it was his contention that Cain, the son of Adam, "was called and reputed for the first and ancient Jupiter," and Adam for the first Saturn, while Jubal, Tubal, and Tubal-Cain were transformed by the later and imitative Greeks into their Mercurius, Vulcan, and Apollo.[44] The argument from similarities in defense of the traditional and theological conception of the chronology of nations is made even clearer by the scholarly treatment of Bishop Stillingfleet. According to his carefully organized *Origines sacrae* (1662), likenesses between the gods of Olympus and the *dramatis personae* of Genesis were never coincidental. They always possessed an historical meaning; they always favored the greater antiquity of the Hebrew people. When we come to the Bishop's discussion of Noah's likeness to the pagan gods, we are told once more that "many parcels of Noahs memory were preserved in the scattered Fragments of many Fables," under the names of Saturn, Janus, Prometheus, and Bacchus. We are reminded that Bochartus insisted on no fewer than fourteen parallels between the Hebrew Noah and the heathen Saturn.

Saturn was said to be the common Parent of Mankind, so was Noah; Saturn was a just King, Noah was not only righteous himself, but a Preacher of Righteousness : . . . The plantation of vines (was) attributed to Saturn by the Heathens, as to Noah by the Scriptures : The Law of Saturn mentioned by the Poets, That none should see the nakedness of the gods without punishment, seems to respect the fact and curse of Cham . . . Saturn and Rhea, and those with them are said to be born of Thetis, or the Ocean, which plainly alludes to Noah and his companies escaping the Flood; thence a ship was the symbol of Saturn : and that

Saturn devoured all his children seems to be nothing else but the destruction of the old world by Noah's Flood.[45]

With these "similarities" the Bishop, a distinguished student of historical method, was satisfied.

In the second Renaissance religious controversy characterized by the employment of correspondences, the contenders were the Reformers versus the Romanists. For one of the many articles in the indictment brought by Protestant spokesmen against the older Church was its toleration in Christian worship of pre-Christian or heathen elements. There were clear and unmistakable similitudes, or so it was said, between the Popish and pagan religions. By changes merely in names, the priests of the new Rome had substituted their saints for the demigods of the old. More indefensibly still, the whole form and outward dress of Catholic worship was grossly idolatrous and extravagant. The ceremonies of the Roman communion appeared "to have been copied from the Rituals of Primitive Paganism, as if handed down in uninterrupted succession" from the priests of paganism to those of the Gospel.

The Roman reply to these charges was cool and judicious. The clergy acknowledged the presence of antique and barbarian elements in contemporary liturgy and belief, but said in extenuation that since avenues for the expression of religious feeling were relatively few, narrow, and old, there was no form of worship, even that of the Reformers, which could clearly escape the charge of including a few elements of paganism. Reproached with being "snared by Paynim superstition," the Roman doctors pointed to the long missionary experience of the elder Church, and the necessity in the conversion situation of making concessions to the religious ideas, customs, and rituals of proselytes; of making delicate adjustments between the heathen conception of the sacred and that contained in Christian doctrine. To evangelize barbarian and savage peoples, missionaries and priests had been compelled to express the piety of the Church through the agency of symbols already known and understood by new communicants. Symbolic usages peculiar to European ritual were often meaningless to Hottentots and Algonquins. Was it not allowable therefore to transfer to pious use practices which these pagans had employed impiously?

While the problem might be new to Protestants, it was old to the Church. It had been confronted first during the missionization of Europe, when both the Church and the Western nations were young. At that time Pope Gregory, sometimes considered the author of the ecclesiastical ritual, had instructed his missionary priests always to destroy idols but to spare idol temples. When attempting the conversion of a heathen people, he directed with wise tolerance, "Let Holy Water be made. Let the temples be sprinkled; let altars be built and relics deposited in them;" but "if the temples be well-built, let them be turned from the service of the Devil to that of the true God, to the intent that these heathen people may the more readily come to worship in accustomed places." Nor did missionaries to the savages of the New World believe differently. Following the counsel of the Holy Father, Joseph de Acosta found it advisable "to leave unto the Indians that which they usually had of custom, so as they be not mingled nor corrupt with their ancient errors, and that their feasts and pastimes may be in the honour of God and the Saints, whose feasts they celebrate." [46] By such a procedure the devil could be tricked. He could be mortified by finding his heathen practices turned to the service of Jesus Christ.

But the Reformers were not to be mollified by either subtlety or greater experience. Wherever a suspected usage was not to be found in the New Testament, it was denounced by Protestants as an illegitimate excrescence on the proper form of worship. Having decided that a Roman practice was similar in a greater or lesser degree to a pagan one, they turned each pair of these minor resemblances into substantial identities. Having converted a pair of resemblances into identities, they denounced the historically recent practice as derived from the historically older. The profound difference which might, and often did, underlie superficial likeness was unrecognized. The new spiritual meaning which might be, and often had been, infused into an old practice was ignored. Similarities, broadly and uncritically construed, were used to document, to prove, and to condemn the Church's pagan past and present.

The literature supporting the Protestant assault was voluminous and circumstantial. In the middle of the sixteenth century, after years of controversy between the contending parties, Guillaume du Choul, an early French antiquary, asserted that if the elements of the existing Roman ritual were compared with those of classical antiquity, it would be found that several institutions in the Romanist religion had been transmitted from the Egyptian and other "gentile" ceremonies. Such, in his opinion, were tunics and surplices; the crowns and tonsures of priests; genuflection at the altar; sacrificial pomp, church music, adorations; prayers, supplications, processions; litanies and many other practices. In this contention he was joined by others, including Polydore Vergil (1470?–?1555) and Pierre Viret (1511–1571).

To Vergil the trimming of Christian temples with flowers, boughs of trees, and garlands, smelled unmistakably of gentility. So also did "the rite of hanging up Images of Wax, and tapers before the Saints;" or, when a member of the body was diseased, its presentation in effigy, "as leggs, arms, feet, Paps, Oxen, Horse or sheep," before the altar of some saint. These practices, he said, came from "an old Heathenish fashion of sacrifice, that the Pagans offered to Saturnus and Pluto." [47] To Viret, friend and disciple of Calvin, Catholic

rites for the dead were also heathenish. "That which superstitious Christians do about the dead, is nothing at all lyke
unto the woord of God, but is altogether taken of the Infidells
& Panims. . . . For to what ende do all those lights serve,
but for to declare that we are the successours of the Panims,
who after the same sort used torches and candels at the burials
and funerals of their dead."[48] It was also Peter Viret who
pointed to St. Thais and St. Mary Magdalen as the Catholic
equivalents of the Roman Flora and Venus.

In the sixth decade of the seventeenth century more than
one hundred years after the publication of Du Choul's
Discours, and again in the eighteenth century, the presence of
pagan "errors" in Roman ceremonials became the occasion
for renewed Protestant criticism. One outspoken critic was
Pierre Mussard, an Huguenot refugee and a minister of the
French Church in Threadneedle Street, London. In his little
book, *Les conformités des cérémonies moderne avec les
anciennes* (1667), there is a relatively well-organized statement of pagan persistencies in the Church.[49] Mussard deals
first with those associated with the office of the pontiff, or the
conformities said to obtain between the Pope and the secular
sovereigns of classical antiquity. This is followed by a chapter
on, "the sundry orders of ecclesiastics," in which a comparison
is drawn between the organization presided over by high
priests among the pagans and that of the Roman hierarchy.
As the ancient Romans had had their grand sacerdotal college,
so the Roman Church had its College of Cardinals. Then came
a description of the mass, ecclesiastical processions, festivals,
holy days, the saints and their canonization, altars, votive
pictures, images, prayers, funerals, and bells. To exhibit
properly these lamentable correspondences, all were carefully
arranged and marshaled with their pagan or heathen counterparts.

Another student of the subject was Conyers Middleton,

principal librarian of the University of Cambridge, man of letters, and author of *A letter from Rome, showing an exact conformity between popery and the religion of the Romans to be derived entirely from that of their heathen ancestors* (1729). To Middleton the similitude "of the Popish and Pagan Religion, seem'd so clear" that he resolved to give himself "the Trouble of searching to the Bottom of the Notion, and to explain and demonstrate the Certainty of it, by exhibiting and comparing together the principle and most obvious Parts of each Worship." [50] On the off-chance that some Romanist might cavil at his charges, his strictures were to be solidly based upon his own observations in the city of Rome; and he promised to produce "vouchers" for every correspondence evoked. But in the end the seventy-page *Letter from Rome* is little more than a summary of Mussard's earlier brochure, which was twice its length; and Mussard, in turn, was heavily indebted to Du Choul, Vergil, Viret, and others of the sixteenth century.

All in all, the controversy over the pagan origin of Roman ritual served merely to underline the obvious—namely, the descent of contemporary religious doctrine and practice from earlier forms of religious expression. As those experienced in the work of the church and in the day-to-day spiritual needs of human beings already knew, it could not well have been otherwise. At the same time, the argument revealed another fact, less well assimilated by thought even today—namely, that the existing elements of all cultures are not of the same age. Each has been practiced or entertained for differing periods of past time—some long, some short. At any given moment of stock-taking, some elements will be found to be derivable from antiquity, some from the Middle Ages, some from more recent cultural experience. In other words, given more insight into these chronological facts, given ideally the dates and places of the earliest acceptance of traits and practices, it is theoretically possible to reconstruct the cultural or institutional past. On the other hand, given similarities, given traits existing in the present purportedly similar to the ancient, the scholars of the seventeenth century believed, as do many at the present day, that the past might be recovered without the aid of dates or places.

While some students of religion thus invoked similarities in culture to fix upon the Roman Church the brand of paganism, or to repel attacks on the orthodox chronology of the Bible, or to lend support to the Noachian or Asiatic provenance of the American Indians, there were publicists, cosmographers, divines, explorers, and even literary critics, who claimed to discern parallels either between Judaism and purportedly earlier religions, or between the customs of contemporary savagery and earlier phases of certain advanced cultures. There were critics of Genesis who sought by means of correspondences to derive some of its incidents and doctrines from lands other than Judea; and there were those who proposed on similar logical grounds to convert the traits of contemporary savagery into historical documents..

In the latter half of the seventeenth century, when Oriental studies were in their infancy, John Spencer (1630–1693), an erudite theologian and Hebraist, shocked some of his colleagues by advancing the theory that the religion of the Jews was not the first to be adopted by mankind. His argument was a simple diffusionist one, supported by the historical fact of the pre-Mosaic period of the Exile, and by an elaborate collection of similarities in Hebrew and Egyptian religious ceremonial, upon which he based the assumption that the Hebrew rites were derived from the Egyptians.[51] But as was usual in such cases, it was easy for critics to invalidate the whole procedure by citing agreements between the Hebrew religion and those of other cultures than that of Egypt. Said the Reverend William Nichols in his *Conference with a theist* (1696), any learned man could readily "prove" that Jewish ceremonies were derived from any other nation in which similitudes were to be found. Was it not true that East Indian priests wore vestments just like the Jewish, and used oil in their rites of consecration? Did not the Brahmins, the Indian high priests, wear bells like the high priests of the Hebrews? Was it not a fact that in both cultures the ears of slaves were pierced; that a perpetual light was maintained in their temples; that women and newborn children were considered unclean? Could it not be shown that "only the Brachmans like the Levites must go into the inward Parts of the Temple"; that "they are defiled by a dead Body, and have Cakes before their Idols like the Shew Bread"; and that

the Brachmans like the Jewish High-Priests must marry virgins? . . . Now when the Jewish and Indian Rites are so very like, why might not I assert, that Moses had them from India, as well as from Egypt? Nay, even the barbarous Tartars have many Things not unlike the Jews. They celebrate the New-Moons with Songs and Compotations; they bewail their Dead thirty Days, they breed no hogs, and punish Adultery with Death. And so as to the new World, the Children of the People of Mexico and Yucatan are circumcised; and the Mexicans keep in a perpetual Fire. The Charibeans celebrate the New-Moon with the Sound of a Trumpet, and abstain from Swine's Flesh . . . all look as like the Jewish Laws, as any Custom in Aegypt. From all which I conclude, that since so many Nations, in so many different parts of the World, have the same Rites as the Jews . . . I am sure it is very great Boldness to say, that all these came to the Jews from the Ægyptians.[52]

As long as the historical priority of any trait or institution rested on similarities alone, or was asserted without other documentation of a more substantial character, historians of human institutions were in methodological trouble. This fact may be easily demonstrated in ethnological and related fields of thought from the seventeenth century to the twentieth; from

John Spencer to Sir Edward Burnett Tylor, to Marx and Engels, to Sigmund Freud and Arnold Toynbee.

The second argument, involving the conversion of the culture traits of living savages into potential documents, or the elevation of savage societies to the status of historical archives, was more recondite, though in the end no less easy to refute. It was formulated, or perhaps revived, soon after the explorations. The nonliterate peoples, whom the explorers to America, Africa, and the islands of the sea had made so well known to Europeans, were to a large degree alien, unintelligible, and repugnant. So too, despite admiration and respect for their literature and art, were many of the customs of Greece and Rome, Egypt, Babylon, Persia, and many other regions of the antique world. Given thus a common unintelligibility in both contemporary savage and in ancient cultures, given a common inconsonance with existing European habits and ideas, given finally a stubborn propensity in the human mind to counteract the stimulus of recognized differences in phenomena by extorting resemblances, the rest followed easily enough. Gradually, step by step, without formal debate, in profound ignorance of the true events and relationships, it became the accepted assumption that if contemporary savagery or barbarism so resembled antiquity, then contemporary savagery and European antiquity must be equally old. "For it hath pleased God," said Francis Bacon, "to ordain and illustrate two exemplar states of the world . . . the state of Graecia and the state of Rome," which also contain the antiquities of the world.[53] It was further agreed that if savage cultures, as they were currently presented to the eyes of the sixteenth and seventeenth centuries, were already old, then wherever they were, they must have been transmitted across the ages from generation to generation, from the ancient past to the existing present, in an unchanged, an unaccountably fixed, primitive, and aboriginal condition. And finally it became axiomatic that contemporary savage cultures, possessed of the properties of oldness and persistence, also possessed historical intimations. They could be used as a form of documentation. With classical or other dated manifestations of high antiquity, their analogues,[54] they possessed the latent power of disclosing an early, aboriginal, or "primitive" condition of mankind.

Now, of course, the full-blown methodological meaning of this use of correspondences—the view of their documentary richness which made a cursory examination of the culture of some contemporary savage tribe the historiographical equivalent of that unperformable feat, an inspection of mankind in his original condition—was not realized at once in the sixteenth century. Full realization came later, or in the eighteenth and nineteenth centuries. Of course, the earliest comparisons and collections of savage parallels, from which the Enlightenment and the nineteenth century were to draw their momentous conclusions, were merely awkward and suggestive. Consequently, their interest for the student of methodological ideas lies in their intent rather than in their accomplishment. In them, he will easily recognize the determination among those who used them to understand the enigmatic savage in a genetic or historical relationship to European culture, and he will see in the crudity of the earliest comparisons a prefiguration of the direction in which ethnological thought was to move for many generations to come.

Crudity and awkwardness were certainly characteristics of the earliest interpretations of savage correspondences. Take those adumbrated by Stephen Batman in his translation of Lycosthenes' *Prodigiorum ac ostentorum* (1557), under the title of *The doome warning all men to the judgment,* published in 1581. Here, in a clumsy effort heavy with medievalisms, Batman spoke all in one breath of anthropophagi, the classical ancients, the American Indians, and the "wilde"

An acephalous monster among the Indians of the Americas, according to Père Lafitau in 1724.

peoples of the sixteenth-century explorer's unfettered imagination. The anthropophagi, in his opinion, were a-social and cannibalistic, living without law and justice. Nevertheless, these man-eaters were also the parents or ethnological precursors or equivalents of savagery. From them, he said gropingly, "may be supposed to proceed those wilde people, whereof some [still] remaine in ye Northwest parts, and the other in ye Southwest parts of the world." [55] It is impossible to divine exactly what Batman intended to convey in this indefinite statement; but it suggests, at the very least, a confused likeness for him among all these strange creatures, and their historical antecedence, together with the classical cultures, to Renaissance Europe. This conclusion is enforced by Batman's *Golden booke of the leaden gods, a study of the classical pantheon,* published a little later in 1577. Here, a similarity between the strange deities of contemporary Africa, the East Indies, and the gods of historically earlier classical antiquity, is more directly indicated. Here again, in a vague way, and by virtue of one of those associations of ideas of which we know only the end result, each comparison conferred age and antiquity upon the contemporary cultures of the American Indians, the Africans, and the East Indians. Furthermore, a fumbling attempt was made to incorporate the savage conceptually in a genetic relationship with the monstrous and the barbarous.

Passing on to something a little less ambiguous, we come to Sebastian Muenster and his *Cosmographia* published in 1544. In this work, the author used another type of comparison which serves to clarify some of the ethnological and historical notions moving in men's minds in the sixteenth century, especially the tendency to regard the elements of classical culture and the traits of savagery as equally ancient and primordial. Unable to conceive of rivals to Christianity or of independently invented religious systems, the great German geographer thought he discerned a connection between the strange gods of the existing European barbarians and those of Greece and Rome, whom he viewed, in their turn, as later distortions of an earlier and original Judeo-Christian truth. In other words, the religion of existing European barbarians was likened to that of the classical peoples, known to be ancient and old, while the classical pantheon, in turn, purportedly exhibited evidences of likeness to Christianity, which was thought to be even more ancient and old. Thus the Gauls, according to Muenster's interpretation of their thought processes, believed themselves to be the descendants of Dis and Pluto; they gave all their war-booty to Mars; and they held Mercury in reverence. Thus the Scythians (of southern Russia) worshiped Vesta, Jupiter, Apollo, Venus, Mars, and Hercules.[56] Thus existing savagery (or barbarism) was endowed conceptually with great age, great antiquity, or an early position in historical time, because it was assumed to be like a people or peoples who were known, through dated history, to be antique and early.

Another and somewhat clearer sixteenth-century comparison of the savage present with the classical or more ancient past is to be found in a remark made by Pedro Mexia in his *Foreste or collection of histories*, written about 1550. Since Christian customs of marriage were well-known to all men, he proposed to "payne" himself by speaking of "certaine aunciente customes, practiced as well in sundrie barbarous countries (such as those of the Massagites, the ancient Britons, and the Arabians), as also among the olde Romaines theim selves."[57] Here, as was usual in this line of argument, there appeared to be no felt need for temporal discrimination among the different historical phases of the Roman institution. There was no realization that the Roman family system, viewed as an historical object, might have been subject to change or modification during its historical career; that it might have had a history composed of several conditions, early and late, some of which might not have corresponded with the marital practices of these barbarous societies. It is tacitly assumed, on the contrary, that the Roman family system, as known to Mexia, had been the system known to the Romans throughout their whole historical experience. Consequently the operative parallel is drawn between the marital customs of existing barbarians or savages and an actually historically late and advanced condition of the Roman family. Nevertheless "sundrie barbarous countries" are indicated as possessing "aunciente customes," and these customs are called "aunciente" or early because they resemble those of the Romans, not the earliest Roman, nor yet the later or latest Romans, just the Romans.

It was by the early explorers of the New World, however, that the purported likeness between savage behaviour and that of men who lived during the period of classical antiquity was stated with the least ambiguity. One good example was Thevet. Having made a voyage to Brazil in the mid-sixteenth century, this cosmographer to the French king and author of *Les singularitez de la France Antarctique* (1556) commented on the nudity of the Indians of South America, and then pointedly recalled that the same custom had once prevailed in Europe during the early days of its settlement, and also in ancient Rome, as shown by the undraped condition of statues and images "reared up in their temples, all naked," without so much as a coif on their heads. For those who charged the Indians with other regrettable practices, Thevet had a ready answer. When first visited in the sixteenth century they were merely conducting themselves in a manner like the ancestors of the complainants, long before in the historical past. If the Americans ate their parents, they were merely observing a practice known also among the Romans under the conditions of warfare; if they ate their enemies, they were merely behaving as had many ancient peoples, such as the Turks, the Moors, and the barbarians. If they counted the moons or months with beads, so also had the Athenians; if they departed from Renaissance standards of European morals and good taste in their marital relations, they were in the company of the ancients. Seneca in one of his *Epistles* and Strabo in his *Cosmography,* said the French explorer, had both written that the Lydians and Armenians carried on similar practices, as did also the Athenians, Turks, and Arabians.[58] But here, once more, temporal institutional differences among these ancient peoples were ignored. The fact that these practices were carried on in what was currently called "antiquity" was enough. It endowed purportedly similar practices among the contemporary American Indians with a corresponding antiquity.

Frequent also were references to similarities between the customs of existing savagery and those of that other claimants to historical venerability, the Hebrews. Antonio Pigafetta, who accompanied Magellan around the world in 1522, and Martin Baumgarten, whose trip up the Nile had been made at a still earlier date, declared that certain African tribes practiced circumcision after the manner of the Israelites; while Grevenbrock, the seventeenth-century author of a letter entitled *An elegant and accurate account of the African race living round the Cape of Good Hope, commonly called the Hottentots* (1695), asserted that the kinship terms of this tribe were similar to those used long before by the Hebrews.[59]

In all of these early examples of the identification of the culture of contemporary savagery with the cultures of the antique world there is the same blind spot, the same perversity of judgment, the same lack of elementary historical insight. In all, correspondences are elicited between an existing condition among a history-less people, a savage or barbarian group, and a purportedly unchanging trait or institution among an ancient historical people. It is naïvely assumed that what the sometimes untutored explorer or missionary happened to know or to remember of the ideas, institutions, and traits of the Greek, Roman, or Hebrew cultures was all there was to know. Effaced from memory, at least for the purposes at hand, were the obvious facts that these ancient peoples, to whom savagery was compared, were themselves not in an original, or even an early historical condition. Forgotten was the fact that the social institutions of these ancient high cultures were products of long histories and a succession of changes. To which period or condition in the long cultural history of Greece, Rome, or the Jews did Thevet, Pigafetta, Baumgarten, or Father de Acosta refer when they likened the savages to the peoples of the ancient or classical world? It would be hard to say, nor did they bother to discriminate. But despite these historical and logical difficulties the comparisons were made, the similarities were found, and the inferences were made.

In Joseph de Acosta's *Natural and moral history of the Indies,* published like Thevet's *Antarctika* in the middle of the sixteenth century, argument and examples are familiar. "If anyone wonder at some fashions and customes of the Indies," said the Father in his Prologue, "and wil scorne them as fooles, or abhorre them as divelish and inhumane people, let him remember that the same things, yea, worse, have beene seene amongst the Greekes and Romans, . . . as we may easily understand, not onely of our Authors, as Eusebius of Caesarea, Clement of Alexandria, and others, but also of their owne, as Plinie, Dionysius of Halicarnaus, and Plutarke : for the Prince of darkness being the head of all Infidelitie, it is no new thing to finde among Infidells, cruelties, filthines, and follies fit for such a master." The Mexicans, he pointed out by way of illustration, attributed natural phenomena such as rain, war, and generation to their idols, "even as the Greeks and Latins have forged Idolls of Phoebus, Mercurie, Jupiter, Minerva, and of Mars." These barbarous people "contented not themselves to have Gods onely, but they had goddesses also, as the Fables of the Poets have brought in, and the blind gentility

of the Greekes and Romans worshipt them." Nor was the purported "oldness" of contemporary Indian behavior "proved"
by these likenesses to the classical peoples alone. Acosta also
pointed out a purported resemblance to the pre-Christian
Britons. The Indians of Peru put to death "above a thousand
persons" to accompany a king into the other life. This superstition, said de Acosta, "is at this day used among the barbarous Nations. And as Polo writes, it hath beene in a maner
generall throughout all the Indies. The venerable Bede
reportes, that before the Englishmen were converted to the
Gospel they had the same custome."[60]

A good idea—good in the sense that it seems to promise
an easy solution to some pressing intellectual problem—
cannot be kept down. It finds its way wherever similar difficulties arise. It should therefore occasion no surprise to find
ethnological similarities freely invoked by literary critics before
the end of the sixteenth century. During the Renaissance,
students of literature, like students of other types of human
behavior, had become uncomfortably aware of the presence
of diversities in forms of literary expression—diversities with
respect to style and form of composition—in diction, rhyme,
and other literary qualities. All of this, taken generally, imparted substance to a vague presumption in favor of an explanation in terms of the operation of a process of change in
literary techniques, or in terms of an historical arrangement
of the diversities in question. "Although poetry is the most
ethereal part of thought and expression," said William Webbe
(fl. 1568–1591) in his *Discourse of English poetrie* (1586),
"yet there is an art of poesy . . . varying with the different
languages and countries, and even with the different ages in
the life of the same country."[61]

But this was not quite enough. Why was it, some commentators asked, that the English poets had failed so far to
avoid the reproach of barbarousness? Why were their poetic

efforts considered less successful than those on the Continent? Here the literary critic, under the influence of current ethnological ideas, called to his aid a theory of diffusion. Early barbarian forms of expression, including "tinkerly" rhyme, had been borrowed in the first instance from the barbarian Goths and the Huns, via Italy, France, and Germany. Then, in the nature of things, custom hardened. Due to "the canckred enmitie of curious custome," or to the fixity of early or "primitive" society, the work of the English poets remained infected with "brutish" habit.

A year or so later Richard Puttenham (1520?–?1601) adopted a different approach to this literary problem, but one based upon similar ideas. Rising to the defense of rhyme, on the score of its antiquity and "primitive" universality, the highly esteemed poetry of the classical Greeks and Romans was said to be merely a later derivation or deviation from an earlier form. For rhymed poetry, Puttenham told his readers, in unconscious anticipation of later communal theories of literary origins, not only antedated classical or civil society, it was the very occasion for the appearance of society itself, the original cause of the formation of the first assemblies among men, "when before the people remained in the woods and mountains, vagrant and dispersed like wild beasts, lawlesse and naked, or verie ill-clad."[62] Like Professor Gummere at least three centuries later, Puttenham derived poetry, like other human institutions, from rude collective beginnings. "At the end of the path" stood "no dignified old gentleman in flowing robe, with a long white beard, upturned eyes, and a harp clasped to his bosom, but rather a ring of savages dancing uncouthly to the sound of their own voices in rhythmic but inharmonious chant."[63] Rhythm and rhyme wrought at the desk of the poet was traced back to the work, play, or dance of the "primitive." Rhyme, or "vulgar running poetry," such as had prevailed until so recently among the English, was an old poetic form, reminiscent of this aboriginal condition. Moreover, it had once long before been common to all the nations of the world. Despite the great antiquity of the poetry of the Greeks and Romans, or that of the Chaldeans and Hebrews which was still older, rhymed verse was the first and oldest verse.

How was this known to Richard Puttenham in the sixteenth century?

His literary theory was in perfect accord with the times and the ideas of the voyagers. It was sustained, said he, "by certificate of marchants & travellers, who by late navigations have surveyed the whole world, and discovered . . . strange peoples, wild and savage . . . the American, the Perusine, & very Canniball"; all of whom sing and also say "their highest and holiest matters in certain rhyming versicles," like our own vulgar poetry.[64] As in the cases of many other forms of cultural expression, the antiquity of rhymed verse had been "proved" to Puttenham by the explorers' reports, and by the common belief in the historical priority of the culture of savagery as they happened to know it. The comparisons, the similitudes, and their results in terms of historical inferences, were again not clearly stated by this literary critic. But they were operative in his thinking. They were his unexamined assumptions. Apparently, the hypothesis and its "proofs" were already too well known and well received to need further exposition or defense.

In 1603, Samuel Daniel's *A defence of rhyme,* a similar line of argument and the same group of ideas were again brought forward, though perhaps with a little less assurance. Replying to those who condemned English poetry because of its contained rhyme, Daniel admitted that "ill customes are to be left, I graunt it : but I see not how that can be taken for an ill custome, which nature . . . hath ratified, all nations received, time so long confirmed." Here, the antiquity of rhyme was "proved" by its assumed universality, and its current likeness to that used in Turkey, Scythia, Arabia, Africa, Muscovy, Hungary, Germany, and among the Britons, Scots, Saxons, and Danes.[65]

Meanwhile, the likeness of existing savagery to the old Mediterranean civilizations having been so frequently used and urged, the range of comparisons and parallelisms began to be expanded. In order to endow history-less savage peoples with the historical attribute of earliness or great age, other peoples nearer at hand in Europe were invoked. Since the actual annals of British history had made it clear that both the Britons and the Saxons had completed their roles early in time, descriptions of the earliest recorded phases of their cultures were frequently accepted as substitutes for the classical cultures, or as acceptable parallels with the existing African and American conditions. Since the German tribes had been described by Caesar and Tacitus in the first century A.D., and were then obviously barbarous, they too were regarded as an appropriate people to be paired off comparatively with the newly discovered savages; as were also the Irish, the Laplanders, the Finns, and other outlying and relatively uncivil European folk.

This variant, this likening of the cultures of European tribal barbarism to Mediterranean antiquity, and of both to New World savagery, began early. Arguing in his *Historia dei riti Ebraici* (1637) that having no temples, the first men worshiped in the open fields and groves, Leon of Modena (1571–1648) cited the Persians, the Getae of Herodotus, the ancient East Indians, the Romans, the people of Guinea, the Negroes, and a European folk, the Lapps.[66] Somewhat later in the seventeenth century, Peter Heylyn remarked that a group of cave-dwelling Spanish "salvages" constituted a "New World" in the midst of modern Castile, and likened the tribes of Borneo to the Saxon ancestors of contemporary Englishmen.[67]

Jobson, an explorer to Africa, observed what he regarded as a parallel in the Irish and African custom of marriage by capture;[68] and the ancient Picts, according to Picart in his *Ceremonies and religious customs of the various nations* (1718), went naked like the Hottentots and other African natives. Nathanael Carpenter, in his *Geography delineated,* published in 1625, declared that in the early days the peoples of Germany and Britain lived on herbs and roots like swine, as in the infancy of the world, and in this were "little different from the present Americans;"[69] and David Persons, the author in 1635 of *Varieties: or, a surveigh of rare and excellent matters,* asserted that when a person died in Greece, "all the women thereabouts after their old heathen custom . . . make lamentable howlings . . . defacing their cheekes and faces," which custom "an ancient Historian of our Country observeth to have been used of Old amongst our British, and yet in our Highlands is observed."[70] At about the same time, William Strachey in his *Historie of travell into Virginia Britania* (1612), observed that had it not been for the civilizing effect of the Roman occupation the Britons "might yet have lyved overgrowne Satyrs, rude, untutred, wandring in the woodes, dwelling in Caves, and hunting for our dynners . . . prostetuting our daughters to straungers, sacrificing our Children to Idolls, nay eating our owne Children, as did the Scots in those dayes." Indeed, in quoting or misquoting St. Hieronymous and the Venerable Bede, Strachey carried the thought still further. "What shall I say," St. Hieronymous is made to remark,

of other Nations, since that when I was a Boy, I saw in Fraunce Scotts, a people of Brittania, eate mans flesh, and when they found in the forrests Heards of Swyne, Beasts, and Cattell, they would cut off the Buttocks of the Boies which kept them, and also the womens Paps, and tooke that to be the most deyntie and delicate meate. As the reverend *Beda* reports (before the *Britons* were converted to the Ghospell) murthering whole Troupes of men, (to accompany and serve their friendes dying in the other life), as they did to the sundry Zemes in the West Indies, at what tyme *Columbus* arryved there and as they did in *Peru,* and *Mexico,* at what tyme Hernando *Cortez* reduced them to Christianity."[71]

What was the religion of the ancient Europeans? asked Alexander Ross in *Pansebia: or, a view of all the religions of the world* (1653). The answer, familiar then, is familiar now: "The same Paganisme was professed among them that was in other parts of the world, and which is yet professed in Lapland, Finland, and some parts of Norway, Lituania, and Samagotia, whose Religion is Idolatrous, whose knowledge is Magick, and whose actions are barbarous."[72]

By appealing to similitudes between the conditions of savagery, barbarousness, or rusticity, and the historically earlier periods of certain historical peoples, no stone was left unturned to confer documentary significance upon these nonliterate conditions. In the seventeenth century, such comparisons and correspondences flowed from every pen. The die was cast. The convention which had bestowed earliness and oldness upon contemporary savagery by comparing it with the cultures of classical antiquity and other purportedly old cultures had hardened. The methodological device which conferred documentary meaning upon geographically remote, history-less, and nonliterate peoples was regarded by a multitude of authors as a truism in a voluminous literature. It was a commonplace to Samuel Purchas. The marginal notes in his voyage collection consist largely of observations of cultural parallels. It was a commonplace also to Pierre d'Avity and to Peter Heylyn. The same comparisons were constantly made by Estienne, Cherbury, Ross, Vossius, Stillingfleet, Huet, Toland, Simon, and a host of others too numerous to discuss separately.

And so they continued to be made throughout the eighteenth, nineteenth, and the twentieth centuries.

In the eighteenth century, after the argument from similarities had achieved the dignity of an accepted procedure and was habitually employed to bestow aboriginal earliness upon the nonliterate cultures whose actual age was unknowable, the occasional mention of parallels was succeeded by their organized collection. Many of the collectors were French, and their primary field of inquiry was religion. While a few of these compendia were written frankly to surprise and entertain, the majority were serious efforts to demonstrate the soundness of some theory or hypothesis.

The fashion was set in 1700 by Père Noël Alexandre in his book the *Conformité des cérémonies chinoises avec l'idolâtrie grecque et romaine*. This was followed four years later by M. de la Créquinière's *Conformité des coutumes des Indiens orientaux avec des Juifs & des autres peuples de l'antiquité*; and in 1724 by Père Joseph Lafitau's *Moeurs des sauvages Amériquains comparée aux moeurs des premiers temps*. In 1760 Charles de Brosses wrote *Le culte des dieux fétiches, ou, Parallèle de l'ancienne religion de l'Egypte avec la religion actuelle de Nigritie;* and in 1799 Joseph Priestley published a *Comparison of the institutions of Moses with those of the Hindoos and other ancient nations*. To grasp the common theme of these books no more than the titles need be read. Like Fontenelle, who before them had discovered "une conformité étonnante" between the myths of the Americans and those of the Greeks, these scholars dealt with the parallels observable between existing savage groups and the conditions revealed in the historical records of civilized peoples.

The argument developed by Père Lafitau is probably the most mature and competently stated of all. Dissatisfied with the fragmentary and casual reports of correspondences made by other travelers, and also with their use by scholars, this

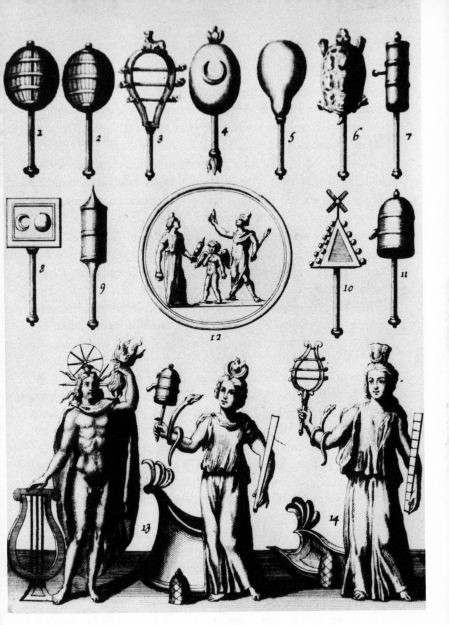

"*A comparison followed by the establishment of likenesses between the timbrels or tamborines of the Brazilians, Iroquois, Hurons, and the classical ancients,*" by Père Lafitau in 1724.

French missionary to the Canadian Indians proposed, first, to complete the stock of correspondences from his own unique American experience; and then when this was done, to demonstrate a much closer parallelism between savagery and the cultures of Mediterranean antiquity than had ever been shown before. "I was not content," he said, "with knowing the nature of the savages and with learning of their customs and practices. I sought to find in these practices and customs vestiges of the most *remote* antiquity [sic]. I have read carefully those earliest authors who have dealt with the customs, laws, and usages of the peoples with whom they had some acquaintance. I have compared these customs, one with another, and I confess that while the ancient authors have given me support for several happy conjectures concerning the savages, the customs of the savages themselves have thrown much more light on the ancient authors [sic]." Not only did Père Lafitau indicate innumerable parallels between the American Indians and the Greeks and Romans, with reference to his chief interest, the institution of religion, but he also showed the same meticulous interest in the collection of correspondences in government, marriage, the family, education, the occupations of men and women, hunting and fishing, the disposition of the dead, and language. Occasionally, the argument is visually enforced with carefully chosen plates. One of these, for example, compares the symbolic figures of antiquity with those of the Indians; another exhibits similitudes in the attire of American Red Men and citizens of Rome; still another displays the conformities between canoes used by the Eskimos and those inscribed on Egyptian monuments.

With materials such as these, could there be any doubt of the existence of the similarities? With the long-standing reliance of ethnological theory upon the validity of similitudes, could there be any question as to the proper historical inferences? Lafitau, along with a host of precursors and successors, thought there could not. In his and their judgment, similitudes showed in multitudinous and self-evident detail that the customs of existing savagery were strikingly and meaningfully similar to those of the Greeks and Romans, as the "earliest" peoples. Without realizing the necessity for discrimination between the varying cultural conditions which succeeded one another in the course of the histories of these two great civilizations, and without realizing the length and cultural variance of the human historical span which preceded them on many areas, the scholar felt safe in inferring that the existing Canadian Indians and savage society had sprung from the same homogeneous stem.

BIBLIOGRAPHY AND NOTES

1. It was inferred that the habits and traits of the European peasanty, their folklore and folk practices, had undergone no change since the time of early tribal conditions, hence that they were like savage tribes elsewhere, and like the Greeks and Romans.

2. Boemus, *Manners, lawes (1611)*, 202–03, 217–19. The Englishman Andrew Boorde tried to awaken interest in cultural similarities in his *Fyrst boke of the introduction of knowledge* in 1542, as did also Montaigne in his *Essayes* at a somewhat later date.

3. Eden, *Briefe collection*, sig. E 3 r; Muenster, *op. cit.*, 45.

4. Muenster, *Cosmographia*, 1052–54.

5. D'Avity, *Estates, empires, and principalities*, 257.

6. Montaigne, *Essayes*, sig. Ff 5 r.

7. André Thevet, *New found worlde*, sig., G viii r – G viii v.

8. Pierre Viret, *De la source et la différence & convenance de la vielle & nouvelle idolatrie, & des vrayes & fausses images & reliques, & du seul & vray Mediateur* (Genève, Jean Gerard, 1551), *passim.*

9. Joseph de Acosta, *The natural and moral history of the Indies, (1588)*, reprinted from the English translation of Edward Grimston, 1604, and edited, with notes and an introduction by Clements R. Markham (London: Hakluyt Society, 1890?), II, 325.

10. Burton, *Anatomy*, III, 321.

11. D'Avity, *op. cit.*, 252.

12. *Infra*, pp. 288, 303, 383, 438–46, 450.

13. Stephen Batman, *The golden booke of the leaden goddes. Wherein is described the vayne imaginations of heathen pagans, and counterfaict Christians: wyth a description of their several tables, what ech of their pictures signified* (London: Thomas Marshe 1577), *passim.*

14. D. C. Allen, *Legend of Noah*, 83.

15. Stillingfleet, *Origines sacrae*, sig. Ffff 3 v – Gggg 1 r.

16. Godwyn, *Moses and Aaron*, 173–75.

17. Hermann J. Weigand, "The two and seventy languages of the world," *Germanic Review*, 17 (1942), 241–60.

18. George J. Metcalf, "Abraham Mylius on historical linguistics," *Publications of the Modern Language Association*, 68 (1955), 536–39.

19. Don Cameron Allen, "Some theories of the growth and origin of language in Milton's age," *Philological Quarterly*, 28 (1949), 8–9; see also Bodin, *Method*, xxiv.

20. Le Roy, *Of the interchangeable course*, sig. D 6 r; Brerewood, *op. cit.*, 16.

21. Metcalf, *op. cit.*, 535–40.

22. John Ogilby, *America: being the latest, and most accurate description of the New World . . .* (London: Printed by the author and are to

be had at his house in White Fryers, 1671), 11–12.

23. Marc Lescarbot, *The history of New France:* with an English translation, notes and appendices by W. L. Grant . . . and an introduction by H. P. Biggar . . . (Toronto, The Champlain Society, 1807–14), I, 47–48.

Everything that was known of ancient and nationalist history contributed to the belief in this explanation. "There is nothing more famous in ancient History," wrote the divine, William Nicholls, "than these Transmigrations of Inhabitants from one Country to another. Everyone knows of *Cadmus's* Plantation in *Boeotia;* of his brother *Cilix's* in *Cilicia,* of *Dido's* in *Africa;* of the *Colonies* setled by *Evander,Æneas,* and *Diomedes* in *Italy;* to say nothing of our *English Brute,* and the swarming Invasions of the *Saxons* and *Danes,* and an hundred other Instances." (William Nicholls, *A conference with a theist; containing an answer to all the most usual objections of the infidels against the Christian religion* [London : J. Holland and J. Boyer etc., 1723], I, 37.)

24. Burnet, *The theory of the earth,* 272.

25. Sir Francis Bacon, *Works,* III, 143.

26. Ogilby, *op. cit.,* 5 ff.

27. *Ibid.,* 5.

28. De Acosta, *op. cit.,* I, 67–68.

29. Lescarbot, *op. cit.,* III, 132–34.

30. Ogilby, *op. cit.,* 29–32.

31. Brerewood, *op. cit.,* 96–97.

32. De Acosta, *op. cit.,* I, 67–68.

33. Ogilby, *op. cit.,* 22–23.

34. Stillingfleet, *op. cit.,* sig. Dddd 2 r – Dddd 2 v.

35. Bodin, *Method,* 319–20. Received ideas on chronology were revolutionized for rational men by Joseph Justus Scaliger (1540–1609), who showed in his *De emendatione temporum* (1583) that ancient history was not confined to the Hebrews or the Greeks and Romans, but had to be carefully reconstructed from Persian, Egyptian, and Babylonian materials as well, and from a critical analysis of their several systems of chronology.

36. Arnold Williams, *Common expositor,* 140.

37. Bodin, *Method,* 319–20.

38. Sir Isaac Newton, "The chronology of ancient kingdoms amended," in *Isaaci Newtoni opera quae extant omnia. Commentariis illustrabat Samuel Horsley . . .* (Londini excudebat J. Nichols, 1779–85), 8.

39. "The Biblical account of the time which elapsed from the creation of Adam to the birth of Christ varies in a hopelessly irreconcilable fashion in different versions of the Scriptures. The Hebrew text assigns 4000 years to it, while the Septuagint reckons it at 6000 years. Gabriel de Mortillet . . . tabulates the various estimates of the duration of this period by no less than 32 different authorities, from which it appears that the highest was 6984 years and the lowest 3784 years—a difference of 3200 years." (Robert Munro, "Chronology," in Hastings, *Encyclopedia of Religion and Ethics,* III, 612.)

40. Paul Harold Kocher, *Christopher Marlowe, a study of his thought,*

learning, and character (Chapel Hill: University of North Carolina Press, 1946), 44.

41. Ralegh, *History*, sig. G 1 r, G 4 r.

42. D. C. Allen, *Legend of Noah*, 83. Jean Seznec, in a recent study of the same materials, shows clearly that, by virtue of the efforts of the Church Fathers and later world historians to fuse all events and characters of the past into one great historical synthesis, the pagan gods lived on into the Middle Ages. Notable among these world histories were Isidore's *Etymologies*, the *Chronicle* of the six ages of the world by Ado of Vienne, the *Historia scholastica* by Peter Comestor, and Brunetto Latini's *Book of the treasure*. No doubt the similarities employed to defend the orthodox position were suggested in this literature. (Jean Seznec, *La survivance des dieux antiques; essai sur la rôle de la tradition mythologique dans l'humanisme et dans l'art de la renaissance* [London: The Warburg Institute, 1940], *passim*.)

43. Bodin, *Method*, 321.

44. Ralegh, *op. cit.*, sig., F 6 r – G 1 r.

45. Stillingfleet, *op. cit.* sig. Ffff 2 r – Ffff 3 r.

46. De Acosta, *op. cit.*, II, 447.

47. Polydore Vergil, *Works*, sig. N 8 r –N 8 v; see also Denys Hay, *Polydore Vergil, Renaissance historian and man of letters* (New York: Oxford University Press, 1952).

48. Pierre Viret, *The Christian disputations. Devided into three partes, Dialogue wise* . . . Translated out of the French into English, by John Brooke of Ashe (London: Thomas East, 1579), sig. D v v, F ii r.

49. Pierre Mussard, *Roma antiqua et recens, or the conformity of antient and modern ceremonies, shewing from indisputable testimonies, that the ceremonies of the Church of Rome are borrowed from the pagans*. Translated from the French (London: C. Smith etc., 1732). Another book of the same type, and also published originally in French, was *Vitis degeneris: the degenerate plant. Being a treatise of antient ceremonies. Containing an historical account of their rise and growth, their first entrance into the church, and their gradual advancement to superstition therein* . . . Thomas Douglas, translator (London. 1668).

50. Conyers Middleton, *A letter from Rome, showing an exact conformity between Popery and paganism; or, the religion of the present Romans to be derived entirely from that of their heathen ancestors* (London: W. Innys, 1729), 14.

51. John Spencer, *De legibus Hebraeorum ritualibus, et earum rationibus libri tres* (Cantabrigiae: Chiswel, 1685), *passim*.

52. Nicholls, *Conference with a theist*, I, 296, 307–309.

53. Sir Francis Bacon, *op. cit.*, III, 335.

54. According to an 1830 definition in the Shorter Oxford Dictionary, an analogue is "a species or tribe in one region, or at one period, which represents a different species or tribe elsewhere or at a different epoch."

55. Stephen Batman, *The doome warning all men to the judgemente* . . . (London: Ralphe Nubery . . . , 1581), sig. A 4 r; according to Henri Estienne in his *World of wonders* (1595) the "God-eaters" of the present

were on the same cultural and historical footing as the Anthropophagi mentioned in Herodotus.

56. Hodgen, "Sebastian Muenster," 522.

57. Mexia, *The foreste,* sig. Q i v ff.

58. Thevet, *op. cit.,* sig. J iii v – J iii r, K i v, sig. G v r – G v v.

59. Katherine Beverly Oakes (Mrs. C. H. George), *Social theory in the early literature of voyage and exploration in Africa* (Ph. D. Dissertation, Department of Social Institutions, University of California, Berkeley, 1944), 200. "The civilized west looks at primitive Africa: 1400–1800. A study in ethnocentrism," *Isis,* 49 (1958), 62–72.

60. Acosta, *op. cit.,* II, 296–97, 305, 321, 313–14. Roger Williams, writing of the Indians of New England in 1643, compared them to the ancient Hebrews. Some words seemed to be like the Hebrew; "they constantly anoint their heads as the Jewes did;" they gave dowries to their wives. (Williams, *op. cit.,* 20.)

61. William Webbe, *A discourse of English poetrie. Together with the authors judgment, touching the reformation of our English verse* (1586). Reprinted in *Ancient and critical essays upon the English poets and poesy,* edited by Joseph Haslewood (London: Bensley, 1815), II, *passim.*

62. Richard Puttenham, *The arte of English poesie. Contrived into three bookes: The first of poets and poesie, the second of proportion, the third of ornament* (1589). Reprinted in Haslewood, *op. cit.,* I, 3. George and Richard Puttenham have each been independently credited with the authorship of this book. (Dictionary of National Biography, XVI, 507.)

63. Francis Barton Gummere, *The beginnings of poetry* (New York, Macmillan, 1901), 347.

64. Puttenham, *op. cit.,* I, 7. It is said that his appeal to the American Indians to support his argument was derived from an Italian source. (Wellek, *Rise of English literary history,* 9.)

65. Samuel Daniel, *A defence of ryme. Against a pamphlet entituled: Observations in the art of English poesie. Wherein is demonstratively proved, that ryme is the fittest harmonie of wordes that comports with our language* (1603), in Haslewood, *op. cit.,* II, 198–99.

66. Bernard Picart, *The ceremonies and religious customs of the various nations of the known world, together with historical annotations, and several curious discources, equally instructive and entertaining* (London: William Jackson, 1733–39), I, i, 3–4.

67. Heylyn, *Cosmographie,* sig. V 3 v.

68. Oakes, *Social theory in the early literature of voyage and exploration in Africa,* 218.

69. Carpenter, *Geography delineated,* sig. II, Nn i r – Nn i v.

70. David Person, *Varieties: or, a surveigh of rare and excellent matters . . .* (London: Richard Badger, 1635), 160.

71. Strachey, *Virginia Britania,* xxi–xxii, 23–25.

72. Ross, *Pansebia,* 121.

CHAPTER IX

The Problem of Savagery

"We need not goe to cull out miracles and strange difficulties: me seemeth, that amongst those things we ordinarily see there are such incomparable rarities as they exceed all difficulties of miracles."—MICHEL DE MONTAIGNE.

BUT WHY THIS INORDINATE EXPENDITURE of energy in eliciting cultural correspondences? The deists, the theists, the atheists, and the infidels, so called by their orthodox brethren, were tireless in their efforts to undermine confidence in many of these too easy-going and uncritical likenesses, but at the same time they proposed some of their own. Why the persistent effort to clothe savagery with documentary significance? Why, indeed, the emphasis upon savagery? With all the problems regarded as subject to solution by the employment of similarities supposedly solved, it still remains far from clear why identifications of contemporary savagery with classical antiquity, or with old phases of other historical cultures, should ever have been made at all.

So much is certain: it was not because of the validity of the correspondences cited. The earmarks of faulty reasoning are on the surface for all to see.

In the first place, to mention only a few difficulties, the number of plausible likenesses elicited between the civil societies of Greece, Rome, or the other old nations and the uncivil agglomerations of tribal Black Africa and the Red Man's America, were at best relatively few and usually trivial.

In the second place, they were offset, and the conclusions derived from them were neutralized, by an overwhelming body of divergences which were seldom mentioned, much less assembled for comparison of relative proportions. The fact, if it was a fact, that the myths, or the marriage rites, or the gods of the Americans and Greeks were similar, was interesting no doubt, but what of it? What meaning was to be inferred? The likeness of a few items could prove nothing concerning the likeness of the totality of traits in any savage culture to the totality in any civilized culture. As between any two cultures, anywhere at any time, likeness in one trait might be accompanied by unlikeness in ninety-nine others. Surely, before conclusions were drawn upon the basis of one pair of similarities, or twenty pairs, or a hundred, the presence of differences should have been acknowledged, and their weight as contrary evidence evaluated.

In the third place, when the terms "savage" and "antique" were applied to large categories of culture under examination for the detection of correspondences, it could by no means be assumed that those elicited for one pair of peoples were true for all members of each category. Though all the cultures in the category of the "antique" may have been in some sense historically ancient, as shown by dates, it fails to follow that all were culturally identical, Greek with Roman, Roman with Egyptian, Egyptian with Persian or Babylonian. Obviously Roman life diverged radically from that of the Greeks, and Greek life from that of all the other ancient civilizations. To place all of them in one classification was by no means to confer identity. And the same divergencies obtained within the category of "savagery"; the Hottentots in Africa differed from the people of Benin, and both of these from the Iroquois and Seminoles of America. Owing to radical differences among members of categories, no one member of the category of "savagery," and no one member of the category of the "antique," could safely be taken as representative of the whole category. Thus an argument from the assumed uniformity of cultures within each category, based upon a handful of likenesses from two peoples or twenty peoples, was fantastically unsound. Though the argument from similarities is still in use, no scholar has produced evidence of taxonomic agreement within either savage cultures or ancient civilized cultures.

In the fourth place, the endowment of specific elements from contemporary savage cultures with documentary significance implies the persistence of savage culture in its presently observable condition at least from the times of the Greeks, Romans, Egyptians, and other ancient peoples with whom they were compared. But who is ready to offer reliable evidence that any existing savage culture has remained fixed or unchanged throughout this long historical interval? Savage cultures are typically history-less cultures, in the sense that little or no documentation is available for the reconstruction of any long past condition. Without such documentation no test can be made of the assumption that they have undergone no change or modification. On the other hand, it is known on unimpeachable historical evidence that civilized cultures have sustained modifications of great magnitude. Why then should savage cultures be considered immune to change? The assumption of great age and persistence among the members of the category of savagery is gratuitous, an interpretation necessary to the argument but unprovable in fact.

In the fifth place, though the Greek, Roman, and other ancient cultures are well known to have existed long ago and to have covered an extended span of time during the course of their achievement of the status of civilizations, it is misleading and historically careless to assume that their purported replicas, the "savage" cultures, are equally old, and equally like them in every phase of their developments. With what period of classical culture have "savage" cultures been equated in the search for similarities? In most cases there is the fact, which must never be forgotten, that the cultures of antiquity, like all other historical cultures, were the products of particular, regional histories; that they became what they once were, high civilizations, as the result of traversing several historical levels or several cultural conditions, which may have been in many respects unique. With which one of these possibly unique cultural conditions, with which civilization, and in which region, does "savagery" in its totality correspond? On this point, users of similarities in the sixteenth and seventeenth centuries, are silent; and so, indeed, are their followers of the eighteenth, nineteenth, and twentieth centuries. To allege, as some have done, that likenesses have not been drawn between high periods of cultural achievement and existing "savagery," but between existing "savagery" and a like condition which antedated high achievement on these areas, is historically imprecise. For interest in the recovery of so-called "primitive" or "savage" periods preceding the civilized condition on civilized areas, such as Greece and Rome, has been recent. Who was to say, in the sixteenth and seventeenth centuries, how the Greeks and Romans lived in those shadowy times before they produced "civilizations"? Certainly, little was then known of any "primitive" condition prevailing on the sites of the ancient civilizations, and much less concerning aboriginal Persia or Mesopotamia. And if later, in the nineteenth and twentieth centuries, archeologists have chanced to unearth a few shards indicative of earlier conditions on these areas, this testimony was not only wanting when the comparisons were first made and the similarities elicited, but is now subject to all the criticism which flows from the presence of differences within the category of "savage" culture.[1]

Were correspondences used then—was savagery clothed with documentary significance—in response to the ambiguities of savage cultures? To make suddenly encountered and unexpected phenomena more intelligible? To assimilate them, however clumsily and falsely, into the already known, or presumed known? To find for them an appropriate, orderly, and satisfying place in the commonly accepted European hierarchical or historical scheme of things? There is much to be said for this proposition. For after all, even though the tribes of the Red Man and the Black Man were sometimes little remarked in Europe, except as figures of curiosity or fun, there were at least a few thoughtful scholars who saw in them a very disturbing and disconcerting intellectual problem.

It is often said that the Renaissance discovered man, and that the perplexities associated with this discovery were profound. But even so, the man discovered was a familiar fellow, a white European. When, at about the same time, the explorers threw the spotlight of publicity upon backward, darker-skinned, non-Europeans, when they brought home and told their stories of naked cannibals, there was something more involved than the enlargement of the European sample of the genus *Homo*. Here, or so it seemed, was a different kind of man. Or was he a man? There were those to say he was not. At all events the discovery of American and African savages introduced a new and different creature to the European world, a more complex problem to thought; and the difficulties of solving the problem of man were multiplied almost beyond management.

It should also be borne in mind, by all those who wish to see the intellectual situation in its less romantic reality, that the Renaissance and Reformation were only in part periods of dazzling enlightenment. They were streaked and furrowed with inherited ignorance, confusion, and traditionalism. Both movements were the outcome of controversies which had had their inception in the Middle Ages or long before, and were just now coming into the open. Both consequently were in part backward-looking, the autumnal flowering of medieval speculation rather than harbingers of a new era. Some men of learning were stirred by the expansion of geographical boundaries and ethnological horizons, but not all of them, nor always profoundly. Erasmus and Luther, leaders of the intellectual and religious Reformation, were little concerned with the facts or problems of New World ethnography. Their minds were elsewhere. Even among the members of the British Royal Society, whose investigations were notable for their multiform variety, other interests came first. Aside from a few philosophers and divines, it was chiefly the seafaring men and the explorers, whose main interest as often as not was commercial profit, who gave thought to the savage. Nor were many of the names associated with "organized" ethnological reflection in any sense renowned. Boemus, Purchas, Heylyn, Ross, d'Avity, Porcacchi, de Gaya, were second-rate at best. There was only a handful of fine scholars, such as the skeptic Montaigne and the Utopians More and Bacon, who could look far enough ahead of their own times to recognize the importance of the natives of America and Africa. But for them also these improbable members of the human species raised innumerable and tantalizing questions.

Were these naked savages, who had grown up outside the framework of the Judeo-Christian ethic, moral beings? Were they capable of practicing the Christian virtues? Such questions, phrased to taste, were subject to debate. And, since the sentiments which inspired comment were predominantly religious or ethical, they were generally explored in relation to current European standards of the good life. By some inquirers attempts were made to measure savage morality by the touchstone of the European conscience; by others, moral criteria were abandoned in favor of an easy-going relativism; while still others, moved by the force of popular theological pessimism, made all members of the human family, including the savage, the tragic remainders of a process of corruption and degeneration.

Throughout the history of Western thought the savage or the barbarian has been envisaged morally in one of two ways. This, at all events, is the thesis authoritatively advanced by Professors Lovejoy and Boas in their monumental work, *The documentary history of primitivism and related ideas* (1935).[2] Here, by means of a confusing terminology (their use, for example, of the word "primitivism" begs the question of the temporal and historical relations of savagery to other cultures), the authors have made it appear that since classical times a choice has always been available between what they have chosen to call a "primitivistic" or favorable estimate of savagery, and an "anti-primitivistic" or unfavorable one.

These authors further imply that the earliest and, throughout the course of Western thought, the most frequent option was the "primitivistic" or favorable one. In selecting their documentary materials they focus attention upon this option almost to the exclusion of the unfavorable view. True, neither author was an anthropologist, nor did either attempt to make a connection between this view and general anthropological theory. They chose rather within the general compass of intellectual history to lay in a useful background for the understanding of later philosophical and literary views, both by stressing the universality of the belief in a paradisaic original condition and by recounting the recurrent appearance of the one interpretation of savagery as morally good, innocent, and noble.

But the anthropologist will know that the very word "primitive," with all the changes which have been rung upon it, carries a heavy semantic burden of confused implications and intimations, impossible to cope with in any discussion which seeks to be precise. He will know also that, while the notion of the "noble savage" seized upon some phases of thought from time to time, it was in direct conflict with both an early and a later ethnological theory, namely, the Renaissance theological position on savagery and the nineteenth-century evolutionary position. Consequently, in simply stated sixteenth- and seventeenth-century fact, and before the rather conspicuous eighteenth-century flare-up of literary "primitivism," an unfavorable verdict upon the newly discovered peoples was far more often employed than a favorable one. And how could it be otherwise? Sixteenth-century theology and seventeenth-century rationalism, being what they were, gave little aid and comfort to a belief in the essential goodness of such examples of "primitive," untutored humanity as were found in Africa and the Americas. In the oft-cited words of Thomas Hobbes, who summarized both a large literature and the existing state of informed opinion, the life of these supposedly society-less, stateless groups of "noble" savages was "solitary, poore, nasty, brutish and short."

On the question, then, of the view to be taken of savagery —a question which ultimately raised the issue of human homogeneity, or the common humanity of the civil and savage peoples—the accounts of Renaissance voyagers were almost unanimous. For upwards of two hundred years an unfavorable, or "anti-primitivistic" verdict was rendered. The Church, with its distaste for the unconventional in marriage and funeral rites, not to mention the non-Christian in religion, may in this have exercised an overwhelming influence upon the explorers. Or it may be that, except by a few well-balanced minds, indelible memories of fantastic medieval ethnological lore made objective observations impossible. Be that as it may, European opinion, during this important period of ethnological reflection, was not "primitivistic"; it was anti-savage, and strongly so. Just as the Hungarians, who had ravaged Europe in the ninth and tenth centuries, were condemned by medieval chroniclers as "hideous, boar-tusked, child-devouring ogres," so the natives of Africa and the Americas, many of whom were gentle and peace-loving peoples on first contact, were defamed and vilified. Seen through the deforming fantasies of Solinus, Mela, Isidore, Mandeville, and their ilk, they were introduced to the European public not as nature's noblemen, endowed with all the innate virtues, and living in romantic communion with rustic surroundings, but as half-human, hairy wild men, degraded by "dayly tumultes, fears, doubts, sispitions, and barbarous cruelties."

The evidence for the generality of this point of view is voluminous. In the *Esmeraldo de situ orbis,* written about 1505, Duarte Pacheco Pereira describes the Negroes on the west coast of Africa as dog-faced, dog-toothed people, satyrs, wild men, and cannibals. In 1511, less than two decades after the first Columbian voyage, a copy of the narrative of Vespucci's travels was lent to the Abbey of Otterburn, and was read by the monks with great interest. Thereupon a grave question, prompted by what Lovejoy and Boas would have called an "anti-primitivistic" bias, was raised. Were these new races to be considered saved or damned? The answer was given in various forms. The state of the East Indians in Calicut, Cannanorre, and Ceylon, rediscovered by Da Gama in 1498, was regarded as bestial. Were the natives of the Dark

Continent of the Americas any better?³ According to the observations of the African traveler Antonio Malefante, writing in the second half of the sixteenth century, the folk south of the Sahara were animals: very wretched, very black, and very bad. According to Captain John Lok who in 1554 was still purveying the clichés of Herodotean legend, the region known as Guinea was inhabited by Troglodites who fed upon serpents; by Blemmines who had eyes and mouths in their chests; and by Satyrs who had nothing to commend them as human but their shape. The historian Gomara, a representative of that type of Christian who found savage custom unacceptable, wrote without sympathy for the New World peoples. They were liars, thieves, perverts, and above all obstinate idolaters. The philosophy of the colonizers in North America was reflected clearly in William Strachey's *Historie of travell into Virginia Britania,* completed in 1612. "I hope," he said of the Indians, "we may wyn them to be willing to heare and learne of us and our Preachers, the more civil use of every particular, in which they now too rudely, and beastly do amisse. All the injury that we purpose unto them, is but the Amendement of these horrible Hethenishnes. . . ."⁴ For a similar reason, all of the unhappiness, all of the persecution, which descended upon the northern tribes of Indians, the Peruvians, the Mexicans, the inhabitants of the Antilles, and Africa, was thought to be well-merited punishment.⁵ By this process of condemnation, New World man or the naked and threatening savage took that place in thought which, during the Middle Ages, had been reserved for human monsters. If human, theirs was a degraded humanity.

Though scholars and geographers should have known better, many whose works achieved great popularity chose to recite the same legendary commonplaces rather than to make sound observations and inductions. Even Bacon berated the

Indians for their rudeness. He found their nakedness a deface-
ment of their humanity, and deplored their cannibalism, of
which he had no doubt.⁶ By a very large fraction of the
voyagers they were habitually described as being given "to
much beastlinesse and void of all goodnesse." And so also the
Africans. Even in an edition as late as 1677, Peter Heylyn's
Cosmography, reported that the inhabitants of Terra Nigritarum were so rude in their behavior that they seemed to lack
that "use of Reason which is peculiar to man"; while Patrick
Gordon, a contemporary popularizer of geographical and ethnological "facts," heaped upon the hapless Negroes the whole
catalogue of vices. The natives of Guinea, it was said, were
proud, lazy, and sluttish; they were great idolaters, very superstitious, and given to stealing and cheating. The Ethiopians
were reported as "rude and beastlie"; the desert nomads as
"bestiall without forsyght." The Egyptians were cowards,
luxurious, cunning, treacherous, and much degenerated from
their ancestors.⁷ Many writers on political theory, influenced
by Hobbes and these explorers, adopted an identical conception of savagery in dealing with the origin of social and political institutions. The same was no less true among men of
letters. To Shakespeare's Prospero, Caliban was "filth . . .
without human care," gabbling like "a thing most brutish."

Nor were judgments of neighboring but outlying European
folk any less harsh. Consider the attitude of the Elizabethan
Englishman toward his kinsmen on Britain's northern and
western borders. Apparently, while sovereigns of the realm
were struggling to pacify the tribal Celts, and the Puritan
colonists in North America were wrestling with the Red
Indian for his soul and his lands, all frontier antagonists looked
more or less alike. Whether Irishmen or Pequots, Scots or
Iroquois, they were enemies, they were ignorant, and they
were animal-like. The only way to regard them was through

the lenses of a quasi-philosophical, quasi-religious, and quasi-political "anti-primitivism," unembarrassed either by any recognition of brotherliness or by a more austere theological assumption of common humanity. Wherever this policy was adopted, the epithets used to describe the folk on Britain's Celtic border were interchangeable with those applied to the Negroes in Africa or to the Indians across the Atlantic.

Writing of the Irish in the sixteenth century, Edmund Spenser (1552?–1599) and William Camden (1551–1623) spoke as if they too were savages. Leaning on a broad knowledge of the voyage literature, Spenser often made beastliness, excess, and irrationality a theme in the *Faerie Queene* (1590). One unfortunate character in the poem was captured by a wild man who had matted hair, tusks, and cannibalistic impulses. The Irish were viewed as "wilde fruit, which salvage soyl hath bred"; their migratory lives, their dress, their "Scythian" habits, "bliendelie and brutishelie enformed," constituted Spenser's evidence for that conclusion. Much other material descriptive of savagery, in the same poem, was reminiscent of the libels then being circulated in the European community concerning the natives of the Americas, Africa, Asia, and the Celtic border lands.⁸ Camden the historian was more restrained. Nevertheless, his *Britannia* of 1586 and Spenser's *View of the present state of Ireland,* written ten years later, were in substantial agreement. The Irish, said Camden, were "in some places wilde and very uncivill." Among the wilder sort he found "neither divine service; nor any forme of Chapelle . . . no Alters at all . . . the Missal or Masse booke all torne." To this disgraceful laxity, superstition was added. "I cannot tell whether the wilder sort of the Irishry yeeld divine honour unto the moone"; said Camden, "for when they see her first after the change, commonly they bow the knee, and say over the Lord's prayer. . . . They take

unto them Wolves to bee their Godsibs. . . . The shoulder
blade bone of a sheepe . . . they use to looke through, and
thereby fortell of some corse shortly to bee carried out of the
house." Indeed, "they are so stifly settled in observing of the
old rites of their country, that not only they cannot be withdrawn from them, but are also able easily to draw the English
unto the same (so prone is mans nature to entertain the worst)
that one would not beleeve in how short a time some English
among them degenerate and grow out of kinde."[9]

Later in the eighteenth century, even after men of letters
became enchanted by the idea of the "noble savage" and made
it a leitmotiv of literary expression, the same unfavorable conception of the real savage was still afloat in the parish ethnology of Britain. Scattered here and there in his diaries and
sermons, John Wesley (1703–1791) referred to peoples all over
the world : to the Chicasaws, Cherokees, Uchees, and Creeks
of the state of Georgia, where he served a missionary appren-
ticeship; to the savages of Siberia and Tartary; to the Fin-
landers, Samoiedes, Laplanders; to the Hottentots, the
Senegalese, and the natives of Benin, the Congo, Angola, and
the three nations of Jalofs, Fulis, and Mandigoes. To none,
however, did he grant even the rudiments of decency or civilization. After the usual formula, the American Indians were
dismissed as possessing no letters, no religion, no laws, no civil
government, no powers either to command or to punish. They
were denounced as implacable and unmerciful; as murderers
of fathers, mothers, and children. Concerning other peoples,
Asian or European, he was equally censorious. "What say
you," he asked, "to thousands of Laplanders, Samoiedes, and
Greenlanders, of all who live in the high northern latitudes?
Are they as civilized as sheep or oxen? Add to these the
myriads of human savages, that are freezing among the snows
of Siberia, and as many, if not more, who are wandering up

and down in the deserts of Tartary. . . . To compare them with horses or any of our domestic animals would be doing them too much honour." As an example of "anti-primitivistic" ideas among the educated and enlightened clergy of the eighteenth century, this statement is of great interest. But Wesley could speak even more plainly. According to the doctrine of Original Sin and the Fall, the Africans and other native folk were condemned as corrupt and degenerate. Some of the inhabitants of Negro Land, indeed, were portrayed by him in repulsive doggerel as lower than brutes:

> Your nicer Hottentots think meet,
> With guts and tripe to deck their feet,
> With down-cast eyes on Totta's legs,
> The love-sick youth most humbly begs,
> She would not from his sight remove,
> At once his breakfast and his love.[10]

At about the same time in the eighteenth century, savage man's supposed kinship with the ape was again broached.

Occasionally, of course, even as early as the sixteenth century, when systematic misrepresentation of the savage was at its height, voices were raised in protest or contradiction. No group of human beings, it was said, could be so wholly evil; a touch of virtue sometimes accompanied vice. Moreover, some of the ancient, almost forgotten, and more generous views acclaiming savagery were revived. To Jean de Léry, who had joined Villegagnon in Brazil in 1556, the South American Indians were men, with the good and bad traits of men. While the lack of religion seemed to place them among the brutes, they were a happy people; while their nudity deserved reproach, it was no worse than the brazen coquetry of Europeans. In saying farewell to his Indian friends, Léry was filled with regret. Declaring that he had always loved his own country, he acknowledged nonetheless that the loyalty of the Americans, contrasted with the faithlessness of the French, made him long to remain among them."

To be sure, the conditions of the first meeting between a group of savages and a boatload of Europeans was crucial. For many voyagers the manner of their reception when they stepped ashore for the first time on the beaches of newly discovered lands determined their conclusions concerning their hosts. If the natives were cordial, obliging and friendly—and often they were, at least at first—then they were so described, and the best face possible was put on habits repugnant to Europeans. If, on the other hand, fear of intruders led to native hostility, the geniality of the ship's company vanished, and they reached for their harshest adjectives.

When John Verrazani, a Florentine, approached the east coast of North America (probably in the neighborhood of what is now Charleston, South Carolina) in 1524, his men were ordered to take a boat ashore. A great crowd ran to the strand to greet the seamen, "seeming to rejoice very much at the sight" of them, and marveling greatly at their apparel, shape, and whiteness. Showing by signs how the ship might easily come in closer to land, the Indian reception committee also offered "their victuals to eate." Then follows a carefully composed physical and cultural description without a syllable implying dislike, fear, or antagonism. When again on the same voyage, the two ships, the *Norman* and the *Dolphin,* put in at another haven, a second hospitable welcome was received. The natives "al made a loud showte together, declaring that they rejoiced." They were very generous and gave the ship's crew something of everything they had on hand. "They came in great companies of their small boats unto the ships with their faces all bepainted with divers colours, showing us yt was a signe of joy bringing us of their victuals." And again a favorable and friendly description was forthcoming." But many voyagers, including Columbus, callously adbucted some of their hosts. From that time on misunderstandings were inevitable. The natives were no longer on their good behavior, nor could they be expected to be.

Sometimes praise of the Indians was a matter of economic policy, or propaganda for the encouragement of the emigration of colonists. For one or the other of these reasons, the explorers Amidae and Barlow, who were sent out to Virginia by Sir Walter Ralegh, described the natives as "very handsome and goodly," and in their behavior "as mannerly and civil as any in Europe." To their kings, nobility, and governors, no people in the world were more respectful than these. The explorers were entertained "with all love and kindness." They found the people "most gentle, loving and faithful, void of any guile or treason." Or sometimes a missionary was well disposed toward his charges. When this was so, savage generosity and other agreeable traits were upheld as virtues which the European community was advised to emulate. With proverbial charity, and despite the difficulties of bringing about the Christianization of Africa or the New World, this type of missionary was inclined to treat the failings of his flock with indulgence, regarding them as "all the more children of God owing to their very lack of capacity and skill." Among such men, the name of Bartholomew Las Casas will never be forgotten, nor his denunciation of Spanish cruelty. His was an immense service in integrating the Indian with the human race. But all in all, the missionary's opinion of savagery differed very little from that of the fault-finding layman. Indeed, in 1724 when Père Lafitau published his *Moeurs des sauvages amériquains,* he found cause to reproach fellow Jesuits for their failure to understand the Indians. He was much distressed, he said, that in the greater part of the *Relations* the barbarous peoples were presented to the world as though they possessed no feeling for religion, no knowledge of the divine, no objects of worship; as peoples, in a word, who could claim nothing human but their shape.[13] And thereafter, he made it his responsibility to overcome this misconception, at least among the clergy.

Meanwhile the literature of geography, travel, and ethnography was haunted by the memory of another conception. Lingering on in the recesses of the European mind, as it survives also in Lovejoy's and Boas' *Documentary history of primitivism,* was an ancient belief in the existence, early in time and remotely in space, of men reputed to be as aboriginal as any savage but happier, more virtuous, and more innocent than civil man. Owing perhaps to Renaissance interest in Greek and Roman literature, or to the morally disturbed conditions which in European capitals had resulted from religious and political controversy, the desire to find some human beings who were worthy of complete admiration was very strong. This, indeed, may be the literature upon which Lovejoy and Boas chiefly relied in drawing conclusions with respect to "primitivism." At all events, the old "primitivistic" convention, conferring approval upon the savage, was granted a new lease on life early in the sixteenth century, paralleling, but always secondary to, the attitude of disapproval and censure. After all, even though the assumption of a contemporary Golden Age was in direct conflict with the doctrine of the Fall of Man, it was a temptation and a relief to think of savage societies according to ancient ideas, in the forms prescribed by classical imagery, as innocent and admirable rather than degraded and repugnant. If these societies were little known, their chances of idealization were good; if they were little known and also very far away, their chances were even better.

Columbus was the first modern voyager to praise a savage people. According to Professor Leonardo Olschki, he looked upon the handsomely formed Caribs with the delight and appreciation of a Renaissance artist. Though the stock phrases associated with the conventional idea of the noble savage are notably absent from his description, yet the natives were presented as virtuous and mild, beautiful in body and countenance, living together in nakedness and innocence, and holding their goods in common.

Again in 1511, less than twenty years after the first Columbian voyage, the revival of the ancient formula of admiration for savagery was carried still further by Peter Martyr. Culling ideas and turns of expression from Empedocles, Ovid, Virgil, and Juvenal, Martyr told the readers of *De novo orbe* that the Indians had "no delyte insuche superfluities, for the whiche in other places men take infinite paynes, and commit manye unlawfull actes"; that "among these symple soules, a fewe clothes serve the naked : weightes and measures are not needeful to suche as . . . have not the use of pestiferous money . . . so that yf we shall not be ashamed to confesse the trueth, they seeme to live in that golden worlde of the whiche the olde wryters speake so muche, wherein men lyved symplye and innocentlye without enforcement of lawes, without quarrelying, judges, and libelles . . . they seeme to lyve in the golden worlde without toyle, lyvynge in open gardens, not intrenched with dyches, divided with hedges, or defended with walles. . . ."[14] After several other uses of these stereotypes, the convention appeared again decades later when, in writing of a certain Brazilian tribe near Rio de Janeiro, Montaigne commented as follows :

They are even savage, as we call those fruites wilde, which nature of hir selfe, and of hir ordinarie progresse hath produced. . . . Those nations seeme therefore so barbarous unto mee, because they have received very-little fashion from humane wit, and are yet neere their originall naturalitie. The lawes of nature do yet commaund them, which are but little bastardized by ours. And that with such puritie, as I am sometimes grieved the knowledge of it came no sooner to light, at what time ther were men, that better than we could have judged of it. I am sorie, Licurgus and Plato had it not : for me seemeth that what in those nations wee see by experience, doth not onelie exceede all the pictures wherewith licentious Poesie hath prowdly imbellished the golden age, & al hir quaint inventions to faine a happy condition of men, but also the conception & desire of Philosophie. They could not imagine a genuitie so pure and simple, as we see it by experience; nor ever beleeve our societie might be maintained with so little arte and humane combination.[15]

The phrase "golden age" appears infrequently in Montaigne's *Essayes;* but who can doubt, given the likeness of his lines to those of Martyr, and of both to classical sources, that this ancient, idealized condition was in their minds?

It can serve no good purpose merely to multiply examples of the resuscitation of this old belief and its application to sixteenth-century breeds of men. The biography of the idea of the noble savage has already been meticulously reconstructed, in so far as it has relevance to the literature of antiquity, the Middle Ages, and the eighteenth century.[16] But even in the latter period, when it became a staple in romanticized social theory, the idea that virtue and happiness were the accompaniments of life in savage societies took a largely aesthetic and didactic form. Literature of this sort discloses an increasing emphasis upon the physical attractiveness of African and American manhood and womanhood. The Negroes had white teeth and enjoyed rugged good health; they were well shaped and well limbed; their eyes were well formed; and so on.[17] Not content with mentioning the gentler and softer traits of savagery, commentators also tried to combat the influence of those who had charged the Negroes and the Indians with brutality and unintelligence. Despite their lack of tools and knowledge of the arts, said one visitor to Virginia, the Indians were ingenious and, when European intruders conducted themselves wisely and courteously, easily civilized and converted. The Mexicans had splendid memories, said another, and were easy to teach.[18] The superiority of the artless, simple, and natural to the artificial and mannered was insisted upon. "If there is one corner of the eartH where decency of conduct and morality is still honored, it finds its temple in the heart of the desert," among the African Negroes.[19] Here, an emergent naturalism is to be detected. The attainments of such savages were not achieved through nurture or education. They were the gifts of nature.

But there was also another side to the ethnological dilemma which suddenly appeared over the narrow horizon of European speculation. To many minds, the employment of a moral standard for judging these strange new human beings was not adequate. The diversity of savage conduct forbade its use. It was not enough to say that this or the other tribe was either good or bad. Disconcerted by opposing standards for evaluating countless kinds of behavior, more than one Renaissance scholar was shocked into an admission of cultural relativism. Merely as a restatement of the fact of cultural diversity, relativism explained nothing. It served its advocates solely as a means of escape from an obligation either to accept an old moral criterion or to find a new one. In another form, however, it was theoretically fruitful in that it stimulated a detached attitude and encouraged the environmental studies of Bodin and his successors.

The troublesome facts were stated early by Peter Martyr and by Montaigne. Martyr's observations led him to remark the presence of relativism in men's opinion of one another, and hence the frailty of any one standard of judgment. "The Aethiopian," he said, "thinketh the blacke colour to be fairer then the white : and the white man thinketh otherwise. Hee that is polled thinketh himselfe more amiable than hee who weareth long hayre, and the bearded man supposeth hee is more comely than hee that wanteth a beard. As appetite therefore moveth, not as reason perswadeth, men run into these vanities, and every province is ruled by its owne sense. . . ."[20] Montaigne, an insatiable reader of travelers and cosmographers, was disturbed by the slenderness of the relation between the particular features of the total array of cultures and any moral criterion. Sharp differences, both in space and time, had long been recognized. "What goodness is that," he asked, "which but yesterday I saw in credite and esteeme, and tomorrow, to have lost all reputation, and that the breadth of a River, is made a crime? What truth is that, which these Mountaines bound, and is a lie in the World beyond them?"[21] The same questions were asked later by others, and often in the same words. The barbarous heathen, said Benjamin Franklin many years later, "are nothing more strange to us than we are to them; savages we call them, because their manners differ from ours, which we think the Perfection of Civility: they think the same of theirs."[22] And John Locke, after a powerful recital of paradoxes, swept all differences in traits and institutions into the one neutralizing net of relativism. Have there not been whole nations, said he, even among the most civilized, in which children have exposed their ageing parents? Are there not others in which babies are buried with mothers who have died in childbirth? The Mingrelians, a people held to be Christian, bury their offspring alive without scruple. Others, such as the Caribbees, fatten and eat them. According to Léry, the Tououpinambos have no name for god, no religion, and no worship. Truly, he who will read the records of the tribes of men will find that there is scarcely a principle of morality or a rule of virtuous behavior which is not somewhere flouted or condemned "by the general fashion of whole societies of men."[23] And in almost the same words, David Hume suggested that somewhere, by some people, even by Europeans, some rule of decency was scorned or held in contempt.

The popular appeal of cultural relativism was the outward

and visible sign of an inward and unresolved difficulty in thought. For some Christians, the realization that heathen cults might possess what appeared to be marriage rites, sacraments, monastic organizations, and tonsured clergy, hitherto regarded as the unique possessions of Christendom, was a dangerous one which shook their faith. The presence among the unbaptized of rites and ceremonies like those of Holy Church suggested that absolute religious truth was unattainable. Difficulty arose for others because there was so little to choose between the morals of professing Christians and those of the pious heathen or the virtuous savage. Nude, dirty, accursed, and rejected of God, the savage, even so, often seemed the better man, endowed with moral qualities denied to priests and bishops. Then there was that other question. How could the God of the medieval imagination, the God worshiped by Christians when the boundaries of Christendom were narrow but coterminous with the known world, be now the sole ruler of a realm in which Christians formed so small a minority? How could all the Chinese and other non-Christians be damned because they knew nothing of an event in Judea which, so far as their knowledge of it at the time was concerned, might have occurred on the moon?

With these aching doubts and anxieties seeping into the very Holy of Holies of theological security, the problem of savagery became more and more insistent. Whence came these creatures, whether human or sub-human, virtuous or bestial? Were the Red Indians and the Black Africans, with all their fantastic and horrid ways, descendants of Adam, and of one blood with their polished and urbane contemporaries, the French, the Italians, and the English? If so, what had happened to them? How had this cleavage in manners between the peoples of the Old World and those of the New occurred in the first place? If due to the deterioration of the wandering progeny of Noah, a condition which no man had wholly escaped, how had the gulf between the culture of Christendom and savagery become so wide? Above all, what was the place of savagery in the general scheme of things?

Quite apart from this peculiar phase of the question (the place of the savage), the larger problem of man's place in nature, or, from a humanistic standpoint, the problem of philosophical anthropology, was endemic in the Renaissance, as it must always be during any period of drastic cosmological or social revision. Profound disturbance in the traditional conception of the universe, and of man's situation in it, contributed to confusion and dissension. Men felt the very foundations of order and intelligibility shifting under their feet, and they could lay their hands on nothing to restore stability. There were those who rejected new-fangled heliocentric ideas, who insisted in and out of season that the world was made for man—that man was its reflection, epitome, and reason for being. There were others who scoffed at every paragraph and clause of the old anthropocentric doctrine. Willingly or unwillingly, man had been set down upon one of the minor planets, and there he was, with no means of accounting for his fate conveniently at hand. The world, said Robert Burton, as he tried to thread his way through the ponderous tangle of argument and counterargument, "is tossed in a blanket." The adherents of different theories "hoist the earth up and down like a ball, make it stand and go at their pleasures."[24]

Meanwhile, to compound the anxieties of the onlookers as a new image of the universe began gradually to take shape, and the old one withered away, mankind itself no longer appeared to be a single homogeneous species or unit. It was cleft to the core into at least two cultural categories, the civil and the barbarous, the polished and the savage.

One of the earliest responses to the problem of savagery, so put and so conceived, came from that wayward genius, Jerome

Cardan (1501–1576), mathematician, physician, astronomer, astrologer. Instructed perhaps by his reading of the experiences of the voyagers, he ascribed the cleavage to an emotional difference between advanced and backward man. Some peoples were properly called "barbarians," not because they were "wild"—some wild men indeed were more humane than the Greeks and Romans—not because they were ignorant, or brutal, but rather because they were psychologically unstable and easily imposed upon. "Before a matter is understood, they begin to rage . . . and it is very difficult to quiet them." [25]

Another widely imitated response was that made by Montaigne in his essay *Of the caniballes* (c. 1580). As has already been mentioned, Montaigne was one of a long line of scholars for whom barbarism was merely civilization stripped of everything that made it admirable and hence was envisaged by a resort to negatives. Using the tribes of Brazil as examples, he attempted to portray savagery as the ethnological antithesis of European society. Here in a primitive social environment, the advantages which the residents of the European peninsula had enjoyed in commerce, in letters, in law, government, the arts and husbandry were absent. [26] The same negative formula of description was subsequently applied by other Europeans when it came time to discuss the natives of North America or Africa, or when the puzzling characteristics of uncivil man were subjects of controversy. It was reiterated by Spenser in his *Faerie Queene,* and by Shakespeare in *The Tempest.* Said Gonzalo, the old counselor:

> Had I plantation of this isle, my lord . . .
> I' th' commonwealth I would by contraries
> Execute all things : for no kind of traffic
> Would I admit; no name of magistrate;
> Letters should not be known; riches, poverty,
> And use of service, none; contract, succession,
> Bourn, bound of land, tilth, vineyard, none;
> No use of metal, corn, or wine, or oil;

No occupation; all men idle, all;
And women too, but innocent and pure;
No sovereignty . . .

(The Tempest, II, i, 143–52)

It appeared also in that learned work *De la vicissitude ou variété des choses en l'univers,* published in 1576 by Louis Le Roy, in Thevet's *Singularitez,* in the *Omnium gentium mores* of Johann Boemus, in William Cunyngham's *Cosmographical glasse,* in Rastall's *Nature of the four elements,* in Samuel Purchas, in Pierre d'Avity, Pedro Mexia, and Thomas Hobbes.

But of all efforts to account for the presence of the savage in the world, the one most congenial to a theological generation was that which was derived from the Scriptural doctrine of the Fall, and attributed his rude presence vis-à-vis the cultivated European to a declension from a higher cultural condition, or to a postlapsarian degeneration. There were many reasons for the prevalence of this theory. Some of them sprang naturally from the condition of savagery itself: its association with dirt, disorder, nudity, immorality; its real or imputed cannibalism or godlessness. But there was also another. Uncompromising and gloomy though it was, the theory of the degeneration of savagery was a corollary of that even gloomier and more inclusive doctrine by which the condition of all men everywhere, uncivil or civil, was regarded as the outcome of corruption. Both the doctrine and the corollary were logical inferences from the ancient and medieval belief, still viable during the Renaissance, that the world and man were subject to inevitable and progressive decay. The savage was only a little more corrupt than anybody else.

It was maintained by travelers to Africa that the natives of the Dark Continent were derived from an earlier and higher condition of barbarism. The existence of the Red Men in the Americas having been accounted for, it was still necessary to account for their savage condition. According to Sir Matthew

Hale in his *Primitive origination of mankind* (1677), migrating men degenerated as they moved from continent to continent.[27] "Differences of degree of savagery or barbarism among New World tribes were explained by the fact that migrations had occurred at successive intervals since the Flood, and hence some groups had had more time in which to degenerate and forget the 'Original' from which they were derived."[28] A similar theory was entertained among English colonists in North America. There it was almost universally agreed that the Indians were of the race of men, not animals; and that they were descendants of Adam, Noah, and the Asiatic Tartars. This opinion, orthodox in the seventeenth century, was also congenial, for it not only allowed the Puritans to draw the Indians into the accepted theological scheme of things, it also distinguished among degrees of corruption. All men were corrupt, but the Indians most of all. The same argument was often braided and interwined with that other conviction which condemned migration and diffusion as evil. Distance was the cause of estrangement from tradition and from a former Noachian condition. Was not the Indian the farthest of all God's creatures from God Himself? "Descended from wanderers, had he not lost his sense of civilization and law and order? Had he not lost—except for a dim recollection—God Himself? And was he not, as a direct result of this loss, in the power of Satan?" To John Eliot, who attempted to Christianize the New England Indians, their way of life was one of satanic degradation; to Cotton Mather, they were "doleful creatures . . . the veriest ruines of mankinde, which were to be found anywhere on the face of the earth."[29] Their religious ideas had degenerated, said Charlevoix. All that was left were the scantiest of remnants.

Over the years, the theory of the degeneracy of the savage races became a hardy perennial. It was the solution to the problem of savagery offered in the eighteenth century by Ber-

nard Mandeville's *Fable of the bees* (1714), and by Père
Lafitau in *Les moeurs des sauvages amériquains* (1724). Since
all men, said Mandeville, "are Descendents of Adam, and
consequently of Noah and his Posterity; how came savages
into the world?" Their advent was obviously ascribable to
conditions associated with the dispersion from the Ark; to
the difficulty of transmitting the Adamic cultural tradition to
scattered tribes, no longer in communication with one another.
In the savage state men were more liable to accidents and
misfortunes in rearing their young than in society; and therefore the children of savages were very often put "to their
shifts," so as hardly to remember, by the time they had grown
up, that they had any parents. Denied tutelage and protection,
as were Cain's posterity and the descendants of the sons of
Noah, those who survived must have been much wilder than
some of their forebears who had enjoyed the advantage of
living "many years under the Tuition of their Parents."[30]

Throughout the seventeenth, eighteenth, and nineteenth
centuries, to the discomfiture of those who desired to gain support for the doctrine of progressivism, the same theory persisted. This notion, or its close relation, the concept of the
unimprovability of savagery, was often employed in response
to the problems of colonization, or in defense of Negro slavery.
British statesmen felt that they could justify their failures of
administration among African peoples by appealing to the
work of Alexander von Humboldt (1769–1859) and James
Hunt (1833–1869). By both the Negro was classified as a
species apart from European man and unimprovable in culture. "No people," said Dr. Hunt firmly, had had "so much
communication with Christian Europeans as the people of
Africa." But the Negro race had "never civilized itself," had
"never accepted any other civilization," and from the most
remote antiquity "seems to have been what it now is." American pro-slavery agitators were equally well served by the

ethnological arguments of J. C. Nott and G. R. Gliddon, who reiterated the old story that the blacks failed to belong to the same creation as the whites, that their organization doomed them to slavery and precluded their improvement. A large literature also accumulated in support of the proposition that the American Indian could likewise never advance beyond his existing aboriginal condition. Indian archeological monuments were interpreted as the work of people greatly superior to the rude tribes found by Europeans in these regions, and were taken, therefore, as indications of degeneration.

Still later, in the early nineteenth century, Richard Whately (1785–1863), Archbishop of Dublin, brought up the matter again. His argument started with a horrified, impressionistic picture of the savage as the defeated missionary saw him— gross, naked, ugly, apelike, deserter of the aged, practicer of polygamy, perpetrator of infanticide and cannibalism. Could this abandoned creature entertain any of the elements of nobility? Could these lowly savages and the most highly civilized specimens of the European cultures be regarded as members of the same species? The Archbishop's answer was an emphatic "No." Nations reported to have risen unaided from the savage state had been found in every instance to have had "the advantage of instruction and example of civilized man living among them." Unassisted change in savage culture, far from being subjected to a law of progress, was to be described in terms of decline and degeneration. And for this conclusion the Archbishop found confirmation in savage legends reminiscent of an earlier and higher state, and the occasional presence in savage cultures of one or two arts "not of a piece with their general rudeness." These he characterized as remnants of a more advanced condition from which they had fallen.

It was to refute Archbishop Whately and other degenerationists that Sir Edward Burnett Tylor wrote his *Primitive culture* (1871), reconsidered the problem of similarities, and revived, in his doctrine of survivals, the earlier concept of "remnants," "remainders," "seeds," "sparks," and "footprints." For these and other services he has been called the Father of Anthropology.[13]

BIBLIOGRAPHY AND NOTES

1. This criticism of the employment of similarities is not a criticism of classification and comparison as such. Both obviously should be used under as many rubrics as may be expected to yield information. It is directed rather toward the association of taxonomic procedures with assumptions underlying the use of the so-called comparative method, conjectural history, developmentalism, and evolutionism.

2. Arthur O. Lovejoy, Gilbert Chinard, George Boas, and Ronald S. Crane, editors, *A documentary history of primitivism and related ideas* (Baltimore: Johns Hopkins Press, 1935), *passim.*

3. Duarte Pacheco Pereira, *Esmeraldo de situ orbis* (London: Hakluyt Society, 1937), 89, 98, 144; P. S. Allen, *Age of Erasmus*, 92–93.

4. Strachey, *Virginia Britania*, 25.

5. Atkinson, *Nouveaux horizons*, 164; Oakes, *Social theory in the early literature of voyage and exploration in Africa*, 96–119.

6. Robert Ralston Cawley, *Unpathed waters: studies in the influence of the voyagers on Elizabethan literature* (Princeton: Princeton University Press, 1940), 245.

7. Oakes, *op. cit.*, 106, 110.

8. Roy Harvey Pearce, "Primitivistic ideas in the Faerie Queene," *Journal of English and Germanic Philology*, 44 (1945), 139–51; M. M. Gray, "The influence of Spenser's Irish experiences on The Faerie Queene," *Review of English Studies*, 6 (1930), 413–28; Edmund Spenser, *A view of the present state of Ireland* edited . . . by W. L. Renwick (London: E. Partridge, 1934), *passim;* William Christie Macleod, *The American Indian frontier* (New York: Knopf, 1928), 152–71. During the sixteenth and seventeenth centuries similar frontier policies were developed by the English government with reference not only to the Indians in North America but also to the Celtic tribes of Britain. As early as the fourteenth century, Ranulf Higden's *Polychronicon*, in the Trevisa version, reported the natives of Ireland as "unseemly" in manners and clothing, "wedding lawfully no wives," forsaking tillage for the pasturage of beasts, and having no knowledge of weaving or metal-working.

9. William Camden, *Britain, or a chorographicall description of the most flourishing kingdomes of England, Scotland, and Ireland* . . . (London: Impensis Georgii Bishop & Ioannis Norton, 1610), sig. Mmmm vi v – Nnnn ii v.

10. Margaret Trabue Hodgen, "The negro in the anthropology of John Wesley," *Journal of Negro History*, 19 (1934), 308–23; R. W. Frantz, "Swift's yahoos and the voyagers," *Modern Philology*, 29 (1931–32), 49–57.

11. Gilbert Chinard, *L'exotisme américaine*, 125–48.

383

12. John Verrazanı, "The relation of John Verarzanus, a Florentine, of the lands by him discovered in the name of his Majestie, written in Diepe the eighth of July 1524," in Richard Hakluyt, *Divers voyages touching the discovery of America and the islands adjacent* . . . , edited, with notes and an introduction by John Winter Jones (London: Printed for the Hakluyt Society, 1850), VII, 56, 64–66.

13. Joseph François Lafitau, *Moeurs des sauvages Amériquains comparées aux moeurs des premiers temps* . . . (Paris: Saugrain l'aîné et Charles Estienne Hochereau, 1724), 1–5.

14. Peter Martyr, "The first booke of the decades of the ocean, written by Peter Martyr of Angleria Milenos." In Eden, *The history of travayle* sig. C vii r, D viii v.

15. Montaigne, *Essayes,* sig. K 3 r – K 3 v̇.

16. Hoxie Neale Fairchild, *The noble savage: a study in romantic naturalism* (New York: Columbia University Press, 1928), *passim;* Lois Whitney, *Primitivism and the idea of progress in English popular literature in the eighteenth century* (Baltimore: Johns Hopkins Press, 1934), *passim.*

17. Oakes, *op. cit.,* 129.

18. Atkinson, *op. cit.,* 149.

19. Oakes, *op. cit.,* 118.

20. Pietro Martire d'Anghiera, *De novo orbe* (1612), sig. Z 2 r.

21. Montaigne, *op. cit.,* sig. Gg i r.

22. Benjamin Franklin, "Remarks concerning the savages of North America," in *The life and writings* . . . collected and edited by . . . Albert Henry Smyth (New York: Macmillan, 1905–07), X, 97–104.

23. John Locke, "An essay concerning the human understanding" (1689), in *Works* (London: C. and J. Rivington, 1824), I, 38–40.

24. Burton, *Anatomy,* II, 57.

25. Thorndike, *Magic and experimental science,* V, 577.

26. Montaigne, *op. cit.,* sig. K 3 v.

27. Sir Matthew Hale, *The primitive origination of mankind, considered and examined according to the light of nature* (London: W. Godbid for W. Shrowsbery, 1677), 195, 197, 318. See also Lewis Paul Kohrs, *The social theory of Sir Matthew Hale's Primitive origination of mankind, considered and examined according to the light of nature* (1677) (Unpublished Ph. D. Dissertation, Department of Social Institutions, University of California [Berkeley], 1952).

28. Kenneth Elliott Bock, *The acceptance of histories: toward a perspective for social science* (Berkeley: University of California Publications in Sociology and Social Institutions, 1956), III, 212.

29. Roy Harvey Pearce, *The savages of America: a study of the Indian and the idea of civilization* (Baltimore: Johns Hopkins University Press, 1953), 25; "The 'Ruines' of mankind: the Indian and the Puritan mind," *Journal of the History of Ideas,* 13 (1952), 207–8, 212.

30. Bernard Mandeville, *The fable of the bees: or, private vices, publick benefits. with a commentary critical, historical, and explanatory* by F. B. Kaye (Oxford: Clarendon Press, 1924), II, 197–99, 240–42, 264.

31. Margaret Trabue Hodgen, *The doctrine of survivals, a chapter in the history of scientific method in the study of man* (London: Allenson, 1936), 20–35.

CHAPTER X

The Place of the Savage in the Chain of Being

"There is in this Universe a Stair, or manifest Scale of creatures, rising not disorderly, or in confusion, but with comely method and proportion."—SIR THOMAS BROWNE.

"Every philosophy is tinged with the colouring of some secret imaginative background, which never emerges explicitly in its trains of reasoning."—ALFRED NORTH WHITEHEAD.

BUT NEITHER THE CULTURAL relativists of the Renaissance, nor the moralists, nor even the degenerationists, were allowed to have the last word in solving the problem of savagery. Their explanations failed to explain. The relativists were too coolly neutral to meet adequately the dramatic challenge of the facts; the moralists and degenerationists were too orthodox to see them in anything other than a theological context. Furthermore, the heart of the difficulty lay elsewhere. It lay in the settled and unshakable belief that the native tribes of the New World were not only alien to Europeans in that minor sense in which one European nation was alien to another, but were a breed apart; that their cultures, if indeed they were the cultures of true men, had departed so far from the accustomed canons of European diversity as to seem polygenetic in origin, or anomalous, aberrant, and intellectually intractable.

No one appeared able to give to savage man a valid and incontrovertible place in the general scheme of things.

To many observers, savage ways of thought and action were, in some sense not easy to put into words, a-human. It followed therefore that if these tribes were to be lived with and understood—if mankind was ever again to be understood—these aberrant men had to be brought conceptually into the framework of European thought. Between civility and incivility a familiar and inoffensive tie of kinship had to be discovered and confirmed.

Thus, while some philosophers and divines declaimed upon the indecorous habits of savages and their shameless moral standards, others looked earnestly about for an intellectual formula which would regularize their existence, "naturalize" them, or draw them into the European system of order. No one said in so many words that it was desirable to make a place for savagery, but in essence that was one of major implications of the interest in comparison and similitudes. However, after making comparisons and converting correspondences into "historical" documents, it was still necessary to confirm the savage as a man, to legitimatize him among men, or failing that, to relegate him to a place among the beasts. How was this difficult maneuver to be accomplished? Whatever the decision, how and upon what logical grounds was this bit of intellectual sleight of hand to be performed?

Though much has already been written on the history of ideas, methological concepts included, we still know too little of the ways and means conjured up by the human mind to meet its problems. One fact alone seems certain. It is usually agreed that man has resisted innovations in thought. When confronted with a new question, he has preferred to resort to old answers, old organizing principles, old presuppositions and procedures, if only to avoid trouble or to take advantage of a relatively stable medium of communication. Old words have been used for new things; old and irreconcilable ideas, remodeled slightly perhaps, have been allowed to lie side by side in explanatory thought, or used in illogical harness, simply because thinkers have found themselves unable to break with immemorial mental habit.

What then was the generally accepted scheme of things into which scholarship, at the time of the discoveries and later, sought to draw the anomalous savage in order to enjoy the repose of presumed understanding and purported kinship? What part was played in the development of this solution by the use of similitudes or correspondences?

It will come as no surprise that answers to these relatively simple questions are not easy to reach. To discover what the generality of men, or even the scholars, of the Renaissance thought of savagery lies deeply embedded in the mental processes of the past, too deeply perhaps ever to be completely and cleanly disengaged. Desirable though it be to recover the history of organizing principles in ethnology, or in the other social studies, and to recover them in their successive usages vis-à-vis successive problems, the obstacles are formidable.

One obstacle lies not only in the soothing security of old ideas but in their malleability in the hands of determined men who have problems to solve. For, as long as they retain some of their familiar lineaments, old mental constructs are unconditionally rigid over vast tracts of time and in every context. It is safe to say that the older the idea, the wider its usefulness; the more comprehensive its field of application, the more it has lent itself to helpful modifications and modulations. Hallowed with age, having been found helpful in one or many fields of inquiry, it has been the lot of every good idea to be borrowed and reborrowed time and time again, always retaining the essence of its old identity, but adding new shades of meaning or losing old ones with every borrowing. To discover a first usage under these conditions, to capture with each new usage each successive implication or nuance of imagery, to follow the detail of each transmission from field to field in thought, while desirable in theory, is desperately difficult in practice.

The best that can be done, therefore, with the problem of savagery, as it was presented to Renaissance Europe, or with the mental constructs that were called upon to solve it, is to point out that once again the procedure of comparison or analogy, and the use of correspondences, were invoked, but in their more medieval form. Making a place for savagery at this time meant a place in scholasticism's hierarchy of being. Once safely there in the shelter of this world picture, and upheld by the Schoolman's logic, the African or American was no longer a stranger or an anomaly, no longer a threat to the accepted envisagement of the organization of things, but kin to everything in nature : to man, to the animals, and to the angels. The critical issue was the determination of his appropriate location in the scale of being, either among men or among the animals. There were those who took both sides of the argument.

It should also be realized that once the savage had been safely introduced into the chain of being, the next step was necessarily historical. For since theologically the European world view was based upon explanation in terms of a succession of events, the next step involved the conversion of the medieval linkage of forms—with its new member, the savage—from a spatially conceived series into a temporal one, thus affiliating the savage to other men or animals not only statically but dynamically. In accomplishing this feat, two old ideas, once separated from one another by divergent functions, had to be welded together, namely, the hierarchical principle of the arrangement of things and the historical or genetic principle of explanation. With the Renaissance revival of historiography, with the decline of degenerationism as a philosophy of history, with the insistence of the "moderns" on their superiority over the "ancients," with the increasing acceptability of the idea of cultural progress, the hierarchy of being had to be converted from a spatial arrangement of forms into an historical, developmental, or evolutionary series.[1]

But perhaps this is going too fast.

It is comparatively easy, when a complex of associated instrumental ideas is inspected as an operating structure, to observe its several components and their logical relation to one another. It is far less easy to discover how the association came about, step by step, modification by modification, in mind after mind, during the history of man's cerebration. Historically, the minglings of ideas, their mergings and remodelings, are labyrinthine. The reconstruction of the intellectual past must be slow and tentative; it can never be rapid and assured.

In the first instance, then, and leaving on one side for the moment the temporalization of the spatially conceived series of forms, the place of the savage in the medieval hierarchy, or in the static or spatially arranged chain of being, was determined by comparison and analogy, two of the oldest and most powerful instruments of thought. Both have occupied respected places in all logics, ancient, medieval, and modern. Abetted by training in logic, analogical thinking formed the cornerstone of Renaissance speculation, theological dogma. During the Middle Ages, not only all Schoolmen but every youth of parts was instructed "in the ready waie to set forthe anythyng plainly," by making comparisons and arguing from similitudes. A similitude, in this medieval and larger than ethnological sense, was "a likenesse when two thynges or mo than two are compared and resembled together, that they bothe in some propertie seme like."

Analogy, on the other hand, was a term referring to the

habit, "deeper than the language of words and underlying their use and formation," of comparing things, not only of detecting resemblance or noting contrast. Essentially a method for persuasion by example, it involved the association of like things and ideas with like, and facilitated their classification. Seeking always to set itself at rest in an ordered world, the mind, then and now, arrives at universals by comparisons and the recognition of resemblances. The primary function of analogy, metaphor, similitude, or imagery, as products of comparison, is to bestow intellectual repose; to instill a feeling in the inquirer that an experience, once enigmatical, is at length understood—that a phenomenon once perplexing and obscure has at last been illumined. Analogical thought directs itself to filling out our knowledge of B by what we already know of A, or to bringing information concerning both into closer correspondence. As a way of assimilating new experiences or strange objects to older and more familiar ones, it permits the embarrassed inquirer to satisfy his longing to understand by transposing the new and strange into the old and customary. Since, moreover, few of the countless phenomena of the universe are directly observable by the senses, or thus amenable to the stricter techniques of comparison, inquiry ultimately comes to rest on imagery and metaphor, on the assumption that relations that cannot be observed directly must be like those that can.[2] By seeking out and establishing likenesses, similitudes, analogies, and correspondences, disorder appears to be replaced by order; darkness and mystery, by the outward seeming of clarity and knowledge.

One of the chief tasks of medieval scholarship was the collection of the fruits of comparison; and certainly one of the most remarkable and voluminous collections was that made in the mid-fourteenth century by Johannes Gorinus de Sancta Gemiano under the title of *Summa de exemplis ac similitudinibus*. Here, in ten books, were recorded the likenesses to be observed in the heavens and the elements, in metals and stones, in plants and animals, birds and fishes, man and his members, arts and artificial things, and even in the actions and customs of men. According to the ancient doctrine of signatures, revived in the sixteenth century by Paracelsus and his disciples, the similitudes informing every aspect of nature bore signs or marks which, if rightly interpreted, pointed to the presence of hidden properties or powers. Such resemblances were to be discerned in all the kingdoms of nature. There were men whose features, bodily habits, and temperament suggested the lion, or the tiger, the bull, ape, cat, or fox; and the doctrine maintained that in their moral natures they reproduced the characteristics of their animal prototypes. In his work *Phytognomonica,* written about 1571, Giovanni Battista Porta devoted the greater part of five hundred pages to the consideration of the likenesses that plants bore to other objects, to animals, or to parts of animals. Here again outward appearance was taken to be an index to inward character and potentiality. On the principle that like cures like, a root resembling the human hand was thought to possess the medicinal virtue of easing painful joints; while bony plants healed bones, plants shaped like the scorpion cooled its sting, and plants and animals which shed their outer integument relieved diseases of the skin.[3] Men's minds were filled with wonder at the analogies, correspondences, or similarities to be found between objects which otherwise had no conceivable connection with one another : at the existence of the seven metals and seven planets; at the seven notes in the harmony of the spheres; the seven days of creation; the seven ages of the world; the seven ages of man; the seven notes of the octave; the seven virtues; the seven deadly sins; the seven wonders of the world; the seven gates of Thebes; the seven sages; and the seven sleepers of Ephesus.

Comparison and the detection of similitudes in every realm of being, which occupied so commanding a place in medieval thought, were continued during the years of the Renaissance, but by this time in the solution of theological, political, and ethnological problems. The *Republic* and the *Method for the easy comprehension of history,* those great sixteenth-century experiments in scientific social theory by Jean Bodin, are comparative throughout. So also were the works of Muenster, the geographer; of Botero, the student of urban life; of Le Roy, and many others of the same period. The northern peoples were contrasted with the southern, the eastern with the western; Athens with Venice, Venice with Rome, Rome with Athens; monarch with monarch, state with state, nation with nation; the prophet Mohamet with other prophets, the modern age with the ancient, contemporary empires with past empires, religion with religion, and so on.

Comparison at this time also found expression in two great analogies, or systems of similitudes, both of which are to be regarded as keys to a wide range of philosophical, political, and ethnological speculation, now and in the past. The first of these analogies, the theory of the macrocosm and microcosm, was originally designed to cope with cosmological questions. Its advocates assumed that all nature, was, like man, alive and sensitive; that the great universe of the sun, moon, and stars (or the macrocosm) was governed by laws which were the same as those obtaining on earth among human beings (or in the microcosm).

Occupying an authoritative position in ancient, medieval, and Renaissance thought, not unlike that of the theory of evolution during the last two centuries, macrocosmic-microcosmic doctrine purportedly exhibited the mimetic relationships which obtained between individual men and the world of which they formed parts. From Aristotle to John of Salisbury, by Occam, Dante, and others of like distinction in the world of thought, no fancied likeness between the parts or members of the human body and the various functions of the church or commonweal was left unexplored. Many sixteenth-century students concerned with social and political phenomena found use for the same analogy. According to Bodin's *Method* and *Republic,* a correspondence or a series of correspondences was observable between the *respublica mundana* and the human body. The philosophers were designated as the intellect of the state, the military its heart, while the workers and farmers performed the customary functions accorded to the liver. Bodin's threefold division of the peoples of the world into those of the north, temperate, and southern zones, corresponded with his threefold partition of the world into the intellectual realm of the mind, the celestial realm of the stars, and the elemental realm of the birth and death of things.[4] And what was true for the theory of Bodin was true also for the theories of many other men throughout the period. Medieval organizing ideas, such as these, the outcome of comparisons and the purported detection of similarities, were in the ascendancy in Renaissance Europe. They exercised a controlling influence over European reflection and speculation. They appeared and reappeared by way of allusion in every form of literature—in poetry, in the drama, in the plays of Shakespeare, in the works of his contemporaries and successors. "Man, thus compounded and formed by God," said Sir Walter Ralegh in the *History of the world,* "was an abstract or modell, or briefe Storie of the Universall . . . the last and most excellent of his Creatures. . . . And whereas God created three sorts of living natures, (to wit) Angelicall, Rationall, and Brutall . . . he vouchsafed unto Man, both the intellectuall of Angels, the sensitive of Beasts, and the proper rationall belonging unto man . . . and because in the little frame of mans body there is a representation of the Universall . . . therefore was man called *Microcosmos,* or the little World."[5]

When Brutus in *Julius Caesar* referred to the state of man as a little kingdom suffering from insurrection, he alluded not only to the commonplace analogy between the body politic and the human body but also to a whole mass of traditional correspondences of which that analogy was composed. It was inferred that the order which prevailed in the heavens was repeated in detail on the earth; that disorder among the stars bred disorder and civil strife among men.[6] Medieval and classical learning were blended in this metaphorical treatment of natural and cultural phenomena, until great complexity was reached. Since physicians, geologists, and astronomers spent most of their time searching for similitudes between the body of man, the body of the earth, and the shape and structure of the cosmic universe, the development of the humane earth and astronomical studies were profoundly delayed. All of which called forth the disapproval of the author of the *Advancement of learning* as early as 1605. The ancient opinion that man was a *microcosmus,* an abstract or model of the world, said Francis Bacon, had been fantastically strained by Paracelsus and the alchemists as if there were to be found in man's body correspondences and parallels which should have respect to all varieties of things, as stars, plants, minerals, which are extant in the great world.[7]

In the meantime in Shakespeare's *Troilus and Cressida,* these eloquent lines were spoken by Ulysses on the second great medieval analogy :

> The heavens themselves, the planets, and this centre
> Observe degree, priority, and place,
> Insisture, course, proportion, season, form,
> Office, and custom, in all line of order;
> . . . . . . O, when degree is shak'd,
> Which is the ladder to all high designs,
> The enterprise is sick ! How could communities,
> Degrees in schools and brotherhoods in cities,
> Peaceful commerce from dividable shores,
> The primogenity and due of birth,

> Prerogative of age, crowns, sceptres, laurels,
> But by degree, stand in authentic place?
> Take but degree away, untune that string,
> And hark what discord follows.
>
> I, iii, 85–110

Here, in beautiful economy and taken for granted as a commonplace in everyday sixteenth-century thought, is an epitome of man's tireless search for an orderly universe, and the assumption that all beings, celestial and terrestrial, are not only classifiable in degrees but arrangeable in a great ordered chain or hierarchy of being stretching from the archangels at the foot of God's throne to the meanest of inanimate objects.[8]

This habit of hierarchical thinking, or of thinking in terms of a highly complex seriation of entities linking together every aspect of spiritual and material reality in a unity of graduated diversity, was not only very old but very quieting. Platonic perhaps in its first European expression, it had been transmitted to medieval and Renaissance theology and philosophy by men such at Plotinus, Boethius, Pico della Mirandola, Ficino, Henry More, John Colet, and others too numerous to need mention. Its earliest and primary function was spiritual or devotional. It was planned and composed to make plain the way of the soul to communion with deity : to teach man how, "rightly apprehending his own position in the chain of being," he might elevate himself "through the next higher order to communion with still higher orders, and finally with God Himself."[9]

But the hierarchy of being also possessed a more secular usefulness. It served as an intellectual instrument for clarifying the muddle of multitudinous earthly and social forms. In it, each creature could be assigned to a precise place in the order of things, angel being set over angel, rank upon rank in the Kingdom of Heaven; man over beast, beast over beast, bird over bird, fish over fish, so that in the end there was no worm that crawled upon the ground, no bird that flew in the air, no fish in the depths, which the chain of being did not bind in orderly, graduated, and harmonious accord. Although there was interminable discussion of the details of these matters between different schools of thought, there was also deep unity of belief. To grasp this unity, says Cassirer, "there is perhaps no better and easier way than to study the two books *On the celestial hierarchy* and *On the ecclesiastical hierarchy*, attributed to Dionysius Areopagita and probably written by a neo-Platonist. According to Dionysius and his disciples, the final cause of all things was the One. The One developed into the multiplicity of things. The multiplicity of things, or the variegated world of nature, was held together by a golden chain, so scaled that the more remote a thing might be from its original source, the lower its grade of perfection."[10] Indeed, at a later date, the same organizing principle, already accepted by the theologians, was ratified in modern biological inquiry by Charles Darwin. "From the first dawn of life," said he in the *Origin of species* (1859), "all organic beings are found to resemble each other in descending degrees, so that they can be classed in groups under groups. . . . Some authors look at it merely as a scheme for arranging together those living objects which are most alike, and for separating those which are most unlike. . . . But many naturalists think that something more is meant by the Natural System; they believe that it reveals the plan of the Creator. . . ."[11]

Nor was this all. The whole universe was eventually envisaged as a series of hierarchies within hierarchies, stretching from one to another in rational chains of being. Hierarchical thought not only gave to every natural entity—metal, plant, animal, man, or God—its logically right, firm, and unquestioned place among other beings in the general scheme of things, it also provided an invaluable and easily picturable, or architectonic, principle for rationalizing the relationships of man to man in

society. This was made clear by many : by St. Hildegard of
Bingen in the twelfth century, St. Thomas Aquinas in the
thirteenth, Raymond de Sebonde in the fourteenth, Bodin in
the sixteenth, Hooker in the seventeenth. "God orders every
man," said St. Hildegard, "so that the lower estate shall not
raise itself above the higher, as once did Satan and the first
man. . . . God divides His people on earth into different
estates, just as His angels in Heaven are divided in different
groups, angels and archangels . . . cherubim and seraphim." [12]
The multitude of individuals in any given society, wrote
Thomas Aquinas, "would be hopelessly confused, if that
society were not divided into different orders," ranked hierarchically. [13]

Raymond de Sebonde, the Spanish philosopher and theologian who died about 1487, and whose *Theologia naturalis
sive liber creaturarum* (1457) was translated by Montaigne,
dwelt upon the same theme. God, he said, had given two books
to mankind. One was the Bible. The other had as its subject
"l'universel ordre des choses ou de la nature," and dealt therefore with as many things and creatures as there were letters on
all its pages. In general, this great and overwhelming diversity
of things was sortable into four "marches" (a word whose
definitions include steady, regular movement; that which
borders upon; or a step in a stairway); and each "marche," in
turn, into numberless orders and species. On the first rung of
the ladder, in a category of beings "sans vie, sans sentiment,
sans intelligence, sans jugement, sans libre volonté," was
placed the earth, the foundation of all, followed, as progres-
sively nobler elements, by air, water, and fire. In the last of the
four major categories, linked to lowly earth and its superiors
by intervening "marches" of flora and fauna, was man. But
when this lofty creature, only a little lower than the angels,
had been reached, it became necessary to recognize "la diversité des estats mondaines," and to reduce them to their proper

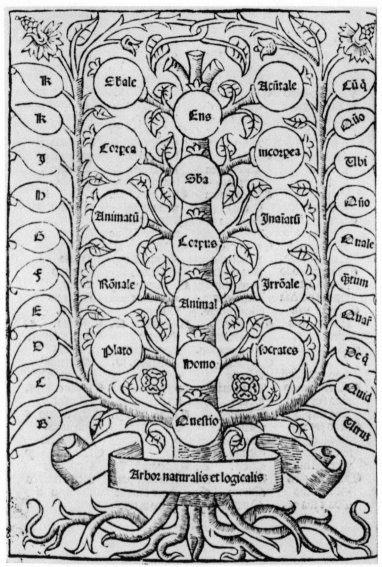

Tree diagram of the hierarchy of being from
Raymond Lull, De nova logica *(1512).*

places and arrangement. "Il y a une perpetuelle diversité d'estats entre nous," said De Sebonde;

celuy des laboureurs va le premier, comme le plus vil, apres vient celuy des marchans et des bourgeois, et puis celuy de la noblesse, qui comprend les Escuyers, les Barons, les Viscomtes, les Comtes et les Ducs : apres viennent les Rois, les Empereurs : et si des Rois il en est beaucoup, et d'Empereurs, il n'en est qu'un. Il y a semblablement de la disparité en l'authorité et en la charge : il y a les juges inférieurs, moyens et souverains, et des puissances ordinaires, moyennes et suprêmes. Une pareille division se voit aussi en l'ordre ecclésiastique : il y a des recteurs Diacres, Archidiacres, Doyens, Prieurs, Abbez, Evesques, Archevesques, et Patriarches.[14]

Bodin's contribution to the application of the hierarchical principle to society appears in his *Théâtre de la nature* (1576–97) and in the third book of the *Commonweale*. Here in the latter, after writing of corporations and colleges, he turned "to speake of the orders and degrees of Citizens. For if it be so that in all things wee desire and seeke after a convenient and decent order," then it is necessary "so to place the Citizens or subjects . . . as that the first may be joyned with the last, and they of the middle sort with both. . . . For why, it is a most antient and received opinion of the wise, Almighty God himselfe . . . that hee divided the mingled and confused parts of the rude *Chaos,* and so setled everie thing in his due place and order." Reproaching those who went about trying to make "all subjects or Citizens equall one unto another," Bodin declared that just as there existed in the body physical some members, such as the feet, which were called upon perpetually to labor and carry about "the whole bulke of the body," so there were slaves, or baser members of society who were "kept under with the most heavie burthens and commaunds of the other citizens." Indeed, said he in summary, "I suppose, that citizens in a monarchie might in this order not

Ladder diagram of the hierarchy from Raymond Lull, Liber de ascensu et descensu intellectus *(1512).*

unaptly be placed. That next unto the king . . . should follow the holie order of the clergie : next unto the sacred order of the clergie, the Senat : after the Senat . . . the martiall men. . . . After them . . . the order of gowne men . . . colledges of magistrats, and companies of judges. . . . Next unto whome should follow the order of physitians, surgeons, and apothecaries. And after them schoole men, such as professed to instruct the youth. . . . After the order of gowne men, I suppose are to be placed marchants, agents, farmers . . . bankers, money chaungers, brokers," and all others who "are most necessarie for the feeding of the citizens," with whom would be joined the handicraftsmen and, finally, the slaves.[15]

According to this hierarchical and feudal principle, there were also settled places for man's religious, political, and economic institutions; and, within each institutional complex (itself a little hierarchy), personnel and functions were graded or ranked on a scale as inflexible as Victorian class distinctions. When applied to the Church, the ecclesiastical orders were named as bishops, priests, and deacons, the function of the bishop being to set forth the mysteries of the Church; of the priest to perform the holy rites; of the deacon to prepare laymen for spiritual participation. Theoretically, the ordered variety of the ecclesiastical hierarchy was meant to repeat on a higher plane, or in the realm of grace, the rationalized diversity of the natural and political order.

When the hierarchical principle was applied to the structure of political society, the emperor or king was endowed with the same pre-eminent position as that assigned in the Church to the Pope. Subject to each lay sovereign, and reaching down gradually to the lowest serf, was an enchainment of "orders" or "estates" composed of individuals or groups with specified duties and qualities. Those considered best and most useful enjoyed a position at the top of scale next to the sovereign; those least useful or least worthy had to be content with places near the bottom. Side by side with the usual feudal order of the three estates of the realm are traces of other social subdivisions. At court, for example, there were "the four estates of the body and mouth," composed of the breadmasters, cup bearers, carvers, cooks, and the like. Chivalry imposed another criterion of classifications and arrangement; the arts and crafts, still another.[16]

The complete acceptance of this system of graduated social stratification is nowhere better illustrated than in the moralities of the popular chess books of the period. As the pieces were placed upon the table, the gentlefolk stood in the rear, "first the bailiff or legate of the king, represented by rook or castle, second the knight, third, the judge . . . fourth the queen . . . fifth the king." The pawns, standing in front, symbolized "the common people in their various ranks, eight very arbitrary divisions of plain men : first, the field-laborer or farmer; second, the smith of every sort; third, the clerk, be he notary, advocate or scrivener; fourth, the merchant or money changer; fifth, the physician and the apothecary; sixth, the tavenner, hostler or victualler; seventh, guards and customs officers; eighth, ribalds and dice-players."[17]

In times of social unrest, when the poor and down-trodden dared to rebel against their betters, they were met with vigorous reassertions of the value of a rigid social scale. This came not only from the libraries of scholars but from the political sources and from the pulpit. To help the lesser orders estimate the value of their contribution to the social whole, they were told that the varying estates in the community were like the strings of a harp. All would give forth sweet melody only when each kept to its own place and tone.[18] It was the duty and high privilege of every man to remain unprotestingly in his own class or kind, and to serve his superiors gladly. In the American colonies, when it was deemed wise to give the New World the same intelligible order as the Old, the doctrine was introduced by the Puritans. Preachers exhorted their congregations not only to maintain a wholesome and right-minded subordination of one calling to another, but to subordinate Indian residents to white.[19] Virtue in this sense was not associated with social change or progressiveness, but with the preservation in every human relationship of a traditional organization of mutual dependencies. Since men's capacities were unequal, since the division of labor was the result of the inequality of powers, an hierarchical organization of society according to class, profession, and function was to be thought of as having been willed by God in accordance with His desire for an harmonious world.[20]

Nearly all efforts to construct a philosophy of nature and man have involved the utilization of some aspect of the hierarchical or architectonic principle in the arrangement of forms, not only during the Middle Ages and the Renaissance but even in the modern period. Scholastic and Renaissance theologians or philosophers went about the congenial task of analysis, classification, and arrangement in a series of three steps. They looked first for similarities or correspondences, asking themselves what was common to groups or to the totality of objects and forms. Second, they looked for diversities, or for that which separated group from group or form from form. And finally, they sought for a principle of connection, for unity in multiplicity. Taxonomic procedures such as these were in perfect accord with the love of categories. They fulfilled the perennial desire of thought to arrange everything in the universe in a systematic list. Hell alone, filled with deviationists or fugitives from the rigidities of the chain of being, could claim emancipation from order and rank.

As soon as the Black African and the Red Indian appeared on the horizon, they too became candidates for induction into the list. For after all, if the good God had ordained special and inalienable places for the snail and the camel, the eagle and the herald angel—if everything else in the universe had its predestined niche in the divine arrangement—it was unthinkable that the Hottentot or Seminole, the Chickasaw or Ashanti, could have been left out. Indeed, the hierarchy of beings seemed to be just that theoretical refuge, expertly designed, to take care of the anomalous savage. It offered some hope of bringing him intellectually into the medieval and Renaissance system of thought.

But where? That was the question, and a hard one. What was his proper position in the natural order?

To those today who may have given the matter any thought, it will be clear that the problem of making a place for savagery in the hierarchy of being turned on a trio of alternatives. First, the savage could be accepted as a man like other men, and inserted in the scale of being with European and other known men; second, he could be regarded as something different from, and less than, European man, and be inserted in the scale in a secondary human category; or third, he could be interpreted as an animal, and given a place, perhaps the highest, among the other animals.

To the orthodox Christian, as to all who subscribed to the Biblical account of the peopling of the world, this choice posed little or no difficulty. Doctrinally, savages were men, first, last, and always—bestial and degenerate in their behavior, perhaps, but still men and thus children of God. This was the logical and unavoidable conclusion from premises written down or logically implied in Genesis concerning the Noachian period of the sacred history. Support was also available from the philosophers of classical antiquity. According to neo-Platonic doctrine which informed much of the thinking of the devout, man as a unit occupied a key position between the beasts and the angels. As an essential link between them, he was both the highest of the animals and the lowest of spiritual beings. During the Middle Ages, this belief in the centrality of man in the natural order could not be repeated too often or too fervently. "The Platonists," said Pico della Mirandola in *A Platonic discourse upon love,* "distinguish Creatures into three degrees. The first comprehends the corporeal and the visible. . . . The last, the invisible and incorporeal, absolutely free from bodies which are properly called Intellectual (by Divines, Angelical) Natures, (while) Man, the chain which ties the world together, is placed in the midst." [21] The whole frame of heaven was established by God with one hand, "but in the creation of Man, he used both. He made not the Heavens to his similitude but Man. He made the Angels to his Ministerie, but Man to his Image." The Church might bid Man to walk humbly with God, and to remember his subordination to the countless spiritual beings who composed the heavenly host, but among the lower animals he was encouraged to mingle with pride. Since, according to more thoughtful theologians, savages were men, they too had been made in the image of God. Any suggestion that a newly discovered tribe somewhere in the wastes of Asia, Africa, or the Americas belonged to a race of beings other than, or lower than, this unique central being, was subversive and unthinkable. Even the Puritan divines, who took up life in the colonies, were sustained through all their conflicts with the Indians by the certainty of this immutable principle, which guaranteed the intelligibility of their relationship with their hostile hosts. They might kill the Indians if they thought they had to; they might mistreat them and defraud them; they might relegate them in the social hierarchy to a status lower than that of the white settlers; but they were under no illusion concerning their manhood. They were not dealing with representatives of the lower animals. Such an inference would have called for a drastic revision of the hierarchical and Biblical scheme at one of its most crucial points. Assuming an unbridgeable cleavage of mankind into civil and uncivil, it would have implied at the same time, and contrary to reason, the division of the image of God into two images, a true and a false. It would have cast doubt upon the Noachian or Adamic descent of all the colonies of mankind, and sapped the foundations of every belief based upon monogenetic premises. For the religious it was far, far better to take refuge in the unquestioning faith of such a man as Du Bartas, who believed that divers tempers and complexions among men existed to manifest the glory of God.

> . . . that his holy name from Isie Scythia
> Might sound unto the sandes of red-hot Africa.[22]

But not all men of the Renaissance were orthodox, and not all were devout. There were reformers, deists, atheists, or infidels in nearly every sizable community. By virtue of their exertions, there was scarcely a phrase in the Old and New Testament which was not torn from its spiritual context for freethinking criticism, or placed upon the Laodicean balances of secular logic. Then, too, there was that large company of uninstructed voyagers upon whom devolved the important task of making the first face-to-face judgments of the native peoples. Hierarchical ideas were used freely in the voyage literature, and in the cosmographies as well, but these works will be searched in vain for a coherent statement of the reasons for their use, or for any uniformity of opinion as to their relation to the status of savage man. This literature abounds with evidence that while some Europeans may have regarded the African and the American as fellow members of their own category of being, there were others in plenty who looked down upon the savage either as an inferior man or as a superior animal.

The first step toward striking down the Christian concept of the unity of mankind, or to toy with the notion that savagery might be included in the hierarchy as a species separate from man proper, was probably taken by the travelers, the sea captains, and especially the hucksters of colonization, either in response to the vulgar cupidity aroused by the riches of the New World, or in honest but uninformed intellectual bewilderment. Through them, the anti-Scriptural solution seeped rapidly into many minds until in 1676–77 it found its way into the formal treatment of the *Scale of creatures* by Dr. Samuel Petty, member of the Royal Society. From that time on, philosophical and ethnological opinion concerning the savage and his place in nature departed from the Christian position. It was no longer possible to hold the mirror up to European man and see in it the reflection of mankind as a whole. It came to be believed that there were multiple kinds of men, each with his rightful place in the natural order but inferior to European man.

A little detailed exposition may make this confusing episode in the history of social thought somewhat clearer.

Among the voyagers and busy promoters of colonization, legend was often more persuasive than the subtleties of theologians in forming judgments of savage peoples. Bred from childhood on the ethnical fables of Pliny, Solinus and Company, they found it easy to mistake what they saw for what they had been told by these fabulists. When confronted with the Red Indian, painted and befeathered, or with the Hottentot, naked and dirty, it seemed only reasonable to see in these specimens the kind of abnormal ethnological phenomena they had been led to expect, especially on the margins of the world. If, for example, a native folk was found to dwell in caves, for most members of a ship's company the matter was settled without further thought. The cave dwellers could not be men in the European sense. They were the Troglodites of ancient story, and all the legendary characteristics of that raffish crew were added unto them. If again, when an explorer and his party stepped ashore, unusually large manlike footprints were found in the sand, it was not necessary to see their makers in the flesh or to measure them. The prints were enough. There were giants in the land. Was not the existence of such creatures vouched for in both sacred and profane literature?

It was never unusual in the sixteenth- and seventeenth centuries to read of the contemporary presence in little-known lands of the most fantastic creatures. In India, as Boemus reported in 1521, "there be a manner of people with heads like dogs, armed and fenced with nayles, and clothed with beast hydes." He said also that there were men and women living on the River Ganges so dainty that they ate no meat at all but survived on the smell of apples. From the earliest times, cannibalism was believed to be widespread in the remoter parts of the world. In the first book on America, published in English in 1511 (or even earlier in a Dutch edition), the Indians were described as "lyke bestes without any reson-ablenes. . . And they ete also on(e) a nother. The man etethe his wyf his chylderne . . . they hange also the bodyes or persons fleeshe in the smoke as men do with us swynes fleshe."[23] In the sixteenth-century, man-eating was ascribed to tribes in both North Africa and America; and the pages of Muenster's *Cosmographia* (1544) were adorned with illustrations of cannibals stirring their cauldrons. Even Sir Walter Ralegh, that scholarly and skeptical traveler, was not immune to the suggestive power of the fabulous. Without hesitation, he reported the existence of semi-human beings or half-men, fit only for a place below man himself in the hierarchy. His informants had told him that there were Amazons in Guiana, and he believed them. Moreover, he reaffirmed the presence there of a people who had "eyes in their shoulders and their mouths in the middle of their breasts." Had a nation been so described by Mandeville, said Ralegh, it would have been taken for a fable; but since the East Indies had been discovered, "wee finde his relations true of such thinges as heeretofore were held incredible."[24]

Naturally the same kind of thing found its way into all branches of literature. Hence Desdemona's interest in Anthropophagi and men whose heads grew beneath their shoulders. Hence *The Tempest's* Caliban, a freckled whelp, "not honour'd with a human shape." These and their like were the persisting images of semihuman monsters, evidences of beast-men, with whom to some observers the savages seemed to correspond.

To other travelers of a more reflective turn of mind, the savages of many regions seemed something less than human, yet more than animal. Comments indicating the frequency of this judgment, and with it, the exercise of some comparative effort, are to be found everywhere—in voyage accounts, in poetry, in the drama, in political theory—with remorseless repetition.

Take the charge that the savage was "unmanly." This accusation went to the very heart of the matter, and led to the inevitable conclusion that certain native folk belonged to another realm of being. One of the spokesmen for this point of view was a "Virginian," a British promoter of colonization, who recited the grounds of England's claim to the new lands overseas. The American Indians, he asserted without hesitation, were a "bad people, having little of Humanitie but shape . . . more brutish than the beasts they hunt, more wild and unmanly than their unmanned wild Countrey which they range rather than inhabite." Englishmen had every right to seek homes in vacant places, especially when the occupiers failed to deserve the name of human beings. The Bishop of Worcester took a similar position. He was charged by John Locke with near denying the manhood of the Cafers of Soldania.[25]

Or take the charge of "beastliness." In the earlier reports on Africa, nearly every voyager spoke of the native peoples as "like to bruite beasts"; or as "rude and beastlie"; or as "bestiall without foresyght." In Terra Nigritarum, according to Purchas' interpretation of Leo Africanus, the blacks lived in utter destitution like the beasts, "without King, Lord, Common-wealth, or any government, scarce knowing to sowe their grounds. . . ."[26] The same idea received a certain amount of traditional embellishment at the hands of Ludovico di Varthema and other travelers. In Mozambique, the Negroes lived in a certain kind of den on the side of the mountains, not differing from those occupied by beasts.[27] In Guinea, there was a region called Trogloditica, "whose inhabitauntes dwelt in caves or dennes." The American Indians, according to Master Martin Frobisher, conducted themselves in the same way, "living in Caves of earth," hunting their dinners "even as the beare and wild beastes" did. By continual repetition, the Hottentots came to occupy the foreground of this unsavory picture. They were described as extremely "ugly and loathe-some." They went about in companies or "heardes" like their animal brethren. Such "ill-look'd stinking, nasty People," it was said in the eighteenth century (and not without hierarchical implications), "scarce deserve to be reckon'd of the Human Kind."[28]

And, as if this were not enough, as if perchance the case against the common humanity of the Indian and the Negro had not yet been adequately made, some observers went still further. Europeans were informed by travelers that these peoples had been denied articulate speech, and with speech that other precious and universal mark of manhood, the faculty of reason. The people of Mozambique spoke "so confoundedly and chatteringly lyke apes" that the voyagers were at a loss to describe what they had heard. The cave dwellers or Troglodites also had "no speache, but rather a grynnyng and chatteryng."[29] The language of the Hottentots was so very harsh and guttural that they seemed "rather to cackle like hens or turkeis, then speak like men."[30] Said Father Merolla, the people of the Cape of Good Hope were not only bereft of human voice, but they understood one another "only by a sort of hissing tone, and motion of the lips."[31] Caliban, Shakespeare's seventeenth-century half-man and half-beast, was denounced for the same lack.

Said Prospero:

> . . . . Abhorred slave,
> Which any print of goodness wilt not take,
> . . . . I pitied thee,
> Took pains to make thee speak, taught thee each hour
> One thing or other. When thou didst not, savage,
> Know thine own meaning, but wouldst gabble like
> A thing most brutish, I endow'd thy purposes
> With words that made them known. But thy vile race,
> Though thou didst learn, had that in't which good natures
> Could not abide to be with.
>
> *The Tempest,* I, ii, 352–60

Hovering precariously between the human and the brute, Caliban and all of his fellows were thought to be incapable of improvement.

As for man's other distinguishing quality, rationality, it was Leo Africanus in the middle of the sixteenth-century who declared that the Negroes not only led a beastly life but "were utterly destitute of reason"; and it was Peter Heylyn and Daniel Beeckman who, many years later, aided in the dissemination of the same idea. Said Heylyn in 1652, the inhabitants of Terra Nigritarum "were for the most part so rude and barbarous, that they seem to want that use of Reason, which is peculiar unto man."[32] Said Beeckman of the Hottentots in 1714: "These filthy animals . . . hardly deserve the name of rational creatures,"[33] a sentiment which was to be revived in the Southern states just before the Civil War and which was incorporated in early American ethnology.

Thanks to a temptation to accept these hasty and prejudiced

findings for what they were, namely : flat denials of the essential humanity of the savage, many learned and responsible Europeans found themselves in the coils of an intellectual dilemma. For the implications were unprecedented; and their ultimate outcome incalculable. The suggestion that speech and reason were lacking in any group of God's children constituted a marked departure from theological dogma with respect to the unity and homogeneity of mankind. This, or any adverse judgment concerning the fundamental humanity of the savage or his attachment to the main body of European mankind, tended to loosen the foundations of the teachings of Moses and the commentators on Genesis. If, on the basis of such judgments, these creatures were to be thrust out of the company of human beings and in the direction of the category of beasts, then a cleavage was implied in the genus Homo which neither difference in color nor wide diversity in religion had ever before suggested. Neither paganism, nor Mohametanism, nor Judaism, nor heathenism had ever held that communicants of other faiths were less than men. Never before had brown skin, yellow skin, or black skin been allied conceptually with irrationality, beastliness, or a-humanity.

What then was to be done? What was to be done with these supposedly man-beasts, these intermediate figures? Where were they to be placed in the hierarchy of being? With man its central figure, or with some category of the animals?

Men of learning everywhere in Europe were aware of the hierarchy of being, of the arguments upon which it was maintained as an analogy, of its function as the framework of thought on the world and on man. The desire to enjoy a rationalized universe found frequent expression in attempts to harmonize this vivid and living "remainder" of neo-Platonism with Moses, or to interpret Genesis by means of that system of graded categories which had become an intimate part of the fabric of Western thought. No doubt these same men of learning possessed some knowledge of what are now called the principles of plenitude and continuity. For the medieval equivalent of the phrase, "Nature never makes leaps," had been discussed, centuries before the time of Charles Darwin, by Albertus Magnus and Nicholas Cusanus. Nature, Albert said, in the thirteenth century, in *De animalibus,* makes no animal kinds separate, or without something intermediate between them. Two hundred years later, Nicholas declared that "all things, however different, are linked together. There is in the genera of things such a connection between the higher and the lower that they meet in a common point; such an order obtains among species that the highest species of one genus coincides with the lowest of the next higher genus, in order that the universe may be one, perfect, and continuous."[34] Like his medieval predecessors, Giordano Bruno was also convinced of the continuity, the unbreached character, of what was commonly called "nature." The members of the external world constituted for him one unified body in which there was no "botch" or gap.[35]

Reflection on the composition of the hierarchy of being, and painful reflection on African and American man in comparison with their fellows in Europe, recalled these old principles to mind. Could it be that thought had failed to recognize a gap between man at the midpoint of the threefold chain of being and the highest of the animals? Could it be that the Africans and Americans, with their distracting characteristics, were designed to fill that breach? Did they belong, for that reason, in a place in the hierarchical series separate from and lower than European man but still higher than the animals? These questions and their like were in many minds in the seventeenth century. They were disquieting in some ways; in others, they offered a possible solution to what was becoming an intolerable difficulty.

Conceivably the hierarchy of being had never been completely analyzed into its several members. Conceivably, as the philosophical theory of plenitude and as these creatures themselves both seemed to suggest, there were more members or links in the finely graduated chain of being than had yet been dreamed of, each differing from its neighbor above and below by a degree as small as, or smaller than, that which obtained between man and some of these "half-men." With this hopeful possibility in mind, it began to dawn upon some scholars that the troublesome problem might yet be solved; that the savage might be installed in the series not as a man as complete and finished as European man, but as a bridge or (missing) "link" between finished man and the animals. It was suggested that he might conceivably be made, as human monster or as bestial man, the terminating member of the animal section of the hierarchy, or a dim, rude, brutal introduction to the human and intellectual series. A few even dared mention the ape as either another species of man or his immediate animal predecessor.

It is unnecessary here to review in detail just when this notable modification in thought occurred; or when the genus *Homo* was bisected; or when and how the savage came to be installed as his immediate predecessor either as the terminal member of the animal section of the hierarchy or the introductory member of the human. Suffice it to say that the transition in opinion was not sudden, nor was the decision always made by men of learning aided by a rich and varied philosophical equipment.

Recalling always that the simple idea of *graduation* in a *spatial* series must be clearly differentiated from the more complex one of *transformation, change,* or *evolution* in a graduated series, it should be pointed out at this juncture that the notion of the existence of transitional forms between man and the animals was already very old. Centuries before the

Christian era, Aristotle had observed that some animals resemble and share in the properties of mankind. This, communicated to his readers and disciples, was never wholly forgotten. Again, ever since antiquity, or when it was thought that the gods had sometimes chosen to take their pleasure on earth disguised as animals, sexual mingling between man and the animals had been taken for granted. The crowd of hybrid creatures known to all Europeans, ancient and modern—the satyrs, the centaurs, the dog-headed, and all the other monsters of mythology—were long believed to be the offspring of these frolics. Again, as early as the fourth century, when the existence of such *similitudines homines* was vouched for by no less an authority than St. Augustine—with only two provisos, namely, that they be mortal, and that they possess the faculty of reason—their status in the world-view of Christendom was established. Thereafter, manlike creatures as well as true men made their appearance in the idiom of Christian art, architecture, drama, and story. Often included, as somehow mysteriously related, were the baboon and the ape, who were thought, like the latter-day savage, to belong to an irrational race incapable of speech, and whose identification with the wild man or *homo sylvestris* was early regarded as highly probable.[36]

As a result of all this, the anthropological scale proposed by Albertus Magnus in the thirteenth century came as close to modern conceptions as the intellectual horizon of the Middle Ages would permit. Man, as the only animal made in the likeness of God, and perfect in mind and body, formed a category of his own. That was clear beyond cavil. But the brutes, as imperfect, fell into two large classes or degrees: the manlike creatures, represented by the pigmies, the apes and others, and then the larger mass of true animals, which were divided from one another by the usual contemporary zoological criteria. In other words, with these *similitudines homines* Albert seems to have introduced into the stream of European thought the concept of the "missing link"; perhaps the earliest attempt, conceptually, to bridge the gap between man and the rest of animate nature. Where other authorities had recognized in addition to vegetable forms the existence of only two main elements in the scale of terrestrial nature—man and the animals—Albert recognized three: these two and a linking element, the manlike creatures. Thus, as early as the thirteenth-century it remained only to find the manlike creatures to prove the linkage.

But in the interval between the thirteenth and seventeenth centuries, or for four hundred years after the writing of Albert's *De animalibus,* little was said of a philosophical or scientific nature concerning the possibility either of a semi-animal link between man and other forms lower in the hier-archy, or of the savage as a possible transitional figure. It was too remote a problem for the times; and its very mention would have offended too many theological sensibilities. The humanity of some tribes was doubted, it is true. There was some reluctance to include Negro and Indian peoples in the same category as Europeans—true. To the Puritan mind in the North American colonies, "Satan had possessed the Indian until he had become virtually a beast." Said Sir Thomas Herbert of the Hottentots in 1626 : "Their words are sounded rather like like that of Apes, then Men . . . And comparing their imitations, speech, and visages, I doubt many of them have no better Predecessors then Monkeys."[37] Lines in contem-porary plays described naked savages as like "Monkeys, Baboons, and Marmosites," and noted that the company kept by the Red Indians was composed of "hound-dogs, apes, asses, lions, barbarians, and hogs."[38] There was long-standing con-fusion concerning the relation between the great apes and the African pigmies. Negroes and Indians, stolen by sailors or slavers, were often exhibited in European capitals side by side with apes and baboons, earning Trinculo's remark that while the curious would not give "a doit to relieve a lame beggar," they would "lay out ten to see a dead Indian."[39] But that was about all. There were no suggested amendments to the human section of the scale of being. The logical implications of these attitudes and observations with respect to the hierarchical position of the savage were not pursued.

The break came in the last quarter of the seventeenth century and the first third of the eighteenth with Sir William Petty's abortive essay entitled *The scale of creatures* (1676–77), Sir William Tyson's *Orang-outang, sive homo silvestris; or, the anatomy of a pygmie* (1708), and Carl Linnaeus' *System of nature* (1735). After the publication of these books mankind was no longer considered a perfect whole, standing alone and indivisible in an unassailable central position in the hierarchy, with the animals classified and ranked below him and the angels classified and ranked above. In both biological and ethnological inquiry the discovery of "missing links" became the order of the day. It became the task of the naturalist to effect a rapprochement between man and the ape and of the student of man to compose an acceptable social or cultural hierarchy as an extension of the biological.

Dr. Tyson (1650–1708), to consider first a younger man and one of the natural scientists, was an anatomist, who accomplished two things of great importance in his chosen field. Before an audience composed of scientific colleagues he proved, first, that in structure the ape was more closely related to man than to any other animal in the animal section of the hierarchy, and second, that the pigmy, sometimes called *Homo sylvestris* and thought by the ancients to be a small man, was more probably an apelike creature. In reaching these conclusions, the doctor was fully aware of their significance in relation to the linkage of forms in the chain of being. He was engaged, he stated, in a "general gradational classification of certain groups of primates"; and he proposed to clarify what he regarded as the hierarchical relationship between his "pygmie," or ape, and man proper. Refusing to be influenced by legend which made the anthropoid the offspring of "mixed generation"—a half-man, or semi-man—he declared him "to be wholly a Brute, tho' in the formation of the Body, and in the Sensitive or Brutal Soul, it may be more resembling a Man than any other animal; so that in this Chain of the Creation, for an intermediate Link between Ape and Man, I would place our Pygmie."[40]

Sir William Petty (1623–1687), though trained as a physician was a man of parts, a statistician, an economist, a musician, inventor, and Latin poet. In other words, his field of interest was broader than that of Tyson. He was concerned with human beings both as physical creatures and as members of organized society. The first time, so far as can be known, that Dr. Petty permitted himself to think out aloud about the ambiguous place of the savage in the universal scheme of things was in 1676, when he delivered an address before the faculty of the Royal College of Physicians in Dublin. Immediately thereafter, or in 1677, several expansions of these ideas were sent in letters to his friend Sir Robert Southwell. The doctor evidently planned to write a book on the scale of creatures in which he proposed to establish "a line of affinity between God 'the architect of the firmament' and mankind, as also between mankind and 'the smallest maggot', or the lowest form of animal life." The first line of affinity between God and man Petty called his "larger" scale; that between man and the animals, his "lesser" scale; while in a third and very significant intermediate series he proposed to offer a classification and gradational arrangement of the tribes or groups of mankind.

Written almost a quarter of a century before Tyson's *Orang-outang,* Petty's contribution to the moot problem of the place of savagery in nature was equally remarkable, though perhaps less well known. The announcement of his subject, "the scale of creatures," was accompanied with an apology. Petty feared that he was unqualified. He had read little on the matter, he said, except in Sir Matthew Hale's *Primitive origination of mankind,* just off the press in 1677. Indeed, up to a point, the analyses of the chain of being by Petty and Hale were very similar. "There are several Ranks of Being in this inferior world, which have various specifical Degrees or Ranks of Perfection one above another," said the Lord Chief Justice of England, with appropriate details and illustrations. From one point of view, this was in the best tradition of hierarchical discussion and therefore acceptable to Petty. But Petty was not entirely satisfied. It seemed to him that Sir Matthew had not gone far enough. "Hales [sic] makes an Affinity between mettals and vegetables," said the doctor, "and another between vegetables and animalls, and a third between animals and man, a fourth between man and his subtile material being; a fifth between those beings and created Intelligences, a sixth, between those Intelligences and the Holy Angells, and another between the Angells and the Creator himselfe." Hale also acknowledged "that the nature of man is very much worth inquiry. . . ." But where, in all the pages of the *Primitive origination of mankind,* was there a close analysis of man's place in nature, including a treatment of the ticklish problem of the savage? Where was there any comparison of "the highest improvements of mankind in his masse, with the rudest condition that man was ever in?" Where was there any realization of the significance of cultural differences among human beings and their bearing on the composition of the hierarchy of being? The problem of the missing link was again raised. Had it not been said "(i) that between Superior and Inferior species there are midle natures, (ii) that man is a meane between Angells and Beastes, or between Intelligent and sencible beings, (iii) and that there is also a meane between inanimate and living natures?"" Where had the Lord Chief Justice dwelt on this important problem of the transitional or "midle" forms, the plurality of human links or kinds in the chain of being?

With this persisting interest in the plural kinds of men in mind, Petty continued in a later fragment of *The scale of creatures* to make comparisons and to set down his observations concerning the "gradations" of the "Lesser Scale of Animalls," the upper end whereof "wee make to be man, and the lower end, the smalest worm or maggott that our senses can take note of." With man at the top of the ladder, the first question to arise dealt with the characteristics of the animal just below him. Was it to be an elephant, because of its superior memory and understanding? Or a drill, because of the nearness of its shape to man? Or a parrot, because of its power to articulate sounds and imitate man's speech? Or a bee, because of its spirituality and power? Or perhaps another sort of man? When none of these seemed to be satisfactory, Petty decided that his criteria of comparison were too complex. He would therefore confine himself to likenesses in shape and visible appearance.[42]

By so modifying his procedure in the direction of simplicity, he was led, first, to the statement of a cardinal assumption, destined to echo down the generations in treatises and tomes on racial and social theory; and, second, to split man, unified by the medieval theologians, into at least two, if not many, potential grades of being. The statement of his cardinal assumption took few words : "Of man itself there seems to bee severall species, To say nothing of Gyants & Pigmyes or of that sort of small men who have little speech and feed cheifly upon Fish called Uries. For of these sorts of men, I venture to say nothing, but that 'tis very possible there may be Races and generations of such." But besides these, and besides individual differences among men, "there be others more considerable, that is, between the Guiny Negros & the Middle Europeans;

& of Negros between those of Guiny and those who live about the Cape of Good Hope, which last are the Most beastlike of all the Souls [? Sorts] of Men with whom our Travellers are well acquainted. I say that the Europeans do not only differ from the aforementioned Africans in Collour . . . but also . . . in Naturall Manners, & in the internall Qualities of their Minds." It was likewise observed, that the people who lived "in the Northernmost parts of the Habitable world and even the Lapplanders" were "a very mean Sort of Men, both in their Statures and understanding. . . ."[43]

Here was set forth for all to see, and perhaps for the first time, a division of man into kinds (other than "nations"), in place of the usual single human unit, homogeneous, uniform, and identical.

With this, Dr. Petty's brief excursion into ethnology came to a halt. But he had said enough to open up the subject. Travelers felt freer to condemn some of the peoples they encountered. In 1696, when John Ovington sailed to Africa as chaplain of the ship *Benjamin,* belonging to the East India company, he denounced the Hottentots as "the very Reverse of Human Kind, Cousin Germans to the *Helachors* [East Indian outcasts] only meaner and more filthy; so that if there is any medium between a Rational animal and a Beast, the Hotantot lays fairest claim to the Species."[44] Philosophers and scientists took a hand in sorting out the kinds of men. In 1684, only a few years after Dr. Petty's effort to construct a human sequence in the scale of being, an anonymous letter in the *Journal de Savans* tried the same thing. Again in 1721, Richard Bradley, author of *A philosophical account of the works of nature, endeavoring to set forth the several gradations remarkable in the mineral, vegetable, and animal parts of the creation, tending to the composition of the scale of life,* offered a short classification. In 1735 Linnaeus offered another; and he was followed by still other zoologists, sociologists, and racialists. What had begun with the careless remarks of a few ignorant sailors or self-seeking colonials, filled to the brim with fables of human monstrosities, became, with Dr. Petty's help, the subject of a serious scientific debate.

None of the early classifications was clear. The criteria employed by an anonymous French human taxonomist were mainly geographical and anatomical, including hair color or texture and pigmentation. Using these as a basis, the author arrived at five confused categories of mankind. Under the first were comprehended the men of Europe, those of a part of Muscovy omitted. To these were added the men of a small part of North Africa, from the Nile to the Pillars of Hercules, and also those of a good part of Asia, including Turkey, Persia, the Mogul, Golconda, Visapore, the Maldivis, and parts of the kingdoms of Arankan, Pegu, Siam, Sumatra, Bantan, and Borneo. In the second category were the peoples of the whole of Africa except those on the Mediterranean coast. The third was composed of a miscellany of folk occupying parts of Arakan, Siam, Sumatra, Borneo, the Philippines, Japan, Pegu, Tonkin, Cochin-China, China, Chinese Tartary, Georgia, Muscovy, Usbekistan, Turkestan, and Zaquetay, along with the little Tartars and the Turcomans who dwelt along the Euphrates toward Aleppo. The Lapps, "wretched animals," constituted a fourth class, described as dwarfs with thick legs, large shoulders, and short necks. The fifth and strangest of all contained the American Indians and the Negroes around the Cape of Good Hope, the latter described as lean, dry, small, ugly, active devourers of raw meat and corpses, drinkers of seawater, whose language sounded like the clucking of turkeys.[45]

Bradley's classification was, if anything, even less competent. "We find," said he, "five sorts of men : the white men, which are Europeans that have beards; and a sort of white man in America (as I am told) that only differ from us in having no beards; the third sort are the Malatoes, which have their skins almost of a copper colour, small eyes, and straight black hair; the fourth kind are the Blacks, which have straight black hair; and fifth are the Blacks of Guiney, whose hair is curled, like the wool of sheep. . . ."[46]

However, it would appear that the main influence of Dr. Petty's *Scale of creatures,* if in fact he alone exerted an influence, was probably upon the botanists, Linnaeus in particular; and that from Linnaeus were transmitted to later scholars and social scientists certain ideas of human classification which might better have remained unpublished. At all events, in the later years of the eighteenth century the collectors of plant-life were in deep trouble. By the year 1600 some six thousand distinct plants had already been described. A century later the number had trebled. The collection owned by Carl Linnaeus, ever increasing by virtue of the co-operative efforts of traveling colleagues, was in a state of confusion. As yet there was no generally accepted scheme for naming and arranging them. Not only was the same plant often designated by a different nomenclature in different places, but different plants were only too often brought together under the same nomenclature.[47]

The *System of nature* by Linnaeus, first published in 1735, was intended to overcome these difficulties. It was composed to give the world of flora an appropriate setting in the universal hierarchy of being. With this in mind, his classification also embraced minerals, animals, and man. In it every geological formation, herb, tree, fish, quadruped, and variety of man was ticketed and arranged in a great catalogue according to an over-arching hierarchical scheme in conformity with the doctrine of immutable design. The scheme had faults which many later students have pointed out, but it appeared to be simple and systematic. It grouped variety under species, species under genera, genera under orders, and orders under classes. Once the system was set up the collector's burden was eased.

To find the appropriate place for a new specimen, or to look up an old one, he had only to open a correctly ticketed drawer or turn to the right page. God, said Linnaeus with undisguised satisfaction, had suffered him to peep into His own secret cabinet.[48]

But whatever the triumphs or blunders of Linnaeus as a botanist, the step taken by him in inserting man into his catalogue, and its import for ethnological thought and future race relations, cannot be over-emphasized. For he not only included man in his arrangement of forms, but divided man as a genus into two species, and these two species in turn into several varieties. The criteria for these divisions were partly physical including skin-color, and partly cultural, including political or social organization and attire.

Homo sapiens, varying by education and situation, was composed of

1. Wild man : four-footed, mute, hairy.
2. American : copper-colored, choleric, erect. Paints self. Regulated by custom.
3. European : fair, sanguine, brawny. Covered with close vestments. Governed by laws.
4. Asiatic : sooty, melancholy, rigid. Covered with loose garments. Governed by opinions.
5. African : black, phlegmatic, relaxed. Anoints himself with grease. Governed by caprice.

Homo monstrosus, varying by climate and art, included

1. Mountaineers : small, inactive, timid.
2. Patagonians : large, indolent.
3. Hottentots : less fertile.
4. American : beardless.
5. Chinese : head conic.
6. Canadian : head flattened.[49]

Thus, though Linnaeus may be generally regarded as one of the chief founders of the botanical and zoological studies, his place in the history of ethnology is less eminent. He not only believed in the existence of human varieties or races, but he failed as a proponent of the hierarchical arrangement of things to preserve any discernible order in their listing. He subscribed to the reality of fabulous, monstrous men. He was subservient to unexamined medieval ideas.

BIBLIOGRAPHY AND NOTES

1. But the various phases of the conversion of the social hierarchy from a spatial arrangement into an historical, developmental, or evolutionary series have not yet been recovered. "So far as I know," said Professor Lovejoy, there as yet exists "no historically and philosophically respectable account of the total development of the idea of evolution before Darwin . . . and we have certainly no adequate history . . . of developmental conceptions in astronomy, geology, anthropology, social philosophy, cosmology, and theology . . . Historically, the various phases of what may be called the genetic way of thinking . . . are closely related . . . but the task . . . can scarcely be executed properly by only one scholar." (Arthur Oncken Lovejoy, "The historiography of ideas," in *Essays in the history of ideas* [Baltimore: Johns Hopkins University Press, 1948], 10–13.) See also Lovejoy's paper entitled "Some eighteenth century evolutionists," *Popular Science,* 65 (1904), 238.

2. Agnes Arber, "Analogy in the history of science," in *Studies and essays in the history of science and learning offered in homage to George Sarton on the occasion of his sixtieth birthday, 31 August, 1944* (New York: Henry Schumann, 1946?), 221–33.

3. Thorndike, *Magic and experimental science,* VI, 294, 422; Frank Dawson Adams, *The birth and development of the geological sciences* (Baltimore: Williams and Wilkins, 1938), 69–73.

4. J. L. Brown, *Methodus ad facilem historiarum,* 95–96.

5. Ralegh, *History of the world,* sig, C i r.

6. Eustace Mandeville Wetenhall Tillyard, *Shakespeare's history plays* (New York: Macmillan, 1946), *passim; The Elizabethan world picture* (London: Chatto and Windus, 1943), *passim.*

7. Bacon, *Works, passim.*

8. Hardin Craig, *The enchanted glass: the Elizabethan mind in literature* (New York: Oxford, 1936), *passim;* Theodore Spencer, *Shakespeare and the nature of man* (New York: Macmillan, 1942), *passim;* "Troilus and Cressida," in *The complete works of Shakespeare,* edited by George Lyman Kittredge (New York: Ginn & Company, 1936), I, iii, 85–110.

9. John Colet, *Two treatises on the hierarchies of Dionysius* . . . now first published with a translation, introduction, and notes by J. H. Lupton (London: Bell and Daldy, 1869), xlii–xliii.

10. Ernst Cassirer, "The place of Vesalius in the culture of the Renaissance," *Yale Journal of Biology and Medicine,* 16 (1943–44), 110–11.

11. Charles Darwin, *The Origin of species* (London: John Murray, 1859), 411–13, Part II, 211–14.

428 *Early Anthropology in the 16th and 17th Centuries*

12. Jacob Peter Mayer, *Political thought: the European tradition* (London: J. M. Dent, 1939), 85.

13. Katherine Oakes George, "The concept of social hierarchy in the writings of St. Thomas Aquinas," *The Historian,* 12 (1949), 28–54.

14. Raymond de Sebonde, "Théologic naturelle de Raymond Sebon," in *Œuvres complètes de Michel de Montaigne.* Preface du Dr. A. Armaingaud (Paris: Louis Conard, 1932), I, 4–5; II, 63–64.

15. Bodin, *Commonweale,* sig. Ll i r – Mm v r.

16. Johan Huizinga, *The waning of the Middle Ages: a study of the forms of life, thought, and art in France and the Netherlands in the XIVth and XVth centuries* (London: Edward Arnold, 1927), 46–55.

17. Frederick Tupper, *Types of society in medieval literature* (New York: Holt, 1926), 22–23; Ruth Mohl, *The three estates in Medieval and Renaissance literature* (New York: Columbia University Press, 1933), *passim;* James Emerson Phillips Jr., *The state in Shakespeare's plays* (New York: Columbia University Press, 1940), *passim.*

18. Gerald Robert Owst, *Literature and pulpit in medieval England* (Cambridge: Cambridge University Press, 1933), *passim.*

19. Helen Constance White, *Social criticism in popular religious literature of the sixteenth century* (New York: Macmillan, 1944), 244–45.

20. Paul Oskar Kristeller, *The philosophy of Marsilio Ficino* (New York: Columbia University Press, 1943), 74–93.

21. Pico della Mirandola, *A Platonick discourse upon love* (Boston: Merrymount Press, 1914), 4, 15.

22. Guillaume de Salluste du Bartas, *The colonies of du Bartas. With the commentarie of S. G. S. in diverse places corrected and enlarged by the Translator* (W. Lisle) (London: Printed by R. F. for Thomas Man, 1598), sig. K 2 r.

23. "The first English book on America," in Edward Arber, *The first three English books on America (?1511)–1555 A.D.* xxvii.

24. Sir Walter Ralegh, *The discovery of the large, rich, and beautiful empire of Guiana, with a relation of the great and golden city of Manoa, (which the Spaniards call Eldorado), etc., performed in the year 1595* . . . edited . . . by Sir Robert Schomburgk (London: Printed for the Hakluyt Society, 1848), 85–86.

25. "Virginias Verger: or a discourse shewing the benefits which may grow to this Kingdome from American English plantations, and specifically those of Virginia and Summer Ilands," in *Hakluytus posthumous or Purchas his pilgrimes* . . . by Samuel Purchas (Glasgow: James Maclehose and Sons, 1906), XIX, 231; Locke, *Works,* I, 61, note.

26. Purchas, *Pilgrimage,* sig. Aaa 3 r.

27. Lodovico di Varthema, "The navigation and vyages of Lewes Vertomannus," in Eden, *History of travayle in the East and West Indies, and other countreys lying eyther way* . . . (London: Richard Iugge, 1577), sig. Hhh iii v – Hhh v v. See also Sir Thomas Herbert, *A relation of some yeares travaile, begunne anno 1626 into Africa and the greater Asia* . . . (London: W. Stansby and J. Bloome, 1634), 14–17.

28. François Leguat, *The voyage of François Leguat of Breese to Rodriguez, Mauritius, Java, and the Cape of Good Hope. Transcribed*

from the first English edition. Edited and annotated by Captain Pasfield Oliver. (London: Printed for the Hakluyt Society, 1841) vol. 83, 287–96; Woodes Rodgers: *A cruising voyage around the world* . . . (London: Printed for A. Bell, 1717), 420.

29. Varthema, *op. cit.*, sig. Hhh iii v – Hhh v v; Yy v v; see also St. Augustine, *Of the citie of God*, sig. Ddd 2 v – Ddd 3 v.

30. Daniel Beeckman, "A voyage to and from the Island of Borneo (1714)," in John Pinkerton, *A general collection of the best and most interesting voyages and travels in all parts of the world* . . . (London: Longman etc., 1812), XI, 152–53.

31. Jerome Merolla, "A voyage to the Congo and several other countries, chiefly in southern Africa, by Father Jerome Merolla da Sorrento, a Capuchin and Apostolic Missioner in the year 1682," in Pinkerton's *Voyages* (1812), XVI, 209.

32. Heylyn, *Cosmography* (1652), sig. Gggg 4 r.

33. Beeckman, *op. cit.*, 152–53. See also the works of James Hunt and J. C. Nott.

34. Raymond Klibansky, *The continuity of the Platonic tradition during the Middle Ages* (London: Warburg Institute, 1939), 28; Arthur Oncken Lovejoy, *The great chain of being: a study of the history of an idea* (Cambridge: Harvard University Press, 1936), 79–80, 198. See Muslim theories of the chain of being in the Middle Ages in M. F. Ashley Montague, *Edward Tyson, M.D., F.R.S.* 1650–1708 (Philadelphia: American Philosophical Society, 1943), xvi–xix.

35. Thorndike, *op. cit.*, VI, 424.

36. Horst Woldemar Janson, *Apes and ape lore in the Middle Ages and the Renaissance* (London: Warburg Institute, 1952), *passim*.

37. Roy Harvey Pearce, "The 'Ruines of Mankind': the Indian and the Puritan mind," *Journal of the History of Ideas*, 13 (1952), 204; Sir Thomas Herbert, *A relation of some yeares travaile, begunne anno 1626* . . . (London: W. Stansby and J. Bloome, 1634), 16–17. Thirty-five years before Herbert undertook his voyages, Bruno, in his book *De universo et immenso*, had also said, "No sound person will refer the Ethiopians to the same protoplast as the Jewish one," thus alluding to the rabbinical idea of three races (T. Bendyshe, "The history of anthropology," in *Memoirs read before the Anthropological Society of London*, 1863–64 [London: Trübner, 1865], 355).

38. Cawley, *Voyages and Elizabethan drama*, 348 and note 36.

39. *The Tempest*, I, ii, 34–36; mentioned by Cawley, *Unpathed waters*, 238–39.

40. Lovejoy, *Chain of being*, 233–34; M. F. Ashley Montague, *Edward Tyson, M.D., F.R.S.* 1650–1708, (243), "This Climax of Gradation can't but be taken notice of . . . It would be the Perfection of Natural History, could it be attained, to enumerate and remark all the different species, and their Gradual Perfections from one to another."

41. *The Petty-Southwell correspondence 1670–1687*, edited from the Bowood Papers by the Marquis of Lansdowne (London: Constable, 1928), 43–48; "The scale of creatures: (a) Synopsis; (b) The scale of animals," in *The Petty Papers. Some unpublished writings of Sir William Petty,*

edited from the Bowood Papers by the Marquis of Lansdowne (London: Constable and Co., 1927), II, 19–26.

42. *Petty Papers,* II, 26, 30.

43. *Ibid.,* II, 30–31.

44. John Ovington *A voyage to Suratt* (1696) (London: Jacob Tonson (1696), 489.

45. Bendyshe, *op. cit.,* 361–63.

46. *Ibid.,* 358–59.

47. Alfred Rupert Hall, *The scientific revolution 1500–1800. The formation of the modern scientific attitude* (London: Longmans, 1954), 283; William Albert Locy, *The growth of biology* (New York: Holt, 1925), 310–18.

48. Hall, *op. cit.,* 293 ff.; Maurice Mandelbaum, "The scientific background of evolutionary theory in biology," *Journal of the History of Ideas,* 18 (1957), 344–46; Henri Daudin, *De Linné a Jussieu. Méthodes de la classification et idée de série en botanique et en zoologie* (Paris: Alcan, 1926), *passim;* Lovejoy, *op. cit.,* 233–35.

49. Sir Charles Linné, *A general system of nature, through the three grand kingdoms of animals, vegetables, minerals, systematically divided into their several classes, orders, genera, species, and variations . . .* (London: Lackington, Allen and Co., 1806), I, 9. Bendyshe shows how vacillating Linnaeus was concerning the precise divisions of mankind. See also Charles E. Raven, *Natural religion and Christian theology* (Cambridge: University Press, 1953), 145–63; John Takman, "Notes on Linnaeus," *Science and Society,* 21, (1957), 193–209; Alfred C. Haddon, *History of anthropology* (London: Watts and Co., 1910) 22–23, 25–27.

The Eighteenth and Nineteenth Centuries

CHAPTER XI

From Hierarchy to History

"What are we to think of the hundreds of earnest, patient, intelligent men . . . whose misfortune it was to devote their whole lives to false hypotheses?"—HARDIN CRAIG.

WHEREVER IN THE CHAIN OF BEING the savage was allotted a place—below or in company with European man—there in theory he was ordained to stay. The medieval mind made no provision for the mutability of animal species, or, among human beings for the transmutation of cultures from incivility to civility. Nor did most minds in the Renaissance. Basically Christian, they adhered to a serial cosmos in which the Good Bookkeeper, God, kept each category in a position eternally fixed, its classificatory bounds firmly established, its value unvarying. One of the major characteristics of the hierarchical view of things, and to many its most reassuring, was this stability. It settled without doubt or debate not only the relation of nature to man but of both to the realm of heaven. For many scholars, it also provided occupation in the task of determining the proper places of the members of the enchainment.

The doctrine and imagery of this immutability was seldom challenged even by those most skilled in metaphysical subtlety. Nature, here and now, or the Creation, exhibited itself in a continuous and unbroken series of members, ranks, or degrees, some still undiscovered perhaps, but each the realization of a changeless archetype existing from the beginning in the mind of deity. Consequently, the chain was not envisaged as a succession in time. Metaphysically and theologically, all members existed simultaneously. In essence the hierarchy was a juxtaposition of the philosophically higher and lower which, if occasion demanded, could be set down on a piece of paper as a simple inventory or list of created things. To its admirers, this orderly, constant, and immobile disposition of the multiplicity of things in space was one of its chief assets; and to the practical men, later collectors particularly, it put an end to argument by permitting the tidy and uncapricious insertion of each specimen in its proper pigeon-hole, each item in its proper rank. Like book titles catalogued by alphabet, each form had a fixed and foreseeable position. It could be readily located when wanted.

Although in an ideal or Aristotelian sense each form might be thought of as striving to perfect itself, the process of perfection, if indeed it involved motion or change in any mundane sense, took place solely within the conceptual boundaries of each category of the scale, not from category to category. No allowance was made for novelty. There was no thought that any form, be it mineral, vegetable, animal, or human, would strive to assume characteristics other than its own. There was no expectation that any member of the spatial enchainment would be tempted to violate the precincts of any other member next succeeding. As late as the eighteenth and even the nineteenth century, this doctrine was held no less faithfully among biologists than among theologians or philosophers. Linnaeus, a Christian taxonomist, who included the ranks or degrees of mankind in his floral and animal hierarchy, accepted the separate and fixed creation of species. And for nearly a century after his death, or well into the Victorian period, the same doctrine was cherished by the vast majority of scientists. The publicity visited upon the few, such as Darwin, who proposed that the enchainment was a record of changes, testifies to the generality of its acceptance.

Given the toughness of this ancient envisagement of an immutable and serialized world, the modern revolution in Western thought was not its abandonment. Indeed, the hierarchical order *per se* remains for most minds today a truism. The intellectual unsettlement took the form of a conversion of the purely architectonic, static, and spatial order of categories into a temporal one. The concept of a timeless inventory of Creation was transformed into one that was viewable as historical, developmental, evolutionary, or progressive —one in which transition from form to form, or from culture to culture, far from being contrary to reason and theoretically disallowed, was accepted as the way things worked.

But how did this drastic modification in a venerable and devoutly respected world view come about? How, logically and historically speaking, was this non-historical, constant, changeless but serial world of beings transmuted into one that was historical, inconstant, and changing? What kind of history did the temporalized series or enchainment become, and what was the influence of this kind of history upon opinion concerning savagery? In the answers to these questions, in the facts and arguments brought forward to give them the semblance of scientific rigor, are to be found the raisons d'être for some of the shapes assumed by eighteenth- and nineteenth-century social theory, and for the first formal drafts of modern ethnology.

The reasons for the conversion of the single, immutable, medieval hierarchy into the several mutable, temporal, developmental, evolutionary, and always historical series which now form the methodological structure of the several natural and social sciences, are still only partially elicited, especially for students of man. The study of ideas by historians has only begun. However, it is not at all unlikely that one reason has been that peculiar bent of the human mind for giving hospitality to mutually exclusive mental constructs. In other words, it seems probable that, despite its apparently viselike grip upon earlier European opinion, Europeans have never been committed to unexamined and uncontaminated hierarchical thought. There have always been deviationists who, given an appropriate moment, have made themselves heard. Another much more demonstrable reason is the existence of that ancient and inveterate inclination of Western reflection to seek solutions of problems, not in contemporary orderliness alone, but in the past, in some kind of genealogical, genetic, or historical explanation. Given both of these tendencies one of three things could happen. The contemporary, immutable, and serial could surrender completely to the temporal, genetic, and historical; the temporal, genealogical, and historical, could give way to the immutable, contemporary, and serial; or some compromise could be reached. In thought, the season for compromise is always open. Therefore, in fact, the serially fixed and spatial was transfigured into the serially mutable and temporal, based upon a well-known group of methodological principles underlying philosophical, logical, or conjectural history, with its progressionism, developmentalism, or evolutionism.

One of the influences leading to a break with the idea of the immutability of an hierarchically arranged order of things, and the adoption of the idea of its mutability, was Scripture. Many of the Books of the Bible are historical narratives from end to end. In Genesis, the Creation, of which the medieval hierarchy was in a sense merely a timeless catalogue or invoice, could also be viewed as a sequence of temporal conditions, while the hexameral literature was nothing more than a somewhat secularized version of the same historical theme. Thus there was unmistakable Biblical support for the contention that the hierarchy itself was the outcome of a series of events, changes, or conditions. Moreover, the Mosaic view of the beginning of things was enough to remind at least some inquirers that any logical and static inventory of an existing array of forms was merely an inventory, not an explanation of an inventory. If all minds were to be satisfied, its existence and serial arrangement required explanation.

But this was not all. During the Renaissance, the temporalization of the chain of being was hastened by influences and ideas associated with the Revival of Learning; by a renewed interest in the problems of historiography; by the belief, widely entertained, that history, as a record of past experience, could be made to serve the public interest; by the introduction of newer forms of documentation, especially those which seemed to lend themselves to the recovery of remoter periods of the past; and, with the ebb of degenerationism, by the conviction that history need not be a mere annalistic statement of local European experiment, but was rather a record of progressive changes in the life of mankind, in the structure of the earth, and the universe.

The fundamental historism of both religious and secular thought was thus in the sixteenth and seventeenth centuries sharply reaffirmed. It was recalled by divines and laymen that the Judeo-Christian faith was a religion of historians; that, with the destiny of the individual placed hazardously between the Fall and the Judgment, the great drama of sin and redemption had been worked out in an historical mood; that the Christian liturgy commemorated not only the historical experience of Jesus but the annals of the Church and the biographies of the saints; that while other "religions," God save the mark, might found their beliefs on myths outside the concept of time and the eventful, the authors of the Hebrew and

Christian Bible were irrevocably committed to a genealogical, genetic, or historiographical exegesis.

Thus, while some of the more conventional scholars of the sixteenth century were still extolling the virtues of the principle of an immutable chain of being, others, more experimental, turned frankly to the construction of dated series, or to history. The *artes historicae* soon came to be a well-defined critical genre. The purposes and procedures of historical investigation were much discussed;[1] and in secular circles political writers affirmed the utility of historical knowledge in the instruction of princes and statesmen. Prominent among these was Niccolò Machiavelli, the Italian humanist, diplomatist, and member of the educated urban laity. Another was Bodin, the French jurist; still another was Le Roy, a student of the vicissitudes of human achievement. These men were followed by a host of others in and out of public life, including Bacon, Shakespeare, Heylyn, Purchas, and Ralegh, each of whom, in his own way and in his own literary medium, looked to history, to the record of man's past experience, for guidance in present dilemmas.

In his *Discourses on the first decade of Titus Livius,* composed in 1516, Machiavelli made the position of the statesman with respect to history clear for generations to come. He proposed what seemed to him a new method of social inquiry, one as perilous for conservative thinkers as the voyages to the New World were for navigators. He called for the writing of historical narrative for something other than entertainment, or the use of the records of the past for the solution of present human predicaments. His remarks were based in essence upon the observation of the recurrent nature of classes of events, though he did not use these terms. "The wise are wont to say," said he, "that he who would forecast what is about to happen should look at what has been; since all events whether present or to come, have their exact counterpart in the past. And this, because the events are brought about by men, whose passions and dispositions remaining in all ages the same, naturally give rise to the same effects."[2] Why was it that in maintaining states, in organizing armies, in dealing with subject nations, and in exercising other governmental functions, no prince or statesman had taken advantage of history, that invaluable record of the accumulated wisdom of earlier men? Such blindness in high places could be due to but one thing: lack of insight into the wealth of information to be found in the historical record, and to an undervaluation of its empirical meaning. Although Machiavelli's empiricism was in no sense modern, consisting as it did of the use of historical examples rather than the rigorous comparison of like events at all times and all places, it served eventually to turn attention to the frequent occurrence of like events and the frequent similarity of human responses to like events.

A generation later, Bodin and Le Roy both affirmed a similar confidence in the potentialities of historical inquiry; and in the case of Bodin a technique was devised for assembling, classifying, and comparing events and epochs which went far beyond not only the rhetorical interests of earlier historians but beyond anything that had been contemplated by Machiavelli. Though Bodin's theoretical conclusions came ultimately to rest upon the subordination of the national and "innate" dispositions of peoples to geographical influences, he was convinced that historical materials should be classified and ordered to facilitate these comparisons. "Such is the multiplicity and disorder of human activities, such the abundant supply of histories, that unless the actions and affairs of men are confined to certain definite types, historical works obviously cannot be understood . . . What scholars, then, are accustomed to do to assist memory in the other arts should . . . be done for history also. That is, similar instances of memorable matters should be placed in a certain definite order, so that from these, as from a treasure chest, we may bring forth a variety of examples to direct our acts."³ Since no satisfactory comparison of all the manifestations of that central institution, the political state, had yet been made in all its forms and changes, Bodin proposed to make it. The study was to be conducted in an historical as well as a contemporary dimension; or in the only way, in his opinion, to determine what rules had been found successful in monarchies, democracies, and aristocracies, and hence applicable to existing political organizations.⁴

Although Machiavelli, Bodin, and Le Roy were all important advocates of the utilization of the records of the past, such confidence in the didactic and utilitarian promise of historical data, properly analyzed and classified, was not confined to any one group of Renaissance scholars. Soon accepted as axiomatic by many practicing historians, it received assent from other quarters. In the *Advancement of learning* Bacon contributed an analysis of the several kinds of historical reconstruction, as he saw them, and in his usual empirical mood advocated recording for posterity what men had done rather than what they ought to have done. This was in accordance with the ruling historiographical presupposition that since history repeats itself, knowledge of man's past behavior should unveil the future. The same assumption was implicit in Shakespeare's historical dramas and in Ralegh's *History of the world*. The frontispiece to the latter shows History, a female figure, treading Death underfoot, "flanked by Truth and Experience supporting the globe."⁵ Closely associated with the same argument was the advocacy of the biological analogy as a pattern of change in time. Since nations were organisms, it was believed that their biographies would exhibit similar sequences of great cycles of advancement and decline.

When once the utility of historical knowledge had taken firm hold on a few European minds, two auxiliary movements made their appearance to give it support and direction, and to lead eventually to the temporalization or historicizing of the hierarchy. One of these movements called for more historical evidence, especially concerning the earliest periods of human existence. If the past was to be as informative in fact as in theory it promised to be, then it seemed only wise to achieve as long a human record as possible by appealing to new documentation. The second movement entailed the restoration of historical optimism and the downfall of the moribund theory of human degeneration. If history was a record of human accomplishment, and if, as many were beginning to believe, the Revival of Learning had been a change for the better, why would it not be wise to find another envisagement of the process of change more in conformity with Renaissance achievement? Both of these movements in thought, this interest in more and earlier historical information and this more sanguine view of the human historical experience, were to have a far-reaching influence on ethnology and the theory of hierarchical immutability: the one, or the search for new documentation, by anticipating Sir Edward Burnett Tylor and his doctrine of survivals; the other, by prompting the so-called Quarrel of the Ancients and Moderns, and so lending support to the doctrine of progressive change.

Turning first to the matter of expanding the documentation of the earlier phases of man's history: the Renaissance antecedents of the concept of mid-nineteenth century "survivals" are not far to seek, nor was their purpose obscure. The use of "survivals" in the recovery of the past requires, as a primary intellectual step, the realization that existing cultures, or systems of behavior, are not historically or temporally all of one piece. They contain ideas, rites, practices, rules, laws, traits, of varying ages: some new, some old. Implicit also is the assumption that older elements, however outmoded, fragmentary, or eroded, possess documentary value. Though often immaterial in character, they may nevertheless be employed like defaced coins or shattered inscriptions to gain insight into early conditions.

Not a little of this was recognized by Herodotus and Thucydides, as also by Meric Casaubon in his *Treatise of use and custome,* written in 1638. There is no kind of knowledge, said Casaubon, that will bring more content to an ingenuous mind than that of the customs of the past. "Hee that knowes certainely . . . what hath been the particular estate . . . (of) most ages of the World, wherein they differed one from another, and wherein they agreed; what peculiar, and what common to every one; he doth as it were enjoy the memorie, of so many yeares, and so many ages past, even as if hee him-selfe had lived all those years, and outlasted all those ages. Hence it is the Antiquarians are so taken with the sight of old things," because of the "visible superviving evidences of antiquitie. . . ."[6] Indeed, by 1638 it would have taken a sub-stantial volume to do justice to this body of materials or to deal with the variety of presuppositions which entered as ingredients into the concept.

Some of these ingredients may be inferred from the imagery associated with the idea of "superviving evidence" when it made its Renaissance debut. In 1566, for example, Henri Estienne in his *Apologie for Herodotus* made reference to the "seeds and sparkes" of the Golden Age remaining visible after the passage of intervening ages.[7] The terms "seeds" and "sparks" were often used later with documentary intent. At about the same time, Bodin advocated that the theories of the origins of peoples, an absorbing subject during the mounting nationalism of the sixteenth century, be tested by "traces" or "remains" of earlier tongues in their current languages, his translator making him say at one point that "we arrive at survivals of words as the most important proof of origin."[8] In 1613 in Purchas' *Pilgrimage* "seeds," "sparks," "traces," and "remains," became "foot-prints," or "shadows," or "stumps." Concerning the religion of the savages of Canada, said this avid and emotional collector of all the religions of the world, "We finde some traces and foot-prints thereof, which neither the dreadful winters have quite frozen to death, nor these great and deep waters wholly drowned, but that some shadow thereof appeareth in these shadowes of men, howsoever wilde and savage, like to them which give her entertainment." Purchas was also responsible for the related idea that the sin of our first parents had not erased all memory of the dignity of God from their posterity. On the contrary, "a remainder or a stumpe thereof continued . . . like the stumpe of Nebuchadnezzars Tree, whose roots were left in the earth, bound with a Band of Iron and Brasse." Or as Samuel Johnson said, "Our first parent, Adam . . . was endowed with most illustrious wisdom of which some sparks remained after the fall."[9] In Heylyn's *Cosmography,* that much published and consulted compendium of information, the author referred constantly to "remainders," or to culture elements which, while being conveyed from past generations to a present one, had lost their clarity of outline and purpose. Christianity, he said, first planted in Egypt by St. Mark, fell into decay, and was represented by a small "remainder" called the Copts.[10] The Christianity introduced into India by St. Thomas was known now only by its "remainders"; while the Druses of Mt. Lebanon were "remainders" of the Frankish Crusaders who had forgotten all principles of the Christian religion except baptism. In 1616 Philip Clüver found "symbols" of the religion of classical antiquity among the Germans. To Sir Francis Bacon, these ancient elements were documents defaced, or "remnants" of what they once had been. They consisted of "monuments, names, words, proverbs, traditions, private records and evidences, fragments of stories, passages from books," which had been rescued in the nick of time from the eroding deluge of onrushing experience." "Although the length and disolving Nature of Time," said Sir Walter Ralegh, "hath worne out or changed the Names and Memory of the Worlds first planters after the floud . . . yet all the foot-steps of Antiquity . . . are not quite worn out nor over growne."[12] Only one form of imagery common in the nineteenth-century use of survivals had been infrequent in the sixteenth and seventeenth centuries. This was the geological or archeological, implying fragmentation, mutilation, or fossilization. A single example comes to hand in Thomas Burnet's *Theory of the earth,* written in 1681, in which the author regrets that "the first and fairest works of Nature should be lost out of the memory of Man, and that we should so much dote upon the Ruines, as never to think upon the Original Structure. As the modern Artists from some broken pieces of an ancient Statue, make out all the other parts and proportions; so from the broken and scatter'd limbs of the first World we have shown you how to raise the whole Fabrick again; and renew the prospect of those pleasant Scenes that first saw the light, and first entertain'd Man, when he came to act on this new erected Stage."[13]

Another of the earlier uses of "remainders" or "footsteps" is to be found in the *Origines sacrae* (1662) by Edward Stillingfleet, who was always profoundly concerned with the documentation of early Biblical conditions. Here, the historical priority and validity of the Hebrew account of human origins was at stake. Pushed to the wall by the reasoning of some of the higher critics, the Bishop was compelled to find some device for confirming the authenticity of the Scriptural account of the distribution of nations, or to give Moses priority to the classical historians. To accomplish this, classical mythology was combed for philological "remnants" of Genesis. But "remnants," "remainders," or "footsteps" had to be recognized before they could be used. How? Granted, said Stillingfleet, that the original Mosaic tradition, passing from age to age and people to people, took on strange disguises and alterations, there were always "certain marks" by which the true original could be detected. To the Bishop, of course, any change of this kind was an instance of corruption; the "remnant" or "remainder" was a defaced or disfigured element. So in order to assist in their detection, he attempted in some detail to show how this process of disfigurement might have operated, especially with respect to religious nomenclature and language."

Though acute anxiety concerning the priority of the account in Genesis had diminished somewhat by the beginning of the eighteenth century, a stereotyped sequence of Scriptural epochs was usually included in an historical work, bolstered by arguments from "survivals." The position of the Abbé Banier, a student of mythology, was substantially the same as that of Bishop Stillingfleet. The classical fables and myths, said he in his *Explication historique des fables,* published in 1710, were not to be regarded as mere fiction. They were treasuries for historians, with their documentary properties concealed by all sorts of "disguises" and "distortions" like the "erosion" or "fragmentation" of all other "remainders" or "remnants." Yet for all that, the hope of finding in them direct clues to the religion of the "primitive Patriarchs," or the true "Remaines of our Mysteries," was illusory." In Banier's judgment, the primordial period of creed and ritual, antecedent to the time of Abraham and prior to Hellenism, was too remote for successful penetration by even this newer form of documentation. It could only be assumed that the religions of earliest man were homogeneous.

The "remnant," "remainder," or "foot-step," once apprehended as such during the years of the Renaissance, thus not only permitted the historian, at least theoretically, to push his reconstruction of the history of a nation farther back into the past, it had other uses. It could be employed—or so it was thought—as Tylor was to employ it: to verify the initiatory position of the savage in the temporalized hierarchy, or to uphold Dr. Petty's decision to insert existing savagery in the enchainment of forms below man but above the ape. The argument adopted by Père Lafitau in 1704 is a case in point. Subscribing, as a cleric, to the dogma of the Fall and corruption of mankind, affecting both savagery and the early civilizations, he desired to prove nevertheless that the savages were not without religion, as had been asserted by some contemporary "atheists." He attempted, therefore, not unlike Tylor at a much later date, to demonstrate that the customs of the American Indians displayed "singular and curious traces" or "vestiges" of the cultures and religions of the earliest historical peoples, namely, the Greeks at the time of Homer and the Hebrews at the time of Moses; that all men came from the same inaugural stem;[16] but that the Indians, as savages, represented an earlier and older phase of human development and occupied a lower place than civil man in the temporalized chain of being.

The traditional tendency of Western thought to solve its problems historically was expressed not only in the use of a new form of documentation, the "survival," and in the temporalization of the hierarchy of being, but in another way as well. This latter movement of thought was of the greatest importance in the history of ethnological theory. It entailed the reenvisagement of the process of change of which the hierarchy had become theoretically the outcome, or the substitution of the doctrine of progress for the doctrine of degeneration.

One of the main results of the Revival of Learning was the establishment of contact between the minds of contemporary scholars and those of antiquity. The outcome was what might have been expected. In the first flush of discovery, the old learning, transmitted by the Greek and Roman literatures, appeared to be more accomplished than anything the Middle

Ages or medieval Scholasticism had to offer. Facing backward, therefore, in the quest for what they took to be a higher truth, many men prepared themselves for the life of scholarship by mastering the ancient languages and reading the ancient philosophers, poets, and historians. They submitted themselves to the authority of classical thought in the belief that in it was to be found the source of all knowledge, to the extent that medieval philosophy began to seem only another inescapable evidence of decay, decline, and degeneration.

But at some time around the middle of the sixteenth century, or even before, the theory of degeneration, as a philosophy of history, began to lose its power to command and depress the human spirit. True, it had long been a hardy perennial among directive concepts. True, it was still due for several revivals: one in eighteenth-century "primitivism," another in the pre-Tylorean theory of the degeneration of savagery. But its days as a prevailing world view were numbered. One important manifestation of its declining influence was a tendency to belittle the achievements of the ancients. In 1565 in France, Henri Estienne had this to say: "As there are many who do highly esteeme Antiquitie," so that "the reverence they beare it, is in the nearest degree to superstitious: so there are others . . . who are so farre from giving it that which of due belongs unto it, that they do not onely disgrace it what they can, but even tread it under foote."[17] Said Le Roy at about the same time: "Let us not be so simple, as to attribute so much unto the Auncients, that wee beleeve that they have knowen all, and said all."[18] Said Ralegh: "I shall never be perswaded, that God hath shut up all light of Learning within the lanthorne of Aristotle's braines: or . . . that God hath given invention but to the Heathen."[19] These men were joined by a host of others, all defending the capacity of the Moderns to equal or outdistance the Ancients.

The expression of this optimistic point of view—the view

that the past was a time of change, and that change was in the direction of advancement—is usually thought of as emerging from a literary controversy, and so in a measure it did. It was maintained by some critics that the Ancients were more gifted as poets and scholars than the Moderns, or visa versa. In actual fact, the Quarrel of the Ancients and Moderns agitated the minds of men in every walk of life in Europe— in religion, in philosophy, in science, in the fine arts, in technology, architecture, invention, and the social studies. It was the current expression of a decisive conflict between traditionalism and modernism, between authority and originality, which was to determine whether thought in the future would continue to follow Greek and Latin models or strike out on its own.

Everyone took a hand in the argument, with the decision finally awarded to the Moderns. According to the French publicist Fontenelle, who availed himself of the Cartesian assumption of the stability, regularity, permanence, and immutability of Nature's laws, "the whole question of pre-eminence . . . reduces itself to knowing whether the trees of yesterday were greater than those of today. If they were, Homer, Plato, and Demosthenes cannot be equalled; but if our trees are as great as those of former times, then we can equal Homer, Plato, and Demosthenes."[20] If the laws of nature were to be regarded as constant, so also were the natural powers of men. Said the Abbé Perrault: "We need only read the French and English journals and glance over the noble achievements of the Academies of these two great kingdoms to be convinced that during the last twenty or thirty years more discoveries have been made in the science of nature than during the whole extent of learned antiquity." The same position was taken by many members of the Royal Society in England who had no doubt of the superiority of their own attainments. Men such as Glanvill and Hakewill delighted in listing the achievements of the Moderns in chemistry, anatomy, mathematics, astronomy, optics, and geography. The inventions of gunpowder, the compass, and the printing press were repeatedly cited as indications of the superiority of modern men and modern times. According to Hakewill, the Moderns had produced more important work in half a dozen years than the Aristotelians in eighteen hundred.²¹ Knowledge had progressed.

The temporalization of the chain of being, with the savage in his place between man and brute, thus came about as the result of the mingling of several ideas and movements of thought. All of them were historical; all implied change in the cultural activities of men rather than fixity; and all led to the theoretical substitution of progressive for degenerative change. But, as Dr. Bock has recently so lucidly pointed out, the idea of progress was something more "than a jubilant expression of hope or self-satisfaction," more than a value judgment celebrating the exalted status of European culture. "It was given formal statement in an age of science when men deliberately sought unequivocal demonstration of their beliefs. So, the idea emerged not as a faith in the possibility of progress, not as a guarded statement of the probability of future advance, but as an unqualified 'law' stating the absolute necessity of continual and never ending improvement."

Some of the axioms and arguments employed for purposes of the "proof" or demonstration of this law of cultural change were derived from the most respectable of contemporary scientific sources. In 1637, Descartes wrote "that there are 'certain laws established in nature by God,' laws that are 'accurately observed in all that exists or takes place in the world.'" If God be the source of natural laws, then it may be said that the world was not "produced at once in a finished and perfect state," but came gradually into existence. The importance of this view, continues Dr. Bock, "lies in the fact that a deity, whose ways are perhaps mysterious and beyond the grasp of human reason, or who might even act arbitrarily," was now replaced by an inexorable regularity and legality operating "uniformly in all times and places." It was this principle of legality and uniformity which was used by the Moderns to demonstrate the inevitability of progressive change in knowledge. "If the laws of nature work with regularity, then men of equal ability must be produced in every age, and mere accumulation of equal efforts will make for advance." Again, "if nature is uniform in her operations and if she works to produce the same effects in every age," then progress, it was argued, is not only a certainty but also a regular, even process. Scholars with ethnological interests thereafter pursued the "scientific" study of man's cultural history by arranging cultures in the usual hierarchical order; but this hierarchical order, no longer static, was assumed to be progressive. As was said by Dr. Petty, when at one and the same time he introduced savagery into the chain of being and envisaged that chain as the product of progressive change, "wee shall also add another Scale [to that of the animals] containing the Severall Stepps and gradations of improuvements which man hath made from the lowest and simplest condition that mankind was ever in, unto the highest that anie man or Company of men hath attained." The acknowledgment that a few elements in the culture of Renaissance Europe were old, or had resisted inevitably progressive change, was allowed to give no trouble. These "seeds" or "sparks," "remnants" or "remainders" of an older, less advanced condition were easily accounted for and employed. They implied that other elements, indeed all other elements, had been subjected to a progressive alteration so complete as to unfit them for the documentation of very early conditions. On the other hand, the resistance of these few to the law of progressive change provided a welcome means of "documenting" the early or earliest members of the progressive and hierarchical order;

and, if anyone questioned the idea of progressive change, they helped to justify its acceptability.

But here it must be said again that while the impact of these several ideas upon the theory of the static chain of being, and through it upon the study of culture, was a turning point of almost inestimable magnitude, none of them, except perhaps those embodied in the controversy between the Ancients and Moderns, has ever received exhaustive discussion. The modification and amalgamation of older ideas went on in the privacy of individual minds, sometimes without trace, except in terms of much later results. Overnight, as it were, and in the almost uncanny silence of unquestioning agreement, the hierarchical concept of nature, which once was taken to be an orderly arrangement of forms in space, became a progressive sequence in time. The savage, who in the context of the medieval schematization of the universe had been given a merely logical and spatial antecedence to European man, was now endowed with temporal or historical priority. Meanwhile, the doctrine of degeneration, which had so long darkened the human spirit, seemed to give way quite suddenly to its opposite, the doctrine of progress. For the zoological world the temporalized hierarchy became natural history, or the evolutionary series; and for the cultural world it became culture history, or the developmental or evolutionary cultural series. Anthropology, or the science of man, said Bendyshe to the Anthropological Society of London in 1863–64, "joins natural history, at one extremity . . . and at the other . . . in its highest and most peculiar department . . . has . . . nothing beyond what is more generally known as the science of history". The whole domain, "from the origin of mankind to its ultimate destiny . . . is embraced in Anthropology."[22]

With early ethnological thought anchored firmly in the early historical chapters of Genesis; with diversities in culture accounted for by diffusion, or the historical wanderings of the patriarchs and their progeny from a tribal center; with correspondences and "remainders" used freely to document other absorbing historical problems; with the Renaissance revival of interest in historiography; with the progressionist theory of cultural change derived, at least in part, from the Quarrel of the Ancients and Moderns, or the comparison of an historically earlier period of European achievement with a later; above all, with the conversion of the a-historical spatial and unchanging hierarchy into one that was temporal, historical, and a reflector of changes—with all of these, it becomes impossible to evaluate the significance of this conversion, or to deal adequately with its role in subsequent ethnological and social thought without dwelling briefly, first, upon the field of inquiry known as history; and then making a distinction between the two major types of history : the hierarchical and that which acquires significance from the use of dates.

Owing to the historical nature of the human being, which resides in his unique possession of dated or historical materials, ethnology, as a discipline devoted to the study of man, can never be safely divorced from an intimate acquaintance with the major details of historiographical theory and practice. The question at issue is this : What kind of history is ethnology to be? Are its conclusions to be based upon "natural" history derived from the conversion of the philosophical and spatial hierarchy into the temporal (the only kind of historical reconstruction permitted to the zoologist and botanist, whose objects of interest, the flora and fauna of the world, frustrate dated investigation by offering no dated records)? Or are ethnologists to recognize fully the historiographical significance of their object of interest, man, which makes it possible for them to escape from merely hierarchical arrangements of cultural data, and to adopt a kind of temporal reconstruction blessed with access to dates and dated evidence, at least for the dated period?

Owing to the conversion of the static hierarchy into a time series, owing to its employment by naturalists as "natural" history, or to its further employment (after Petty's introduction of the savage into the chain of being) as the core of developmental or evolutionary anthropology, this question has been and still remains one of the most crucial in the whole field of the social studies. Far from being a "dead horse," as so many would like to think it, cultural or social evolutionism versus dated history remains *the* intellectual dilemma in the study of man in the twentieth century. On a clear-headed realization of its central importance in ethnological theory, on an accomplished understanding of the various forms of historiography, rests the conscious and informed direction of the future of social thought.

What then is history? What should the student of man know about the basic assumptions of historians? How many kinds of history are there? What is the relation of dated historical thought to hierarchical thought? What is the relation of the culture of savagery to hierarchical and historical inquiry? To what extent should ethnologists give their attention to the histories of the cultures of the historical peoples? What, in the methodological sense, is "natural" history? What is culture history?

When once the puzzle is broken down into questions such as these, it will become apparent that there are at least two major kinds of historical inquiry. One is dependent upon the accessibility of dated documentation for insuring the correct temporal arrangement of human activities. The other, possessing few or no dated resources, resorts to philosophical, metaphysical, logical, or hierarchical procedures for arriving at purportedly temporal arrangements. It will also become apparent that the device of correspondences, so closely associated with the construction of the medieval hierarchy, is imported into the latter type of "historical" effort for the purpose, in the absence of dated evidence, of sustaining the logically constructed "historical" series.

Apart from the recognition of these two types of historical effort and the function in one of them of correspondences, the above questions appear simple enough. But to answer them intelligibly, to make clear the relationship between historiographical assumptions *per se* and those which lie at the foundation of the temporalized scale of being, it will be necessary, first, to recall some of the traditional features of the method of dated history; and then to compare dated history with philosophically or logically constructed temporal series.

At the outset, the very word "history" may be a source of confusion to unwary readers. In English, it is an omnibus word, endowed with many meanings for the performance of multiple services. It may be used merely as a synonym for "the past," when it is said, for example, that "history" or the "past" has much to teach the present. It may refer to the general course of events in the past, or to that vast, chaotic body of documentary material available to the historian for the recovery of the past. Finally, it may pertain broadly to the finished products of historical endeavor—to the dated historical narrative, to the historical monograph, to the philosophy of history; to natural history in the fields of zoology and geology; or indeed to all the books which line the shelves of the so-called historical subjects, and to all subjects "historically" treated.

To add to this initial confusion, history in its various guises has itself a long history. It is not a recently and hastily conceived speciality of social investigation, without traditional intellectual substance, and therefore easily dismissed. Historical inquiry of one kind or another is very old, and has been conducted on the basis of several old and very tenacious organizing principles. Though not always so recognized, it rests upon a serial as well as temporal arrangement of data, superficially not unlike an hierarchical series. In addition to this and briefly sketched, the traditional model of historiography rests upon three assumptions leading to the construction of temporal series or sequences. Some of these are dated, but some are logically achieved, as was the hierarchical type of series.

In accordance with these traditional organizing principles, it is assumed, first, that the present for which the historian seeks to account, or in which he finds his problem, can best be understood if it be regarded as the result of something which has happened in the past, and if that past be recovered. This, it need not be said, is an assumption of some magnitude. It all but declares that knowledge of the little-known present is dependent upon the recovery of the less knowable past.

It is assumed, second, that the past can be best understood if it be envisaged in terms of the phenomena of human generation; if each event chosen by the historian to form an element in an event series, or every member of an hierarchical sequence, be thought of as bearing the same relation to preceding and subsequent events or members as the human elements of a genealogical or genetic series; as having begotten a subsequent event or member of the hierarchy; as having a natural antecedent event or member in somewhat the same sense as a child possesses a natural antecedent in his father, and his father in a preceding parent, and so on.

It is assumed finally that the world, man, and all of the activities carried on by man, are not eternal, but have had a beginning or origin recoverable by appropriate types of investigation. It is believed that every series of events selected by an historian as significant, or every sequence of members in a logically constructed hierarchical series, proceeds from some first or original event or member, and that this original event or member is discoverable.

However audacious the historian may be in making his initial assumption, the second, derived ultimately from the phenomena of generation, is well founded in tradition. In dealing with the problem of the present as the outcome of what has happened in the past, man is "an incorrigible genealogist who spends his whole lifetime in search of a father. He longs for a chain of gold or blood to fasten himself to the universe in which he is committed to live."[23] Ever since the writing of history began, the events which constitute the backbone of dated historical narration have been fitted conceptually into a traditional framework which perpetuates the genealogical method of the early peoples—the ancient Hebrews, the Greeks, and the Romans. Just as a genealogy possesses three elements —a person present or spoken of, a series of ancestors, and a specific first progenitor, source or origin—so, in the large, the historical method envisages the past in three major terms : first, as a problem, or an existing present to be accounted for; second, as a point of departure or first event, or origin; and third, as a series of selected events or members connecting the origin with the present.[24]

In this confusion of ancestry with explanation, the genealogical frame of reference, as employed among the ancient Mediterranean peoples, has provided a form into which all types of historical reconstruction may be fitted, whether dated or undated, whether referring to situations in the affairs of men or to conditions in the world of nature. The Bible, with its surfeit of genealogies, offers one example from one Mediterranean people. Many others appear in the Greek and other ancient literatures. Herodotus relates that when Hecateus, a previous Greek visitor to Egypt, had traced his own ancestry back to a god in the sixteenth generation, the Egyptian priests took him into a temple containing 345 statues. Each one of these was the son of another in unbroken descent, without reaching back to a god. The Biblical genealogies, or "begats," began with the generations of Heaven and Earth, and passed thereafter by successive steps from Adam and Eve to Jacob and his sons, to the tribes founded by Jacob's sons, to the subdivisions of each tribe, and thence to some form of dated reconstruction, or to the selection of a dated series of events. (Note that the dated part of this series was joined on to the specifically genealogical or undated genetic section without comment or indication of difference.) Theoretically each Israelite could trace his descent back to Jacob, the father of the whole nation, and finally back to Noah and to Adam. This genetic form of explanation was also extended in the books of the Bible to problems outside the range of Old Testament tribal, military, or political history. The author of the Book of Genesis took delight in pointing out the origin of human institutions, in explaining how agriculture, pastoralism, music, metallurgy, and language came into existence; who the Moabites, Ammonites, Canaanites, and Edomites were, their tribal sources usually being "discovered" in a significant first action of some hero, or in the oracular pronouncement of some patriarch.[25]

To enforce the argument, only a passing reference need be made to the intricate genealogies also to be found in classical literature, which, in a like manner and on like assumptions, made the gods the forefathers of heroes, tribes, cities, and individuals, in somewhat that order. A more poetic example of the genealogical solution of a problem, or in that sense a genetic or historical explanation, is to be found in the *Iliad*, where the narrator sought to account for the power which was vested in Agamemnon and symbolized by his scepter. The genetic explanation of Agamemnon's authority thus became a genealogy of the scepter as it was passed from hand to hand, from the high gods to man, and thence to Agamemnon.

. . . The place of assemblage was in turmoil, and the earth groaned beneath them, as the people sate them down . . . [And] hardly at the last were the people made to sit, and were stayed in their places, ceasing from their clamour. Then among them lord Agamemnon uprose, bearing in his hands the sceptre which Hephaestus had wrought with toil. Hephaestus gave it to king Zeus, son of Cronos, and Zeus gave it to the messenger Argeï-phontes; and Hermes, the lord, gave it to Pelops, driver of horses, and Pelops in turn gave it to Atreus, shepherd of the host; and Atreus at his death left it to Thyestes, rich in flocks, and Thyestes again left it to Agamemnon to bear, that he might be lord of many isles and of all Argos.[26]

In later times the same genealogical pattern shows through the opaque pages of detail introduced by medieval historiographers or their renaissance successors. In Boccaccio's *De genealogia deorum,* first written in the third quarter of the fourteenth century and printed frequently after 1472, the genetic plan was arboreal rather than unilinear, recalling the neo-Platonic Tree of Porphyry and other early hierarchical schemes. Boccaccio's first concern was to find a classical deity who could stand as the founder of the race of gods; then the greater divinities were arranged on the branches of the family tree with the lesser gods grouped around them.[27] In Muenster's *Cosmographia* and in the Nuremberg *Chronicle* the history of a country or a city was often similarly expressed in drawings of vinelike designs bearing in sequence the medallion likenesses of the nation's sovereigns.[28]

But despite the fact that genealogy constitutes the basic and traditional pattern of conventional historical enterprise, history in this sense is divisible into two categories, the touchstone of classification being dates: the availability of dates for the accurate chronological arrangement of the historical sequence, or the willingness of the historian to use them. Since narrative history proper, nationalist history, world or universal history, and the history of civilization are in varying degrees datable, the historian in these areas usually avails himself of dated evidence—some more, some less. Consequently, the order of events in political history, or the order of the appearance of periods of high achievement in world history, may, within certain well-defined limits, be achieved chronologically. It is inferred that since events, empires, or periods of supreme accomplishment have taken place in dated time, and since there is only one order or direction in time, these entities can and must fit meaningfully into some kind of dated or time series, the members of which are viewed as intimately related to one another "causally" or genealogically.

But of equal or even greater importance to all students in the social studies is a clear understanding of the make-up and import of the second category of historical types of inquiry, composed of those reconstructions of the past which have been accomplished without benefit of dates in establishing sequences. No less genealogical in spirit than the dated type, this kind of historiographical enterprise is variously and properly known as logical, ideal, hypothetical, conjectural, or speculative history; and the temporalized hierarchy, especially as it came to be manifested in "natural" or cultural history, is to be included under this rubric.

Concerned more or less ideally or abstractly with the total experience of mankind in time, or with the total array of cultures past and present, or, as in natural history with the total array of species, this logical or conjectural type of so-called "historical" series assumes the complexion of a sequence of conditions; and the order of conditions in time is achieved, not with the aid of dates, but on *a priori* grounds, or with the aid of logic. That is to say, the array of flora, fauna, or cultures, are first given a logical *present* arrangement in *space,* usually hierarchical; and then this present hierarchical arrangement is converted into a time or historical series.

Thus though there are unmistakable likenesses between dated and philosophical or speculative forms of historical reconstruction, in the sense that each presents the reader with a

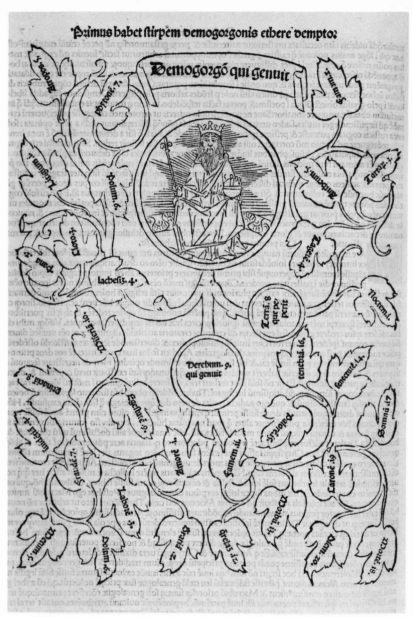

Boccaccio's "Genealogia deorum," from his Genealogiae deorum *(1494).*

"time" series in which one event or one member is assumed to follow genetically from the event or member just preceding it in the series, history of the logical or conjectural or philosophical type is actually history abstracted from specific dates or places. It is universal in intent. It deals with flora, fauna, cultures in general. The relation between the members of such sequences may not be identifiable in years, the earmark of the historian's history. Like the temporalized hierarchy, a logical construct, their sequential relationship is conceptual and ideal, not necessarily chronological or assignable to dates.

The methodological details of the dated type of historical investigation is probably too well known to require further analysis or illustration at this time, except perhaps in the form of a reminder of the genealogical relationship which theoretically obtains between the members of every dated event series selected by each individual historian. For no matter how many historians may have worked on a given historical problem, each perhaps selecting a different series of antecedent events as its historical solution; no matter how widely separated in time and place may be the events chosen in each historian's sequence; no matter how difficult may be the demonstration of connection between events chosen; an earlier event in every dated sequence theoretically gives rise to a later just succeeding event, is "causally" or genetically related to it; else why the selection of the sequence?

The second type of historiographical thought, on the other hand—the ideal, the logical, the philosophical, or conjectural —should be carefully examined and illustrated. For this type is not only less well recognized as a distinct and pervasive type of historical reconstruction but is widely used in the social studies in several forms. Some of these are on the borderline between the dated and the undated, such as the important sequences of empires popular among Renaissance historians, and inherited perhaps with the medieval interest in the Four

Monarchies. Some rest flatly and undatably upon organismic ideas inferring a common succession of sequences of stages in social phenomena. Some have been concerned with the determination of the first or original stage, the first member of the hierarchy—or, in anthropology, with savage culture.

Though Bodin and Le Roy did much to commend the historical studies to discriminating men, to discourage flights of the historical imagination, and to convert historians from artists into scientists, both believed that there was something to be gained by pressing the cause of the already popular type of universal history, or history of civilization. Typically, this consisted of a time series composed of descriptions of celebrated empires or cultures at the moment of their *greatest* worldly success, and *omitting* all other historical periods, either preceding or following the celebrated one. In many cases these sequences or periods of high achievement, either chronologically arranged or datable, were given a geographical explanation as a movement of high attainment from east to west. According to Bodin, the torch of civilization passed from the Chaldeans, the most ancient of peoples, to the Mediterranean nations of antiquity, and thence to the northern Europeans.[29] In the words of Le Roy in the *Vicissitudes* : "I thinke that God being carefull of all parts of the world, doth grant the excellencie of Armes and Learning, sometimes unto Asia, sometimes unto Africk, sometimes unto Europe; . . . and suffering vertue and vice, valancie and cowardice, sobrietie and delicacie, knowledge and ignorance, to go from countrie to countrie, honouring and diffaming the Nations at divers times."[30] Speaking probably for many other members of the Royal Society, Thomas Sprat pointed out that the Greeks "took their first hints from the East; but outdid them in Music, in Statuary, in Graving, in Limning, in Navigation, in Horsemanship, in Husbandry, as much as the Ægyptians or Assyrians exceeded their unskilful Ancestors in Architecture, Astronomy or

Geometry. The Germans, the French, the Britains, the Spaniards, and the modern Italians, had their light from the Romans; but surpass'd them in most of their own Arts."[31] As Lord Berkeley was later to remark—along with Vico, Hegel, and their many nineteenth-century followers, the dates and geographical stations of civility showed conclusively that westward the course of empire took its way. The members of this kind of series, partially dated and partially logical, might be and usually were widely separated from one another in space and time, but theoretically were closely connected by virtue of their adjacency on the printed page as elements of a genetic or genealogical order.

From the earliest times, and prevalent again during the Renaissance and its long aftermath, another conjectural sequence was based upon the ancient idea that the career of a nation was analogous to the life cycle of the individual man or organism; that the historical process, or the process of change, was cyclical in character, with each cycle divided into a conventional number of members, periods, conditions, or stages. All human beings, said Le Roy, in this spirit, "have their beginning, progresse, perfection, corruption, and end; and being rude at first do afterwards polish themselves, with civilitie of maners and knowledge; . . . The Greekes at first were but rude, and grosse . . . and the first which became civill amongst them were the Athenians, who polished their language, which they also brought unto perfection; where it remained not long : but was corrupted, and lost, togither with the libertie of the Countrey, being supplanted by the Macedonians, Romains, and other strawngers, which have ruled there."[32] The cyclical or organic theory lent itself to a theory either of degenerative change or of progressionism, depending upon which arm of the cyclical movement was stressed.

With this analogy in mind, many conjectural historians spoke of the history of a nation as traversing the seven ages of

man. Shakespeare's famous passage in *As you like it* is said
to have been taken from a school text-book by Marcellus
Palingenius (fl. 1528), and was therefore old and conventional.
But there were also many other seven-member sequences of
the same kind by men such as Lemnius, Pedro Mexia, and
Pierre de la Primaudaye.[33] There was an even more popular
three-member series harking back to St. Augustine, with the
epochs named as ancient, medieval, and modern, or as youth,
manhood, and old age. The rebirth of art and letters was
associated from the beginning with a vague idea of a middle
period between a decline of the ancient culture and a modern
revival. Following this more or less unconscious assumption
underlying the thought of all humanists, Giorgio Vasari (1512–
1574) presented a conception of art as an organic whole
destined to pass through these clearly marked stages; and his
Lives of the great painters, sculptors, and architects, written in
1550, remained a model for all Renaissance histories of art
for upwards of a century and a half.[34] Another who accepted
the validity of a three-member series was Thomas Sprat. The
historian of the Royal Society, followed by many others,
envisaged the stages of the human past as the Greek, Roman,
and Renaissance, combined with an assumed east-west march
of the empire of knowledge.[35] Still others were the Jesuits in
seventeenth-century America; Bernard Mandeville in the
eighteenth century; and the founder of the so-called science
of sociology, Auguste Comte, in the nineteenth. "It was the
opinion of Aristotle," according to the Jesuit *Relations,*

that the world had taken as it were three steps in order to arrive
at the perfection which it possessed in his time. At first men contented themselves with life, seeking purely and simply for the
things just necessary and useful for its conservation. At the
second, they united the agreeable with the necessary, and civility
with necessity. They found food first, then the seasoning; they
covered themselves in the beginning against the rigor of the
weather, and afterward they gave grace and charm to their dress;

Vine-like succession of England's kings as presented in Muenster, Cosmographie Universelle *(1552).*

they made houses in the first ages simply to use, and afterward they made them to be seen. At the third step, men of intellect, seeing that the world was enjoying the things which were necessary and pleasant for life, gave themselves to the contemplation of the things of nature and to the investigation of the sciences, so that the great republic of men has perfected itself little by little, necessity marching ahead, civility and well-being coming after, and the sciences bringing up in the rear.[36]

In *The fable of the bees* (1714) it was indicated that the first forced association of men (to protect themselves against wild animals) was followed by a second condition in which they were compelled to protect themselves from each other, and a last which was signalized by the invention of letters. Achieving a temporal series through philosophic analysis of the past and through generous borrowings from predecessors, Auguste Comte developed the "science" of society on the basis of his famous triad of universal epochs.

While these three- or seven-stage philosophical or conjectural histories of mankind were being outlined, there were also many logical and undated reconstructions of technological history. "In the beginning," said Robert Allott in 1552, indicating that he was quoting Strabo, "they writ in ashes, next in the barks of trees, then in leaves of Laurell, afterwards in Sheets of leade, & at last they came to write in paper."[37] Moved by the influence of collections of weapons, or the need for some criterion for arranging them for exhibition, Pedro Mexia in his *Foreste, or collection of histories,* written first in Spanish in the mid-sixteenth century, called Lucretius to his aid. According to this ancient authority, men first defended themselves with "the nailes and teeth," and after that acquainted themselves with the staff and stones, "which this daie yet are onely used of certaine barbarous Nations."[38] Le Roy presented this series in another technological dimension, "Now whereas men have taken nourishment, first of tame beasts, before either of graine, or of fruits : there is no doubt but that pasturage, grasing, & and shepheardie, were before husbandrie & tillage . . . The tilling and planting of the earth have bin both invented after pasturage, and unto both have bin added hunting, fouling, and fishing."[39] Repetitions of Le Roy's series, attempts to prove it, to disprove it, or to replace it with some other, have absorbed the efforts of countless scholars; and statements like it, whether sound or unsound, have become the commonplaces of ethnological and economic discourse.

Conjectural or philosophical stage series such as these were especially popular among the members of the so-called Historical School of economic thought in Germany in the nineteenth century. Frederick List distinguished five stages of economic development : a wild or uncivilized condition, followed by pastoralism, agriculture, agriculture plus manufacturing, and agriculture plus both manufacturing and commerce. Roscher suggested that the economic history of every more advanced people had traversed three stages of development. Hildebrand, reacting against Roscher, formulated a sequence consisting of three modes of distribution : barter economy, money economy, and credit economy. Schmoller, differing from both Roscher and Hildebrand, would have nothing less than five stages, beginning with a tribal or agricultural condition and ending with a world economy. In the twentieth century, Marx, Marshall, and Veblen, each in his own way, followed suit;[40] though by this time all memory of the earlier sources of the procedure had been lost and each man thought of himself as an original thinker.

Moreover, as time went on, it seems certain that hierarchical ideas, temporalized to suit the needs of the conjectural historian of culture, were mingled with historical assumptions concerning the savage as a conjectural first member of these conjectural series. One such argument was advanced by those who, believing in the static chain of being, faced the necessity for finding in it an appropriate place for the hitherto unheard-of savage. Long before 1677, when Dr. Petty installed the Hottentot between beast and man in the medieval static hierarchy, the savage had already been introduced to Europeans as a kind of man peculiar to earlier times or the beginning of things. "Our world," said Montaigne in the sixteenth century, "has of late discovered another . . . so fresh and infantile that he is still being taught his ABC." Ralegh spoke of the aborigines as men without ancestors; Bacon, as the human contingent of an infant world; Estienne, as rustics; Purchas, as originaries, or naturals. In a striking argument, developed in 1589 by Richard Puttenham, and obviously familiar to all of his readers, the origin of verse was ascribed to those who lived "before any civil society was among men," or to wild and savage people who remained, like New World man, in the woods and mountains, "dispersed like wild beasts, lawlesse and naked." In clarification of this concept, Pierre d'Avity became, in 1614, the author of an analysis of barbarousness which attempted to distinguish from among all savage tribes those which were the most infantile, most natural, or most aboriginal—and therefore earliest. The political counterpart of Puttenham's theory is to be found in Hobbes' *Leviathan* seventy-five years later. In short, this traditional temporalization of savagery, together with certain philosophical difficulties with the notion of a merely static hierarchy of beings, may have operated as an entering wedge in bringing about the ultimate temporalization of the whole hierarchy.[41] Such concepts, obviously merely logical or conjectural, were part of the ethnological imagery of the sixteenth and seventeenth centuries. They were taken for granted, constantly repeated, never analyzed, never challenged;[42] and so they remain today, except for a few critics, as almost ineradicable elements in thought, both lay and professional.

Curiously enough, the temporalization of the zoological and botanical sections of the hierarchy of being, their conversion into a conjectural or philosophical history of living forms, was far slower in finding acceptance than its social or cultural counterpart. Or putting it in another way, theories of social development or evolution were not derived from or imitative of the theory of biological evolution; they anticipated it. Since change had long been remarked as a characteristic of human behavior (from some points of view a very disturbing characteristic), belief in the immutability of culture was abandoned in Europe long before the abandonment of a belief in a concomitant idea, the fixity of species. No doubt historical evidence, its accessibility to historians and its absence in the life sciences, had much to do with this difference in timing. Certainly no one familiar with the mass of historical documentation attesting to cultural change in past time could long avoid its implications. That point being settled early, the question at issue was transformed early into how the process was to be envisaged hypothetically. Cyclical theories in their legions, the intervention of Providence, degenerationism, and progressionism were some of the answers.

No such body of dated, chronologically arrangeable fact ever confronted the early naturalists, the collectors of beasts, birds, fishes, or flowers. Unlike man, the "lower" forms of life were not equipped with historical memory or the power of conveying to others what was remembered, or with historians to jot down events for the benefit or confusion of posterity. For a long time no evidence cropped up to suggest that any form, floral or faunal, was different, as the result of change, from any of its forebears. In Aristotle and Theophrastus, to be sure, an attentuated expression of belief in transmutation may be discerned. Similar opinions were occasionally expressed during the Middle Ages, in the sixteenth century by William Turner,[43] and by others who observed cases of hybridization, but never with enough conviction to undermine confidence in the fundamental immobility of the hierarchy of nature.

The break came in the eighteenth century with Leibniz and Erasmus Darwin. "The different classes of beings," said the great German philosopher, "the totality of which forms the universe, are in the ideas of God, who knows distinctly their essential gradations. . . . Accordingly men are linked with animals, these with plants, and these again with fossils. . . . All the orders of natural beings must necessarily form only one chain, in which the different classes, like so many links, are so closely connected . . . that it is impossible for sense or imagination to determine where any of them begins or ends; . . . [and all are] pregnant with a future state . . . [or] orderly change." Dr. Darwin went further, in comments that would have filled earlier zoologists and botanists with horror.[44] Anticipating Lamarck by fifteen years, he remarked that "when we revolve in our minds . . . the great changes, which we see naturally produced in animals after their nativity . . . we cannot but be convinced, that . . . all animals undergo perpetual transformations . . . and many of these acquired forms or propensities are transmitted to their posterity."[45] Nevertheless, during the lifetime of Linnaeus and for many decades thereafter a belief in the fixity of species was as respectable among scientists as a belief in God. God was still thought of as the personal fabricator of every kind of gnat and bramble. Recalling that Adam's chief responsibility in the Garden had been the naming of animals and plants, Linnaeus took pride in following the same calling. And while his passion for orderly classification and arrangement led him to follow hierarchical principles, he stoutly resisted the evidences and meaning of hybridization, and with them the idea of the mutability of species. It was Charles Darwin, generations later, who made the first clear statement implying the temporalization of the biological hierarchy and the envisagement of that converted series as a natural, ideal, logical, or conjectural history, based upon genealogical principles. From the most remote period in the history of the world, said he, "organized beings have been found to resemble each other in descending degrees, so that they can be classed in groups under groups. . . . I believe that the *arrangement* of the groups within each class . . . must be strictly genealogical in order to be natural. . . . Thus . . . the natural system [of classification] is genealogical in its arrangement, like a pedigree. . . ."[46]

BIBLIOGRAPHY AND NOTES

1. Bodin, *Method,* as cited, *passim;* Wallace K. Ferguson, *The Renaissance in historical thought: five centuries of interpretation* (Boston: Houghton Mifflin, 1948), *passim;* Robin George Collingwood, *The Idea of history* (Oxford: Clarendon Press, 1946), 57–61; Teggart, *Theory of history, passim.*

2. Niccolò Machiavelli, *Discourses on the first decade of Titus Livius,* translated from the Italian by Ninian Hill Thomson (London: Kegan Paul, Trench and Co., 1883), 475.

3. Bodin, *op. cit.,* 28.

4. J. L. Brown, *Methodus ad facilem historiarum,* 122–23.

5. Tillyard, *Shakespeare's history plays,* 9.

6. Casaubon, *Use and custome,* sig. N 3 r – N 3 v. See note 42 below for the views of Herodotus and Thucydides on "survivals."

7. Estienne, *A world of wonders,* sig. D 3 r.

8. Bodin, *Method,* 336, 338, 352, 358.

9. Purchas, *Pilgrimage,* To the reader; sig. Hhh 6 r. Perry Miller, *op. cit.,* 192.

10. Heylyn, *Cosmographie* (1652), *passim.*

11. Bacon, *Works,* III, 333–34.

12. Ralegh, *History,* sig. N 4 r.

13. Burnet, *Theory of the earth First Two Books,* 263.

14. Stillingfleet, *Origines sacrae,* sig. Aaaa 4 r–Ffff i v. Evidence of the use of another historical device, the "age and area theory," is to be found in students such as Purchas and Stillingfleet.

15. Antoine Banier, *The mythology and fables of the ancients explained from history* (London: A. Millar, 1739), vi, x, 10, 12.

16. Joseph François Lafitau, "The customs of American savages compared with the customs of primitive times," in *The idea of progress; a collection of readings,* selected by Frederick J. Teggart. Revised edition, with an introduction by George H. Hildebrand (Berkeley: University of California Press, 1949), 223–25.

17. Estienne, *op. cit.,* sig. C 3 r.

18. Le Roy, *Of the interchangeable course,* sig. Z 1 r.

19. Ralegh, *op. cit.,* Preface, sig. B 6 r.

20. Teggart, *The idea of progress; a collection of readings.* 176.

21. Robert Foster Jones, *Ancients and moderns: a study of the background of the battle of the books* (St. Louis: Washington University Studies, New Series, Language and Literature, No. 6, 1936), 248–51.

22. Kenneth E. Bock, *Acceptance of histories,* 63–65; Lansdowne, *Petty Papers,* II, 26; Bendyshe, "History of anthropology," 335.

23. D. C. Allen, *Legend of Noah,* 113.

24. Teggart, *Theory of history,* 76–78.

472

25. Stanley Arthur Cook "Genealogy," in *Encyclopedia Britannica,* 14th edition (1929), X, 101–02.

26. Homer, *The Iliad,* by A. T. Murray (London: Heineman, 1924) II, 95–110.

27. Ernest Hatch Wilkins, *The trees of the "Genealogia Deorum" of Boccaccio* (Chicago: The Caxton Club, 1923), *passim;* George Boas, *The major traditions of European philosophy* (New York: Harper, 1929), 111–12, 122–23.

28. Cornelia C. Coulter, "The genealogy of the Gods," in *Vassar Medieval Studies* (New Haven: Yale University Press, 1923), 336–40.

29. Bodin, *op. cit.,* 337; Joseph Ward Swain, "The theory of the four monarchies: opposition history under the Roman empire," *Classical Philology* 35 (1940) 1–21.

30. Le Roy, *op. cit.,* sig. G 2 v.

31. Sprat, *Royal Society,* 390.

32. Le Roy, *op. cit.,* sig. E 6 v; Rexmond C. Cochrane, "Bishop Berkeley and the progress of arts and learning; notes on a literary convention," *Huntington Library Quarterly,* 17 (1953–54), 229–50.

33. Virgil Keeble Whitaker, *Shakespeare's use of learning; an inquiry into the growth of his mind and art* (San Marino: Huntington Library, 1953), 8 and note 10. See also John W. Draper, "Jaques' 'Seven Ages' and Bartholomaeus Anglicus," *Modern Language Notes,* LIV (1939), 273–76; Don Cameron Allen, "Jaques' 'Seven Ages' and Pedro Mexia," *Modern Language Notes,* LVI (1941), 601–603.

34. Ferguson, *Renaissance,* 73–77.

35. Sprat, *op. cit.,* 55.

36. Quoted in Kennedy, *Jesuit and savage in New France,* 99.

37. Robert Allott, *Wits theater of the little world* (London: Printed by I.R. for N.L., 1599), sig. V 4 r. One of the earliest formulations of a technological series for the prehistoric period was made by Michele Mercato (1541–93), keeper of the botanic garden of Pius V. A collector of flints and arrowheads, he refers to flint knives among the Jews, and to the employment of stone for tools and weapons by the American Indians. He also thought the early inhabitants of Italy had used stone, which gave way to iron. (Murray, *Museums,* I, 28–29, 82.)

38. Mexia, *Foreste,* sig. D ii r.

39. Le Roy, *op. cit.,* sig. F 4 r.

40. Herman Schumacher, "The Historical School of economics," in *Encyclopedia of the Social Sciences* (New York: Macmillan, 1935), V, 371–76. An important anticipation of the technological series later adopted by the Historical School of economics is to be found in John Millar, *The origin and distinction of ranks* (1806). Here again economic origins were found in hunting and fishing, followed by taming and pasturing cattle, the introduction of tillage, and finally manufacture. See also Henry William Spiegel, "Theories of economic development, history and classification," *Journal of the History of Ideas,* 16 (1955), 518–39; William Burton Cherin, *The German Historical School of economics* (Unpublished Ph. D. Dissertation in the Department of Social Institutions, University of California, Berkeley, 1933), *passim;* M. J.

Herskovits, *The economic life of primitive peoples* (New York: Knopf, 1940), *passim;* Margaret T. Hodgen, *Change and history: a study of the dated distributions of technological innovations in England* (New York: Wenner–Gren Foundation for Anthropological Research, 1952), 23–31; Alexander Vucinich, "Soviet theory of social development in the early Middle Ages," *Speculum,* 26 (1951), 243–54; "Ages of the world," in Hastings, *Encyclopedia of Religion and Ethics,* I, 183–210.

41. Lovejoy, *Chain of being,* 242–87.

42. What kind of proofs were available to uphold the idea of the priority of the savage to man proper in the spatial hierarchy? Sheer belief was very important. Apart from this, and apart from Petty's argument, based upon the principles of plenitude and a meager use of correspondences, there were only two, or possibly three other "proofs." Two of these came dripping from the well of legend, and are to be found in the Book of Genesis and in the classical philosophers and historians. A third involves the use of similarities between non-European savagery and northern European barbarism before the latter's subjection to Christianization and the civilizing influences of the south — in other words, the use of survivals, antedating not only Tylor's but also all Renaissance "remains" and "remainders."

According to one legend, found in both Hebrew and Hellenic sources, man's career began in Paradise or a Golden Age, after whose tragic loss humanity was condemned to a succession of disasters, a continuous process of decadence or decline. Another theory inverted this process. Life in the beginning was far from golden, peaceful, or secure. It was a time of misery, deprivation, and discord, succeeded by a process of amelioration and improvement. Neither legend needed any documentation. For by the time the elements of each had been incorporated into Genesis by Moses, or into the *Odyssey* and the *Works and days* by Homer and Hesiod, each was already so old that it could be advocated on the authority of a simple declarative sentence.

The likenesses between these two Old-World theories are interesting, their differences significant. In both, the attainment of knowledge of the arts by man was climactic. In Genesis, where the first human condition was described as felicitous, man nevertheless was ignorant and destitute of the rudiments of culture. Placed in a garden planted to trees of every kind pleasant to see and useful for food, there was only one the fruit of which he was forbidden to taste. Eve violated the prohibition. Man and his helpmate were expelled from Paradise and subjected to a life of unremitting toil. On the relation of this painful denouement to the acquirement of the arts the author of the Book fails to make himself clear. But most commentators are certain that the corruption which began with the Fall was accelerated by Jubal's invention of the lyre and pipe, and by the technological skill of Tubal Cain.

According to Hesiod, the tribes of old likewise lived free from pain and travail. But despite warnings another inquisitive woman lifted the lid of a forbidden jar. Out rushed all the ills of the world, and man was plagued with them forever after. Concerning the part played by technological innovation in subsequent events, the Greeks, like the Hebrews, are not clear; or they allowed the story to be concluded in two different ways. When their imaginations were haunted by dreams of a lost paradise, they adopted Hesiod's version of the Prometheus legend, which inferred that man was not intended by the gods to possess and practice the arts and crafts, and that his degradation was precipitated by the gift of fire. When, on the other hand, man's first condition was thought to be only a little less degraded than that of the beasts, and when he was still ignorant of how to clothe himself with skins or to work metals with fire, the first culture-bringer or inventor was a savior, and the gift of the arts the first step in amelioration, improvement, and progress.

Meanwhile, the relation between Greek theories of social origins and Greek acquaintance with their savage contemporaries was very close. Anthropological information or misinformation was usually cited in support of each shade of any theory. Not unlike Renaissance Europe, the ancient Greeks relied for ethnological information upon observations made by merchants, explorers, and colonizers, whose voyages took them along the shores of the Mediterranean and to the east as far as India. In the eighth century B.C., Homer was thus made aware that there were several kinds of human beings: cave dwellers, nomads, and others, all more or less alien to the Greek political way of life. He was also told of several groups of barbarous peoples, known as the Abioi and Scyths. Beyond these, imagination peopled the fringes of the world with pigmies, half-dogs, big-heads, one-eyed folk, and other biological and ethnological marvels; and to these were added in good time the greater range of cultures known to Herodotus, a list which exceeded fifty in number. So great among the ancients became their absorption in strange, un-Greek practices, that many followed the example of Aristotle and made collections of savage customs. (Sikes, *Anthropology of the Greeks, passim.*)

But to Homer and others, the primeval way of life, which they took to be one of ease and abundance, possessed a spatial or geographical significance only. It was to be associated not with the past but with the present in certain remote spots on the earth's surface: at a great distance, among the furthermost of men, at world's end. Some of the peoples mentioned were frankly mythical or semi-mythical. They lived in legendary Elysiums in odd corners of the earth, or on the edges of the known world. In one happy land, far away in the extreme north, dwelt the Hyperboreans, a sacred race which, never ill, never old, lived forever surrounded by music, the voices of maidens, and the sounds of the lyre and flute. Across the sea in the furthermost south lived the blameless Ethiopians, proverbially the happiest of men; tall and beautiful in body; followers of nature rather than custom; peace-loving and uncontentious. Whether mythical or real, such qualities placed both of these peoples in the category of those living contemporaneously in the Golden Age.

The literature also mentions flesh-and-blood groups possessing similar qualities. These, in conformity with the idea that the first era was a golden one, are presented as superlatively happy, kind, innocent, and good. The milk-drinking Abioi, mentioned by both Homer and Aeschylus, were the best of men whose lands, untouched by plow or mattock, bore profusely. The Argippeans, known to Herodotus, were described as a sacred folk who, possessing no martial weapons, wronged no one but spent their lives settling the differences of others. Another tribe, the Tibareni, refused to engage in battle unless the hour, day, and place were announced beforehand; and their lives were filled with good humor and merriment. And so it went. (Lovejoy and Boas, *Primitivism, passim.*)

Just why any of these peoples should ever have come to be regarded as existing representatives of earliest man, and just how the Greek mind worked—whether in the actual sequence of ideas a conception of some savage culture was evolved first, to be reflected later in a theory of origins, or whether this order was reversed, with prior theory coloring subsequent interpretation of savage fact—cannot now be known with certainty. What seems to have happened was the failure to satisfy some Greek minds of Homer's purely geographical conception of savagery, and the substitution of another. It seems to be true that some one among the early Greeks, an historically-minded people, became conscious of a likeness between the ways of their own ancestors and the ways of known barbarians, or of a more historically significant type of correspondence than that usually employed during the Renaissance. They observed the perpetuation in contemporary Greek culture of ancient elements associated also with a barbarian and early condition, and at least inferred their documentary import.

The first inkling of the use of this type of correspondence, so far-reaching in its consequences for the history of thought, appears in the *Histories* of Herodotus in the fifth century B.C. Here, the old historian noted that from the earliest times, the Ionians had called the papyrus sheets (upon which they wrote) "skins," because formerly, for the lack of that valuable plant, they had used the leather of sheep and goats. "And even to this day," he remarked, but without drawing further inferences," there are many foreigners (barbarians) who write on such skins." (Herodotus, *op. cit.,* Bk. V, 58.)

To Thucydides, perhaps only a few years later, the parallel between contemporary barbarism and an early condition of the Hellenes had apparently become an accepted historical conclusion. He stated not only the principle involved but also the kind of evidence that could be brought forward to support it. "It should be explained," he said, "that in *early times* both the Hellenes and the Barbarians who dwelt on the mainland near the sea . . . turned to piracy. . . . For this occupation did not as yet involve disgrace, but rather conferred something even of glory. This is shown by the practice, even *at the present day,* of some of the people on the mainland, who *still* hold it an honour to be successful in this business. . . . On the mainland also the men plundered one another; and *even today* in many parts of Hellas life goes on under the same conditions." The habit of the mainlanders of carrying arms, even as Thucydides wrote, was taken by him to be evidence of the persistence of the ancient freebooting life common to both Hellenes and barbarians. (*Thucydides with an English translation by Charles Forster Smith* [London, 1921], I, v–vii.) Still later, the principle, with an illustration, was mentioned by Aristotle in the *Politics.* Some people, he said, raise the question of altering the ancestral laws, supposing that another law is better, is harmful, or is advantageous to states. It should be borne in mind, he answered, that the laws of ancient times were too simple and uncivilized: the Hellenes, for instance, used to carry arms and purchase their wives from one another. Since primitive men were just like ordinary foolish people, it is odd that we should consider abiding by their notions (Sikes, *op. cit.*, 11–12). From the fourth century onward, the Scythians seemed to serve the same purpose in Greek hypothetical history as the American Indians and Africans for cosmographers and philosophers in sixteenth-and seventeenth-century Europe. They portrayed to the eyes of living men the kind of life which purportedly had been lived by their first ancestors; and the adjectives applied to all three were "simple," "rude," "rustic." The Greeks were ready to concede that their ancestors were savages, though they made no serious effort to understand savage modes of action and thought (*Ibid.*, 22).

43. Charles Earle Raven, *English naturalists from Neckham to Ray; a study in the making of the modern world* (Cambridge: University Press, 1947), 131; *Synthetic philosophy in the seventeenth century; a study in early science, being the Herbert Spencer lecture for 1945* (Oxford: B. Blackwell, 1945); *Natural religion and Christian theology. The Gifford Lectures 1951, first series: Science and religion* (Cambridge: University Press, 1953), *passim;* Kenneth E. Bock, "Darwin and Social Theory," *Philosophy of Science,* 22 (1955), 123–34; "Evolution and the historical process," *American Anthropologist,* 54 (1952), 486–96.

44. Clark Emery, "Scientific theory in Erasmus Darwin's *The Botanic Garden,*" *Isis,* 33 (1944), 486–96.

45. Ernst Ludwig Krause, *Erasmus Darwin* [London: John Murray, 1879) 175–78, quoted by Emery, *op. cit.* 325].

46. Darwin, *Origin,* 411, 420, 422.

CHAPTER XII

Aftermath

"Every once in a while we come across phenomena that look back reproachfully at the man who is studying them and cause him to ask whether his way of thinking about things is entirely straight. That is what happened in atomic physics; and these experiences give to physicists a certain sense of humility as to the power of human thought, as to the things that are built into it by accident or custom. . . ."—J. ROBERT OPPENHEIMER

THE MIND'S FIDELITY to the old has left its mark on anthropology as well as on other fields of thought. Modern cultural investigation has taken up its abode in a mansion of organizing ideas already designed, built, and richly furnished with traditional assumptions more closely related to the early levels of Western theology and philosophy than to the data of human history. Nearly all the principles of inquiry employed by recent generations of scholars in Europe and elsewhere are of great age and authority. Were their genealogies consulted, it would become quickly apparent that their antecedents are to be found in the Judeo-Christian Scriptures, in the classics, or in the derivative Christian literature of the Middle Ages. Non-European folk have had no part in their formulation. Buddhist ideas, Muslim ideas, East Indian or Chinese ideas on cultural problems are unrepresented. Moreover, though European field workers, collectors of artifacts,

478

and describers of the nonliterate cultures of the world have done admirable work, their strength has resided less in doctrinal inventiveness than in industrious observation. There have been few Galileos, Newtons, or Einsteins in anthropology or sociology.

Unquestionably, these long-lived and prescriptive organizing ideas have often been a source of uneasiness to critical minds. Recent years have seen occasional debate over which among them are suited, in a modern European world, for the solution of problems stated in more or less modern terms. Evolutionary doctrine, for example, so long regarded as a welcome theory for imposing order upon the array of the world's cultures, has been widely attacked by men such as Graebner, Koppers, Rivers, and others. Diffusionism and functionalism have produced competing schools, a sure sign that a satisfactory procedure in this realm has not yet been reached.

While drift and imitation have abounded during the last three hundred years, little methodological tension appeared until very late or after the middle of the nineteenth century. It was then that Sir Edward Burnett Tylor fought so successfully to repel a flurry of degenerationism as applied to savagery, which would have wrecked the logical foundations of current development or evolutionary theory—and this, be it noted, not by suggesting some drastically new principle, but by the revival of the seventeenth-century theory of "remainders" or "remnants" in the nineteenth-century terminological dress of "survivals."

Soon after this episode, so triumphant for the maintenance of the *status quo ante,* modernism in ethnology and related subjects became expressed either in the collection of "survivals" in the spirit of Lang or Frazer, William Graham Sumner or Carl Jung; or, with the assistance of "survivals" and similarities, the elaboration of differing hierarchical, developmental, or evolutionary series by Bachofen, Lewis Henry

Morgan, Marx and Engels, Herbert Spencer, Sumner and Keller, and countless others, together with borrowings in adjoining fields by current idols such as Freud, Durkheim, and Veblen. "What has greatly influenced anthropology mainly to its damage," declared Alfred Kroeber out of his long experience, has not been Darwinism (actually a later arrival on the intellectual scene), "but the vague idea of evolution. . . . It became a common practice in social anthropology to 'explain' any part of human civilization by arranging its several forms in an evolutionary sequence . . . allowing each successive stage to flow spontaneously from the preceding . . . without cause. At bottom this logical procedure was astonishingly naïve."[1]

No old problem known to sixteenth- or seventeenth-century ethnology, and no old solution, has been wholly abandoned or become obsolete. If not preserved in the very structure of the language, it has passed out of fashion for a while only to return, more acceptable than ever; or more often, a minor idea, split off from its source and refreshed with a new terminology, has temporarily been given the limelight. Whether actively followed, or respectfully laid on the shelf, theories of earlier anthropologists are often presented not as false starts based upon faulty logic or infirm conceptualization, but as "current" schools of thought among which many anthropologists prefer to maintain a tolerant eclecticism. Seldom are such theories subjected to anything more exacting than courteous re-examination or minor modification. If, from time to time, changes have occurred in teaching or research methods, these changes have been temporary, not the products of dramatically original thought. Regrettably, as Agnes Arber has pointed out, "the general intellectual atmosphere of any given moment has an effect" on the choice of problems of investigation and their solution "which is compulsive to a humiliating degree. . . ."[2] Despite advances in biology, physics, and chemistry, students of man have seldom ventured beyond the conceptual schemes of previous generations. They have remained indifferent to the import of the history of ideas in their own fields of study, including its Europocentrism. Seldom, even by scholars of the most elevated philosophical and historical vision, have widely entertained and cherished principles been brought before the bar of conscious and rigorous judgment.

Should these old organizing principles, which seem already to have achieved immortality, be summarized again? Will still another brief statement clarify their influence upon the ethnological thought of the Enlightenment, of the Encyclopedists, and of the Scottish Moral Philosophers, to whom nineteenth- and twentieth-century social thought is so heavily indebted?

Well, whenever and wherever in Europe or around the Mediterranean the collection and description of the manners and customs of mankind have assumed considerable volume, or when new and astonishing types of human behavior have been called to the attention of Europeans, there and then the arresting problem of cultural diversity, or some one of its subordinate problems, has emerged—not only for the Hebrews, the Greeks, and the Romans, not only for the amateur anthropologists of the sixteenth and seventeenth centuries, but also for the moderns. There and then, an ancient and unexamined European monogenism, an ineradicable belief in the one-time physical and cultural uniformity of mankind has raised the question of how that original uniformity became splintered into existing diversity. This question and its answer were of course traditional. Save for tradition, Scripture, and logic, there is not one scintilla of evidence that the original culture of mankind was ever either uniform or not uniform; or, if uniform, was ever disevered into the array of existing cultures.

Reliable historical evidence begins ages after the primordial uniformity assumed. Nevertheless, diversity is the problem which underlies and qualifies the statement of all other problems in modern anthropology. Old Testament embellishments may have been rejected along the way. The argument may have been almost entirely secularized. But the form of the problem and solution remains recognizably the same as in the Book of Genesis.

More than this, the so-called problem of similarities in its several expressions is both logically and historically dependent upon a prior acknowledgment of that diversity in culture which is believed to have supervened upon an original uniformity. No question having cultural similarities as its subject matter could have been framed at all in absence from an assumption of an anterior onset of diversity after an initial period of uniformity. The recent admirable attempts by such men as Boas, Sapir, and others, to arrive at cultural time sequences by importing a chronology into the undated and undatable distributions of nonliterate similarities share the same logical or traditional background. Their solutions are tied by many threads of argument to earlier solutions of the problem of differences; and in many cases these innovations in method are based upon an "age and area" theory known to and used by seventeenth-century scholars.

During the last four hundred years, from the sixteenth to the twentieth century, anthropological inquiry, as expressed in the Scripturally inspired problem of cultural differences, has formulated or inherited three major types of solutions, each sanctioned by age and authority. With varying degrees of emphasis these solutions have been found along old avenues of diffusionist doctrine, environmental doctrine, or in doctrines of cultural change framed in long banks of time, and enriched with copious illustrations (not proofs) culled from the files of history, or documented with similarities.

Doctrines of social change may in turn be divided into three categories. One, now out of favor but likely to recover its influence with the increasing popularity of cyclical theories of history, is degenerationism. A second, once widely held but now dismissed as a result of the secularization of thought, is providentialism. A third, the official doctrine not only of anthropology but of many other fields of social inquiry, appears under several designations. In its most general sense, it may be referred to simply as progressivism. By some it has been called developmentalism. More recently in the study of society and culture it has been known as social evolutionism. Whatever the differences in nomenclature, however, this theory is to be noted, first, for its dependence upon earlier hierarchical notions of arrangement; and second, upon its inflexible Europocentrism, which has consistently belittled the mentality of the aborigine by installing him at the bottom of some scale of being. As Tylor once said almost a hundred years ago, the educated world of Europe and America has practically settled the matter "by placing its own nations at one end of the social series, and the savage tribes at the other, arranging the rest of mankind between these limits according as they correspond more closely to savage or cultural life."[3]

Obviously, these three theories of cultural change, including evolutionism, have never been more than hypotheses—verbal or conceptual descriptions of purported processes, involving value judgments among peoples and periods of history. And hypotheses they must remain. We have the word of many fine scholars that for them no scrap of confirmatory evidence was, is, or can be forthcoming. From the standpoint of scientific method, the intrusion of moral or ethical judgments into the making of hypotheses renders proof illusory. This scientific blunder has been pointed out again and again with reference to progressionist, developmental, and evolutionary social doctrines. Nevertheless, "proofs" are still tendered, and always take one form : the form of appeals to hierarchical arrangements of cultures, logically rather than historically arrived at. There have been countless constructions and varieties of unilinear cultural series, each differing from all others except in basic model and basic assumptions, and none subject to scientific corroboration. Nor are the diffusionists exempt from the same criticism. Even when the criteria for the historical interpretation of their geographical distributions of traits bear inspection, they have seldom made the transition from the contemplation of these to a general theory of change without resorting to the same errors. They, too, often fall back upon an unverifiable evolutionism inherited from their forefathers.[4]

Meanwhile, certain eighteenth- and nineteenth-century scholars succeeded with considerable adroitness in "harmonizing" these hierarchical, developmental, or evolutionary theories, so ignoring incongruities and expanding "testimonies" collected from Old and New World materials, so modernizing superficial terminologies, as to make old principles appear to be newly minted by original minds. Here one thinks of Voltaire during the French Enlightenment; of Adam Smith, Adam Ferguson, and other Scots; of Herder during the *Aufklärung,* of Engels and Marx in the mid-nineteenth century, and of Veblen in the twentieth. But apart from substituting the idea of progress for that of providence, or using the term development or evolution in place of progress; apart from the important amendment of diffusionist doctrine by the acculturationists, apart from a determined effort to collect and describe the existing customs of existing nonliterate peoples of the world, recent centuries have witnessed little that warrants the title of theoretical innovation.

Lest the above indictment appear too severe, let us review the ethnological work of a few major figures in the eighteenth century, especially those who have exerted a profound influence upon their successors in the nineteenth and twentieth.

In partial extenuation of the modern championship of the intellectually old and doubtful, let it be conceded that no investigator can undertake an inquiry *de novo*. He must have somewhere to start in his thinking. Nor can any inquirer lavish all of his working hours on the intricacies of methodological debate. On grounds such as these, organizing principles were, after all, no less necessary to the Enlightenment and to the scientific endeavors of the following two centuries than they were to the Age of Faith. The only question is, what principles were used, those that were old and fallible or those which were new and promising?

Though eighteenth-century thought has often been praised for its skepticism, or for its unwillingness to accept any theory based on Scriptural premises, the ethnology of the period was characterized by the consolidation of old solutions: first, by the environmentalists; second, by some of the diffusionists; and third, by the developmentalists or evolutionists. All of these carried with them to a greater or lesser degree the more imaginative glosses of the Old Testament commentators.

Among the environmentalists of the Enlightenment, the ancient explanation of cultural differences, revived by Bodin during the Renaissance as an alternative to Biblical diffusionism, was again called into service by Sir William Temple in the field of literary criticism, and was soon extended into other fields of social inquiry. Dating back, as a commonplace, to Plato, Aristotle, Hippocrates, Strabo, and Vitruvius, it appeared again in Temple's essay *Of poetry* (1690), to account for the alleged superiority of English comedy. By this critic, the British propensity for humor was explained as the result of the variability of the island climate, the native plenty of British soil, the ease of the King's government, and the liberty of his subjects to profess divergent opinions and factions. Plenty begets wantonness and pride, and wantonness, said Sir William, "is apt to invent and pride scorns to imitate. Liberty begets stomach or heart, and stomach will not be constrained. Thus we have more originals. . . ."[5]

Not long afterwards the Abbé Dubos expressed similar views, and so did Thomas Blackwell, the Greek scholar. According to the Abbé's *Reflexions critiques sur la poésie et sur la peinture,* published in 1719, natural influences controlled the development of the human spirit, either by encouraging or by retarding its expression. According to Blackwell, in his *Enquiry into the life and writings of Homer* (1735), the climate of Asia Minor was one of the favorable environmental features operating to produce the supreme genius of the great epic poet.[6] A few years later, in 1748, the same general theory was given a broader application by Montesquieu in his *Spirit of the laws.* In the discussion of law in its relation to external nature and slavery, servitude, civil or domestic, was said to depend upon climate or soil. "We ought not then to be astonished that the effeminacy of the people in hot climates has almost always rendered them slaves; and that the bravery of those in cold climates has enabled them to maintain their liberties." The goodness of the land in any country, it was said in the latter connection, "naturally establishes subjection and dependence. . . . Thus monarchy is more frequently found in fruitful countries, and a republican government in those which are not so. . . ."[7]

Similar ideas, accompanied with great collections of "proofs," or rather illustrations, were later advanced in every field of social investigation, including ethnology, throughout the nineteenth and twentieth centuries. The materials are massive and persuasive. But the critical literature is also well developed. Consequently, he who seeks in these latter days to gain acceptance for a theory of the geographical determinism of culture has a hard road to travel.

Among those committed to the revival of diffusionism during the Enlightenment, David Hume must be mentioned. Always skeptical of the purported high correlation between the manners of men and their external surroundings, Hume leaned heavily on the efficacy of contact among peoples as an explanation of differences. In his *Essay of national characters,* published in 1741, several years before the monumental *Spirit of the laws,* his readers were reminded that there were substantial faults in the environmental explanation of human behavior, that there were moral as well as physical antecedents to the appearance of cultural diversity. With reference to those said to be physical, Hume found reason to doubt the universality of their operation. The Greeks and Romans were charged with having mistakenly "confined genius and fine understanding to the more southern climates," whereas Hume took pride in pointing out that his own northern home had produced "as great men, either for action or learning," as the classical empires. Moreover, and this was a formidable obstacle to simonpure environmentalism, it could no longer be denied that while geographical stations remained unmodified, the manners of peoples could change "very considerably from age to age." Was this due to concomitant changes in climate, as some environmentalists wished to insist, or to changes in government and the intermixture of peoples? Hume leaned toward the latter, in effect sending his readers back to one of the theses of Moses. From this Scripturally descended theory of Hume's only the corollary of the degeneration of diffused traits was omitted, the original terminology and illustrations being altered. Ararat was no longer considered the center of the effective dispersion. Students were no longer urged to regard movement away from some tribal hearthside as a first step in cultural corruption. On the contrary, "if we run over the globe," said this historian and philosopher, "or revolve the annals of history, we shall discover everywhere signs of sympathy and contagion in manners, none of the influence of air or climate."[8]

Inspired in part by Hume, the theory of diffusion has since been granted a ready hearing among ethnographers, though occasional details in their thinking have more than once suggested the pervasive spell of the evolutionists. Here, for one we may recall Tylor, who tried so hard during his young manhood to deal even-handedly with both hypotheses. Also to be remembered, in the nineteenth and twentieth centuries, are men such as Graebner, Father Schmidt, Koppers, Wissler, Rivers, Elliot Smith, and Perry. Little need be said here to distinguish among their several views, but it may be observed that the theories of the English diffusionists Smith and Perry exhibit in their extreme pan-Egyptianism how any hypothesis of migration from a single center (derivable ultimately from the Mosaic model), can be done to death.[9] The members of the Kulturkreise School, historically trained and historically oriented, are important examples of a more promising treatment.

To some writers, the third theory of cultural change—progressionism, developmentalism or evolutionism—has seemed to emerge, unheralded and without precursory intimations, in eighteenth-century thought as something radically new and different from anything that had gone before. For this reason the men of the Enlightenment have often been fulsomely acclaimed. The late Ernst Cassirer was one who held them in exaggerated esteem. Through the philosophes, he declared, European thought sought hitherto unknown goals; it confronted the world with the fresh joy of courage and discovery, "daily expecting new revelations."[10] A similar tribute has also been paid to the Scots across the Channel. As philosophers, they have been designated as the "founders" of that empirical study of mankind which made economic, social, and institutional relationships definitive fields of inquiry with respect to the operation of natural and moral law. In short, the Enlightenment is often regarded as an extraordinary age in which

Nature's laws were first fully explained by the New Philosophy.

But what justification exists for celebrating the accomplishments of this period of Western thought, when, as Basil Willey has it, "biology had as yet revealed no disturbing ancestries, and man was still unassailed by anthropology and psychoanalysis"?[11] How judicious is an evaluation of an era which describes it "as the silver age of the European Renaissance," when "sanity, culture, and civilization had revived; and at last across the vast gulf of the monkish and deluded past, one could salute the ancients from an eminence perhaps as lofty as their own"?[12] Certainly, so far as ethnology was concerned, little that was noteworthy or original was accomplished. Praise of the Enlightenment, if grounded upon purportedly new insights into the manners of man, overlooks the persistent and uncritical use by still another company of learned men of the same old body of doctrine, the same old organizing ideas and principles.

Canon Raven has intimated that the French Encyclopedists were pretty dull fellows, whose best could never be anything more than an imitation of their predecessors.[13] Be that as it may, all scholars at the time, other than the diffusionists, relied upon hierarchical presuppositions known since the Middle Ages. As gifted propagandists, they were engrossed in the exposition and extension of this central organizing doctrine.[14] Professor Cassirer and other uninhibited admirers of the Enlightenment are at least in partial error. They have failed utterly to mark the dependence of their idols upon seventeenth-century ideas of which they were not the authors but the purveyors. Like many an earlier thinker who turned to an unmodified analogy with periods of organic rise and decline, these newer men fell under the influence of progressionism. They either sheared off the declining arm of the cultural cycle, replacing it with an ascending one; or, by underestimating the evidences of human corruption, they allowed this element in an older envisagement of cultural change to go by default. When this was done, Dr. Petty's earlier seventeenth-century view of the place of the savage in the chain of being was readily adoptable.

Logically speaking, if an eighteenth-century progressive or developmental sequence of cultural stages was to withstand criticism, then the theory of Adamic innocence and subsequent degradation, and the classical theory of the noble savage, would have had to be abandoned as acceptable conceptions of human beginnings. It is notable that all of this had already been accomplished before the Encyclopedists or their Scottish colleagues, were born. Neither Purchas in 1613, nor Heylyn in 1620, cherished any admiration for savagery. But both spoke of the natives of America, Africa, and the South Seas as examples of "originall mankind," "naturals," or "first men." Another early and even bolder advocate of the same position was Thomas Hobbes. It was his opinion in 1651 that European mankind had passed from a pre-political to a political condition. Nothing was said in the *Leviathan* about a Fall, recurrent degenerations, or recurrent historical cycles. Humanity had started at the bottom, and the bottom was a brutish condition of *bellum omnium contra omnes,* like that reportedly existing in savage America. Hobbes's influence upon subsequent thought was immense.

To observe the impact of seventeenth-century or earlier ideas upon the supposedly original but actually imitative scholarship of the early Enlightenment, the reader may turn among others, to the jurist Von Pufendorf (1632–1694), the satirist Bernard Mandeville (1670?–1733), the Jesuit missionary Père Lafitau (1670–1746), the statesman Turgot (1727–1781), the historian-philosopher Vico (1694–1724), and to Goguet (1716–1757) and de Brosses (1709–1777). To observe the borrowings of the men of the later Enlightenment from

these same sources the reader may refer among the Encyclopedists to Voltaire (1694–1778) and Condorcet (1743–1794);
among the Scottish moral philosophers, to Dugald Stewart
(1753–1828), Adam Smith (1723–1790), Adam Ferguson
(1723–1816), the putative founder of sociology, and Lord
Kames (1696–1782); among the Germans, to Kant (1723–
1808) and Herder (1744–1803), and many others.

Leaning markedly upon Hobbes, Samuel von Pufendorf
in *De jure naturae et gentium* (1672) was one of the more
famous seventeenth-century scholars, who asserted that the
condition of men in a presocial, savage condition had been
deplorable until societies "had been set on foot."[15] With a few
notable exceptions this was the common view. "All nations,"
said Bernard Mandeville in 1714, "must have had mean beginnings." Charles de Brosses in his *Du culte de dieux fétiches*
(1760) set forth the theory that fetishism, as exemplified by the
West African Negroes, was the fundamental and earliest form of
religious worship. This doctrine was not only widely disseminated but became, in the thirties of the nineteenth century
the slender "factual" foundation of Auguste Comte's primary,
fetishistic, or theological stage in the development of society.[16]
As early as 1724 in the Jesuit *Relations* Pére Lafitau testified
to the prevalence of the same view of savagery among the
clergy. Many of the missionaries who had written upon the
manners of their charges had described them as devoid of
religion, law, or any form of government. This description,
declared Lafitau, was false,[17] if it meant that they were also
beasts. His object was to demonstrate that they were merely
early and barbarous.

But logic is ever a frail reed against tradition, especially
tradition as embedded in Scripture. Though an hierarchical
and progressive plan might be wholly acceptable to a collector
faced with the simple spatial problem of arranging items on
cabinet shelves, it was not quite so easy to accept in a temporal

or historical version. The introduction of the existing savage as the first member of a series assumed to be ever advancing toward perfection was not in accord with the events of the Adamic period, the expulsion from Eden, and the onset of corruption. Accordingly, throughout the eighteenth century, when the idea of progress seemed to threaten the authority of other organizing ideas, there were frequent and tortuous efforts both to accept it and at the same time to reject it; to appear secular in secular company, but Scripturally orthodox as occasion seemed to demand. Turgot's was one of these. Disinclined in his *Discourse* at the Sorbonne to question the historicity of the Book of Genesis, he avoided that pitfall by skipping the first few chapters, and taking up the Mosaic story only after the Fall, or at the time of the dispersion after the Deluge. For him, as for others, these older and Biblical conceptions were still to be reckoned with, but sometimes by compromise or suppression.[18] Vico chose suppression, excluding all disturbing Hebrew materials from theoretical consideration in his theory of change. Goguet was less drastic. Not unlike Turgot, he chose compromise, admitting to argument only that part of the account in Genesis which dealt with post-Adamic, post-Deluge events susceptible to a progressionist interpretation.

The *Nuove scienza* (1725) of Giambattista Vico (1668–1744) is very instructive both as an illustration of the problem of handling Biblical tradition and as an essay in the secularization of hierarchical ideas. Essentially a philosophy of history—"an ideal eternal history traversed in time by the histories of all nations"—it stands today as an early and notable attempt to arrive at a statement of a universal historical process by the winnowing of the common in human experience from that which is nonrecurrent and irrelevant. Vico also made a somewhat important departure from the historiographical habits of fellow historians. Adopting the position that the historical process was one whereby human beings built up relatively permanent systems of behavior, called social institutions, he made these institutional systems, rather than the flashy careers of princes and potentates, the subject matter of his inquiry. How had the law, marriage, government, and language, in all their diverse forms, come to be as they were? This was his central question. By virtue of concentrating his attention upon these institutional entities; by trying to form a clear idea of what was actually involved in what he regarded as the historical method; by extending his investigations backward into remote and remoter times; and by comparing histories or periods of history, he became convinced that the sequence of cultural epochs in all historical areas, the destinies of social institutions in all areas, exhibited a similar character and a similar temporal order. "Our New Science," he declared, "must be a history of the form of order," universal and eternal, and bound together by a chain of causes. His science of history was thus "far removed from history itself." The series of social forms possessed for him attenuated but familiar and unavoidable hierarchical and progressive implications.

Incidentally, Vico was conspicuous among the very few students of the cultural hierarchy who ever attempted to recover, not only social origins, but all the members of the developmental series. In so doing he became an advocate of the old-fashioned triadic division of the cultural past, an economical procedure frequently used, and later embodied in Auguste Comte's *Cours,* by which it was transmitted to twentieth-century sociology. But in his *New science,* the rule of three was sometimes carried to ludicrous extremes. It was impressed upon every possible sequence, and upon some that were impossible. "The nations," Vico declared, "will be seen to develop . . . through three kinds of natures. From these natures arise three kinds of customs; and in virtue of these customs three kinds of natural laws of nations are observed; and in consequence of these laws three kinds of civil states or commonwealths are established. And in order that men, having reached the stage of human society, may . . . communicate with each other . . . three kinds of languages and as many characters are formed; and in order that they may on the other hand justify them, three kinds of jurisprudence assisted by three kinds of authority and three kinds of reason in as many judgements."[19] According to the Italian philosopher-historian, there were three poetic characters in Greek mythology, Vulcan, Mars, and Venus; there were three ages of poets before Homer; and fathers could sell their children three times. Not content with this, he preserved the three-fold symmetry of his plan of organization throughout every step of his analysis. A classifier of historico-cultural data rather than a narrative political historian, he observed "that all nations, barbarous as well as civilized, though separately founded because remote from one another in time and space, keep these three human customs: all have some religion, all contract solemn marriages, all bury their dead."[20] A broad law of nations, proceeding through three stages, governed aristocratic commonwealths, popular commonwealths, and monarchies alike.[21]

Of more substantive interest, especially since Vico emphasized the problem of the reconstruction of the earliest and most obscure period of human temporal experience (or the first member of his triads), was his advocacy of what he misconceived as a new form of documentation, the place he allotted in his many three-stage sequences to ancient and existing savagery, and the theoretical relationship thus suggested between savagery, early European man, and the acceptance of progressionist doctrine. Indeed, some of Vico's supposed originality arose from his familiarity with classical literature, and the free use that he made of it, in conjunction with materials on savagery, to illuminate a supposedly primordial condition of culture. As a student of philology and religion, he was sensitively aware of the documentary potentialities of language and myth. The vulgar tongues of European rustics, created in a remote past before refinements had been imposed, were freighted, in his judgment, with potential evidence of what that past had been like. By using philological procedures, especially by examining the speech of country people or the folk, he proposed to recover the kind of life led by all peoples when the world was young, or when the peoples were first forming their languages. The same was true of myth. Mythologies were the civil histories of the first nations. Composed by natural poets, they presented in fragmentary outline the political structures of early societies.[22]

After this, however, Vico adopted a more familiar method. Though it might well be true that whenever men found it difficult to form an idea of ancient and unknown things they judged them by what was familiar and near at hand,[23] that procedure, he felt sure, should be checked with "fact." Hence it is that we find this Italian historian proceeding in the opening decades of the Enlightenment, in a manner already made familiar as early as the sixteenth century. For purposes of proof or documentation, comparisons were made, first, between the early institutional forms recovered or documented by means of language or myth, and with the practices of European tribalism as reported by Caesar, Tacitus, and Procopius; then, second, with the behavior of existing savages, as observed in the Americas by Lescarbot, Oviedo, and Acosta, in Guinea by Van Linshooten, in Siam by Joost Shouten, and in Virginia by Harriot. Over and over again it was said that the rude and simple nations "help us to a much better understanding of the founders of the gentile world."[24] The common, if erroneous, assumption that savages were culturally identical at all times and in all places, was again put to work. For, said Vico, the first of all men, like his nonliterate contemporaries, did their thinking under the "strong impulsion of violent passions, as beasts do";[25] and we, of the modern European present, possessors now of humane and refined natures, are descendants of the same kind of wild and bloodthirsty creatures.[26]

Biblical history meanwhile was a source of acute embarassment to Vico. It could neither be woven logically into his secular historico-philosophical system, nor be comfortably left out. In the end, therefore, although there is some treatment of some of the episodes narrated in Genesis, although in piety he lost no opportunity to adduce proofs from gentile sources of the reliability of Jewish historians, the whole early Hebrew period, together with the irreconcilable episode of the degeneration of Adamic man, was more or less reverently set on one side as irrelevant to generalizations concerning the progressiveness of the remainder of human history. Jewish historical experience, as the outcome of the direct intervention of God, could not be regarded as subject to the laws of secular history, or so Vico made himself believe. Its course was unique. Harmony between the historically sacred and the historically profane was achievable, but only by giving to each a respected place of its own.[27]

As for Vico's role among the progressionists of the eighteenth century, some commentators will have it that he was an adherent of the theory of historical cycles—a claim which can be supported by isolated sentences here and there. In accordance with this theory, it must be acknowledged that for him, as a classifier rather than a narrator of history, certain periods had a general character and an order of appearance which was repeated from place to place and time to time. But decline, that element usually inseparable from cyclical theory, was never stressed. The cyclical movement in the *Nuove scienza,* as Collingwood says, was never a mere rotation; it was a spiral.[28] History never fatuously repeated itself. It was always creating novelties. It came around to each new phase in a form different from any that had appeared before. Hence Vico was a progressionist.

Another eighteenth-century figure, whose work provides an illuminating example of the conflict between the tormented conscience of the believer and the secular philosopher of history, is the French jurist and historian Antoine Yves Goguet (1716–1758). Far less original than Vico's *Nuova scienza,* indeed a potboiler by comparison, this work published a quarter of a century later, in 1758, was described as "un des bons écrits du temps . . . plein d'érudition, de recherches, et d'une critique aussi judicieuse que profonde." Actually commonplace, but widely read and translated, it may be taken as even more instructive concerning the general level of educated European opinion at this time than its Italian predecessor.

Goguet states frankly in his preface that he is interested in recovering the earliest condition of human beings, and in this only. He is one among many scholars who, believing in progressionism, and admitting the desirability of demonstrating it with the reconstruction of the whole progressive series, nevertheless restricted his attention to social origins. The book is entitled *The origin of laws, arts, and sciences, and their progress among the ancient nations,* and is completely orthodox in that it made no effort, such as was made in Vico's work, to exclude Hebrew or Biblical history. Goguet merely insisted with a straight face that since Moses had chosen to inform posterity only of those grander events which it seemed necessary for mankind to know, and had suppressed all others, "which would have served only to gratify an idle curiosity," he had included too little in Genesis to justify a modern reference to the Adamic or antediluvian period. The book starts, therefore, with the days just following the Flood, "as in some sort the first age and infancy of the world," and proceeds to a consideration of life and knowledge among the ancient historical peoples : the Hebrews, first, the Babylonians, the Assyrians, the Medes,

Lydians, Phoenicians, Egyptians, Greeks, and finally the Romans. This constituted for Goguet a progressionist study of origins. All the discoveries made by these peoples "belong entirely to the ages included in this work"; and these discoveries "undoubtedly comprehend the origin of laws, arts, sciences and their first improvements." [29]

Concerning the adequacy of the documentation of the postdiluvian period of social origins, Goguet felt no misgivings. Mankind, he said, is not "condemned to the hard necessity of fluctuating in perpetual doubt, about the principal facts which have been transmitted to us by history and tradition. The most important events, such as the formation of nations, the origins of laws, arts, and sciences, are known." [30] Faithful, therefore, to the common practice, he availed himself of the customary kind of "evidence." When he found himself destitute of hard, dated facts and historical monuments, he turned without hesitation to what had been said by ancient and modern writers on the manners of savage nations. These, too, were "ancient" in the historiographical sense he wished to employ. Like others before him in the sixteenth and seventeenth centuries, or while the earlier explorations to the New World were under way, Goguet felt sure that these descriptive materials could be made to contribute clear and just ideas of the state of the first wandering colonies of the Noachidae, immediately after the confusion of tongues and the dispersion of families. He regarded narratives concerning the American Indians as extremely valuable. We may judge the state of the ancient world, he said, "by the condition of the greatest part of the New World when it was first discovered." He often compared the reports of modern travelers with those of ancient historians, "and mingled their narratives." Like Vico and others both before and since, he declared that they mutually supported one another. They laid a solid foundation for everything he had to say concerning social origins and the progress of the human understanding.[31]

From the second half of the eighteenth century, and well into the nineteenth and twentieth, the same objectives prevailed, except for occasional examinations by way of environmentalism or diffusionism. That half-century was once again a period of reliance upon hierarchical and related ideas, as well as one of secularization. As a result, Genesis, with its accounts of the Creation, the Fall, and the Deluge, was rejected out of hand. Nevertheless, anthropological thought continued to take its inspiration from concepts which were nothing other than disguises of what had been discarded. Moreover, when developmental series of cultures were presented, less and less evidence was produced, even of the commonest and most questionable sort. Less and less time was allotted to the detailed recapitulation of the whole series of stages in the conjectural cultural sequence; and less also to the assemblage of savage materials intended to shore up proposed theories of social and institutional "origins." Where once the hierarchical and evolutionary hypothesis had demanded at least some argument and a solid body of "testimony" to ensure the acceptance of its astonishing inferences, these were now taken for granted. Students dealt no longer with an extremely difficult and unsolved historical problem, but with finding a few illustrations whose attenuation was in itself symbolic. The French Encyclopedists, in some respects so skeptical, constitute one illustration of this perfunctory and naïve type of inquiry which adhered to precarious intellectual positions without intellectual discomfort. The Scottish moral philosophers, with their offspring the sociologists, were another in the nineteenth and twentieth centuries of the many followers of each school.

Caught in a revolutionary situation which played its part

in the religious reformation, the Encyclopedists contended that an ancient and powerful clerical tradition had obstructed intellectual advancement. Since the theological postulates of preceding generations were denied intellectual value, assumptions in ethnological reflection thought to stem from them, were considered "sheer error, due to the unscrupulous and calculating hypocrisy" of the priesthood. In attacking this fortress of dogma and superstition, an attempt was made to replace every presupposition recognized as Scriptural or theological with another presumably more in harmony with natural science. For one example, the supernatural mission of the Hebrews was denounced. The true authors of civilization, said these detectors of error, were the Egyptians. Recurring often to a much earlier and ever-attractive hypothesis of the westward or northward diffusion of civilization, French savants insisted that civilized achievement had taken a meandering geographical course, from the cities of the Nile and the coasts of Phoenicia to Greece and Rome, and thence to northern Europe. Recent discoveries in geology, paleontology, and chronology, in so far as they seemed to possess an anti-Scriptural bias, were also of absorbing interest. By means of these and other borrowings from their predecessors during the Renaissance, the Book of Genesis was thought once and for all to have been laid to rest.

But unfortunately, French intellectuals, their Scottish colleagues and German sympathizers were far less successful in abstaining from an enveloping Scriptural tradition than they fondly supposed. Knowing little of the permeating theological sources of ethnology, they permitted much of the Bible to slip through their fingers and back into their theories. Omitting the more obvious theological principles enunciated by Moses, they unwittingly accepted the less obvious. Among the latter was their wholehearted adoption once more of an hierarchical type of explanation of the phenomenon of cultural diversification, slightly transfigured as the plan of Nature rather than of God. Apart from ideas such as these, the convictions of the Encyclopedists are not easily distinguishable from those of other progressionists. The *Encyclopédie* contains relatively little discussion of the process of cultural change itself. But when it does, the *notions directrices* are the same. There is the same developmental, genetic arrangement of peoples and nations, with the same Europocentrism; there is the same stress upon the description of social origins; and the same use of travelers' reports to substantiate the assumption that existing savagery is representative of the culturally low, brutal, and early.

Belief in the villainy of savagery as a whole, and hence in the propriety of regarding any representative of the nonliterate group of mankind as an acceptable illustration of the first stage of development, became so self evident that little effort was expended in amassing documentary materials. Not only was savagery seldom defined, but it was assumed without argument to belong on the lowest rung of the cultural ladder; and all the origins of civilized institutions were said to be found in some phase of its deplorable activities.

What else was there to say? What other alternatives were there? There were none.

Two men among the Encyclopedists, honored ever since the eighteenth century, may be taken as examples of this practice. One was Voltaire (1694–1778); the other was Condorcet (1743–1794).

The late Professor Cassirer, misled by his exaggerated conception of the originality of the period, praises Voltaire for his contribution to the so-called eighteenth-century "conquest" of the historical world. Though merely a popularizer of Newton in the natural sciences, he is applauded as an innovator in history, sociology, and ethnology. According to the German philosopher, the *Essai sur les moeurs* (1748) is nothing less than "an original and independent conception, a new methodological plan." With the publication of this work the center of gravity in European thought shifted overnight from "political history to cultural history by conscious methodological intention."[32] Thereafter, all great works of the eighteenth century were written "under the influence of this achievement."

More correctly, Voltaire's essay, written for Madame Chatelet about 1740, was neither original nor profound. It was slight and superficial, merely repeating many of the questions and conclusions of earlier times. What of the peoples of the Near and Far East, he cried, that "nursery of the arts," from whence everything enjoyed by European civility had been derived? This was patently not a new thought peculiar to the Enlightenment; it was merely a reiteration of a reiteration. What of the old inhabitants of Europe, known and described by Caesar and Tacitus as existing in a condition similar, and in many respects inferior, to that of brutes? The implication of this question was not new. It was part of the same tottering logical bridge over which many others had arrived at the assumption that the cultures of existing savagery, like those of the earlier tribal inhabitants of Europe, were brutal, old, and possessed of documentary qualities. Should not the customs of all peoples, whether highly advanced or lowly, be considered a part of universal history? No doubt they should. But this view had been a commonplace in European thought long before Voltaire lived.

In a later and shorter work entitled *La philosophie de l'histoire,* published in 1765[33] and afterwards affixed to the *Essai,* Voltaire again showed himself to be completely subservient to conventional ideas. He began by exclaiming that nothing could be more interesting than racial differences among men—a fruitful subject. But from this he turned without explanation to other exclamatory remarks upon the terrifying antiquity of the nations of Asia, a brief consideration of the religious ideas of the "first" men, and a few questions relating to savagery: What did the condition involve? Was it the outcome of degeneration? Where did the Americans come from? All of these may have been new to his readers but were stale elements in the literature. There is not one word in the fifty-odd pages of the *Philosophy of history* which deals technically with that subject or adds a new methodological insight.

Though pervaded with all of the hopefulness and apocalyptic enthusiasm of the Enlightenment, Condorcet's widely known little book, the *Esquisse d'un tableau historique des progrès de l'esprit humain* (1793) is only a little better. It may be said in his favor that, unlike Voltaire but much like Vico, Condorcet was one of the few progressionists in either the eighteenth or nineteenth century who took the trouble to distinguish with clarity among the several members of the hierarchy of cultures along which man's inevitable development was destined to lead on to a glorious future. In so doing, he expanded the usual three stages to nine and departed from convention by naming all and submitting all to a short description.

Where did the author get them? This is a question of some interest to a student of the history of scientific method in the social studies. Concerning the first four stages—horde society, pastoral society, agricultural society, and its successor initiated by the invention of hieroglyphics—he made no claim to direct information, apart from a vague reference to unnamed savage tribes and the mention of travelers' reports. He confessed that for this part of the series he had been obliged to guess.[34] Obviously, had he retraced the history of his thinking, he would have found that his guess was a memory; that the same series had been frequently proposed in the sixteenth and seventeenth centuries, if not before; and that the descriptive material employed by him to give it cultural substance had been part of the mental furniture of most educated men for more than two hundred years. After these first four stages, the picture began "to take its coloring in great measure from the series of facts transmitted . . . by history." But here, said the author, it became necessary to be selective [a dangerous procedure]; to choose data from the experience of a wide range of different nations, and at the same time to compare and combine them, "to form the supposed history of a single people [sic], and delineate its progress." The final series of five stages was therefore of familiar European provenience. It included "the progress of the human mind in Greece; the decline of learning and its restoration; the progress of the sciences to the period when philosophy threw off the yoke of authority; and the time of Descartes to the formation of the French Republic." Condorcet was wholly Europocentric. There is no suggestion of the participation in human progress of any of the Eastern or Asian nations.[35]

When we turn from the Encyclopedists to their contemporaries across the Channel, the same idea system is discernible, but with a difference. Like their French colleagues, the Scottish moral philosophers were committed to hierarchical ideas, to the determination of social origins in the usual way, and to the construction of developmental series. To all this some of them added a certain insight into method and a desire to make its elements more explicit. The man chiefly responsible for this signal departure was Dugald Stewart, whose sagacious comments on *conjectural* history, as he wisely called any hierarchical cultural series, appeared in his study of the life and works of Adam Smith, published in 1810.

As a moralist and progressionist, Smith began very early in his career, said Stewart, to make use of the currently popular methodological approach to the problem of cultural differences by planning to write a "general history of human improvement." In this he proposed not only to account for the origin of arts and sciences, but to show "by what chain" [sic] human minds had been led "from their first rudiments to their last and most refined improvements." This project, set up in a familiar progressionist frame of reference, was started in his early essay on the *Origin of language,* appended in 1761 to the second edition of *The theory of moral sentiments.* Writing with his usual abstractness and independence of evidence, Smith stated in his first sentence that "the assignation of particular names to denote particular objects . . . *would probably be* [sic] one of the first steps towards the formation of language." In his second sentence, the conventional and conjectural argument from nonliterate origins begins. "Two savages," said he, "who had never been taught to speak, but had been bred up remote from the societies of men, would naturally begin to form that language by which they would endeavor to make their mutual wants intelligible to each other. . . . The particular cave whose covering sheltered them from the weather, the particular tree whose fruit relieved their hunger, the particular fountain whose water allayed their thirst, would first be denominated by the words *cave, tree, fountain*" in their primitive jargon.

How could Smith know this? Smith did not say. Stewart did.

This essay, said Smith's expositor, was one of "great ingenuity," and deserved attention less on account of the opinions it contained "than as a specimen of a particular sort of inquiry," which, so far as Stewart knew, was "entirely of modern origin." Something akin to it, continued Stewart, could be traced in all of Smith's other works, whether moral, political, or literary; and "on all these subjects he . . . exemplified it with the happiest success." For "when in such a period of society as that in which we live, we compare our intellectual acquirements, our opinions, manners, and institutions with those which prevail among *rude* tribes, it cannot fail to occur to us as an interesting question, by what *gradual* steps the transition has been made from the first simple efforts of *uncultivated* nature, to a state of things so wonderfully artificial and complicated." On most of these subjects, Stewart acknowledged, "very little information is to be expected from history; for long before that stage of society when men begin to think of recording their transactions, many of the most important steps of their progress have been made." When, therefore, in examining the records of the past, "we cannot trace the process by which an event *has been* produced, it is often of importance to be able to show how it *may have been* produced by natural causes." Thus, in the instance of Smith's *Dissertation on the origin of language,* which had suggested these remarks, Stewart observed that "although it is impossible to determine with certainty what the steps were by which any particular language was formed," yet if it could be shown, by logical analysis "from the *known* principles of human nature, how all its various parts *might* gradually have arisen," the mind was not only to a certain degree satisfied, but a check was given to indolent philosophy.[36] [Italics added.]

So much for Adam Smith's conception of the origin of language in the fancied activity of unspecified nonliterate peoples; and so much for Dugald Stewart's shrewd, respectful, but historically uninformed analysis of the procedure which Smith employed. Taken together they indicate that the provisional or tentative verb form *it may have been* had become the sign manual of conjectural history as a formally accepted procedure of the Scottish school, and was transmitted to its direct and legitimate offspring in the social sciences of today. Since neither the philosophes nor the moral philosophers could think of a better approach to the problem of cultural diversification, it was assumed out of hand that none could be found. In 1811–12, when Stewart's analysis was published, the procedure of conjectural history, involving an hierarchical arrangement of elements interpreted as either progressive or evolutionary, was recognized as invalid for the determination of *what was*; but even that clever man who could see its faults had no alternative to suggest. Apart from Stewart's exceptional perspicacity in recognizing the principles of the favored historiographical or hierarchical method, apart from an even more frugal use of evidence, none of the Scottish school, with the notable exception of the diffusionist David Hume, departed one jot from the hierarchical assumptions made by their French colleagues.

As illustrations of the use of the same procedure in later social theory, two other members of the same school of thought may also be mentioned. The first was Adam Ferguson (1725–1816), often regarded as a "father" of modern sociology; the other was Henry Home, Lord Kames (1696–1782). Since 1930, when Ferguson was recalled from oblivion as an eighteenth-century founder of social theory,[37] his *Essay on the history of civil society,* published in 1766, has generally been regarded as more sociological than ethnological. And so it is. But to a certain extent this emphasis distorts his fundamental argument and method. For whatever his excursions into the hazier precincts of sociological speculation, his term "civil society" contains several important ethnological overtones. For one thing, it implies the acceptance of that already well-known evaluation of all existing cultures which gave to "civility," or European culture, the most exalted place in an already assumed hierarchical series; and it also affirms an hierarchical arrangement of nations as the order of progressive change in past time.

There is no doubt of his reliance upon the idea of the chain of being, transmuted by the chemistry of ideas into a developmental or evolutionary series of cultures. In the variety of things, he wrote, "we observe the gradation of excellence displayed on a scale of great extent. The parts rise above one another by slow and almost insensible steps. That man is placed at the top of this visible scale has never been questioned."[38] In order to account for the existing array of differing peoples he turned without hesitation to the several principles of organization underlying what Dugald Stewart was soon to call conjectural history; and in his adherence to a process of change operating within in this hierarchy, Ferguson comes very close, as Professor Whitney points out, to a theory of the evolution of species.[39]

Not unexpectedly, one result of Ferguson's efforts was a theory of social origins, based upon slender descriptions of a few nonliterate peoples. The first member of his hierarchical and progressive series was reconstructed by the examination of a rude existing folk, namely, the ever-useful American Indians. Convinced that what was already known of living Red Men was true also for historically earliest man, Ferguson remarked confidently that "it is in their present condition, that we are to behold, as in a mirrour, the features of our own progenitors."[40] But the reports on the Indians read by him, or the sources employed to accomplish this astonishing historical feat, were surprisingly few. Like many others of his generation, he failed to regard it as necessary to amass great bodies of "savage" evidence, since its interpretation was already known. The most frequently cited travelers were Lafitau, Charlevoix, Colden, a *History of the Caribees* [author unknown], D'Arvieux, Chardin, and our old friends the thirteenth century missionaries to the Mongols, Carpini and Rubruck.

Another sign of Ferguson's traditionalism was the formulation of several three-member progressive series. One of these, composed of the already commonplace sequence of savagery, barbarism, and civility, he held to be supported by Tacitus' description of the German tribes in the first century, and by the thirteenth-century descriptions of the Tartars.[41] A second suggested triad recalled to life the timeworn technological succession of hunters, shepherds, and farmers. The third combined these two series with a vaguely realized conception of the development of the institution of property.

The work of Henry Home, Lord Kames, though written in much the same theoretical vein, was more voluminous than Ferguson's and marked by an uncomfortable awareness of logical and historical difficulties. That awareness, discussed in his *Sketches of the history of man* (1774), not only made him an unhappy environmentalist and polygenist, but led him to subscribe to the doctrine that God had created the differing races of men in order that they might better adapt themselves to the various geographical and climatic conditions encountered during the course of the Dispersion. Indeed, had logic rather than methodological convention always remained Kames's guide, this theory would have barred him forever from the company of progressionists, or from among those who aspired to the reconstruction of a uniform, unilinear, hierarchical history of mankind. But by using the device of endowing all men, wherever they happened to be created, with the same powers of understanding, or with the same capacity for improvement, logic (at least for him) could be brushed aside. He proceeded thereafter, unembarrassed, to the delineation of a sequence of uniform stages in the development of the arts, as man everywhere passed from hunting and gathering to fishing, from fishing to pastoral pursuits, and from pastoral pursuits to agriculture. As Professor Bock has pointed out, "We are also indebted to Kames for making explicit the fact that before the comparative method can be employed a principle of arrangement that is itself a theory of history must be adopted."[42] The Comparative Method, as it came to be employed by Kames and many others in eighteenth-century ethnology, despite its good name in the natural sciences was not a means for obtaining knowledge. It was merely a device for illustrating that which—as based upon a pyramid of value judgment—was ultimately unprovable.

The Scots were perhaps more elegant than the French in their elucidation of doctrines, and less addicted to propagandist devices; but all of them—Hutcheson, Smith, Ferguson, Monboddo, Kames, and Dunbar, as well as a host of their followers elsewhere in Europe—were progressionists, with all that term had come to imply. Few were harassed by doubts. All were perfunctory in assembling "evidences" of their logically derived "historical" findings. None made substantive departures in methodological ideas. The idea of a unilinear series of stages, hierarchically arranged and "leading up to the present European society seemed to explain so much . . . and was so agreeable to the high European estimate of European achievement, that recalcitrant facts contradicting the theory were easily disposed of as exceptions or accidents or special effects."[43]

The main difficulty for these scholars as for all social evolutionists was to hit upon that nonliterate people which was demonstrably lowest, nearest the beast, and hence oldest. On this matter agreement has never been achieved. In an earlier period of ethnological controversy, now beginning to be forgotten, Cook, Fitzroy, and Wallis were said to be in favor of the Fuegians, as was true also for Karl Marx and Charles Darwin; "Burchell maintained that the Bushmen [were] the lowest. D'Urville voted for the Australians and Tasmanians; Foster said that the people of Mallicolo 'bordered the nearest on the tribe of monkeys'; Owen [inclined] toward the Andamaners; others . . . supported the American Root-Diggers; and one French writer even [suggested] that monkeys were more human than Laplanders."[44] Nor has the controversy been resolved by geographical discovery. As Sir John Linton Myres pointed out some years ago, a matrilineal theory of social origins followed hard upon the exploration of matriarchal areas of social organization in southern India, Africa, and

North America, only to be displaced by the discovery of totemistic societies in other regions.

Certainly no more need be said to impress upon the reader that in all of these undated, logical, ideal, evolutionary, and conjectural philosophies of history there are unmistakable overtones and reminders of the medieval chain of being, of the medieval conceptual inventory and schematization of things. In its earlier forms this inventory was no more genealogical or historical than a telephone book, or a series of beetles in a museum cabinet. Though pious commentators might suggest that the enchainment constituted the pathway of ascent to or descent from the divine, they did not prove thereby that each member of the scale was in any sense fathered by or causally related to a member just preceding. The medieval mentality avoided this trap by using the happy device of insulating its ideas one from another.

It should be clear also that when the logically arranged spatial hierarchy found its way into the seventeenth-century inquiries of Dr. William Petty, and later into the work of social scientists in the nineteenth and twentieth centuries, it lost none of its scholastic, philosophical, or conjectural characteristics. Its use does not result in the construction of dated histories of human institutions, or provide the assurance which resides in the use of dates. The Comparative Method is a fine piece of circular, Europocentric reasoning which rejects the nonliterate tribes as on a par, mentally and morally, with the peoples of Western Civilizations. What would have happened to such a body of doctrine had a prescient mind foreseen the ultimate literacy and westernization of the nonliterate peoples of Asia, South America, and Africa, it would be hard to say.

BIBLIOGRAPHY AND NOTES

1. Alfred Louis Kroeber, *Anthropology* (New York: Harcourt, Brace, 1923), 8.

2. Agnes Arber, *The mind and the eye: a study of the biologist's standpoint* (Cambridge: University Press, 1954), 7–8. See also Leslie Stephen, *History of English thought in the eighteenth century* (London: Smith, Elder, 1876), I, 1–19.

3. Quoted in David Bidney, *Theoretical anthropology* (New York: Columbia University Press, 1953), 193–94; Wilhelm Koppers, *Primitive man and his world picture* (London: Sheed and Ward, 1952), 2.

4. Paul Radin, *The method and theory of ethnology: an essay in criticism* (New York: McGraw-Hill Book Company, 1933), 76, 166.

5. Quoted in Wellek, *English literary history*, 32.

6. *Ibid.*, 55.

7. Charles Louis, Baron de Secondat, Baron de Montesquieu, *The spirit of the laws,* translated from the French with corrections and additions by the author (London: J. Nourse and P. Vaillant, 1750), I, 377–78; 386.

8. David Hume, *Essays moral and political* (London: Henry Frowde, 1904), 209 214.

9. Koppers, *op. cit.*, 16–17.

10. Ernst Cassirer, *The philosophy of the Enlightenment,* translated by Fritz C. A. Koelln and James P. Pettegrove (Princeton: University Press) 4–5; Nelly Noémie Schargo, *History in the Encyclopédie* (New York: Columbia University Press, 1947); Réne Hubert, *Les sciences sociales dans l'Encyclopédie; la philosophie de l'histoire et le probleme des origines sociales* (Paris: F. Alcan, 1923); Lynn Thorndike, *"L'Encyclopédie* and the history of science," *Isis,* 6 (1924), 261–86.

11. Basil Willey, *The eighteenth century background* (London: Chatto and Windus, 1940), 5.

12. *Ibid.*, 1.

13. Charles E. Raven, *Natural religion and Christian theology,* 145.

14. John Bagnall Bury, *The idea of progress: an inquiry into its origin and growth* (London: Macmillan, 1928), 159–77.

15. Samuel von Pufendorf, *Of the law of nature and nations,* eight books . . . done into English by Basil Kennet . . . (London: R. Sare, 1717), Bk. II, 105.

16. Frederick Schleiter, *Religion and culture: a critical survey of methods of approach to religious phenomena* (New York: Columbia University Press, 1919), 31–32.

17. Lafitau, *Moeurs des sauvages,* I, 5.

18. Anne Robert Jacques Turgot, "On the successive advances of the

human mind," in Frederick J. Teggart, *The idea of progress, a collection of readings* (Berkeley: University of California Press, 1949), 243.

19. Giambattista Vico, *The new science of Giambattista Vico*, translated from the third edition (1744) by Thomas Goddard Bergin and Max Harold Fisch (Ithaca: Cornell University Press, 1948), ¶ 915. See Brown, *Methodus of Bodin*, 97, 103, 104, for similarities between the theories of the two men. Francis Bacon also found it convenient to deal in threes: three great realms of poetry, history, and philosophy ruled over three faculties of the imagination, memory, and understanding; there were three kinds of civil history.

20. *Ibid.*, ¶ 333, ¶ 582.

21. *Ibid.*, ¶ 31.

22. Collingwood, *Idea of history*, 60–70.

23. Vico, *op. cit.*, ¶ 122.

24. *Ibid.*, ¶ 375.

25. *Ibid.*, ¶ 340.

26. *Ibid.*, ¶ 338.

27. Benedetto Croce, *The philosophy of Giambattista Vico*, translated by R. G. Collingwood (New York: Macmillan, 1913), 145–46. Vico's explanation of savagery as the result of degeneration was wholly orthodox. It will be found, he said, "that the races, first of Ham, then of Japheth, and finally of Shem, without the religion of their father Noah, . . . were lost from one another by roving wild in the great forest of the earth, pursuing shy and indocile women, fleeing from wild animals . . . They were scattered further in search of pasture and water, and as the result of it all were reduced, at the end of a long period, to the condition of beasts." (Vico, *New science*, ¶ 13.)

28. Collingwood, *op. cit.*, 67–68.

29. Antoine Yves Goguet, *The origin of laws, arts, and sciences, and their progress among the most ancient nations*, translated from the French of the President de Goguet (Edinburgh: Alex. Donaldson and John Reid, 1761), I, xi.

30. *Ibid.*, I, xiv.

31. *Ibid.*, I, xv.

32. Cassirer, *Philosophy of the Enlightenment*, 216–23; Paul Honigsheim, "The American Indians in the philosophy of the Enlightenment," *Osiris* (1932).

33. François-Marie Arouet de Voltaire, *The complete romance of Voltaire. Also the philosophy of history, dialogues, and philosophic criticisms*, eight volumes in one (New York: Walter J. Black, 1927), 375–77; Jean David, "Voltaire et des Indiens d'Amerique," *Modern Language Quarterly*, 9 (1948), 90–103; Jerome Rosenthal, "Voltaire's philosophy of history," *Journal of the History of Ideas*, 16 (1955), 151–78; Robert Flint, *The philosophy of history in Germany and France* (Edinburgh and London: William Blackwood, 1874), 290–94; Paul Honigsheim, "Voltaire as an anthropologist," *American Anthropologist*, 47 (1945), 104–108).

34. Marie Jean Antoine Nicolas de Caritat, Marquis de Condorcet, *Outlines of an historical view of the progress of the human mind: being*

a posthumous work, translated from the French (Baltimore: Printed by G. Fryer for J. Frank, 1802), *passim.*

35. Writers like Voltaire and Condorcet did little to improve historical research. They took over the methods devised by the preceding generation, and even these methods they did not use in a really scholarly spirit. "They were not sufficiently interested in history of remote and obscure periods." (Collingwood, *op. cit.,* 77.) See also Réne Hubert, "Introduction bibliographique à l'étude des sources de la science ethnographique dans l'Encyclopédie," *Revue d'Histoire de la Philosophie et d'Histoire Generale de la Civilization* (1933), 163.

36. Adam Smith, *The works of Adam Smith,* with an account of his life and writings, edited by Dugald Stewart (London: T. Cadell and W. Davies, etc., 1811–12), V, 3–4, 447–50.

37. In a book by William Christian Lehman, *Adam Ferguson and the beginnings of modern sociology: an analysis of the sociological elements in his writings with some suggestions as to his place in the history of social theory* (New York: Columbia University Press, 1930).

38. Quoted in Lois Whitney, *Primitiveness and the idea of progress in English popular literature of the eighteenth century* (Baltimore: The Johns Hopkins Press, 1934), 151.

39. *Ibid.,* 151–52. See also Roy Harvey Pearce, "The eighteenth century Scottish primitivists: some reconsiderations," *English Literary History,* 12 (1945), 203–20; Gladys Bryson, *Man and society. The Scottish inquiry of the eighteenth century* (Princeton: University Press, 1945), 78–113.

40. Adam Ferguson, *An essay on the history of civil society* (London: A. Miller and T. Caddel, 1767), 122; see also Whitney, *op. cit.,* 145–54.

41. Lehman, *op. cit.,* 59 note 4.

42. Henry Home, Lord Kames, *Sketches of the history of man. Considerably enlarged by the last additions and corrections of the author* (London: A. Strahan and T. Caddel, 1783), I, 74–75; 163–65.

43. Bock, *Acceptance of histories,* 80.

44. John Lubbock, Lord Avebury, *Prehistoric times, as illustrated by ancient remains and the manners and customs of modern savages* (London, 1865) 445–46; Myres, "Anthropology and political science," 65. It must be borne in mind that the current enthusiasm for the Marxist philosophy of history and for Freudian psychology marches forward on the basis of unexamined assumptions, formulated long ago, with respect to savagery; as does also the Darwinian concept of the descent of man. There can hardly be any doubt, said Darwin, "that we are descended from barbarians. The astonishment which I felt on first seeing a party of Fuegians on a wild and broken shore will never be forgotten by me, for the reflection at once rushed into my mind—such were our ancestors. These men were absolutely naked and bedaubed with paint, their long hair was tangled, their mouths frothed with excitement. . . . They possessed hardly any arts, and, like wild animals lived on what they could catch; they had no government, and were merciless to everyone not of their own small tribe. He who has seen a savage in his native land will not feel much shame if forced to acknowledge that the blood of

some more humble creature flows in his veins. For my own part, I would as soon be descended from that heroic little monkey . . . as from a savage who delights to torture his enemies, offers up bloody sacrifices, practices infanticide without remorse, treats his wives like slaves, knows no decency, and is haunted by the grossest of superstitions." (Charles Darwin, *The descent of man and selection in relation to sex* [London: John Murray, 1871], II, 404–405.) So do the anthropological ideas of the sixteenth century find reiteration in the nineteenth.

Index

517